ARCHITECTURE AND RITUAL

Transformations
Shelley Nordlund, founder
1417 Queen Anne Ave. N.,#208
Seattle, WA 98109

ARCHITECTURE AND RITUAL

HOW BUILDINGS SHAPE SOCIETY

Peter Blundell Jones

Bloomsbury Academic
An imprint of Bloomsbury Publishing Plc

B L O O M S B U R Y
LONDON · OXFORD · NEW YORK · NEW DELHI · SYDNEY

Bloomsbury Academic

An imprint of Bloomsbury Publishing Plc

50 Bedford Square
London
WC1B 3DP
UK

1385 Broadway
New York
NY 10018
USA

www.bloomsbury.com

BLOOMSBURY and the Diana logo are trademarks of Bloomsbury Publishing Plc

First published 2016

© Peter Blundell Jones, 2016

British Library Cataloguing-in-Publication Data
A catalogue record for this book is available from the British Library.

ISBN: HB: 9781472577474
       PB: 9781472577481
       ePub: 9781472577498
       ePDF: 9781472577504

Library of Congress Cataloging-in-Publication Data
A catalog record for this book is available from the Library of Congress.

Cover design: Paul Burgess

Cover images courtesy the author and Getty Images

Typeset by Fakenham Prepress Solutions, Fakenham, Norfolk NR21 8NN
Printed and bound in India

CONTENTS

LIST OF ILLUSTRATIONS

List of Illustrations

PROLOGUE AND ACKNOWLEDGEMENTS

This book follows on from a series of monographs on twentieth-century architects, for which close reading of buildings was required, along with a questioning of circumstances under which they had come about. Being a critic under the patronage of Peter Davey at *The Architectural Review* also involved dipping into case studies, while contributions to Dan Cruickshank's series *Masters of Building* in *Architects' Journal*, shifted to more historic territory. A general history, *Modern Architecture through Case Studies* of 2002, devoted each chapter to one building by one architect, with cases assembled in chronological order and linked top to tail. Distrusting styles, isms, and the established hierarchy of masters, it celebrated the creative diversity of a more broadly conceived modernism. Further shifts took me backwards into architectural history and sideways into what architecture might be. Seemingly endless admirable buildings existed outside the traditional canon of architectural history, often under the rubric 'vernacular', and the inventiveness of the craft-builder needed more acknowledgement. Readings in anthropology revealed how differently people have organised their worlds under different assumptions, requiring re-evaluation of the 'primitive' and 'illiterate' and questioning the dominant value hitherto attributed to 'civilisation'. Human existence until relatively recently relied on oral communication, with more weight on the mnemonic value of landscapes and buildings. Those locally produced or modified by many hands could involve greater social commitment and reflect greater shared investment of meaning than we experience today. Following a second volume of *Modern Architecture Through Case Studies* the idea grew of a larger, deeper, case study book, taking a longer view and including an alternative history about how people built for themselves. The central issue was how buildings might express or embody social institutions, understood as part of the social construction of reality, and therefore resistant to reductive laws like 'form follows function'. It has become a series of essays, each adding fresh insights, intended to work both as an unfolding narrative and standing on its own.

Thanks to the patronage of Peter Davey, a first sketch of these concerns appeared as *Implicit Meanings* in *The Architectural Review* thirty years ago, the title a homage to Mary Douglas. It prompted a first investigation into the structuring of the Palace of Westminster, the subject of Chapter One. In taking that further, the idea arose of including the Guildhall and the Lord Mayor's show, to embrace the scale of the city. Interest in the law court, also noted in *Implicit Meanings*, led to a PhD undertaken by Clare Graham, later published as *Ordering Law*, while the pursuit of a specific Chinese case in Chapter four grew out of work with the Centre for East-West Studies at the University of Sheffield, in collaboration with Jan Woudstra. Engagement with that group also inspired the Dong chapter, drawing particularly on PhD theses by Xuemei Li and Derong Kong, and a field visit generously organized by Lingjun Kong and Huiqiong Yao in May 2014. Engagement with the Nuremberg Rallies dates back to a debate in the Festival Hall organised by the 20th Century Society in 1996, where I opposed the idea that Speer's Classicism was merely incidental. The earliest anthropological case study addressed the Dogon, to which my attention was first drawn by Joseph Rykwert's *The Idea of a Town.* The case study on the Tukanoan Maloca arose from contact with Stephen Hugh-Jones. The third part of the book, Modernities, makes a bridge with the anthropological material by considering a traditional farm, and then moves to a modern reinterpretation by Hugo Häring. This and the study of Hans Scharoun's Philharmonie loop back to my earlier work on these architects and their bid for specificity. Contrasting the Philharmonie with Garnier's Opéra was prompted by exposure to Garnier's book, but happily also allowed some unravelling of the conventions of high culture against a changing political background. In contrast, Powell and Moya's hospital exemplifies the modernist orthodoxy of around 1960 and the way it was propagated, the Kings' Fund's *The Hospital Description* being as interesting for its omissions as for its statements. The idealistic aims of Cedric Price and Joan Littlewood's Fun Palace deserve applause, but Price more than anyone shows the will to de-ritualise architecture. If underestimating the importance of memory, he also reminds us that the casting of habits in buildings is always both a comfort and a tyranny. The book ends with an example of participation, a theme first broached in *The Architectural Review* of 1985, and later celebrated in *Architecture and Participation,* edited jointly with Sheffield colleagues Jeremy Till and Doina Petrescu. Further participative work conducted by Peter Hübner was presented in detail in my Hübner monograph of 2007. His type of agency proposes no universal solution, but the small scale operation and specificity to local context suggest manageable goals. Such projects show that commitment and joy in creation can still be awakened.

I thank colleagues too numerous to list from my days at Cambridge, South Bank and Sheffield for hints and corrections, and more generally for providing an arena of debate. Particular thanks go to Bryan Lawson, Jeremy Till, Roger Plank and Flora Samuel as Heads at Sheffield who allowed me to plough my own furrow. I thank also my many PhD, Masters, and Dissertation students, who made me think and think again. Journal editors have shaped my work, among them Peter Davey, Peter Carolin, Dan Cruickshank, Cathy Slessor and Charlotte Ellis. The following persons and institutions have provided material without which this book would not have been possible: Akademie der Künste Berlin, Architectural Association Library Eleanor Gawne and Sue Barr, Claire Blundell Jones, British Library, Bundesarchiv Koblenz, Bundesarchiv-Filmarchiv Berlin, Canadian Centre for Architecture, Diego Carrasco, Jianyu Chen, Flickr, John Haworth, Peter Hübner, Archiv Museumsdorf Hösseringen, Stephen and Christine Hugh-Jones, LVR-Freilichtmuseum Kommern, Derong Kong, Peter Lathey, London Metropolitan Archive, Brian Moser, Stadtarchiv Nuremberg, People's History Museum Manchester, Richard Rogers, Pascale Scheurer, Smithsonian Institution, Spencer and Gillen Archive, Richard Weston and Xiang Ren.

CHAPTER 1
INTRODUCTION

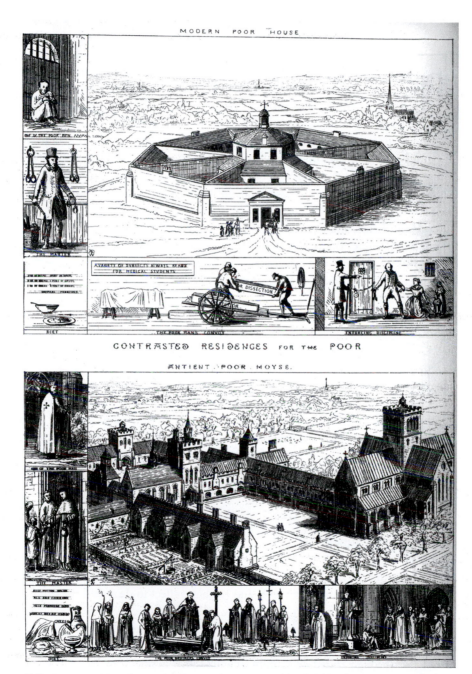

Figure 1.1 Contrasted 'residences for the poor' from A. W. N. Pugin's book *Contrasts* of 1836.

Architecture and Ritual

Augustus Welby Pugin, leader of the Gothic Revival in Britain, was a key figure in proposing a link between architecture and society, but he was perhaps more effective with his drawings than with his writings or buildings. In his book *Contrasts* of 1836 he set out to prove the virtue of fourteenth-century Gothic in comparison with what he regarded as the degraded architecture of his own day, but much of the textual argument is about the Reformation, polemical rather than factual, and no longer pertinent or credible, so we scarcely attend to it today. The drawings, though, still resonate (Figure 1.1). Here we are shown comparative poor houses: above is a parody of the workhouse, playing on the utilitarian philosopher Jeremy Bentham's panoptican concept,[1] below an idealized depiction of a medieval hospice. Quite as interesting as the views of the buildings themselves are the marginal scenes of life within them, presented like a strip cartoon around the edge. Top left in each case shows one of the poor men, the modern one apparently in a prison with a high barred window sitting in a state of relative undress on straw, while his medieval counterpart stands cloaked and hatted before the church door. Moving on down, Pugin depicts the master: the top-hatted modern one brandishing a cat-o'-nine-tails with manacles on the wall, while the medieval one is a priest ministering to a woman and child, again at the church door. The lower strips show other aspects of life: a diet of thin gruel as opposed to bread, cheese, ham and ale; a body being taken away for dissection as opposed to receiving a Christian burial; and the enforcement of discipline in the modern case with prison, chains, and force, in the medieval one with admonishment from the pulpit towards good behaviour. The polemic is visually compelling, all the more so for its almost Dickensian satire and social concern, and the twenty-four-year-old Pugin was surprisingly astute in the choice of things to connect with architecture: food, clothes, discipline, and the death ritual (or lack of it in the modern case). It was a knowing choice, and one that would satisfy a modern anthropologist. Food is not only considered an essential factor in establishing human society,[2] but also involves taste, not by mere accident the key term used for aesthetic judgement. Clothes are indicators of social position and rank, as explained in the almost contemporary anti-utilitarian book *Sartor Resartus* by Thomas Carlyle, though we do not know whether Pugin read it.[3] Discipline is the common instrument of social control and was to become by the mid-twentieth century the focal point of Foucault's revolution in theory.[4] Burying the dead has long been considered a defining characteristic of humanity.[5] Some of Pugin's points might have been substantiated with carefully chosen evidence, but he had neither the time nor the patience to gather it, and the images poured out of his fervent imagination.[6] All who feel the efficacy of architecture might concur with the sentiment, but the connection is objectively hard to substantiate.

Beyond the 'merely functional'

This is a book about how architecture affects people's lives. It will attempt to penetrate beyond traditional assumptions about utility, style and aesthetic effect to deal with the implicit, with the way that architecture shapes our experience without our conscious awareness. It will show that by providing a background for our lives, buildings tacitly suggest and sustain a classification of people and things that contributes to the constitution of a shared reality. Buildings do this not just through coded decoration or intentional aesthetic message – though these may be part of the story – but more essentially by how they are used, and by the meanings established during use, during the relationships that people enact with them. Accepting that buildings have some kind of shaping influence on life is not to say that architecture determines behaviour, or that 'form follows function', as Louis Sullivan so simply and famously put it.[7] By suggesting a kind of hand-to-glove fit, this oversimplified formula based on the Darwinian evolutionary principle concealed a much more complex interaction between people and their habitat.[8] Most buildings apart from prisons are not physically coercive, nor do they force people to behave in particular ways, yet all buildings limit the available possibilities and can by their organization suggest or persuade towards particular courses of action.[9] To give a simple example, whether you enter a theatre by the box-office or the stage door confirms your role as spectator or actor, dividing spatially between separated frontstage and backstage worlds which reinforce those roles, so obliging you to behave as one or the other. Failure to comply with these conventions is almost unthinkable, as we know that it is 'not our place' to presume to enter by the stage door, just as we should not enter the main door without a ticket or inappropriately dressed.

But how far does this go? My teacher James Gowan, no stranger to functionalist planning concepts, once rebuked me for erring in the determinist direction by declaring sceptically: 'I can eat a sandwich in a room of any shape: you try me!'[10] As a student I was somewhat floored by this and never took him up on his offer, but I think it would be possible to create a room nasty enough to put him off his sandwich. More to the point, most people would agree that some rooms are better to eat sandwiches in than others, even if Gowan had cunningly chosen an activity that tends to be independent of site.[11] The relationship between space and activity is evidently neither a compelling certainty nor open and random, but complex and variable. What makes it so hard to pin down is that it is a two-way process involving a 'reading' as well as a 'doing', so that there must be some complicity between user and building. In other words the arrangement of the building has somehow to mesh with a set of habits, beliefs, and expectations held by the person who experiences and uses it, a matter of what Marcel Mauss and Pierre Bourdieu have called the 'habitus'.[12]

Once such 'meshing' between spaces and rituals of use is achieved, buildings and activities tend to reinforce each other, for besides the sheer convenience of 'fit', buildings go on to reassure their users by reinforcing their beliefs and intentions, substantiating their world. Buildings provide prompts for action and frameworks to define relationships with fellow human beings in forming societies or communities. This is why variations in buildings and social practices expose differences in understanding and in conceptions of the world, causing the questioning of things normally taken for granted. The naming of rooms, for example is but the tip of an iceberg of classification rooted in language, perception, and in the metaphorical construction by which shared worlds are ordered. Beyond the question of rooms lie greater differences in spatial usages and the application of meaning, differences one could never guess at without knowledge of practices. And buildings reflect not only relationships between persons but also those between humans and deities, humans and cosmos. In many if not most pre-modern societies practical tasks embraced a religious and cosmological dimension, allowing no clear division between the utilitarian and the ceremonial. In summary, buildings provide a mirror that reflects our world, our knowledge about it, and the way we interact with it.

This was well understood by William Lethaby, Pugin's inheritor and the most serious architectural theorist of the following generation, who pushed the link between architecture and society further. The pursuit of 'style pretences' was, according to him, all wrong. 'Art is the well-doing of what needs doing',[13] he said repeatedly, and he found in farm carts and hayricks objects of beauty, the way of finishing a loaf of bread a source of local pride and identity. Even in gardening 'great thought is given to laying out cottage vegetable gardens to get the rows straight and right'.[14] The well-organized and skilful activity knowingly done produces a beautiful and poetic result, which is 'shipshape' and 'tidy', two of Lethaby's favourite words of approval. This spirit can also rise into communal celebration in 'work festivals' which mark calendrical events like harvests and raise work to the level of play: 'almost a ritual' he says at one point, taking the word in its usual narrow sense.[15] But Lethaby also perceived the link between architecture and cosmology. In the most original of all his written works, *Architecture, Mysticism and Myth*, a cross-cultural survey by an architect drawing for the first time on the discipline of anthropology, he sought the basis of architectural order in the beliefs and cosmologies of the peoples concerned. In the preface to the later version, *Architecture, Nature and Magic* published in 1928, he claimed: 'The main thesis that the development of building practice and ideas of the world structure acted and reacted on one another I still believe to be sound'.[16] An abundance of evidence accumulated by anthropologists and historians since Lethaby's time supports his basic thesis and the validity of his pioneering enterprise, if undermining some of the detail.

Architecture as memory and as promise

A further complication of the way architecture reflects society is the element of time and memory. The space–activity relationship does not simply and nakedly exist at a particular moment as the phrase 'form follows function' seems to imply, but is necessarily more protracted, involving duration, memory, and anticipation. The sense of duration, so easily overlooked, is essential to consciousness, for we have to locate ourselves in time and are always aware of temporal relations beyond the present instant.[17] A simple illustration of this is the experience of music: hearing a single note means little, for it is the relation of notes that matters and the way they unfold in time, which we have to 'bear in mind' in order to experience it.[18] A parallel in architecture is the need to walk around and through a building to experience it while at the same time somehow constructing in mind an idea of the whole. We generally use the word 'memory' for a rather longer term process, but it is essential to everything we do and think.[19] Memory is engaged on a personal level in our interaction with, and understanding of, the spaces we occupy not only because of the movement and sequence essential to experience and appreciation as noted above, but also because we tend to compare what we do now with what we did last time. It is further engaged on a social level because shared social activities leave traces that can be read.[20] Anticipation is involved because we have to decide what to do next, and to fit it into the structure of relations in which we find ourselves. As David Lowenthal put it:

> The prime function of memory is not to preserve the past but to adapt it so as to enrich and manipulate the present. Far from simply holding on to previous experiences, memory helps us to understand them. Memories are not ready made reflections of the past, but eclectic, selective reconstructions based on subsequent actions and perceptions and on ever-changing codes by which we delineate, symbolize, and classify the world around us.[21]

The inevitable remembering and anticipation mean that the use of buildings is no mere matter of 'functioning' in the present tense, but also of what the sculptor Horatio Greenough called 'the promise of function', involving a reading of use-meaning by an observer or by a prospective user. Greenough was attempting to explain the beauty of a frigate in full sail, but the idea applies equally to simpler examples.[22] Ernst Gombrich raised the question of a child's hobby horse, pointing out that a stick with a head and reins could hardly be considered a good 'image' of a horse but was much more of 'a substitute for a horse', a necessary adjunct to imagined riding.[23] It is therefore not only a 'promised function' but an imitated one. To take an even more basic example, a door handle serves to open a door, but it also invites the approaching visitor to enter, and if it fails to indicate this purpose, the door will never be opened. The handle therefore also serves as a sign, but not merely as a sign. Its signing role is logically connected with its function, which unites eye and hand, vision and activity. Some visitors open the door for the first time, in which case its promise of openability relates it to other door handles, involving a known typology of them. In addition, no sooner is it glimpsed than subconscious comparisons are made.

Some handles (Figure 1.2) – those designed by Gunnar Asplund or Alvar Aalto, for example – welcome the hand and encourage the grasp: others can be sharp and geometrical, sacrificing ergonomic comfort to visual display. But if we see a handle covered in grease, wreathed in barbed wire, or visibly wired to a high-voltage source, the avoidance is visceral, for we imagine the experience in an empathic, emotional manner. Refusal in such cases is no considered decision and requires no prior reflection.[24] Our inward assessment takes place without conscious effort before we reach the door, let alone pass through it, and this judgement surely counts among the aesthetic experiences offered by architecture, which can be negative as well as positive: the gate may welcome us, but the jagged edge of broken glass (Figure 1.3) topping the wall makes us flinch at the imagined cuts on climbing over it; the bench invites us to sit, but not when an upturned drawing pin is placed on it. As we shall see in chapters to come, principles observed in such simple examples expand to cover whole buildings and many of their features, and the essential point is that the 'promise of function' addresses both anticipation and memory, for we are trying to decide how and if to enter, while at the same time relating our present experience to past doors and past entries. Repetition of the activity is essential to establish both the fit between space and action and the meanings attached to doors and thresholds. Repetition is essential to, if not definitive of, ritual.

Scaling up from the door handle to the door, and reconsidering the example of the stage door versus the theatre's main entrance, it is clear that entrances stand for the whole building beyond, often addressed to specific groups of people and involving particular rules of use. The actors' entrance signed 'stage door' is set discreetly in a side-street policed by a porter, but the theatre's main entry, set in an elaborate front with multiple doors and surrounded by images of the current production, does not have to be labelled. Lest anyone miss the point there is an enlarged title naming the theatre as a whole, but set in the upper façade, addressing a wider public. Everyone in the city recognizes it, even if they are not regular theatregoers, and they also associate the word 'theatre' with such kinds of place, no longer expecting a show mounted in the street or an inn yard as it was a few centuries ago.[25] Theatres are part of a well-established tradition with its own highly evolved building type designed to support its many rituals, which occur backstage and frontstage as well as on the stage itself. The audience dress up to be seen and to see others when 'going to the theatre', which may be of as much interest as the content

Figure 1.2 Doorhandle at the Academic Bookshop, Helsinki, by Alvar Aalto, which shows the door swing and encourages the grasp (author's photograph).

Figure 1.3 Broken glass topping a wall, the traditional way to discourage trespassers (author's photograph, St Valéry, France).

of the play.[26] The whole setting and its ornamentation contributes to the effect, but the spatial arrangements are essential not only in controlling the relations between actors and audience, but also in defining the audience to and for itself. A disconcerting commentary on this occurs in the movie *The Discreet Charm of the Bourgeoisie* by Luis Buñuel, in which a group of people in evening dress gather for a dinner party only to discover in mid-conversation that they are on the stage of a theatre, apparently acting out a play. The surrealist film director was underlining the framing of cinematic experience by creating the frame of theatre within it, as well as reminding us of the embarrassing juxtapositions that often occur in dreams.[27]

That we are accustomed to playing roles and imagining ourselves into situations is clear from childhood games and fictional narratives,[28] but the spaces required may be fleeting in character, short-lived, and dependent on a particular interpretation. The metaphor of theatrical space has nonetheless great potency and gave rise in the middle of the last century to a whole school of sociology. This was founded by Erving Goffman, who extended the concepts 'frontstage' and 'backstage' far from the theatre and into everyday life.[29] His famous book *The Presentation of the Self in Everyday Life* starts with a domestic front door and the house owner putting on a face to face the world, but in later chapters Goffman persuades the reader that frontstage and backstage are ubiquitous: the shop and its storeroom, the restaurant and its kitchen, the garage with its neat front office and receptionist in jacket and tie as opposed to the dirty workshop behind. Once you start to look at human institutions in this way, examples are legion. All kinds of activities need settings, and these settings are nearly always both functional and symbolic. They must both signal and accommodate the activity, and afterwards they tend to become mnemonics of it, at least for those who were involved. This is why architecture and ritual are so closely related.

Definitions: Architecture

This book's title connects the words 'architecture' and 'ritual', implying the interrelation of the two. On one side stand the buildings, on the other the habits and beliefs: the question is how these two fit together or how each reflects the other. To explore it we need to expand the roles of both 'architecture' and 'ritual' beyond familiar usage, for both have suffered the fate of being ascribed presumptuously to a special realm above and beyond the everyday. There are historical reasons why 'architecture' has usually been seen as designating a cultural superstructure added to 'building' or somehow going beyond it, and it is commonplace to reserve the word for buildings of ceremonial function, buildings that show artistic intention, or buildings made by people called architects. But none of these categories is satisfactorily definitive, and it is essential to the purpose of this book to challenge the widely assumed dichotomy between the utilitarian and the ceremonial. I therefore respectfully disagree with Nikolaus Pevsner's famous definition: 'A bicycle shed is a building, Lincoln Cathedral is a piece of architecture',[30] for while the cathedral is obviously more ceremonial and more loaded with cultural significance, the bicycle shed is not devoid of meaning. Bicycle sheds reveal the status of the bicycle as a mode of transport, and to have bicycles poorly rather than well-housed also communicates. Pevsner's subsequent insistence that architecture 'applies only to buildings designed with a view to aesthetic appeal'[31] is neither sufficient nor necessary: for the intention may not be achieved, or a building may be found beautiful without it. There is a 'reader' involved as well as a maker. Furthermore, any shed can be well or badly built, which leaves scope for a type of aesthetic judgement overlooked by Pevsner though evident to Lethaby as cited above: the pleasure of the job well done. The aesthetic cannot be turned off for mere building: instead its possibility becomes ubiquitous, multifaceted. Following Nelson Goodman's arguments in *Languages of Art*, it must be regarded as integral to the work and its context, as cognitively engaged in a cultural system.[32]

Rather than using the term 'architecture' I could have stayed with 'building' as consciously adopted by Lethaby[33] and by the German architect Hugo Häring,[34] and as more recently deployed by Thomas Markus,[35] but it is part of my purpose to question this long assumed distinction. To abandon 'architecture' to exclusive use of the so-called classical tradition, or to limit it to the productions of so-called architects, would only substantiate institutions whose very limits I am attempting to challenge.[36] In this book, therefore, 'architecture' is taken to apply to all buildings and even to landscapes modified by human intervention, and it is chosen because it traditionally refers to the meaningful, spiritual, social, and cultural aspects of buildings and the thinking behind them, as opposed to aspects that can be identified from a narrowly material or technical point of view.

Definitions: Ritual

The word 'ritual' is taken in an equally expanded sense, for it has suffered a similar restriction. In everyday usage we tend to apply it to church services, weddings, and funerals – in other words to special occasions with explicit religious content – while not regarding it as applying to simpler everyday events. Furthermore, as with the word 'architecture', we tend to think of 'ritual' as a superstructure of display or symbolism, and as giving expression to a substrate of underlying beliefs rather than having a legitimate existence of its own. That 'ritual' implies a connection between practices and beliefs or views of the world – realities even – is crucial to this enquiry, although how the connection works and what is to be regarded as primary have been among the most vexed questions in anthropology. Some leading figures of that discipline have been exasperated enough by the confusion to suggest abandoning the word altogether,[37] and the extensive literature leaves little hope of tying it down to a final definition by pursuing it through thickets of theory.[38] The question of what it is and how it works must be allowed to cross our path in various ways throughout the book, but as a starting point take dictionary definitions. The Concise Oxford gives two: 'a prescribed order of performing rites' and 'a procedure regularly followed'. Only on turning to its definitions of 'rite' does the religious element emerge: 'a religious or solemn observance or act (burial rites)'.[39] The Random House Dictionary is broader, for after several definitions concerned with religious practices it adds a secular one: 'a prescribed code of behaviour regulating social conduct, as that exemplified by the raising of one's hat or the shaking of hands in greeting'. Similarly, its sixth and last definition of 'rite' is 'any customary observance or practice', giving as examples; 'the elegant rite of afternoon tea; the white collar rite of the 10 a.m. coffee break'.[40]

The longer Oxford with its dated citations shows rite to be derived from the latin 'ritus' and in use since the fourteenth century.[41] Clearly the word opened in what could be called its religious mode, though what constituted 'religion' in a world of churchgoers for whom science was not yet separable from theology, was hardly how we think of it today. By 1570 the sense of superfluity was already present in Foxe's mention of 'certain ritual decrees of no purpose', and by 1865 Dickens was using 'rite' in a decidedly secular sense when he referred in *Our Mutual Friend* to 'the rites of hospitality'. All the same, the 'religious' emphasis remained, becoming a convenient 'other' within the scientific world view, for the OED reveals that the archaeologist's use of 'ritual' for finds of presumed religious as opposed to practical function dates back to Arthur Evans's Mycenaean digs of 1901.[42] In contrast a specialist social science dictionary hands the term over to the anthropologists, attributing its broadening to encompass things like handshakes and tea breaks to Edmund Leach in 1954.[43] The section's author traces a lineage of further development through Claude Levi-Strauss and Rodney Needham to Victor Turner, Max Gluckman, and Mary Douglas. It is no accident that the period 1950 to 1990, which saw this development of ritual theory, was also a period of increasing atheism and crisis for the Church. A further marginal usage of 'ritual' is found in the medical dictionary describing obsessive–compulsive behaviour. The OED traces this back to a translation of Piaget in 1932.[44] Such usage stresses the repetitive element of ritual while isolating it from the social, involving the pursuit of repetitive personal practices which look as though they should be social. Precisely this underlines the pathology: ritual is a shared interaction with the world and its displacement into private obsession identifies the disorder.

Ritual and classification

Handshakes and coffee breaks bring ritual into the realm of everyday life and necessary social behaviour. If we fail to greet each other, we are condemned as 'rude' for having omitted to observe the rules, and the coffee break is both a device for structuring the timetable of the day and an opportunity for conversation. It may even be regarded as a small meal, and meals are surely ritualistic, whether or not a grace is said before them. As Mary Douglas pointed out in a seminal essay, they give rhythm to social and bodily experience, mapping out the day between breakfast, lunch, tea, and dinner, each of which involves distinct food types and settings.[45] They break out of the normal rhythm to mark anniversaries and to define friendships, and the sharing of food is both an ancient defining characteristic of humanity and a persistent way of marking our most valued social occasions through feasts.[46] While nobody would deny that a feast is a ritual, many would quibble about the coffee break. What Douglas points out is that meals necessarily exist in a structured contrast with each other, in terms of timing, setting, company, number of courses, accompanying drinks, etc. If wedding feasts at the high end involve maximum elaboration and expensive foods such as caviar and champagne, prisoners at the low end were supposedly reduced to the bare minimum, bread and water, and there are many stages in between. When friends drop in, we feel obliged to offer them at least a cup of tea as a register of our hospitality, but opening a bottle of wine is better, inviting them to stay for a meal better still. Hot food is better than cold, three courses better than two, and so on. We can all judge the relative ceremony of a meal and how much trouble our hosts have gone to in preparing it, and our meals can be set on a continuous scale between the most and the least elaborate. Even munching a Mars Bar while walking in the street has its place in the system, for although it involves no fixed time and location, no special dress or equipment, and is a lone experience apart from nods to passers-by, it sits close to the bottom of the range. But the Mars Bar itself, dressed in a wrapper for ritual opening, combines various layers which, on Douglas's system, symbolize the assembly of ingredients on a plate.[47]

The point here is that with ritual, as with architecture, no hard line can be drawn between the utilitarian and the ceremonial, between the practical and the symbolic, because they exist along a continuous scale in contrast with one another. In this sense ritual is ever present, marked by repetition and rules. Most of the time it is evidently and positively social, invested in things done together and agreements about how to behave, but it also necessarily involves the antisocial, the rules dedicated to keeping us apart. Defecation is among the most private of activities, performed within a locked room within sight of nobody and often set within a gender-designated enclave defended by a threshold of purification through washing. Only for the very young or the sick is the rule of confinement broken, and then in a restricted manner, for in a hospital it may be necessary to break many conventions about ordinary intimacy, which is one reason for the high degree of discipline and control found in them. This is normally regarded as a matter of practical hygiene, of pathogens suppressed, but as Mary Douglas pointed out in *Purity and Danger*, pollution behaviour is always symbolic, and its rules vary from culture to culture.[48] As she explains:

> Dirt is never a unique isolated event. Where there is dirt there is system. Dirt is a by-product of a systematic ordering and classification of matter, in so far as ordering involves rejecting inappropriate elements. This idea of dirt takes us straight into the field of symbolism and promises a link-up with more obviously symbolic systems of purity.[49]

She illustrates this with familiar domestic examples:

> It is a relative idea. Shoes are not dirty in themselves, but it is dirty to place them on the dining table; food is not dirty in itself, but it is dirty to leave cooking utensils in

the bedroom, or food bespattered on clothing; similarly, bathroom equipment in the drawing room; clothing lying on chairs; out-door things in-doors, upstairs things downstairs.[50]

With their strong sense of appropriate place, such examples are already architectural, but yet more architectural is Douglas's description in her preface of *Purity and Danger* about a house belonging to friends where she sometimes stayed. They had constructed a bathroom in a converted corridor but continued to use it also as the store for garden equipment and muddy gumboots, the outside things in the intimate inside, destroying all sense of repose. Reflecting on this, she admits that 'in chasing dirt, in papering, decorating, tidying we are not governed by anxiety to escape disease, but are positively reordering our environment, making it conform to an idea'.[51]

Rituals involve both practices and beliefs, which reinforce each other.[52] Grace before a meal is a shared acceptance of divine providence, a social agreement about the order of things, as well as setting a necessary punctuation in time and place. Ritual practices always reflect shared ideas and are hedged about with rules, many of which are implicit. Because they occur in space, they usually require a specific location, and the definition and embellishment of that location is arguably among architecture's primary tasks. When created for or adapted to ritual processes, buildings reinforce their efficacy, carry memories of them in their organization, and both guide and encourage their repetition. This depends on interaction between the structures laid out in physical space and the accompanying structures of ritual, along with the beliefs and states of mind that sustain them.

Thick description and necessary material

Studying the relation between architecture and ritual, both writ large as just explained, requires two kinds of information. On the one hand there has to be detailed descriptions of buildings and places, usually through maps, scale drawings, and photographs. On the other there must be detailed information about how the building or place is used and what people believe about it while they are using it. It is surprisingly difficult to find cases with enough evidence of both kinds to allow a sophisticated reading, and never could any collection of such evidence be called complete. Usually it amounts to a pretty thin description, not at all what Clifford Geertz would call a thick one.[53] To understand a building adequately, accurate plans and sections are needed to show the relative sizes and positions of rooms. Although photographs might seem closer to what we actually see, they are limited and selective in viewpoint, and relative sizes and positions can be difficult to gauge. We also need a large number of them to attain any sense of completeness, and even then we lack continuity. Plans and sections do not reveal what we experience, but they do display the building's anatomy, enabling those familiar with the conventions to assemble it in imagination. To show usage, drawings need to include furnishing, and to explore the relationship with the context, a local map or site plan is needed. These are normal tools in the world of the architect, and there is some truth in Henri Lefebvre's claim that they are instruments of power, conditioning what is produced.[54] But it is also both possible and necessary to make drawings of buildings whose production never required them: in fact all serious study of vernacular architecture depends on this. Without drawings, discussion of how architecture works is severely limited, for there is no substitute. Film may appear to show spaces better in three dimensions, but the frame is restrictive and the sense of movement blinded by lack of haptic and binocular data.[55] Indeed, the history of cinema demonstrates only too well that its key device of montage enables it far more effectively to create fictional spaces than to depict real ones.[56]

For the other kind of data – the social content – full descriptions are needed of buildings being used in time, including evidence about the positions of events and how they occurred. We also need to know what people thought they were doing, the rules they were consciously or unconsciously following, and why they were doing it. Since much of this is taken for granted in everyday life, it usually goes unreported and needs to be gathered – sociologists and anthropologists are the experts – or it must be read between the lines of reports and descriptions, even fictional ones.[57] Because it necessarily deals with questions of belief and meaning as well as apparently straightforward questions about who put what where, it is always a matter of interpretation, and often involves layer after layer of information. As Clifford Geertz put it 'what we call our data are really our own constructions of other people's constructions of what they and their compatriots are up to'.[58] To get a really thick description we must obtain as much data as possible, and as it piles up the interpretation gets more complicated if also richer.

Limitations of the 'programme'

In traditional architectural discourse the interaction between information about buildings and information about rituals was often considered as the relationship between the building and its 'programme', the programme being a summary of the building's social content taken as the starting point for design and the client's brief.[59] But architects' briefs tend to be thin. They are generally short and uncomplicated, often consisting of mere lists of rooms with given sizes and surface areas, then going on to describe the special demands of some of them, and perhaps also how they interrelate. Briefs contain much hidden or implied information. First the names of the rooms – living room, bedroom, bathroom, and kitchen in the case of a dwelling – have established associations which are mostly taken for granted, yet which carry a considerable cultural load. It is only when faced with different patterns of use in unfamiliar cultures – the Japanese habit of unrolling bedding on the floor instead of having bedrooms, for example – that we realize it can be otherwise. Furthermore most architects, on receiving a brief, imagine the purposes and relationships of rooms in relation to rooms and buildings that they have known, past experience supplying preconceptions about how such buildings have worked and looked. Their efforts at individual expression therefore tend to take place against an underlying conformity to these implicit standards. Although the current situation relating to recent buildings often appears chaotic, half a century's hindsight shows the emergence of clear building types for any period. There have also increasingly been rules, regulations and standards about how buildings should be planned, including technical demands and cost limits. Although taken for granted in practice as inevitable or even as mere 'common sense', from an anthropological viewpoint such textual prescriptions can be seen as strong cultural impositions.[60]

If the brief is often a laconic document taking too much for granted, critiques and historical accounts of buildings can also be thin on social content. This is due partly to an art-historical discipline dedicated to a genealogy of style, which began its studies with the world's great religious monuments. Typically a sophisticated analysis of form and ornament was pursued with hardly a mention about how, where, or when worship was performed.[61] In the last half century cross-disciplinary work has filled gaps and resulted in much better understanding, and a surprising degree of information about the social side can be inferred. But even though we know the general purposes of worshipping Athena at the Parthenon, for example, and the periodicity of the various rituals, such details as how many people took part, how long each presentation lasted, and who stood where, will probably remain obscure.[62] Stonehenge sets yet a more difficult puzzle. For centuries declared a 'ritual site', with astronomical alignments to show its builders' interest in defining a calendar, it provokes tantalizing questions which archaeologists are pursuing enthusiastically, and new techniques continue to expand the evidence in surprising ways to give more of a general sense of period,[63] but there seems scant hope of recovering detailed data about ritual practices of millennia ago, let alone about the supporting beliefs behind them. When such monuments existed in continuous use for millennia, there is also the problem of changing meanings with changing generations or dynasties.

If archaeologists and architectural historians face cases where fabric has survived but practices have ceased, social anthropologists approach it the other way round. Their prime concern is with living people, their activities and beliefs. The raw material is direct observation of practices and oral accounts about what people do and why they do it, but for this reason it is primarily in the present tense. With pre-industrial peoples there seems often to have been little architecture to record, for buildings were simple and short-lived, and the means of recording them were also often limited. When enough spatial information has been gathered, though, it has often proved rich and significant, showing that lack of a developed architecture entails no lack of interest in space or its possible meanings: indeed, as we shall see, technologically primitive examples can be all the richer in meaning because of the greater use of buildings as mnemonics and the social involvement in making.

Structure of the book

This book consists of a series of case studies, chosen for the possibility of combining descriptions of architecture with descriptions of ways of life. In an exploratory way they are distributed across time and across the globe, to show how social conventions vary with spaces from time to time and place to place, and to begin to tease out what they have in common. The difficulty of finding examples replete with both social and architectural information is just the start: there follows the problem of translation, not only of language but of unfamiliar cultural habits, to say nothing of the added lens of the historian or anthropologist. Then there is the problem that the relevant background of habit, belief, history, myth and world view becomes ever larger and more intricate, tempting one to stray ever deeper into that other world. But the shutters have to come down on a manageable length of text, which necessarily sets the limit.

The studies divide into three groups under the headings *Power and Politics; People and Their Territories;* and *Modernities. Power* opens the field with political rituals, showing not only how the social order can be defined spatially, but also how memories of the social order are carried on, how it develops in time. Political rituals are often regarded as superfluous to the political process, as instanced by the late Anthony Howard's remark in 2009 that the

Queen's opening of Parliament in Britain was an archaic and outdated process that the British people could well do without,[64] or the more recent debates about deteriorating fabric, a £3 billion pound repair bill, and the possibility of moving elsewhere. But as David Kertzer lucidly explains in *Ritual, Politics and Power*, no modern state could exist without the extensive symbolization and reification that give politics its form and substance.[65] This book begins with the British Parliamentary opening, examining the still existing rituals within the Palace of Westminster, the way they were redefined by Barry and Pugin when the buildings were rebuilt after the fire, and the way they have developed subsequently. Chapter 3 remains in London, but moves on to consider a larger field both spatially and temporally with the Lord Mayor's Show and Banquet, concentrating on an eyewitness report from 1680. Chapter 4 maintains almost the same date but moves to Imperial China, depending on the detailed descriptions of daily life written by a provincial magistrate, governor of a small region. The interest here is to see what is common between Europe and the other great independently founded culture of Asia. Chapter 5 considers the Nuremberg rally of 1934, and the way the ritual organization in its spatial setting helped substantiate a modern and short-lived political regime, providing an illusion of cultural depth. All four examples involve processions and axes, which bear different meanings and are used in different ways, with contrasts between long-evolving democracy, imperial hegemony and newly invented fascism.

The subject matter of the middle section, *People and Their Territories*, has been gathered largely from anthropological fieldwork of the last century, so the focus shifts somewhat from cases of individual buildings to group culture. The section is concerned with the dwellings of people who had survived into the modern world with their building culture largely intact. Since such building traditions are mainly unselfconscious, generally unburdened by theory, and handed down from generation to generation, they do not usually have histories, and as the buildings concerned are often lightweight and short-lived, the archaeology is often also thin. This has meant studies normally confined largely to the current or recent time, for all cultures are in transition, and when communal memory rapidly merges into myth the diachronic is difficult. The advantage of anthropological studies, though, is that people exist alongside their buildings and are able to explain what they are up to. This allows a view not only of how the structures are used and who sleeps where, but also what they are considered to mean and how they relate to ideas of the cosmos.

The section starts in Chapter 6 with the Australian Aboriginal People as reported by Spencer and Gillen in the 1890s. These researchers might with hindsight be accused of 'orientalism', but were on the scene early and wrote remarkably detailed and sympathetic accounts. For architecture the Aboriginal People would at first seem a marginal case, but precisely the marginality is interesting. Their traditional manner of possessing territory through a mythical reading of the landscape was sensitive, and the barely physical ceremonial grounds that they created suggest an alternative origin for architecture in place of the usual assumption about shelter. The following chapters 7 to 10 take examples from Native Americans, Tukanoans in Amazonia, Dogon in Africa, and Dong in China, to engage accounts about contrasting and independent cultures to test similarities and differences. Deployed in that sequence they present a progressive series in which buildings become specialized and differentiated, from shelter to house and on to town. The Dong example adds a detailed description of building rituals, charting the ways spatial and symbolic readings are inscribed and reinforced during construction.

The last section, *Modernities*, applies the same kind of analytical approach to modern industrial society, showing how radically the relationship between architecture and society has changed. The cases shift back to specific buildings and also to architects as authors and commentators. In contrast with the attacks on straw-man modernism by so-called post-modernists, this section takes a wider sweep by reconsidering the effects of technical and bureaucratic aspects of modernization, and the concomitant changes in the way buildings are procured. Chapter 11 on the farmstead makes a bridge with the previous section, showing how the kind of spatial structures found in remote anthropological examples existed also in rural Europe until fairly recently. A comparison is made with a farm project by Hugo Häring, one of the most serious of modernist architects who took a special interest in the farm as a type, and who tried to retain the ritual structures of agriculture within a modern setting. The remaining chapters concern buildings devised around 1960. Chapter 12 undertakes the study of the British hospital that was chosen by the King's Fund as an exemplary work for its book *The Hospital Description*, this text being as much the object of study as the building. The natural science-based approach conceals implicit ideas about purity and pathology, and documents the effects of an increasingly complex bureaucratic process that was soon to prove alienating. Chapter 13 takes in contrast the Berlin Philharmonie of 1956–63, an extraordinarily bold attempt by a modernist architect to maintain an intense sense of place and occasion in the modern world. It is contrasted in the same chapter with the more traditionally monumental Paris Opéra of the previous century, to reveal not only the intricate social and architectural structures required for musical events, but also the changes in the audience and in its expectations between late-nineteenth and mid-twentieth centuries. The subsequent study of the proposed Fun Palace and the Centre Pompidou in Chapter 14, both almost contemporary with the Philharmonie, goes to the opposite extreme. It shows the point at which architecture almost deritualized itself in the name of freedom, but came instead to monumentalize its own technical apparatus. Through the case studies some general observations will be allowed to emerge, and the Conclusion, Chapter 15, will draw together common threads.

Notes

1   Jeremy Bentham was the originator of the principle of greatest happiness and devised a prison design which he called the Panopticon, based on the idea of a radial plan with central supervision. It was published in London in 1798 entitled 'Proposal for a New and Less Expensive Mode of Reforming Convicts'.

2   See Martin Jones, *Feast: Why Humans Share Food*, 2007.

3   *Sartor Resartus*, Carlyle, 1833–4, written just before *Contrasts* of 1836; Pugin and the Carlyles were later neighbours in Chelsea, see Hill 2007, pp. 158, 188.

4   Foucault 1979.

5   Davies 1999.

6   As Part One of Rosemary Hill's biography *God's Architect* makes clear (Hill 2007), Pugin learned much from his draughtsman father, who took him on trips to draw and record medieval buildings from an early age, and from his intellectual mother, who was encouraging and ambitious on his behalf. Auguste Pugin's collaborations with the cartoonist Thomas Rowlandson, especially on *The Microcosm of London* (1808–11) combined architecture with social ritual in a way that anticipates the plates of *Contrasts*.

7   It is usually attributed to Sullivan, but became synonymous with many aspects of modernism in architecture; for a dated but intelligent treatment of the subject see De Zurko 1957.

8   The idea of fitness for purpose, still widespread, began with theories of evolution and natural selection. It seemed very straightforward with examples like giraffes having long necks to feed off trees and anteaters' specialized snouts for licking up ants. For a detailed treatment of this analogy applied to design see Steadman 1979.

9   Even with prisons the locked doors do not become coercive until they are instruments in possession of the guards, and panopticon planning for surveillance requires establishment of roles between the watchers and the watched. On the social and functional nature of prisons see Evans 1982 and his source, Foucault 1979.

10 Remembered from studies at the Architectural Association, London, in 1971–2. An analysis of Leicester University Engineering Building, Gowan's key work with James Stirling, is included in Blundell Jones and Canniffe 2007, pp. 71–88. Gowan supplied material and approved our functionalist reading.

11 The sandwich is an informal type of food designed to be consumed on the move or at picnics, unlike formal meals. The picnic place is a rather complex case, as certainly choice matters, but it is neither designed for the event nor is the interaction necessarily repeated. A discussion on the significance of settings for meals follows on pages 9, 29.

12 See Bourdieu 1977, pp. 78–87. I have not adopted this term in my title because it is neither widely known nor easily definable.

13 Lethaby 1922, essentially the refrain of the whole book, but explicitly p. 209, the essay 'Art and Workmanship' of 1913.

14 Lethaby 1923, p. 109

15 Ibid., pp. 95–108.

16 Lethaby 1956, pp. 15–16. The original *Architecture, Mysticism and Myth* was published in 1891, but dated 1892. Lethaby revised and republished it under the new title in *The Builder* of 1928, three years before his death in 1931. This version was republished by Duckworth in 1956 with an introduction by Alfred Powell.

17 On the interaction of time and space and the problem of duration see Bergson 1910, pp. 99–110.

18 See Bergson 1910, pp. 100–1. On the necessary role of memory in appreciating music see also Meyer 1956.

19 F. C. Bartlett's book *Remembering* (1932), though rather old, is lucid about the way memory is necessarily concerned with meaning and is both selective and constructive; see particularly its presentation of serial experiments with stories and drawings. A more recent study that cuts across commonsense assumptions to reveal the complexities of memory is Draaisma 2001.

20 On collective memory see Lowenthal 1985, pp. 185–214.

21 Lowenthal 1985, p. 210.

22 Greenough 1947.

23 Gombrich, *Meditations on a Hobby Horse*, 1963.

24 The nature and value of such immediate and intuitive reactions as opposed to reflective thought is explained in Kahneman's *Thinking, Fast and Slow* (2011), especially chapter 4.

25 For a brief summary of the development of the theatre building see Pevsner's *Building Types* (1976), pp. 63–90.

26 See Chapter 13, and its main source Garnier 1871.

27 *Le charme discret de la bourgeoisie*, with Fernando Rey, Delphine Seyrig and Jean-Pierre Cassel, script by Luis Buñuel and Jean-Claude Carriere, France 1972.

28 I am reminded of an occasion when looking through some books with a two-year-old, I pretended to pick up and read a non-existent one, tracing the text with a finger. The child not only got the point but was delighted, remembered it, and demanded a repetition the following day. The sharing of make-believe seems fundamental.

29 Goffman 1956.

30 Pevsner 1963 (1943) p. 15, opening line of Introduction.

31 Ibid., fourth line.

32 Goodman 1976, 'Symbolization is to be judged fundamentally by how well it serves the cognitive purpose: by the delicacy of its discriminations and the aptness of its allusions; by the way it works in grasping, exploring, and informing the world; by how it analyzes, sorts, orders, and organises; by how it participates in the making, manipulation, retention, and transformation of knowledge', p. 258. The strength of Goodman's book lies in comparison of operating procedures between the various arts. It does not much engage architecture, but he later took on this subject in *How Buildings Mean* in Goodman and Elgin 1988, pp. 31–48. The discussion there is illuminating if largely concerned with external symbolic readings rather than the matters of space and use. Also to the point is an essay on aesthetics pursued by an anthropologist: Clifford Geertz's 'Art as a Cultural System', included in Geertz 1983, pp. 94–120.

33 Lethaby, as the main theorist of the Arts and Crafts, wanted to play up honest building and to play down artistic pretension, see Lethaby 1922, p. 31.

34 Häring preferred the term *Baukunst*, building art, as the imported *Architektur* betrayed its latin root, see Blundell Jones 1999.

35 In the very title of his book *Buildings and Power*, Markus 1993.

36 The title 'Architect' was not protected in Britain until 1931, and architectural education only started in an organized way around 1900. In the eighteenth century the architect could be a gentleman amateur expecting to provide the icing for an aristocratic cake; nowadays he or she is a cog in the building bureaucracy without much artistic aspiration. For a history of architectural education see Saint 2007.

37 Jack Goody, 'Against Ritual', in Moore and Myerhoff 1977, pp. 25–35.

38 The problems are well rehearsed in Bell 1992.

39 *The Concise Oxford Dictionary*, Ninth Edition. Oxford: Clarendon Press, 1995, p. 1189.

40 *The Random House Dictionary of the English Language*. New York: Random House, 1967, p. 1237.

41 *OED* Second Edn, vol. XIII, pp. 990–2.

42 Ibid.

43 Smelser and Baltes, *International Encyclopaedia of the Social and Behavioural Sciences* (2001), 'Ritual', D. Parkin, vol. 20, pp. 1368–71.

44 *OED* Second Edn, vol. XIII, pp. 990–2.

45 'Deciphering a Meal', in Douglas 1975, pp. 249–75.

46 See *Feast: Why Humans Share Food* by Martin Jones, 2007.

47 Meat and 2 veg, decoded into A+2B, can be reapplied in many other ways, see Douglas 1975, pp. 249–75.

48 Douglas 1966.

49 Ibid., p. 35.

50 Ibid., pp. 35–6.

51 Ibid., p. 2.

52 Anthropologists argue endlessly about what is primary and about how ritual works. Theorizing

about it in pursuit of a final definition is perhaps a vain quest and certainly beyond the limit of our concerns here: for a history of the arguments see Bell 1992.

53 See 'Thick Description: Towards an Interpretive Theory of Culture', in Geertz 1993, pp. 3–30. He cites Gilbert Ryle as the source of the term.

54 Lefebvre 1991, p. 361.

55 Walking through a space, one feels one's progress in the body and one also decides where to look, but film does not permit this interaction. Lack of binocular vision also restricts cues about depth. The same principles apply to computer-created fly-throughs which seem oddly disembodied precisely for these reasons.

56 Hugo Häring, after having designed film sets for the director Theodor Dreyer's *Mikael*, wrote an article precisely about this: see Blundell Jones 1999, p. 35.

57 The experiences of places in novels cannot simply be 'made-up' but are inevitably based on the author's earlier experience, so they still have some degree of truth to them. The more closely one examines the line between 'fiction' and 'non-fiction' of the modern library, the more unsustainable it seems.

58 Geertz 1993, p. 9.

59 Summerson 1949, pp. 195–218.

60 See Clifford Geertz's essay 'Common sense as a cultural system', in Geertz 1983, pp. 73–93.

61 Such concerns were almost completely missing from the primary textbooks of my generation such as Pevsner's *Outline* (1963) and Banister Fletcher (1943), and although the balance has since shifted in favour of social studies, most books in the architectural section of university libraries still assume a technical or aesthetic/art-historical view.

62 For a clear and relatively recent summary of the state of knowledge see Pedley 2005, pp. 202–4.

63 See Pryor 2014, pp. 147–84.

64 Anthony Howard on the BBC Radio Four News, following the opening in the autumn of 2009.

65 Kertzer 1988, Chapter 1.

PART 1
POWER AND POLITICS

Figure 2.1 Black Rod knocks at the door of the Commons, Opening of Parliament 2014 (photograph by Jessica Taylor, licensed under the Open Parliament Licence v3.0).

Figure 2.2 Black Rod approaching the Commons (photograph by Jessica Taylor, licensed under the Open Parliament Licence v3.0).

Figure 2.3 Black Rod summons the Members (photograph by Jessica Taylor, licensed under the Open Parliament Licence v3.0).

Figure 2.4 The procession returns to the Lords, led by Black Rod and the Speaker, 2014 (photograph by Jessica Taylor, licensed under the Open Parliament Licence v3.0).

CHAPTER 2
BLACK ROD AND THE THREE KNOCKS ON THE DOOR

We shape our buildings, and afterwards our buildings shape us.

Winston Churchill, 1943[1]

Every autumn the opening of the British Parliament is marked by 'The Queen's Speech', a statement of policy addressed to the assembled members of the House of Commons and the House of Lords. The text read by the Queen is not of her own composition, but describes the intentions of the party in power. It is prepared by the current Prime Minister, and the Queen is obliged neither to comment upon it nor to deviate from it. Such is the nature of the precarious balance gradually established and adjusted over centuries in Britain that allows royalty to persist within democracy: but to bolster the Sovereign's dignity and remaining potential power the speech is held on the territory of the old aristocracy, the Lords. The holders of real power, the democratically elected Members of the Commons, are summoned by the Queen to attend,

Figure 2.5 House of Lords during the Queen's speech in 2014, with the Lords and Bishops assembled before her, the Members of Commons at the low end beneath the gallery (photograph by Roger Harris, licensed under the Open Parliament Licence v3.0).

Figure 2.6 The Queen reads her speech (photograph by Roger Harris, licensed under the Open Parliament Licence v3.0).

Figure 2.7 Speaker and Commons stand opposite (photograph by pru@parliament, licensed under the Open Parliament Licence v3.0 check Flickr.

and that summons is a highly ritualized process. When the appointed time has arrived and the Queen is present on the throne at the south end of the Lords, her representative the Lord Great Chamberlain raises his white rod of office to signal to another official, The Gentleman Usher of the Black Rod, to go and fetch the Members of the Commons. Accompanied by his minions, and with his route lined by police and attendants standing to either side, Black Rod leaves the Lords' chamber, marches across the peer's lobby, down the peer's corridor, across the polygonal central hall and on down the commons corridor to the members' lobby. As he crosses the latter, the door to the Commons is abruptly slammed in his face. He knocks three times on the door using the head of his black rod of office. The Sergeant at Arms, responsible for discipline in the Commons, checks his identity from the other side via a small grille in the door before announcing and admitting him. Having entered the Commons, Black Rod stops to bow respectfully at the bar of the house, the notional boundary of the arena of debate, then proceeds to the table of the house to summon the members. They return following him and the Speaker in procession two by two, led by the Prime Minister on the right and the leader of the opposition on the left. The procession takes its dignified course back to the Lords where the members gather and stand at the lower end of that house – the humblest position below the bar of that house – to hear the Queen read her speech. She has her robes and crown, the Lords their wigs and red gowns, but the members are in their everyday suits.[2]

The office of Black Rod has a long and complicated history originating in the fourteenth century with the Knights of the Garter, an élite group founded by Edward III. As their usher he kept order, led processions, and was guardian of the doors at Windsor Castle where they met, policing the membership as well as controlling the spaces on behalf of the King. The military implications of the role continue in modern times, for it is held by retired leaders of the three armed forces in rotation. Not until the seventeenth century was Black Rod's role in summoning the Commons recorded, and it was around that time that the door-knocking ceremony was established. The reason was that on two earlier occasions the Commons had found the behaviour of Black Rod presumptuous and disrespectful: in 1628 when he merely sent a deputy in his place, and later in 1641 when he arrived without his rod of office and entered prematurely before being called. Then to add insult to injury, in 1642 King Charles I tried to have five members arrested by Black Rod, at once overstepping the limit of his power and violating the independence of the House of Commons.[3] Thereafter members wanted to make it clear that it was beneath their dignity to be pushed around by the representative of the King, and that if they had to show deference to the Sovereign, they would do so only on their own terms. The persisting ritual, with its gentle suggestion that one day Black Rod might be refused, is a regularly re-enacted reminder of this balance of power.

Black Rod's progress as ritual

Probably nobody would doubt that this event falls within the definition of a ritual. It is of national importance, highly organized, involves large numbers of people, many of whom wear uniforms, happens repetitively in the same order at annual intervals, requires a particular spatial setting, and carries a significant symbolic content. So loaded is it symbolically that many might consider it merely symbolic, superfluous to the real business of government, but deeper scrutiny shows it to be a defining element in the longer chain of government rituals. These control how the governing process occurs and what it means, as well as carrying memories of its history. The threat of superfluity begs the question of how far it could be dismantled before the process fell apart, for at least it has the role of reminding the experienced of where things happen, and of initiating the newly arrived into a proper respect for the process. But it also creates order both in time and in space. Its temporal function is in ordering the parliamentary year, the annual ritual being the big brother of weekly rituals like Prime Minister's Questions and, lower in the hierarchy, the daily opening and closing of parliamentary sessions. A parliament can only work if people agree in advance to meet for discussion in a given place and at a given time, and these places and times necessarily take on a repetitive and rhythmic character. The ritual's spatial function lies in defining, separating and combining the territories of groups within the seat of government. The Queen's presence on the throne of the Lords sets her at the head of the traditional aristocracy, the Lords Temporal and Spiritual, and remembers the days when parliament was merely an advisory body to the King or Queen, called irregularly at his or her will. In those days the King or Queen's speech really was just that: the Sovereign's own declaration of the reason why parliament had been called and revelation of the business to be discussed.[4] The throne of the Lords is the Sovereign's place, not to be usurped by anyone else, for it remains empty while the Lord Chancellor runs the everyday business of the Lords from the more centrally placed but still axial Woolsack. One might think that as the Commons is the more powerful house, the Queen should make her speech there, but as the ritual makes clear she has no place in that House, nor should she threaten its independence, hence the three knocks. It would be as inappropriate for her to assume the place of the Speaker as it would be for the Speaker to usurp her place: they are key roles mediating different kinds of power, and are appropriately placed at opposite ends. There could hardly be more contrast, too, between the Queen's elaborate Gothic throne with its richly gilt canopy and the Speaker's relatively plain and sober chair, designed to give him dignity and precedence over the chamber but no further glorification.[5] The Speaker, a temporary role, is the impartial controller of debates in the Commons and is so-called because it was initially his job to report proceedings to the King or Queen. His special uniform like that of Black Rod and others is a necessary ingredient, along with the set patterns of etiquette, all of which help to define and confirm the roles of participants.

Figure 2.8 The Palace of Westminster in modern times, with the south end of Westminster Hall on the left (author's photograph).

The Palace of Westminster as we know it today is largely due to the rebuilding and reorganization by Charles Barry and Augustus Welby Pugin after a disastrous fire in 1834 and Barry's success in the open architectural competition.[6] It was one of the greatest monuments of the Victorian age and not completed until the 1860s. Spatially, Black Rod's progress traces on foot the connection between Sovereign, Lords, and Commons. Looking at the plan of the rebuilt Palace (Figure 2.10) the entire organization seems to hang on his route (Figure 2.11), for the building centres on an axis that links the Queen's throne in the Lords with the Speaker's chair in the Commons, terminating with each. The rooms linking these two highly symbolic terminations are all symmetrical, and they centre on the octagonal hall which leads westwards through the rebuilt St Stephen's chapel as vestibule to the main public entrance, eastward to the wing of libraries and consultation rooms overlooking the river: a crossing of axes. Each House is traversed along its main axis towards its respective focal seat, giving a powerful sense of centrality to the whole building. This layout by Barry and Pugin was something entirely new, as the two Houses had never before been linked in this way. Nor had they before enjoyed purpose-built accommodation, having been allotted rooms adapted from other purposes. Before the fire the Lords sat in the former Court of Requests (3 in Figure 2.12), the Commons in the much adapted former St Stephen's Chapel (2). These rooms stood almost at right angles to each other at the end of Westminster Hall (1) in no clear formal relation, and transition between Commons and Lords involved fourteen steps down and seven up.[7] The only grand architectural route in the pre-fire Palace (apart from Westminster Hall itself, which we shall come to) was the recently added Scala Regia built by Soane in the 1820s at the request of

Figure 2.9 Palace of Westminster seen across the river, with Victoria Tower on the West End and the Big Ben Clock Tower on the right (author's photograph).

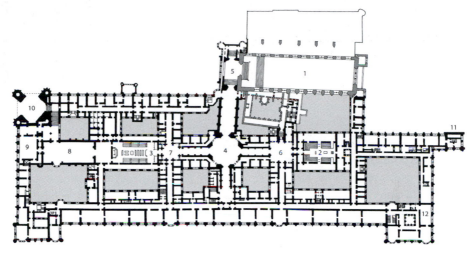

Figure 2.10 Plan of the Palace of Westminster as rebuilt by Barry and Pugin, main floor. The surviving medieval Westminster Hall is top right, its walls in dark grey, open courts are in light grey, north is right. Key: 1. Westminster Hall; 2. House of Commons; 3. House of Lords; 4. Central Hall; 5. Main Entrance; 6. Commons Lobby; 7. Peers Lobby; 8. Royal Gallery; 9. Queen's Robing; 10. Victoria Tower; 11. Clock Tower; 12. Speaker's House (redrawn by author after Hastings 1950 after Barry).

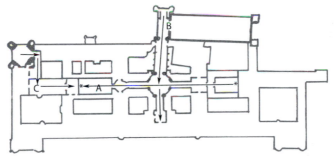

Figure 2.11 Diagram to accompany 2.10, identifying the principal axes of the plan. A links the Royal Throne with the Speaker's Chair and so defines the territory walked by Black Rod; B is the main entrance leading through to central hall and on to members' facilities; C is the route taken by the arriving Monarch (author's drawing).

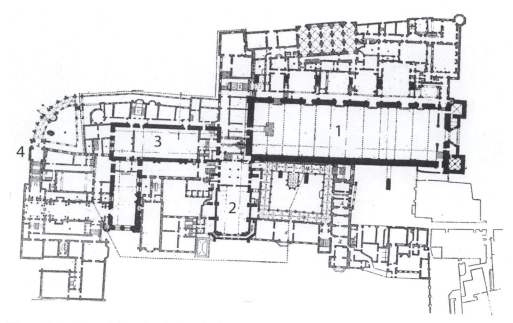

Figure 2.12 Plan of the Palace before the fire of 1836 at approximately the same orientation as 2.10. Key: 1. Westminster Hall; 2. Commons in former St Stephen's Chapel; 3. The Lords in former Court of Requests; 4. Royal Entrance and Scala Regia (redrawn by author after Hastings 1950).

George IV (4). As a ceremonial route this also served the opening of parliament, but it concentrated on the glorification of the King parading before the aristocracy. Surviving watercolour perspectives (Figure 2.13) show Soane's concern with the *promenade architecturale* of the King's entry and progress from his carriage, up the Scala Regia, through the Royal Gallery, then through the Painted Chamber and on to the Royal Robing Room just behind the throne of the Lords (Figure 2.12).[8]

This example was not neglected by Barry and Pugin, who set the royal entrance beneath what was the tallest secular Gothic tower not only in the complex, but in the country. They repeated the grand stair for the Sovereign (Figure 2.14) leading from the great vaulted entrance porch to the Robing Room, and they provided a sumptuously decorated Royal Gallery larger even than the House of Lords, but in their much larger scheme the royal element was limited to the south end. It was subtly balanced by the substantial Speaker's house around its own entrance court at the north-east corner, and Victoria Tower in the south was balanced by the clock tower in the north that we know by its bell, Big Ben. The Speaker's house had only been part of the Palace of Westminster since 1794, but had become increasingly important with the growing dominance of the Commons. Its several rituals, including ministerial dinners and so-called Speaker's levees, were accommodated in a range of elaborate state rooms and there was even a state bed.[9] Barry and Pugin played up its polar partnership with the royal quarters, giving the Speaker's house a similar weight in the plan, if denying it equivalent grand halls and axial connections. The clock tower stands in a balanced but differentiated relationship to the Victoria Tower (Figure 2.9), a vivid instance of how Gothic Revival asymmetry could achieve a kind of rhetorical differentiation that would be repressed by automatic classical symmetry.[10] Although smaller, the clock tower is much more elaborate, and more focal in relation to the

Figure 2.13 Soane's Scala Regia (courtesy of the Trustees of Sir John Soane's Museum).

Figure 2.14 Barry and Pugin's Royal Stair in the Victoria Tower (photograph by Roger Harris 2014, licensed under the Open Parliament Licence v3.0).

rest of the city. Its success as a monument is constantly demonstrated by use of its photographed image to represent London and Britain. It carries its authority in its famous clock, ordering the nation's time as the government orders its laws, an effect now extended through radio and television, for its image daily introduces the news. The chimes are carried by BBC radio as the auditory equivalent, and it was fascinating to witness when the clock needed repairs in 2006 that the BBC felt it necessary to mark the absence of the chimes by replacing them with birdsong rather than filling them in with a recording, which would have been technically easier and indistinguishable from the real thing. Despite worldwide establishment of international time and the unseen rule of the atomic clock, the acoustically relayed chimes of Big Ben still carry a sense of authenticity, while the clock tower's appearance still gives a necessary sense of place to the political process.

The subtlety of Barry and Pugin's reworking of the Palace lay in the asymmetrical balance of plan which made things roughly equivalent without being the same, and everything centred

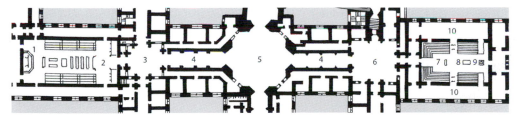

Figure 2.15 Palace of Westminster: extract from Barry's plan (Figure 2.10) showing the axial connection of the Lords, left, and the Commons, right. Key: 1. Queen's Throne, 2. House of Lords, 3. Peers' Lobby, 4. Corridor, 5. Central Hall, 6. Commons Lobby, 7. House of Commons, 8. Table of the House, 9. Speaker's Chair, 10. Division Lobbies.

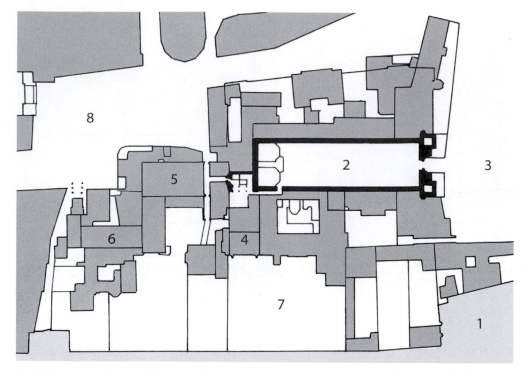

Figure 2.16 Palace of Westminster 1761. Key: 1. River Thames; 2. Westminster Hall; 3. New Palace Yard; 4. Commons in former St Stephen's Chapel; 5. Court of Requests; 6. House of Peers; 7. Gardens; 8. Old Palace Yard (redrawn by the author after a plan in the British Library, Crace Collection).

on the axial partnership, again balanced but differentiated, between House of Commons and House of Lords (Figure 2.15).[11] This came to dominate the whole complex as the real focus of power, and Black Rod's ritual call increased in importance. This has gradually assumed the dominant role in what was once a tripartite ritual, for in the early nineteenth century the main public experience of the opening of parliament was the royal progress by carriage from residence to Westminster along a crowd-lined route with flags and decorated windows. This was the main annual occasion when the King would show himself, and before photography or film even a glimpse was exciting. The subsequent and second rite of the King's internal passage to the Lords was a more restricted affair reserved for members of the aristocracy and their wives, but Black Rod's call to the Commons was an event witnessed only by the Commons themselves, not even by the Sovereign who was already installed on the throne.[12] This third part, the least important in George IV's day, has grown steadily in significance with increasing democracy until assumed by the television age as the focal event, while direct experience of royal progress through city streets has largely lost its appeal.

Westminster Hall as precedent

Another great change between the plans of the pre-fire Palace and those of Barry and Pugin is the decline in importance of Westminster Hall. Before the fire the pattern of a great hall

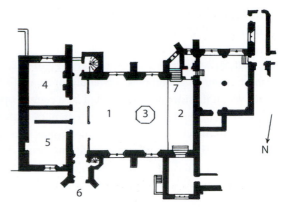

Figure 2.17 Hall at Penshurst Place (author's photograph).

Figure 2.18 Penshurst Hall plan (redrawn by the author after Banister Fletcher, 7th edn, 1924).

for audiences and public events, to which private apartments were added for the Sovereign beyond the high end, had remained unbroken for centuries. A plan dated 1761 (Figure 2.16) beautifully indicates the still central role of the hall in the eighteenth century, with its thick wall and subordinate buildings for law courts and administration accumulated around it. It was entered from the east off New Palace Yard, site of the main landing stage from the river and also the main approach to Westminster Abbey,[13] so it was the definitive entrance to the whole complex. A pair of law courts is shown within its west end to either side of the main connecting stairs.

Barry and Pugin deliberately sidelined the Hall, leaving it mainly for the use of the Law Courts which had grown up around it, and shifting politics onto their new centre line.[14] From being the very focus of political life, Westminster Hall was therefore reduced, and the removal of the Law Courts in 1883 to G. E. Street's new building in the Strand brought further decline, so that by now it has become a mere memorial hall for special occasions like state funerals. But Westminster Hall had been the birthplace of Westminster politics. The royal presence on a damp island somewhat west of London began with the adoption of Westminster Abbey as royal church and the building of a first palace nearby, probably by Edward the Confessor in the eleventh century. The Hall was added by King William Rufus in 1097–9, and although its elaboration with the famous hammerbeam roof dates only from the 1390s, the full outline and unprecedented 68-foot width were originally present. The precedent of a hall as place of government and authority went back to the Roman basilica, but the type was visible in medieval times across the country in the hall houses of lords of the manor, the halls at the hearts of castles, the halls of bishops and abbots, the halls of colleges at Oxford and Cambridge, and the halls of companies and guilds.[15] As long rectangular spaces, they conformed to a common pattern conditioned by the prevailing technology of masonry walls and steeply pitched timber trussed roofs, but they also had a common internal layout and the common function of bringing a social group together to share feasts, to show solidarity, to declare policies, and to make judgements. As Michael Thompson explains:

the hall was not just a dining room, a cookhouse, but something much more than that – a theatre where many aspects of life were played. Service and subordination held the household together and it was during meals in hall that this was demonstrated most dramatically, with all its members arranged in due degree.[16]

The pattern was remarkably consistent (Figures 2.17 and 2.18). The hall was the largest and highest room in a complex, generally open to the full height of its elaborate roof. It had windows on its sides and was heated by a central open fire whose smoke escaped via a louvre in the roof above: this smokey arrangement persisted into the fourteenth century in buildings of great architectural sophistication despite the availability of a well developed chimney technology. The hall had a high and a low end. The high end, marked by a raised dais for the lord or master, was where he and his close relatives sat centrally at high table looking down the main axis. Their private apartments, often on two storeys, lay behind the end wall, immediately accessible. An oriel window projecting from one side at the high end provided extra light as well as adding an architectural flourish visible from within and without. The hall was entered from the low end at the side, via a screens passage which often linked opposite doorways. Having entered at the door, guests and appellants would turn at the centre of the screen to find themselves looking up the axis towards the higher-seated and well-lit lord. They would need to traverse the entire room to obtain an audience. Behind the screens passage three doors in the low end's wall led to buttery, pantry and kitchen where drink and food were prepared. The manor house often adopted an H-shaped plan, with the dominant double-height hall linking the two-storey end blocks of services and apartments.

Westminster Hall was the great grand-daddy of them all. It was used for audiences and feasts, for legal trials, and for every kind of royal occasion. It was large enough even for five performers to enter abreast on horseback during the Coronation Feast of Queen Anne.[17] Illustrations of it down the ages confirm the Sovereign's constant central and axial place on a raised throne at the south end (Figures 2.19 and 2.20), but the most detailed evidence about

Figure 2.19 Westminster Hall during the coronation feast of George IV in 1821 (London Metropolitan Archives, Collage 18665).

Figure 2.20 Westminster Hall during the trial of Lord Lovat 1747 (London Metropolitan Archives, Collage 18665).

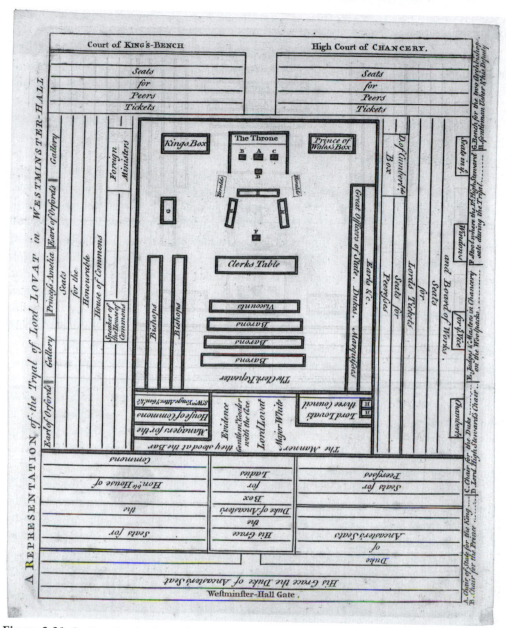

Figure 2.21 Seating plan for the trial of Lord Lovat (British Library, Crace Collection: Crace Port.II.38).

the use and meaning of the space can be gleaned from published seating plans. A convenient sample is the one recording the layout for the trial of Lord Lovat in 1747[18] (Figure 2.21). It shows the attention that went into providing appropriate places for all according to rank and role, not only within the central arena of the court where the trial actually took place, but also in spectators' galleries which were constructed with temporary scaffolding for the occasion. The symmetrical plan emphasizes the axis with the King's throne at the middle of the south end, flanked by side chairs for the Prince and the Duke. The King's box and that of the Prince of Wales are set to either side for members of the royal household, and heralds (dotted) stand on either side to perform fanfares. Before the King, forming the centre of the proceedings, sit the Judges and Masters in Chancery on their ceremonial woolsacks, the side seats slightly skewed to turn them towards the accused. In the centre we find the Lord High Steward acting as prosecutor, then comes the clerk's table at which proceedings are recorded. Moving on down we find a kind of inner audience consisting of Barons seated behind viscounts, with earls and marquises on one side and bishops on the other. The two archbishops occupy a special bench pulled forward to align them with the woolsacks.

This is just the inner arena of the court, a space to which the accused and his representatives are not admitted. Lovat stands at the Bar which completes the north side of the inner space, centrally placed and guarded by his jailer wielding the axe of judgment. Witnesses present evidence at the same Bar, and there are boxes to either side with lawyers for the accused and lawyers for the government, the latter seated on the King's right. For such popular pieces of national theatre the outer galleries were bursting with eager spectators, and the allocation reveals wealth and aristocracy. The Duke of Ancaster's 'Box for Ladies' takes axial precedence, for example, over the seating for Members of the Commons,[19] and despite the lower status of women, peeresses have equal and opposite positions to the members, though the latter are again on the King's right. In the front row of the side galleries the Duke of Cumberland and Foreign Ministers are flattered by sharing the line of the King, while the Speaker of the Commons must make do with a position further down, behind the bishops, though well placed to hear everything that is said. Perspective drawings of the trial represent it, unsurprisingly, seen from the middle of the north end looking axially towards the throne (Figure 2.20), and in three dimensions the axis is reinforced by the banked galleries, the centrally peaking roof, and beyond the fixed partitions of the courts of King's Bench and Chancery the vast south window of the hall, perhaps with the sun streaming in. It seems self-evident that there is no other way to give the King and his agents such clear precedence.

Several implied principles can be identified behind this layout. Most obvious is the symmetry and axiality of the hall, and the idea of low and high ends, metaphorically reinforced, incidentally, by the vertical printing of the plan on the page. There is also a division of centre and periphery, reinforced by the thickly drawn barrier around the arena of the court and by the stepping of the spectator's galleries. Social hierarchies operate centrally, since only those of highest rank involved in the judgment are admitted within the arena, but around the periphery there is ranking of seats. More important than the central hierarchy though is the longitudinal one, with the King at the high end and the prisoner brought to the Bar at the low end. The Bar is a physical barrier, but more importantly a symbolic division, a line beyond which the unprivileged dare not go. The prisoner is called there after others are in place, having arrived in due procession, so a temporal hierarchy also obtains.[20] The bilateral symmetry of the layout accepts the hierarchy of direction given by the shape of the hall, setting all principal actions to operate longitudinally. The lateral divisions are then balanced to left and right, but persons placed on the left of the hall – that is to the King's right – are superior. Here are not only the Prince of Wales' throne as opposed to the Duke's, and the King's box as opposed to the Prince's, but the Lords Spiritual (bishops) sit to the King's right as opposed to the Lords Temporal (earls and dukes) to his left. The Lord High Steward has two seats because he plays two roles. In the opening ceremony he represents the King as prosecutor and sits axially before and beneath the throne, but for the process of the trial he moves to a stool in the arena, still on axis but able to reverse position to address the King and Judges.[21]

Layouts of the Lords and Commons

If Westminster Hall helped define for the whole country the nature of a hall as the seat of power, it provided the key example for ritual use, setting precedents for other hall-like spaces such as the Houses of Lords and Commons. Early depictions of parliamentary assemblies, if giving relatively little idea of the architectural setting, reveal the roles, uniforms and spatial organization much as they still exist in the House of Lords today. A print by John Pine of 1749 (Figure 2.22) is particularly informative because it sets seating plans of the houses of Peers and Commons to either side of Westminster Hall, which is depicted in ritual use. Pine based his layout of Westminster Hall on a 'drawing in the Herald's office' showing the 'creation of Charles Brandon Duke of Suffolk in the 5th year of Henry VIII', 1514. We see the King on his throne at the end of the hall with other members of the royal household behind. To the King's right are earls holding the Sword of State and the Cap of Maintenance, and the King's man leads the procession, holding the Mace, symbol of his power. Brandon is brought in at the low end of the hall by two earls, and five others proceeding before him carry his mantle, sword, coronet and

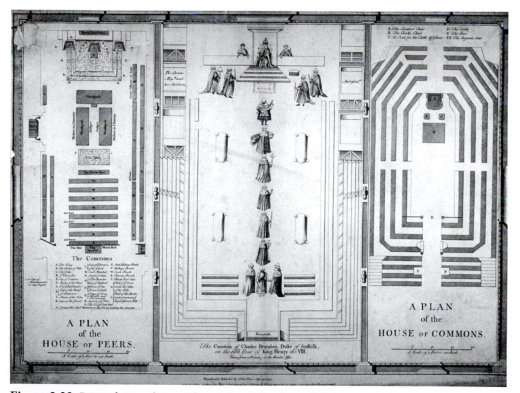

Figure 2.22 Print of 1741, showing from left to right plans of the Lords, Westminster Hall and the Commons, with detailed seating layouts. Westminster Hall is shown during the ceremony of Henry VIII creating the Duke of Suffolk (London Metropolitan Archives, Collage 29049).

Figure 2.23 The Commons in St Stephen's 1656, with the chapel's gothic window behind the Speaker, The opposed benches, central Speaker in his chair, and table of the house remain the same, as do the bar of the house at the bottom and the axial stance of the artist in each case. This image relates to the right hand plan of Figure 2.22 (London Metropolitan Archives, Collage 26906).

Figure 2.24 The Commons in 1700 after Wren's conversion (London Metropolitan Archives, Collage 29278).

Figure 2.25 The modern Commons in session, Speaker in his chair behind the Table of the House, Government and Opposition occupying the front benches to left and right (Flickr: Commons Civil Service Local Parliament/Flickr licensed under the Open Parliament Licence v3.0).

other ceremonial gear with which his transformation to Duke will be accomplished, the King dubbing him with his own sword before returning it to him. Seats indicated on all three sides show this to have been a very public occasion, but only the Queen's box to right of the King and Ambassadors' to his left are labelled, while at the door 'trumpets' are noted, so entry was made with a fanfare. This drawing pushes a plan into projection with exaggerated figures and could hardly stress the axis of the hall more as the way a subject presents himself to his King. Correct symbolism of garments and objects was the evident concern of the original artist at the College of Heralds, which regulated such things.

The accompanying plan to left is the House of Peers (Lords), with no drawn figures but detailed identification of roles and positions. At the top end is the throne, with the King seated on the dais three steps up, the Prince of Wales to his right one step lower, and 'The Duke' symmetrically to his left. Behind are the peers' eldest sons. Surrounding the King guards and officers of the royal household have specific positions. At the centre on the woolsacks are Judges and Masters in Chancery, and below them the table on which the clerks record proceedings. Outer benches to the King's right are occupied by Bishops, the Lords Spiritual, the Archbishop's seat being closest to the King and opposite the primary woolpack. Closest to the King on his left are the Great Officers of State, and beyond them the Lords Temporal, Earls and Barons, more of whom also occupy the middle, seated beyond the clerks. At the bottom of the plan is the Bar of the House, with the Speaker standing at the centre reporting to the King, and Black Rod to his right, the latter also allowed a special seat in the bottom right corner. The Commons are only designated by a label. We can easily recognize in this arrangement the essential hierarchical layout of the modern Opening of Parliament.

The third plan shows the House of Commons in St Stephen's Chapel, a far more centralized arrangement with only a few roles noted: the Speaker in his central seat, the Clerks in front of him, the Table at which they wrote, and the Sergeants at Arms beside the entrance. Prominent at E, bounding the central arena, is the Bar of the House. The lack of designation of Government and Opposition, or of front bench for Ministers, perhaps indicates the fluidity of these positions and the ideal of a representative parliament where all discuss on equal terms. The engraving in Figure 2.23 concurs with this plan version and shows the Gothic windows of the old chapel, seen as usual axially from the low end. The parliamentary system grew in stages, for the hereditary aristocracy (Lords Temporal) had been part of the royal court, and the bishops and abbots (Lords Spiritual) had been a powerful force before the Reformation, the Catholic Church being not only possessed of power and wealth, but also the fount of knowledge and truth before our secular and scientific age. Commoners first became involved with Simon de Montfort's parliament of 1265, which invited the attendance of two knights from each shire, two citizens from each city, and two burgesses from each borough. Early parliaments were called by the still-powerful Sovereign and met somewhat irregularly in various places, but the process gradually consolidated itself at Westminster, where the two social groups of Lords and Commons separated, each holding its own meetings. The Lords long occupied what was known as the Old Parliament Chamber, then from 1801 sat in the Court of Requests (Figures 2.12 and 2.16). The early Commons met in various places, including the polygonal Chapter House of Westminster Abbey, until they were given the former royal Chapel of St Stephen by the ten-year-old King Edward VI in 1547.[22] The Court of Requests and St Stephen's were the largest rooms in the pre-fire complex apart from Westminster Hall, the former with a width of 36 feet, the latter 32 feet (in contrast with Westminster Hall's 68 feet).

The chamber used by the Lords in 1834 was thus both larger and more prominently positioned than that of the Commons.

St Stephen's Chapel (Figures 2.22 and 2.23) had been one of the most elaborate Gothic buildings in England, started by King Edward 1 in 1292 but not roofed until 1348, when Edward III also turned it into a college (in the original sense), with a dean, twelve canons and thirteen vicars, who sang the offices to connect with the divine presence at regular intervals each day. Their prayers on the King's behalf were thought to improve his position in the afterlife, hence the expenditure both on the building and on its rituals. Edward VI's handing of it over to the secular purpose of parliament following the reformation was not merely a practical redesignation of usable space but a deliberate and insulting rejection of Catholic rites. As built, St Stephen's was a tall vaulted space with decorated Gothic windows down the sides and across the east end. Conventional Christian orientation made it face the river. The main axis terminated in the altar which was raised by a few steps, and lateral benches accommodated a choir in two halves following the long-established tradition of antiphonal singing. This duality, taken over by the Commons, provided the basis of our two-party politics of government and opposition, with two groups of people symmetrically disposed for an alternating series of speeches (Figures 2.23, 2.24 and 2.25). The axial position of the altar, formerly designating the divine presence, was taken up instead by the Speaker's chair, though Members continued to nod to the lost altar. The Speaker, as controller of the whole proceedings, was given the prime position, which also located him impartially between the factions of Government and Opposition: Government on his right, Opposition on his left.

At the opposite end of the chapel was a screen with two doorways which was adopted as a device for voting at the end of the debate, members being counted as they walked through; 'Ayes to the right, Noes to the left' as the speaker still calls today. Cross benches were set up for observers, and a bar was added in front of them to mark the edge of the territory occupied by participating members. It was also the point where petitioners and persons tried by the house might be interrogated. A table in the central space was provided early on for the two clerks writing the record of the debate, and this evolved into the centrepiece between opposed parties, with a dispatch box added on each side to mark the place from which the main speeches were to be made. The table also became the site for the placing of the Mace, the symbolic object that signifies parliament is in session. The arena at the centre needed to retain a certain width, both to allow movement in and out and to separate the parties, and in the space of the rebuilt Victorian Commons, red lines were made in the carpet to mark the distance apart, defined as two sword lengths. The lines indicated the limits beyond which each side was forbidden to pass, preventing the anger of the debate erupting into physical violence.

Between the moment when the King handed over the chapel for the Commons' use in 1547 and its destruction by fire nearly 300 years later, the building went through extensive alterations and adjustments of form and organization. Extra tiers of seats were added to accommodate more Members, extending them around the corners behind the Speaker, but the chamber was never large enough for all, and Members took their places as they arrived, still the practice today apart from the reserved front benches. The vividly painted and decorated sides of the Gothic chapel were suppressed first with tapestries, then with panelling, partly to cover up the religious iconography of a building associated with 'popery', partly to improve the acoustics which must at first have been excessively resonant. In the 1690s all visible memory of the Gothic building was expunged by Christopher Wren (Figure 2.24), who lowered the ceiling, added galleries, and replaced the great pointed window of the east end with three round-headed lights of his own.[23] Attempts were made to improve the ventilation, for the room became hot and stale, but with limited success. All in all, with the help of some distinguished builders and architects, the room was gradually adapted to the Members' needs.

Rebuilding after the fire, Barry and Pugin were obliged to transpose the spatial organization of each House as it had evolved up to that point (Figures 2.10, 2.11 and 2.15). Despite their symmetrical placing and some intended equivalence, contrasts in internal organization based on their different histories and uses were played up. The Lords is a longer chamber, with clear space around the Sovereign at the south end, and space for the gathered visitors from the Commons at the north. The equivalent of the Commons Speaker is the Lord Chancellor, who sits on the woolsack, historic symbol of trade, set on the axis of the chamber towards the south end, but below and directly in front of the normally vacant throne. The main party benches occupy the two sides of the chamber, but there are also cross benches in the middle for judges and bishops with no party attachment. With its smaller number of occupants, the Lords has only minimal galleries in contrast with the extensive ones in the Commons, and is noticeably looser in its general organization. The continuing tradition of colour coding makes leather seating in the Lords red, while that in the Commons it is green. Despite the continuities, there were many readjustments and even substantial rearrangement in the making of the new Commons. Most of all, the members objected during experimental sittings of 1850 to the new high ceiling, which proved an acoustic disaster, and they insisted on having it lowered.[24] Thereafter the chamber was accepted and even loved, though Barry himself felt it had been ruined.[25] There are other differences between the two Houses. One crucial improvement added by the architects was the division lobbies set alongside the chamber, rooms in which members gather as they are counted, and which may draw in the whole membership if the vote looks to be close. These lateral chambers dramatize the physical process of voting and the responsibility of being seen to take a stand on an issue.

Each chamber had its own programme of decoration, part of a representational programme for the Palace that, properly described, would need another chapter to itself. In an age of highly decorated buildings it was taken for granted that leading painters and sculptors would provide embellishment, being given subjects intended to represent the nation. Thus the Queen's robing room has morally loaded fresoces by Dyce of Arthurian scenes, there are statues in the Lords representing the barons supposed to have instituted Magna Carta, and the octagonal central lobby is dominated by mosaics of St George, St David, St Andrew, and St Patrick proclaiming the union of the kingdom.[26]

Conclusion: Rituals and spatial hierarchies

As an event of national significance, the Black Rod ritual has the advantage of good documentation, and there is also no lack of material on the buildings in which it occurs. That they carry such a heavy iconographic programme and are at the same time so spatially elaborated has provided rich material for our first case study, while also engaging a necessary chronological dimension. The account *Duties of Black Rod Today* dates from 1976 and is presented essentially as a present-tense story,[27] but the buildings were designed and completed mainly in the mid-nineteenth century. The narrative has necessarily introduced many other dates both before and between these two, revealing that neither the ritual nor the setting can be regarded as fixed in time or constant in form. They exist in a mutual state of evolution that must be understood within a temporal continuum. The ritual is both present and historic, as matters of habit and memory are bound to be. Styles might be identified in both practices and buildings, but again they are not fixed or isolated, and always subject to understanding and interpretation. Within all this complexity and specificity can any general or universal principles be discerned?

We might first look at spatial arrangements within the halls themselves. Putting a powerful person such as the Queen or Speaker in the highest seat on the end of the main axis seems to be a universal phenomenon.[28] It combines three factors: relative height, lateral centrality and longitudinal culmination. The queen sits on a throne at the top of a dais ascended by multiple steps, so all must look up at her unless in distant galleries and safely marginalized by being so far from the action. If groups of thrones are involved to accommodate princes or consorts, the relative heights are seen as critical to the social hierarchy, both as regards level of seat and the seat-back or canopy. Height and vertical progressions obey gravity, a given of living on this planet that we cannot escape or imagine being without. It is constantly reflected in metaphorical references within everyday language which automatically privilege height, such as high quality versus low quality, the cream rising to the top, being top of the form or on the top of one's form, and so on. Being at the top of the list is usually advantageous, and we read from the top down. Some usages are directly political, such as upper class versus lower class, rising through the ranks, or being elevated to the peerage as opposed to being sent down from university. More anciently, heaven and gods were regarded as being above, hell below.[29]

Centrality in the hall seems equally important, depending on the symmetry both of the building and of the layout. Perception of symmetry relates to our symmetrical bodies and our recognition of faces, and the very basic register with us and the other higher animals of the difference between looking at the axially symmetrical front as opposed to the asymmetrical side. A roof peaking at the centre of the gable and an elaborated roof structure as at Westminster Hall enhance symmetry, as do centrally placed end doors and windows, and it is surely significant that depictions of events in parliaments and halls, whether painted or photographed, are usually presented on axis. Symmetry of layout with persons seated to the sides in equivalent and balanced arrangements reinforces the sense of centrality.

That the Queen sits at the end terminating the main axis of the space adds the third factor. She sits directly opposite the entrance, commanding with her gaze the main route through the space along which she may process on ceremonial occasions, but also along which appellants may be obliged to approach her as she presides, stressing the confrontation. In the case of the trial of Lord Lovat the central route was not traversed ceremonially, for the hall had been subdivided to create a central arena for the court, but the confrontational nature of the axis was exploited in the central placing of the accused at the bar, standing opposite his accuser, the King. This polarity left no doubt about the relative status of the two persons, no danger of mistaking the prisoner for the King, because of the different treatments of the two ends. It followed the long-standing convention about a hall having a 'high' end and 'low' end, incidentally a reapplication of the height metaphor to the longitudinal direction.

Door, longitudinal route, throne, and end window all fall on the axis of the hall, and there is no doubt that this axis is the main one, even though the hall is also symmetrical in the other direction and has cross-axes which also dictate alignments. The long axis becomes the main one not only because it is longer and follows the building's structure, but also because it becomes the main route, and the principal persons involved in the ritual move along it, gaze at each other down it, and have their conversations on it. When the primary movement is to and fro along the main axis, the symmetrical sides of the hall present themselves as left and right, and can be read either way round depending on whether one is entering the space from the entrance or looking back when seated on the throne. The long-standing custom of seating the most honoured persons on one's right, or the governing party on the Speaker's right, seems to be based on an almost universal and cross-cultural convention that allows precedence to the right hand, the dextrous one as opposed to the sinister one.[30] The point here is that the two axes are treated differently in ways which relate to longitudinal as opposed to lateral movements and postures of the human body, the lateral being more or less symmetrical. This difference is reflected in the layout of the House of Commons in that longitudinally the dominance of the Speaker opposite the door is assured by the main axis, while laterally there is a symmetrical balance between the parties and an expectation of even-handed debate across the chamber.

Although all the examples considered are essentially linear, there is in every case also a crucial difference between centre and periphery. When Westminster Hall was used for the Lovat trial, a defined central arena for those conducting and recording proceedings was surrounded on all sides by an audience ranked in terms of closeness to the action and progress towards the royal end. In the House of Commons the central action revolves around the Speaker, Table, and dispatch boxes. There are front benches and back benches in hierarchy, with more distant galleries for observers. The ultimate expression of centre and periphery is a circular layout, and people do tend to gather around focal events in a circle. The circus big-top is an obvious way to make the action available to as many spectators as possible, and the circle is also a well-known model for democratic discussion on equal terms, as with King Arthur's legendary round table or the term 'round-table discussion'. In medieval monasteries the Chapter House was often polygonal to express the idea that brothers shared their gatherings on equal terms, even if the Abbot took the seat opposite the door, reawakening the axial principle. It is revealing, incidentally, that the Commons, having borrowed this kind of space in Westminster Abbey in its early days, did not choose to cling to the polygonal form.

A key early precedent for the centre and periphery layout is the antique Greek theatre (Figure 2.26), bringing the whole of society to contemplate the play. Many modern parliaments

Figure 2.26 Theatre at Epidaurus (author's photograph).

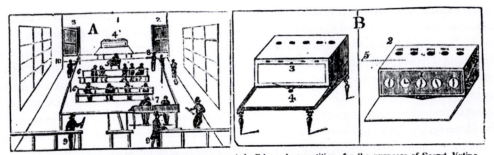

Schedule A, the Balloting Place.—1. The space separated off by a close partition, for the purposes of Secret Voting 2. The entrance to the Ballot Box, where the voter gives his vote. 3. The door by which the voter retires. 4. The front of the Ballot Box, placed on a stand with an inclined plane, down which the balloting ball descends, to be ready for the next voter. 5. The seat of the Deputy returning Officer. 6. The seats of the Agents of the Candidates. 7. The desk of the Registration Clerk and his Assistant. 8. The Assistant, who delivers the balloting ball to the voters. 9. Assistants and Constables at the doors and barriers, who examine the certificates, and let the voter pass on to the ballot. 10. A Constable, to stop any voter who may vote unfairly.

Figure 2.27 Perspective of voting room from Chartist pamphlet, 1838. Voters move down the right side and across the stage then back on the left while observers in the middle look on (People's History Museum Manchester, LHASC. VIN/6).

follow a circular layout to stress the equality of members in representing their constituencies, but the parties still tend to align themselves in segments between extreme right and extreme left, a spatial designation of political leaning that goes back to the French National Assembly of 1789 where the so-called First Estate of conservatives took the right side and the Third Estate of revolutionaries the left.

The ubiquitous nature of the axial spatial arrangement in political buildings is not restricted to strong political hierarchies, but can be found reinterpreted at the egalitarian end of the political spectrum in a fascinating nineteenth century proposal. Two years after the fire at the Palace of Westminster and six years after the Great Reform Bill, suffrage was still restricted, representation varied, and Members of Parliament, being unpaid, were drawn only from the propertied classes. The Chartist Movement of 1838 sought to correct all this in the name of just representation for all, but despite wide popular support it was ignored by parliament. Of interest for our purposes are the drawings on the cover of its pamphlet (Figure 2.27) depicting how the secret ballot could be conducted. There is a voting machine with counters operated by means of a dropping ball, and a room in which this apparatus was set. In the axial and symmetrically organized hall the voting machine has pride of place, set axially on the dais. Directly in front sits the deputy returning officer to witness the casting of votes, and behind him are two rows of benches for agents of the candidates, present to assure fair play. Voters arrive at the back, register, move down the right hand side (dominant hand for the active agent), and receive a voting ball as they arrive at the dais which they enter by a door. The visit reaches a climax with the voter's passage across the dais and the dropping of the ball: he then passes through the opposite door to leave by the passage on the left, passing two constables who react to any irregularity. This idealized arrangement may never have been built, but its intended spatial hierarchy puts the ballot box where the king or lord might have been expected to sit, and makes each member of the public momentarily player on stage and focus of interest. As well as walking the entire perimeter of the hall, the voter crosses no less than four thresholds, the doors to the dais added to stress the drama of transition and temporary ownership of the space by a single person.

This discussion has concerned only the single room, but in most buildings rooms are put together, which also has hierarchical implications. Add a second room or a forecourt in front of the door and the route is extended, the impressiveness of the axis increased every time it is framed by a new threshold or centred on another symmetrical space. The procession following Black Rod back to the Lords passes axially through five separate rooms – wide, narrow, wide, narrow, and wide again – before entering the Lords. Each narrow room is divided into four vaulted bays further stressing the rhythm and centrality. During the opening of parliament ritual, the great crossroads of the polygonal central hall is traversed specifically to unite the two Houses, while normally it is the daily point at which arriving visitors turn right to Lords or left to Commons. Rooms can be assembled in numerous ways, but always they fall into relationships significant in terms of adjacencies or polarities. We experience them as we move through and between them, so they exist for us as a progression, and the movement always has a direction. Our consciousness of the way spaces unfold normally goes unremarked, and yet we daily remember new sequences as we encounter hitherto unknown buildings, if only to be able to find our way out again. Our ability to negotiate stairs at home in complete darkness without missing a step is a reminder that the body knows the space and has subconsciously choreographed itself for the interaction. Spatial sequences and a sense of direction are always sought, and we look to the building to inform us where to go next. Moving from one room to the next also involves doors and thresholds as definers of territory. The door to the Commons with its inspection grille is largely symbolic, for any real invaders could quickly find a way around, but the ritual use makes it seem defensive, and the knocking with the rod is almost violent. On the other hand both Houses have bars which are largely symbolic fences dividing the space, and spatial definitions can be set by as little as a line on a carpet. In everyday life we obey the most minimal spatial divisions once the convention is established and understood. Respect for thresholds and the crossing of them is an essential part of our ritual behaviour.

Parliament and the progress of time

As well as setting up order in space, this chapter has also shown the crucial importance of time and the need to understand the spatial ordering in terms of its chronological evolution. Because the spatial arrangement needs to mesh with the choreography of human actions, it also remembers and prompts them, both in the way it tacitly carries forward the hierarchies and polarities of political life, and in the way it reminds and teaches the reassembled members of parliament about the history of the balance of power. But the clock keeps ticking and life changes. Barry and Pugin's arrangement freezes an order thought appropriate in the 1840s, when the Lords enjoyed more power than today, and the Sovereign was a more elevated if more remote presence. There have since been radical political changes, including growth and loss of empire, the arrival of universal suffrage, joining Europe, the devolution of power, and globalization.[31] The Lords has been weakened and even threatened with abolition, and should that happen the current arrangements would become inappropriate. The ritual would have to be revised, the Lords' chamber perhaps converted to another purpose. Similarly, although the Commons seems yet alive and well, its chamber with the stress on opposed benches makes it difficult for third and fourth political parties to establish any physical presence, and might thereby be restricting the growth of our democracy.[32] Furthermore, the overplayed Victorian 'inventions of tradition', both in the setting and the ritual, may have encouraged an illusion of permanence that is unjustified, obstructing development and change. After all, the story of the developing parliamentary process over a thousand years suggests not constancy but change, and there is no reason to suppose this evolution has stopped.

This chapter has shown how a reciprocal relationship exists between a ritual and its setting. Sometimes the setting is needed to make the ritual possible: for example, Black Rod could not knock if there were no door. Sometimes the setting is required to organize and orientate the participants, so that they have a stage to act out their parts which defines their relationships spatially. The setting may be merely helpful and suggestive, supporting the proceedings with suitable symbolism and with costumes helping the general make-believe. But equally, the destruction of a setting can deny a ritual and prevent it taking place, as often happens with rebuilding and reorganization. This might remind us that our daily relationships with space, though unnoticed and taken for granted, are always engaged by our bodies if not by our consciously attentive minds, for we need to recognize where we are, where we have come from, and where we are going. It is this that gives architecture a necessary guiding role, ensuring that places and spaces are riddled with memories and suggestions, hopes and opportunities. In later examples, through which the definition of ritual will be extended, we shall see that the relationship between setting and ritual depends on an essential feedback between buildings and practices.

Notes

1   Winston S. Churchill, speech to the House of Commons, 28 October 1943 about the necessary rebuilding of the House after bombing in 1941.

2   Bond and Beamish 1976, pp. 12–13.

3   Ibid., p. 5.

4   See Henry S. Cobb, 'The Staging Ceremonies of State in the House of Lords', in Riding 2000, pp. 31–48.

5   See Christine Riding, 'The Aura of Sacred Mystery: Thrones in the New Place of Westminster', in Riding 2000, pp. 179–94.

6   Barry was the principal and Pugin the assistant, and the competition was submitted and won under Barry's name. That Pugin supplied most of the decorative schemes seems without doubt, particularly as he had studied the Gothic with his father and became the passionate leader of the Gothic Revival, but he also drew the competition drawings. It is often assumed that Barry was wholly responsible for the planning, but plan and elevation must develop and interact, and Pugin was a forceful and knowledgeable character never afraid to criticize his elders and collaborators, as reported by Margaret Belcher, editor of his letters. It is hard to imagine him, when acting as draughtsman, not suggesting potential improvements as he drew, so helping to steer the design towards its successful conclusion. Besides, he was an avid proponent of asymmetry and of the idea that the parts of a building should articulate its social structure, neither of which were among the classical-minded Barry's primary interests, and it is the balanced asymmetry of the building that for our purposes is most important. Pugin is reported as having been critical of the symmetry of the east front, but more specific evidence we do not have. The original competition drawings and some crucial letters between the two architects which might have shed more light on Pugin's role were unfortunately lost: see Colvin et al., 1973, pp. 573–626, and the essays by Andrea Fredericksen and Alexandra Wedgwood in Riding 2000, pp. 99–112, 113–36. Later letters

from Barry to Pugin published in Port 1976, pp. 85–6, reveal a close and working relationship, with Pugin very well paid by a respectful Barry for elaborating and detailing parts of the building in relative freedom and independence.

7   Port 1976, p. 9. An earlier arrangement recorded in a plan of 1793 placed the House of Lords further south and must have involved Black Rod and the Commons processing through the Long Gallery and turning through the Painted Chamber, which at least gave them ceremonial space but involved three turns; see Colvin et al., 1973, p. 496 and figure opposite.

8   See Sean Sawyer, 'Sir John Soane and the Late Georgian Origins of the Royal Entrance', in Riding 2000, pp. 137-48.

9   Riding speaker's house.

10 This was made explicit in Pugin's *True Principles*: 'many architects apply the details and minor features of the pointed style to classic *masses* and arrangements … They must have two of everything, one on each side … Because a man has a real door to enter his house by on one side, he must have a mock one through which he cannot get in on the other' Pugin 1853, pp. 51–2. Ruskin often made the same point.

11 The other surviving competition entries show substantial struggles with this, tending towards a kind of total and automatic symmetry. Thomas Hopper even suggested a twin for Westminster Hall in order to achieve it (see Riding 2000, p. 104). Port 1976, the most detailed published source on the competition, includes the principal floor plans of the second, third and fourth prize winners, all of which adopted an axial relationship between Commons and Lords, but less clearly than Barry and Pugin. Buckler set a stair between them, Hamilton blocked them with a committee room as well as placing them back to back, and Railton isolated them by a long central corridor (Port 1976, pp. 41–9).

12 See Henry. S. Cobb, 'The Staging of Ceremonies of State in the House of Lords', in Riding 2000, pp. 31–48. Interestingly, in a chronological treatment beginning in the Middle Ages, Cobb hardly mentions the Black Rod element.

13 Westminster Bridge was completed around 1750, so this plan from the Crace Collection was retrospective.

14 As the making of laws and keeping them was part of the same process, the main courts had long been there with new buildings by Soane on the west side of the hall, but all moved out in 1883 to occupy G. E. Street's new building in the Strand.

15 For the latter, including several illustrations, see Unwin 1908.

16 Thompson 1995, p. 115.

17 Ibid., p. 186.

18 Tried for treason after taking part in the Jacobite rebellion, found guilty, and publically beheaded at Tower Hill on 9 April 1747. The trial took a week.

19 The Duke of Ancaster had the hereditary role of Lord Great Chamberlain, controller of ceremonial at Westminster Hall, so presumably this box was among his perks: see Colvin et al., 1973, p. 500.

20 The full order of procession is given for the first day in Mackay 1911.

21 The change of position is allowed with formal permission after the opening of proceedings each day, see Mackay 1911.

22 Presumably arranged by his protector Somerset. The gift of the chapel reflected the sweeping changes of the reformation, pushed through by Charles's father Henry VIII, and intended to show a rejection of the Roman Catholic heritage (Jones 1983, p. 49).

23 Jones 1983, p. 79.

24 See account by M. H. Port in Colvin et al., 1973, p. 624.

25 Ibid., also Hastings 1950. It was later changed again in ways that need not detain us here. As

a result of heavy bomb damage in the Second World War, the Commons was rebuilt by Giles Gilbert Scott on the same layout but with simplified Gothic detail. See Gavin Stamp '"We Shape Our Buildings and Afterwards Out Buildings Shape Us": Sir Giles Gilbert Scott and the Rebuilding of the House of Commons' in Riding 2000, pp. 149–61.

26 A useful general summary is given in the first volume of the London Pevsner, Pevsner 1973, pp. 520–32. A detailed account of the stylistic evolution is given in Colvin et al., 1973, pp 573–626. For detailed descriptions and illustrations of the painting, sculpture, furnishing, and many other aspects see Riding 2000.

27 Bond 1976.

28 Examples from other cultures will be given. This is not to say that everyone necessarily does it, for there are other patterns, such as the radial one of centre and periphery discussed later, but I have yet to find cases that contradict or reverse it.

29 Lakoff and Johnson 1980.

30 Sinistra and dextra are latin for left and right. There is undoubtedly much cultural construction around right-handedness, but there also seems to be an underlying biological basis. For a sophisticated discussion see Needham 1973.

31 David Cannadine discusses all these and more in 'The Palace of Westminster as Palace of Varieties' in Riding 2000, pp. 11–30.

32 Churchill argued for the recreation of the double-sided chamber on the basis that the adversarial system of government and opposition was positive and essential, and he also opposed making the chamber large enough to take all members on the basis that its intimacy would be destroyed. It is interesting too that early use by the Commons of the apparently more egalitarian polygonal Chapter House of Westminster Abbey seems not to have left any lasting legacy.

CHAPTER 3
THE LORD MAYOR'S BANQUET

Figure 3.1 Lord Mayor's Banquet in the Guildhall in 1914 (colour print of a painting, artist unknown, from a magazine c. 1925, found in a collection of cuttings, author's photograph).

Figure 3.2 The Guildhall south side today with George Dance's Portico and enlarged courtyard (author's photograph).

Figure 3.3 Guildhall and surrounding buildings in 1884. (North is top) Key: 1. Guildhall; 2. Guildhall Yard; 3. Library; 4. Council Chamber; 5. Committee Rooms; 6. Court of Exchequer; 7. Courts of Justice; 8. Bankruptcy Court (author's redrawing after a ward map in Guildhall Library, now in the London Metropolitan Archives).

Figure 3.4 Guildhall Yard in the nineteenth century dominated by George Dance's Portico with the Hall behind (from Thornbury 1871).

Figure 3.5 Interior of the 'Old Library' added to the complex by Horace Jones in 1870–3 (from Thornbury 1871).

Just as Black Rod's procession marks the annual opening of Parliament, linking Commons, Lords and Sovereign, so with a curious symmetry the Lord Mayor's Banquet links the British Government with the City of London, for it is the annual occasion that synchronizes the arrival of the newly elected Lord Mayor with the Prime Minister's major public speech about government policy. Taking place in November,[1] somewhat later in the year than the opening of Parliament, it is a different kind of government speech from that read by the Queen. Rather than outlining any specific legislation to be pursued, it tends to concern policies and general intentions often related to foreign or economic policy, but it has also been used effectively as a means to rally the nation, as with Churchill's wartime speeches of 1941 and 1942.[2] On Monday, 16 November 2009, Gordon Brown's speech was largely about the war in Afghanistan. Whatever the content, it is the focus of much subsequent commentary and speculation, and is therefore prepared with much forethought by the Prime Minister, his colleagues, and his staff. Although its effect is now felt largely through the newspapers, radio and television, and although it would presumably be reported to the nation wherever it was held, the choice of the Lord Mayor's Banquet as a venue has a tradition reaching back to the mid-nineteenth century, and like the reading of the Queen's speech in the Lords, it represents a balance of power. This time the balance is not between the elected government and the Sovereign, but between the elected government and the economic powerhouse of the City. It has become the newly elected Lord Mayor's privilege that the speech be given on his or her territory, where he or she is symbolically the first to hear it.

The speech and banquet usually take place at the Guildhall, sited at the very heart of the City.[3] Constructed between 1411 and 1440 by John Croxton, this is what remains of one of the major medieval buildings of London: a Gothic Hall 160 feet long, second in size only to Westminster Hall. It was built to represent the great combined power of the medieval guilds, and has remained the focal point of City administration. Nowadays the whole block is owned by the City Corporation, and the buildings immediately surrounding the old hall are mainly rebuilds from the 1970s, but an accumulation of subsidiary law courts and offices has surrounded the hall for centuries (Figure 3.3), knitting it into the dense urban context. Until modern times the hall had to be approached through the narrow courtyard of Guildhall Yard, and entered via the new eclectic face given to it in 1788–9 by George Dance the younger (Figures 3.2 and 3.4). The external form of the hall proper could long be seen only as a roof from afar, but now the larger pedestrian square leaves much of the south side visible, even if lower buildings still block it at ground level. For the purposes of this chapter the only subsidiary parts of the complex that need concern us are the so-called Old Library (only old since the new one was added in the 1970s) beyond the hall's east end (Figure 3.5), and the Old Print Room, both added by Sir Horace Jones in 1870–3 in a Neo-Gothic manner.[4]

The banquet

The ritual of the banquet begins with the arrival of the new Lord Mayor and his wife in front of the Guildhall at 18.00, along with the Sheriffs and their wives. He inspects the guard of honour awaiting him, which then leads off in a hierarchical procession into the building, all those involved wearing their appropriate uniforms. First come the Trumpeters, followed by the City Marshalls, then the Under-Sheriff, the Deputation of the Mayor, the Sheriffs, the Mayor's Chaplain, and finally the Lord Mayor himself. The procession leads to the Old Library, the second largest room in the complex, where the company assemble on a raised dais at the far end in order to welcome their principal guests.[5] The Lord Mayor takes centre stage with his wife beside him to his left, his Sword-bearer and Sergeant at Arms standing slightly behind them to either side. All take up their appropriate positions in the essentially symmetrical layout. Sheriffs take front places to the Lord Mayor's right, their wives the opposite places to the left. Beyond them stand Aldermen to the Mayor's right, other favoured guests to his left. The City contingent is now ready to face the principal guests, who are admitted to fanfares of trumpets and greeted by the Lord Mayor in reverse order of seniority. First comes the Lord Chief Justice with the senior Judges, then the Speaker of the Commons, then the Lord Chancellor followed by the Archbishop of Canterbury. Next come the Late Lord Mayor and Lady Mayoress, who occupied the role in the previous year, and in whose honour the banquet is supposedly held. But nobody is allowed to trump the Prime Minister, who arrives with his escort at 18.55, to the last fanfare of trumpets.

The Remembrancer in charge of proceedings then announces the passage of the procession to the Old Print Room, where the principal guests wait while everyone else is taking their place in the hall. This procession is formed according to the Taking-in List, even the short progress to the Old Print Room being arranged in hierarchical order, with the Lord Mayor escorting the Prime Minister followed by the previous Lord Mayor and the Sheriffs. When the lesser guests have all found their places at table in the hall, the Lord Mayor and principal guests emerge in procession preceded by the playing trumpeters, a deputation of the Lord Mayor and Sheriff's committee, the City Marshall, the Under-Sheriff, the Lord Mayor's Chaplain, and the bearers of sword and mace. Having made a dignified circuit of the centre tables, they take their places at the centre of the south side. That the hall was long used in the traditional manner like Westminster Hall, with dais and high table at the east end, is proved by many images (Figure 3.6), and such layouts can be found until the end of the nineteenth century, especially if royalty was present. Walter Thornbury reports that the Lord Mayor actually waited on George III along with the City Aldermen, showing great deference to the King,[6] but the predominant practice in the twentieth century avoided the longitudinal form in favour of a transverse arrangement that is still current (Figure 3.7). Orientated on the cross-axis, the Lord Mayor and his guests sit at a table on the same level as the rest, but still called high table. His position is nonetheless central, taking the axis of the horseshoe-shaped table which defines the centre of the room. He occupies a high-backed chair in front of a Gothic canopy to give him the necessary precedence (Figure 3.1). Despite the preference for a central rather than a linear hierarchical position – an arrangement that brings the Lord Mayor closest to his guests – the seating layout nevertheless tells an ordered story. The great horseshoe-shaped table reserves its inner seats for Aldermen, while its outer corners are dominated by Sheriffs. The Lord Mayor in the central seat has the Late Lord Mayor, the Late Lady Mayoress and the Lord Chancellor on his right; the Prime Minister, the Lady Mayoress and the Archbishop of Canterbury sit on his left. The six tables embraced by the main one are for senior officers and friends of the Lord Mayor, but the outer tables and those on the gallery are divided up territorially to represent the wards of the City, its political territories which are in the ritual both individually recognized and assembled into a unity. With Lord Mayor and guests in their places, the Chaplain says grace, the sword and mace are put on their bracket, and dinner can begin. The menu is always elaborate, with numerous dishes accompanied by several different kinds of wine. Traditionally the central course was Baron of Beef which involved a whole spit-roasted animal, at once a display of extravagance suited to the grandeur of the occasion and the visible sharing of a single sacrificial beast. The 1914 menu (Figure 3.8) shows this item in larger type as the central element in a sequence of five main courses: fillets of sole and mutton cutlets being served before it, casserole of pheasant and smoked tongue after. There was also soup before all of these, and a choice of seven puddings after, followed by yet more 'ices and dessert': eight courses in all. Wines included sherry, three kinds of eight-year-old champagne, fifteen-year-old La Rose claret, port, and brandy.[7] With 750 guests, such a setting, and such a menu, this was intended as meal of the year with no expense spared, and the incoming Lord Mayor was obliged to reach deep into his pocket to fund this once-in-a-lifetime peak of his glory.

The toasts and speeches

Great meals often involve toasts and speeches, in which the principal hosts and guests acknowledge and flatter one another in front of the whole assembly, cementing their relationships, and these usually take place at the end of the meal. At the Lord Mayor's Banquet they are highly organized and arranged in hierarchical order, each acknowledged if possible by an appropriate other. At the banquet of 1914 there were eight toasts (Figure 3.9). The first two were given by the Lord Mayor to the King and the Queen, but went unacknowledged since Royalty was not present. As the First World War was in progress, the Prime Minister gave the third toast to 'Our Allies', acknowledged by the French Ambassador, and for the fourth the Sheriff toasted 'The Imperial Forces of the Crown', answered by Winston Churchill, First Lord of the Admiralty. The fifth toast, again raised by the Lord Mayor, addressed 'His Majesty's Ministers' and was answered by the Prime Minister, H. H. Asquith, at length. The next two toasts were addressed to the 'Judges and the Bar', and 'The Late Lord Mayor and Court of Aldermen', while the final one, given by the Prime Minister and answered by the new Lord Mayor was for 'The

THE ROYAL BANQUET IN GUILDHALL. *From a Contemporary Print.* (*See page* 326.)

Figure 3.6 Lord Mayor's Day in Guildhall 1761 with the high table at the east end and galleries for spectators (from Thornbury 1871).

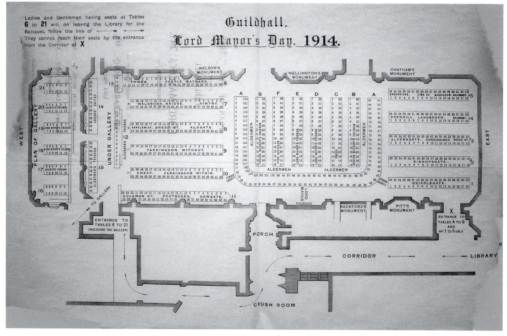

Figure 3.7 Seating layout for Lord Mayor's Day 1914, with the Lord Mayor's seat at the centre of the U-shaped table on the south side, close to the main entrance. Aldermen sit around the U, special guests at the central tables, and representatives of the city wards at the outer ones (London Metropolitan Archives, author's photograph).

Menu

Wines

TURTLE   CLEAR TURTLE

SHERRY:
AMONTILLADO

FRIED FILLETS OF SOLES

TARTARE SAUCE

CHAMPAGNE:
CLICQUOT, 1906
BOLLINGER, 1906
ROEDERER, 1906

MUTTON CUTLETS ROYALE

BARON OF BEEF

CLARET:
LA ROSE, 1899

CASSEROLE OF PHEASANT

SMOKED TONGUE

PORT:
GONZALEZ'
OLD PORTUGAL

ORANGE JELLY   CHARLOTTE RUSSE

CREAMS   BAVAROIS

BRANDY:
DENIS MOUNIÉ, 1865

MERINGUES

MAIDS OF HONOUR

PETITS GATEAUX

SCHWEPPES'
MALVERN AND
SODA WATERS

ICES   DESSERT

Ring & Brymer

Figure 3.8 Lord Mayor's Banquet 1914, the menu card (London Metropolitan Archives, author's photograph).

GUILDHALL BANQUET
1914

TOASTS.	GIVEN BY	ACKNOWLEDGED BY
1. THE KING	THE LORD MAYOR	
2. THE QUEEN, QUEEN ALEXANDRA, THE PRINCE OF WALES, AND THE OTHER MEMBERS OF THE ROYAL FAMILY	THE LORD MAYOR	
3. OUR ALLIES	THE RT. HON. ARTHUR J. BALFOUR, M.P.	HIS EXCELLENCY THE FRENCH AMBASSADOR
4. THE IMPERIAL FORCES OF THE CROWN	MR. ALDERMAN AND SHERIFF MOORE	THE RT. HON. WINSTON SPENCER CHURCHILL (FIRST LORD OF THE ADMIRALTY) FIELD MARSHAL THE RT. HON. EARL KITCHENER OF KHARTOUM (SECRETARY OF STATE FOR WAR)
5. HIS MAJESTY'S MINISTERS	THE LORD MAYOR	THE RT. HON. H. H. ASQUITH (PRIME MINISTER)
6. THE JUDGES AND THE BAR OF ENGLAND	SHERIFF THE REV. H. CART DE LAFONTAINE	THE LORD CHIEF JUSTICE OF ENGLAND THE ATTORNEY GENERAL
7. THE LATE LORD MAYOR & COURT OF ALDERMEN	HIS GRACE THE ARCHBISHOP OF CANTERBURY	THE LATE LORD MAYOR
8. THE LORD MAYOR AND THE SHERIFFS, "THE HOSTS"	THE RT. HON. H. H. ASQUITH (PRIME MINISTER)	THE LORD MAYOR

BLADES, PRINTERS, LONDON, E.C.

Figure 3.9 The programme of toasts (London Metropolitan Archives, author's photograph).

ANCIENT VIEW OF CHEAPSIDE.
(From La Serre's "Entrée de la Reyne Mère du Roy," showing the Procession of Mary de Medicis.)

Figure 3.10 A Lord Mayor's Procession in Cheapside in 1639. This occasion was the welcome of Marie de Medicis to the city, but it shows both the form of the parade and London's main street with its four and five-storey timber-framed houses, all burned twenty-seven years later (from Thornbury 1871).

Hosts'. The banquet's list of toasts sets the almost centrally placed 'His Majesty's Ministers' equal with the others, and registers Asquith's reply only as the acknowledgement; yet by that time the Prime Minister's speech had already assumed the dominant role, displacing the change of Lord Mayor as the focus of a national rather than local event. It was a relatively late adjustment to the 500-year-old ritual, for the ministerial toast was not firmly established until 1831, and only in subsequent decades did prime ministers begin to sense the banquet's efficacy as an occasion for propaganda, giving increasingly longer speeches. A Guildhall historian notes: 'Palmerston's reply in 1857 was more extensive than anything that had come before, but in 1858 the Earl of Derby produced a speech more comparable in length and scope with those of today.'[8] In keeping with the increased importance of the Prime Minister's speech, his place at table changed in the mid-twentieth century from two seats right of the Lord Mayor to the seat directly on the Lord Mayor's left, displacing the Lady Mayoress. Even so, the seat of honour on the Lord Mayor's right remains that of the Late Lord Mayor.

Lord Mayor's Day

The other great change in the Lord Mayor's Banquet in recent times was its detachment from the Lord Mayor's Show. Originally both were part of Lord Mayor's Day, and the banquet provided the culmination to the day's proceedings. It started in the thirteenth century when the role of Lord Mayor was established by royal charter, and centred on the legal duty of swearing-in the new Lord Mayor by the Sovereign's representative, an acknowledgement of the City's right to its own political organization. It occurred on a fixed date every year: 29 October from 1253 until 1752, thereafter corrected to 9 November with the adoption of the Gregorian calendar. It persisted as an integrated process on that date until 1939, but the timing was revised after the Second World War. To fit in more pragmatically with modern traffic and communications, the Lord Mayor's Show was then moved to a Saturday when it would not disrupt the work of the City, while the banquet shifted to the following Monday evening, turning it into a separate event and weakening its link with the legal ceremony. For centuries Lord Mayor's Day had been important enough to defy the order of the week as Christmas still does, but no longer. That the City finds it unnecessary to cease its work for the sake of its Lord Mayor indicates the reduced nature of the role, just as the hijacking of the banquet by the Prime Minister diverts it to a new political purpose. London possessed a mayor from 1189. He was elected annually from a class of aldermen (derived from 'elder-men' of Saxon times), each representing an area of the city called a ward. Initially these positions had been held by landholders or royal officials, but the city guilds gradually took over. They were groupings of merchants and craftsmen which had grown with the city, bringing into existence a new political middle class. Their leaders joined the ranks of aldermen, some even going on to become mayor, since the occupant of this role was elected from among them, and by the mid-thirteenth century they wielded the whole power of municipal government in London, including the enactment of the law.[9]

Within their ranks – which included trades like the Goldsmiths, Merchant Taylors, Mercers, Fishmongers, Drapers, and Skinners – they regulated their own markets and set rules for their workers. Typically they demanded an entrance fee, insisted on an oath of initiation, and set strict rules for apprenticeship within their profession, a period of normally around seven years. They held formal business meetings three or four times a year operating within strict rules, and settled disputes between their members and those of other guilds. They collected common funds to provide for sickness and accidents, and they obliged their living members to attend funerals, bearing the body and causing masses to be said for the soul, which before the Reformation was an important consideration.[10] Each major guild built its hall for meeting and administration, usually sited close to streets where its members practised their trade, for medieval London grew up around streets dedicated to a trade or craft, many still remembered in street names.[11] Some of the halls survive today in modified form, swallowed by huge office blocks and available for hire for private social occasions, but in the London of before the fire in 1666 they stood as major landmarks in a sea of houses, distinctive in size, shape, and elaboration (Figures 3.11 and 3.13).

The thirteenth and fourteenth centuries saw frequent power struggles between guild organizations, each seeking advantages and monopolies for its trade, so in the fifteenth century they were reformed by royal charters of incorporation as livery companies, an arrangement that survives in ceremonial form to this day.[12] Livery is a kind of uniform that identifies the members of a company, giving them both the privilege of recognition and the solidarity of a group. The Grocers, for example wore a scarlet gown with a green hood in 1414,[13] and the day of the year to present these uniforms in contrast with others was the occasion of the Lord Mayor's Show. Since the mayoralty was held only for a year and involved considerable political power and responsibility, including being the principal magistrate, the change of mayor was a major civic event involving a significant handover of power. The privileges of the City were enjoyed at the discretion of the Sovereign, which necessitated a swearing-in ceremony, the outgoing mayor accompanying the new one to register the transfer of responsibility. From 1215, when King John set up the charter, until 1882, when the law courts moved to the Strand, the newly elected mayor was obliged to travel out of his territory of the City of London and down to Westminster, the seat of national power, set originally in open country. This was where the Royal Courts of Justice had developed, so was where the swearing-in usually took place.[14] From around 1422 until 1856 the Lord Mayor travelled in a highly decorated barge rowed ceremonially up the Thames (Figures 3.12 and 3.14).

The Lord Mayor's Show originated in the accompanying procession, which set off in the morning from the Lord Mayor's seat of power at the Guildhall, made its way in due order down to the river bank, continued in part as a flotilla of boats and barges upriver to Westminster, waited until the swearing-in had taken place, then accompanied the newly legitimated Lord Mayor back to the City. Here he was welcomed with performances and pageants set up in the street, which by the seventeenth century had become extremely elaborate, including theatrical pieces written by leading playwrights and sets by such well-known architects as Inigo Jones. Some productions commented on contemporary political concerns, particularly the dangers

Figure 3.11 Drapers', Fishmongers', and Vintners' Halls (as depicted in Unwin 1908).

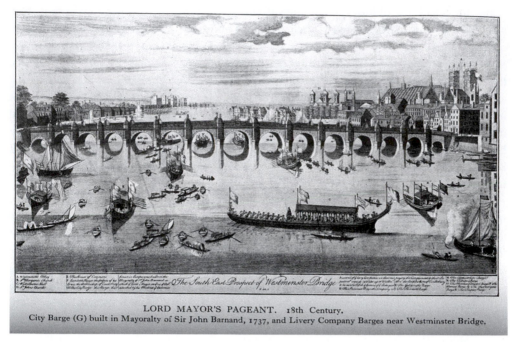

LORD MAYOR'S PAGEANT. 18th Century.
City Barge (G) built in Mayoralty of Sir John Barnand, 1737, and Livery Company Barges near Westminster Bridge.

Figure 3.12 Lord Mayor en route to Westminster Hall (top right) in 1747. His is the large barge, built 1737; those accompanying belong to livery companies (print by Benjamin Cole based on a painting by Canaletto, London Metropolitan Archives, Collage 18312).

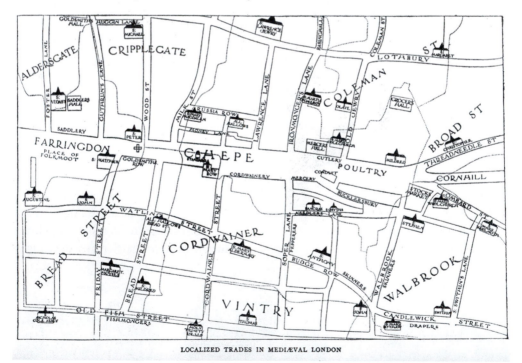

LOCALIZED TRADES IN MEDIÆVAL LONDON

Figure 3.13 Localized trades in medieval London and their various halls, distributed in the area around Cheapside (Chepe). The wards are also named (from Unwin 1908).

Figure 3.14 The Lord Mayor's Barge passing Somerset House, early nineteenth century (from Thornbury 1871).

of papist plots, while others encouraged the new Lord Mayor to moral probity. The banquet at Guildhall was the culminating event of this long progress, regarded as the gift of the new Lord Mayor to his predecessor, showing mutual respect and continuity of the role, as well as gratitude for the power symbolically transferred.

The Lord Mayor's Procession in 1680

The origins of the procession are obscure, but probably from the beginning the Mayor was attended by officials and servants, and by 1401 'minstrels' are mentioned, the celebration already being primarily organized by the city guilds. Pageants were in place by 1553, reaching a peak of elaboration between 1585 and 1708.[15] The visual evidence is selective and sporadic, but one of the fullest written descriptions is Thomas Jordan's pamphlet of 1680.[16] Unfortunately no surviving drawings match the detailed descriptions, though drawings of other pageants are included below. Since the incoming Lord Mayor, Sir Patience Ward, was of the Merchant Taylors' Company, that company organized the procession and much of the show. The day started with the gathering of around 400 persons at seven in the morning in their various uniforms at Merchant Taylors' Hall in Threadneedle Street.[17] The Foot Marshall took charge and arranged them in processional order by pairs in three sections, punctuated with flags and banners, musicians playing trumpets or fife and drums, and coats of arms carried at strategic points. Jordan lists no less than twenty-six groups in their various uniforms, some including forty or more persons. They were arranged in order of seniority, for the procession started with

Figure 3.15 John Overton's map of London, 1676, showing the street pattern, Tower of London, single bridge, and medieval wall. Streets arriving through separate gates from the west combine as Cheapside close to St Paul's. The new King and Queen streets run vertically crossing Cheapside to connect Guildhall in the north with river to south (British Library, Crace Collection, Crace II: 69).

Figure 3.16 Author's diagram identifying Lord Mayor's route. St Paul's, Guildhall and City Wall are blacked.

Figure 3.17 Pageant put on by the Fishmongers Guild in 1616 with at least sixteen actors, as represented in a contemporary print (from Unwin 1908).

Figure 3.18 Pageant put on by the Merchant Taylors in 1580: reconstructive sketch based on the description in Jordan's pamphlet and showing the hierarchical disposition of figures (drawing by the author and Claire Blundell Jones).

'poor pensioners' and ended with 'masters and wardens of the company'. Once assembled, all marched off to the Lord Mayor's House where the Lord Mayor and aldermen joined them on horseback, and the party proceeded from there to Guildhall, the ranks of the procession being completed by the addition of the Late Lord Mayor with his 'knights, esquires, and gentlemen'. The full procession, with bands playing, now set off down King's Street towards the Thames. It arrived at Three Cranes Wharf (Figures 3.15 and 3.16), where the Lord Mayor's barge waited at the west end of the quay and another for the court of assistants and gentlemen ushers – those privileged to accompany him – at the east. Other elements of the procession waited to form up again on the Mayor's return. The two oar-driven barges set off upriver accompanied by the elaborately decorated craft of the other city livery companies.

The water passage was again an organized progression, for a dispute between the Merchant Taylors and Skinners in 1484 about whose boat should go first had forced the imposition of an order of priority, worked out for all forty-eight companies by 1516. Jordan is silent on the size of this flotilla, which was presumably large, but he does report a salute of great guns from 'a pleasure boat' along the way. Having arrived at New Palace Stairs, the attendants formed an orderly 'lane' through which the two mayors were conducted to their business with the justices in Westminster Hall. The oath and transfer of power completed, they re-emerged and the new Lord Mayor made a 'liberal donation to the poor of Westminster' before re-embarking with his retinue for the return voyage. Rowing downriver, they did not return to Three Cranes Wharf but landed further upriver at Blackfriars Stairs, allowing a westerly entrance to the City. Their arrival was greeted with beating drums and a salute of three volleys from the Artillery Company in best ceremonial armour, who then served as escort for the reassembled procession. Set in order once again by the Foot Marshall, the whole company proceeded up the channel (the newly canalized river fleet) to Ludgate Hill, through Ludgate, on through St Paul's Churchyard and Cheapside, and eventually back to Guildhall for the banquet (Figure 3.16). But the new Lord Mayor's progress was now slow, interrupted by four separate pageants set up along the broad central street of London, Cheapside. These had elaborate settings with many actors and props, each with a spokesman primed to deliver a well-rehearsed speech of thirty or forty lines to the Lord Mayor, which the latter was obliged politely to acknowledge. These structures had also been assembled and funded by the Merchant Taylors' company, overtly advertising its virtues. Jordan describes them in detail, identifying the characters, the elaborate costumes, and the speeches given, which he printed verbatim.

The first pageant

Cloth being their main concern, the Merchant Taylors' coat of arms depicted a royal tent, which was taken as the basis of the set, with a central stage for the 'large imperial pavilion, red fringed and richly garnished and adorned, lined faced and doubled ermine'. Alongside were a pair of symmetrical side stages bearing 'carved camels', another main element of the company's coat of arms, presumably expressing its pride at trading with exotic places (Figure 3.18). To drive the point home, the camels had riders, exotic dark-skinned persons from India and the West Indies lavishly dressed with gold and jewels, one holding the company's banner and the other the Lord Mayor's. A further twenty-four actors, elaborately dressed to support the characters and qualities portrayed, were symmetrically disposed. Ladies representing

Diligence, Industry, Ingenuity and Success struck poses on pedestals on the right-hand side stage, their equivalents on the left being Mediocrity, Amity, Verity and Variety, at that time considered the more feminine set of virtues.[18] Supporting the open curtains to the sides of the main tent and flanking the central display were two figures described as Ministers of State, representing on one side Royalty and on the other Loyalty. The central group of fourteen persons in or before the tent was ranked in four layers: at the top the single figure Sovereignty:

> In the highest and most eminent seat of a throne like ascension, in royal posture alone, sitteth Sovereignty, in a robe of purple velvet, lined faced and caped with ermine, a black curled hair, on his head an imperial diadem, about his shoulders a rich collar of esses, with a George Pendent. In one hand he beareth a golden globe, in the other he guideth a royal sceptre.[19]

On the next tier down were three figures side by side representing Principality, Nobility and Honour, while a further three figures on the third represented Gentility, Integrity and Commonalty. Jordan describes their dress and equipment in detail, as with Sovereignty, but we need not repeat it here. Finally at the base stage level, in front, stood the spokesman for the whole event, whose job it was, having caught the Lord Mayor's attention, to deliver a speech explaining the desirable virtues portrayed, and exhorting him to use his power wisely. This actor portrayed a character from history, 'an ancient English hero, habited in antick habiliaments of war such as were worn by the chief commanders; under the conduct of Edward the third, when he conquered France'.[20] Armed with sword and a quiver of arrows hanging from a golden belt, and wearing a silver helmet and plume, he carried a bow in one hand and a spear in the other. His speech addressed the Lord Mayor in his role as chief magistrate, and after clarifying the part the actor played, he explained the set:

> This object you are pleased to look upon
> Is an imperial pavilion.
> The Merchant Taylors' coat of arms within,
> On a throne-like ascension may be seen
> A royal sovereign and beneath him lie
> All those gradations of nobility,
> Who of the Merchant Taylors have been free:
> In all their royal robes, they are arrayed
> Which with great ingenuity were made
> By the most curious Merchant-Taylor's trade.
> Thus you are dignified, my lord and now
> All London's expectation is on you.
> That in this vertical and doubtful year
> You will so equally poise love and fear,
> That you may add new honours to the chair
> And all may bless the time that you came there,
> And, call you prudent, pious, just Lord Mayor.[21]

The other pageants

The other three pageants can be dealt with more briefly. The second was 'a chariot of ovation, or peaceful triumph' drawn by a golden lion and a lamb, the lion ridden by a 'negro prince', the lamb by a 'seraphim-like creature', both elaborately dressed. In the chariot were seven persons: Concordia, Unamina, Pacifia, Consentiana, Melodia, Benevolentia and Harmonia. Sitting alone at the front, Harmonia stood to address the Lord Mayor with a speech about the need for concord, union and harmony, including reference to the Merchant Taylors' motto, and including the observation that 'by fruitful concord small things do increase, but dismal discord will make great things less'. Again the Lord Mayor is entreated to behave well:

> To move men to agree and to concurr,
> Is the great art of a good governor.
> With your praetorian power, mix harmony,
> I make the lion and the lamb agree
> To draw my chariot; If they fall out
> My little commonwealth, and I, no doubt,
> Should run to ruin, and receive the rout.[22]

The third pageant was 'a ship called the patience, fully accommodated with all her masts, sails, cordage, tackling, cables, anchors, ordnance; and manned by a captain, master, boatswain, steers-man and seamen'. Jordan does not concern himself with further details, but goes straight to the captain's speech, which tells of the mercantile and political advantages of trade, comparing the ship's voyage to the Lord Mayor's voyage through the coming year, which will doubtless bring 'cross winds', but they can be met with patience.

The fourth pageant is described as 'a palace of pleasure in the form of a triumphal arch of excellent form according to the ionick order of architecture'. In it sit nine ladies who are Jollity, Delight, Fancy, Felicity, Wit, Invention, Tumult, Laughter and Gladness. A group of musicians perform 'a ditty in commendation of the Merchant-Taylors' trade'. This Jordan includes in full, along with several printed bars of the music. It is more substantial in length than the other pageant speeches, providing a myth of origin for the Merchant Taylors' Company:

> When Adam and Eve out of Eden were hurled,
> They were at that time King and Queen of the world:
> Yet this royal couple were forced to play,
> The Taylers, and put themselves in green array;
> For modesty and for necessity's sake,
> They had figs for the belly, and leaves for the back;
> And afterward clothing of sheepskins they made,
> Then judge if a Tayler was not the first trade,
> The oldest profession ...[23]

After the Lord Mayor had heard and acknowledged this performance, the Foot Marshall reorganized everyone to line the route into King Street to salute him as he entered Guildhall for the feast. Three final volleys were fired by the artillery as they went in to dinner.

The Lord Mayor's Show still exists, involving uniformed marchers and motor-powered floats, a procession three miles long with aircraft flying overhead and other modern elaborations. It provides an afternoon of passing amusement for locals and a picturesque spectacle for tourists, but with the reduction of the Lord Mayor's role it has lost its calendrical impact and political force. These days the Lord Mayor finds himself in competition with another mayor: that of Greater London, sited in his own new castle-like headquarters just outside the City, and given real power. Nor has the show adapted well to the media: in the early days of television it was among the first outside events broadcast, but in a media-dominated world it has not kept up. The banquet now belongs to the Prime Minister. In 2009 national news covered Gordon Brown's speech only, the television camera isolating him from his dinner companions, and the context shot showing the hall lasted only a couple of seconds. That the speech being given at the Lord Mayor's Banquet was mentioned only in passing, and the Lord Mayor was not seen at all.[24]

Conclusion: Ritual, power and display

This chapter has been about the relationship between national and local power and how that has been expressed in spaces and rituals. The Lord Mayor's Banquet reminds us of the importance of feasts in expressing relationships and the symbolic role of food and consumption, as discussed in the introduction. More specifically, it has been an important political opportunity, persisting as the occasion when the Prime Minister, with his or her speech, acknowledges the place of the City of London in the national economy. But this event used to be the occasion when London renewed itself, readjusting its power structure, and proudly remembering its political origins in the growth of its guilds and livery companies, as well as the geographical structure of its wards. All this was laid out in space for the 1914 banquet quite as clearly as in the parliamentary Houses or in Westminster Hall for the trial of Lord Lovat in the preceding chapter. But the processional use of the Guildhall complex has none of the clarity of Black Rod's passage. Lacking the kind of major architectural reorganization implemented by Barry and Pugin, its internal organization, the result of piecemeal aggregation, has remained somewhat shambolic, obliging the processions to take place as and where they could, rather than enhancing their progress, and extensive bomb damage in 1942 removed much of the charm of the historic layers. As with the parliamentary ritual, that at Guildhall has also shifted markedly in emphasis with time, and we should not be surprised. It is a paradox that rituals invite and accept reinterpretation while at the same time seeming to provide the stability of a continuing tradition. Certainly they really do serve the preservation of communal memory, but it is also their role to provide an illusion of continuity during change.

In the first chapter we saw how in hall buildings such as parliamentary chambers the far end of the major axis is the prime place of importance, while the cross-axis lends itself to adversarial polarities. The seating plan of the Lord Mayor's banquet shows a similar order, for although the seat of honour is now on the cross-axis, where it can be more central – the Lord Mayor being more 'one of the people' than the King – there is nonetheless a balanced symmetrical arrangement of seating that is familiarly hierarchical and handed. There is a notable replication in this kind of static spatial positioning of the dynamic order of the parades and processions, which follow a similar hierarchy in time as well as in space. The various

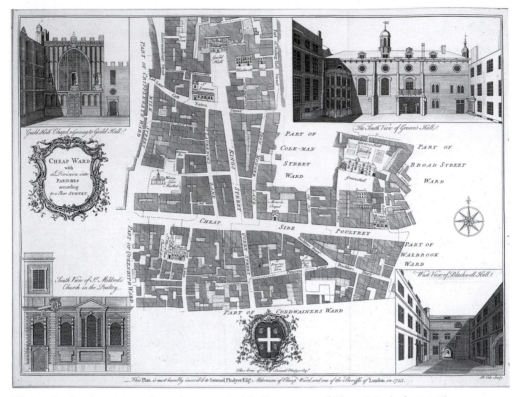

Figure 3.19 Cheapside and its relation to Guildhall, in a map of Cheap Ward of 1756. The corner images of Guildhall Chapel, Grocers' Hall, St Mildred's Church and Blackwell Hall are also picked out as elevated versions in the map, so there is no doubting their primary importance (British Library, Crace Collection, Port 8.15).

marchers, grouped by rank or profession, appear hierarchically, lesser mortals paving the way for greater, and they must be lined up in order before moving off, presenting a temporary spatial ranking. The process is reversed when the processional order on the move is decanted into a fixed spatial setting, as with the Lord Mayor's arrival at table. We might notice too that the spatial structure within the Lord Mayor's pageants, as far as it can be deduced from the text, followed the rules of centrality, polarity and relative height already seen in hall layouts and parades. The dominance of the 'Sovereignty' figure in the first pageant, for example, is assured not merely by his single central position but also by his being the highest, lording it over six others. This precedence is maintained even though the speaking part is given to the 'Ancient English Hero' placed in front at the bottom.

The distinctive uniforms and banners used in the parades are not incidental but absolutely essential, since they provide an identity for each character or group, and it is unsurprising that descriptions of costumes take up so much of Jordan's account. In the text of one of the pageants they are actively justified:

> If princes and people stark naked should go,
> Who could their gradations of dignity know?
> It would pretty modest fair virgins perplex,

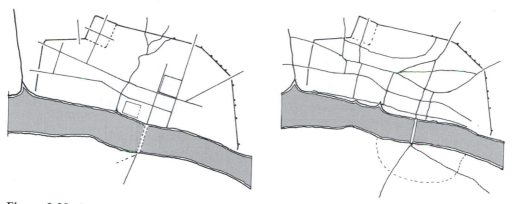

Figure 3.20 Comparative plans of Late Roman London, left, and Saxon London, right suggesting the origin of Cheapside as part of Roman London's principal east–west street (redrawn by author after Biddle et al., 1973).

'Cause nakedness shews the distinction of sex.
And, therefore the Tayler to fortify nature
By Art, in formalities, covers the creature:
To every person he gives a due dress,
Which doth in fit order their calling express.[25]

Not only the Merchant Taylors but all the other livery companies wore uniforms of several kinds with different kinds of trim: Jordan describes 'budge bachelors' and 'foyns bachelors', identifying subgroups by whether their gowns are trimmed with the fur of the lamb or that of the martin. These uniforms showed the hierarchical order within a company as well as advertising to the general public the overall size and power of each group, and the Lord Mayor's procession was the day of the year when each city company could compare and compete with the others, making their relative powers visible. No wonder they spent so extravagantly on their pageants once they had managed to land the mayorship, an opportunity that might not recur for several years. Uniforms unify and promote solidarity, and on the field of battle they differentiate friend from foe, so it is not surprising that they have often been restricted by legislation and made subject to license.

From buildings to city

Along with banners and uniforms, building types are also markers of identity. The point of origin and final destination of the Lord Mayor's procession is the Guildhall, for centuries the largest and most elaborate secular space in the City, while the outward goal of the procession is Westminster Hall, its national big brother. Also mentioned by Jordan is Merchant Taylors' Hall, a reminder that in London such halls stood out against the background of ordinary housing as landmarks, expressing the competing factions of trade and power. But more important than any of these were the streets of the city, the outdoor rooms to which the processional route gave definition. Cheapside, where the pageants were held, was for probably a thousand years London's principal street (Figures 3.19 and 3.20). It was the leading market, but it was also a place where political struggles, riots, and demonstrations took place, royal news was proclaimed (occasionally with free wine), tournaments were held, and public punishments including the pillory and even executions were meted out. Market rules were frequently enacted and enforced, and illegal goods were publicly destroyed by burning. As sites along Cheapside's edge were prestigious, an epidemic of projecting signs had to be curtailed, and there was competition between trades for pitches. Eventually Charles I gave precedence to the Goldsmiths in the 1630s in order to raise the tone.[26]

The importance of Cheapside was due to its advantageous position. It originated as the course of the main east–west artery of Roman London, which connected the gate from Praetorian Way to the Forum, there meeting at right angles the street from the only bridge, its angle having been set perpendicular to the axis of the Roman fort. By Late Saxon times it had developed its triple fork to the east at Cornhill, and once linked by the site of St Paul's, it drew from both gates and roads from the west. It was allowed to remain two or three times as wide as all other streets in the otherwise cramped town for use as a market (Figures 3.10 and 3.20). The Guildhall stood to its north, on the end of the axis of King's Street, being linked straight through to the river by the new Queen Street, cleared after the fire of 1666 to improve the route to the quay. The Lord Mayor's passage by water from there is a reminder that the Thames was the main traffic artery of London, the City's position being at the lowest crossing point, and nationally the best-placed port for the continent. The symbolic value of taking to water was underlined by a contemporary commentator:

> His Lordship once a year (as the Duke of Venice to the sea) weds himself to the Thames with a ring of surrounding barges, that being also part of his dominion.[27]

The river trip served to open the procession to more eyes, while dramatizing the Lord Mayor's transit to Westminster for the formalities. The return voyage deposited the whole company at Blackfriars, next to the mouth of the river Fleet outside the City, allowing progress up the channel to the Fleet bridge with a right turn up Ludgate Hill (Figures 3.15 and 3.16). The City was then ceremonially re-entered by its new-born Lord Mayor via one of its main gates, the procession taking in St Paul's Church Yard before engaging with the pageants lined up along Cheapside. For the Lord Mayor to have passed the other way in the morning would surely have defeated the object, for he would have disturbed the pageants while they were in preparation and seen them in advance. The whole progress counted as a symbolic tracing of territory, and its start and finish involved streets that could be considered the main axes of the City, crossing at its very centre: north–south King St/Queen St and east–west Cheapside. This delineation of space with bodily movement is reminiscent of ancient traditions of 'beating the bounds', when parishioners would annually parade around the entire border of the parish to define their home territory, presumably also passing on the knowledge of ownership to their children.[28] Many other such ceremonies of spatial definition, including religious processions and pilgrimages, still occur. A world famous example is the annual Palio at Siena, a horse race held in the main square between competitors from the quarters of the city, who identify themselves with contrasting banners and uniforms.

Pageant and theatre

Looking back to the 1680s, it is the sheer elaboration of the pageants that surprises. The performance of the Merchant Taylors in 1680 was not exceptional: in 1687 one of the Goldsmiths' pageants was a merchant ship called 'Unity' 145 feet long, 45 feet wide, and 45 feet high at the stern, fully manned and equipped with twenty-two guns.[29] The pageants provided an opportunity for competitive display, allowing city companies to express their pride and prowess to each other and to the citizens of London. In a city of about half a million people,[30] the expense and elaboration per citizen must have been considerable, and the whole business focused on just a single day, but that day provided the greatest entertainment of the year when few travelled, few could read, and shared events within the local community were the sole form of social expression and exchange. Everyone was involved, the route known in advance, and spectators appeared at every window along with banners and other decorations. Although the actual speech to the Lord Mayor took but a few minutes, publications like Jordan's show the high value attached to the content. The pageants were open to the general gaze throughout the day, unmissed by friends and competitors, as everyone joined the crowd.

It is hard not to think of the pageants as theatre. They follow the tradition of medieval mystery plays, also played in the street. But by 1680 Shakespeare's Globe, the Rose, and other Elizabethan theatres had come and gone, suppressed in mid-century by Puritanism.[31] The drama stood at a world peak, yet was enacted in a relatively crude setting developed from a tradition of inn courtyards: it had even been driven outside the city walls as dangerous and anomalous. There were court performances, but the respected architectural institution of 'theatre' did not yet exist, nor did the framing restrictions that set a play within its polite bourgeois context, in some ways emasculating it.[32] The pageants temporarily took over the key street of the city, and in the absence of a framing building, scenery and costumes did the work. Their temporary nature made the pageants ephemeral, but also allowed – even forced – constant reinvention. Pageant and procession acted together as preservers of memory, definers of myth, and presenters of a moral ideal.

Notes

1   The Monday evening after the second Saturday of the month, the Saturday being the day for the Lord Mayor's Show.

2   Which included such memorable phrases as 'Here we are and here we stand, a veritable rock of salvation in this drifting world', reported in *The Times*, New York edition, 11 November 1942. Speeches available online: www.britishpathe.com/workspaces/BritishPathe/QAhWzN46.

3   Though it is often and confusingly called the Mansion House Speech, after the alternative and more modern venue, the Mayor's house established in the early eighteenth century.

4   For Guildhall's history see John Edward Price *A Descriptive Account of the Guildhall of the City of London*. Corporation of the City of London, 1886: also Caroline M. Barron, *The Medieval Guildhall of London*. Corporation of London, 1974.

5   All this description is based on John Arthur Harris, *Ceremonials of the Corporation of London, A Handbook prepared by authority of the Court of Lord Mayor and Aldermen for the guidance of the Lord Mayor etc* … Corporation of London 1991, pp. 40–3.

6   Thornbury 1871, p. 326.

7   Menu card for 1914, Guildhall Library files.

8   Unsigned typescript in files of the Guildhall Library, Noble. C. 22/3.

9   George Unwin, *The Gilds and Companies of London*. London: Methuen, 1908, pp. 61, 76.

10 Ibid., p. 53.

11 In the reign of Richard II there were probably only two or three halls, but by that of Richard III there were thirty-eight, and the hall of the Merchant Taylors would hold 200 guests: Unwin 1908, p. 176.

12 Unwin 1908, p. 155 ff.

13 Ibid., p. 191.

14 There were occasions when the Tower of London was used.

15 These dates are from a letter about the history of Lord Mayor's Day by A. H. Thomas of the Guildhall Records Office to the Town Clerk, 7 December 1932, preserved in the files of the Guildhall Library.

16 Jordan, Thomas, *London's Glory or the Lord Mayor's Show etc.* printed for John and Henry Playford, London 1680. The original is available online: Jordan_Thomas-Londons_glory_or_ The_Lord_mayors-Wing-J1037-459_34-p11.pdf. Easier to read is William Hone's transcription in Hone 1823, pp. 246–61.

17 Jordan's verse account, more geared to literary flourish than to providing an accurate inventory, clearly identifies 290, including 51 musicians, but some evidently substantial groups are listed without numbers.

18 'Mediocrity' is a surprising virtue, but presumably indicates a positive lack of arrogance. That these virtues could be read as feminine in opposition to the masculine ones opposite relates to other left–right gender divisions noted in later chapters.

19 Jordan 1680, p. 5.

20 Ibid., p. 6.

21 Ibid., p. 7.

22 Ibid., p. 10.

23 Ibid., p. 12.

24 It has not evolved into a national event like the Last Night of the Proms, a clear example of the priority now given to televisual experience. Originally celebrating the conclusion to the concert series for its specific audience, the Last Night has gradually turned into a patriotic jamboree, spawning satellite events around the kingdom with which it is now intercut. The audience at the Albert Hall no longer get the full show, and seem less interested in listening to the music than in 'being on telly'. No live event competes with media events for size of audience, and no Lord Mayor competes with a young and glamorous 'presenter' from the virtual family that television opens to us.

25 Jordan, p. 12.

26 All this from Thornbury 1871, pp. 304–15.

27 Matthew Taubman 1687 quoted in Hone 1823, p. 257.

28 A fascinating parallel to European examples is the Iraqw of Tanzania as analysed by Robert J. Thornton (Thornton 1980).

29 Hone 1823, pp. 257–8.

30 Its population in 1680 was 450,000, occupying 4 square miles according to demographia.com. Available online: http://www.demographia.com/db-lonuza1680.htm (accessed 29 January 2016).

31 The Globe was first built in 1599 amid a rash of other theatres outside the City, and rebuilt after a fire, but it was pulled down under Puritan pressure in 1644. See Day 1996, pp. 5–16.

32 I am thinking of the efforts of Bertold Brecht and others during the twentieth century to overcome the bourgeois conventions and reconnect theatre with political reality.

CHAPTER 4
THE IMPERIAL CHINESE MAGISTRATE AND HIS YAMEN

Figure 4.1 Inner gate of the Neixiang Yamen leading to the third court, halfway through the spatial sequence (author's photograph, May 2009).

Architecture and Ritual

Just as Jordan witnessed and wrote about the Lord Mayor's Show in London, on the other side of the world Liuhung Huang was ruminating over his experiences of acting as magistrate in two regions of China in preparation for his *Complete Book Concerning Happiness and Benevolence* published in 1694.[1] It is a remarkably detailed account of the role and duties of the seventeenth century Chinese magistrate, the effective ruler of a provincial city, and it provides a wealth of information about the ritual operation of the Yamen, his official residence and seat of government.[2] Although we cannot fit his descriptions to precisely the buildings and cities in which he operated, the architectural form of the Yamen was relatively standardized. Surviving examples and others known through drawings provide a remarkably consistent picture of form and layout. China was the other great ancient civilization to rival Greece and Rome, a competitor in scholarship, philosophy and science, and with an early established and highly centralized political organization. At the end of the seventeenth century its traditions were still intact and relatively undisturbed by the west.[3] It provides an illuminating cross-cultural comparison in the use and meaning of space.

Our expansion of the concept of 'ritual' beyond its reduced modern and Western usage is well supported by Chinese traditional practice, where it was not only essential to the ideology of Confucianism, but even the title of one of the six departments of government. As Arthur Waley explained in the preface to *The Analects of Confucius*:

> The word li ('ritual') is expressed in writing by a picture of a ritual vessel. The original meaning is said to be 'arranging ritual vessels', and this may very well be true, for it appears to be cognate to a number of words meaning 'to arrange in proper order', 'to put in sequence' etc… But as used in early China li would cover everything from the opening of the great doors of St Peter's down to saying 'Bless you' when someone sneezes.[4]

From the time of Confucius at least (around 500 BCE) ritual in China had been the basis of social order and of the believed connection with the powers of heaven, so that correct performance by the Emperor (the Son of Heaven) and all his subordinates was considered essential to assure agricultural fertility and avoid disaster. Tradition had it that there were 300 major and 3,000 minor rules to be mastered and observed. Correct behaviour was definitive of both status and virtue, and is a constant concern of the Chinese classics, the basic texts of education for the civil service. As *The Analects* puts it:

> The master [Confucius] said, to look at nothing in defiance of ritual, to listen to nothing in defiance of ritual, never to stir hand or foot in defiance of ritual… If a gentleman attends to business and does not idle away his time, if he behaves with courtesy to others and observes the rules of ritual, then all within the Four Seas are his brothers.[5]

The magistrate and his role

The seventeenth-century local magistrate in China was not just judge of the local court and settler of local disputes but the organizer of the constables and militia, the collector of taxes, the head of the local bureaucracy and the supplicant in public worship, making regular observances at various temples.[6] He was also responsible for public works and maintenance, disaster relief, and for the local part of the horse-based postal system which transmitted instructions across the empire. Although his powers over his own locality were great, even permitting summary executions in exceptional cases, he was constantly answerable to his superiors, obliged to pass serious cases on up to the superior Yamen and to send frequent reports on many issues. He suffered a full and merciless inspection of his books and premises every three years. He was expected both to preserve the peace and to keep the local economy in balance, and Huang's book is full of cautionary tales not only about detecting and preventing sharp practice among inferiors, but also about dealing tactfully and cautiously with superiors.

It comes to life particularly in the long anecdotes about how he dealt with specific criminals and solved difficult cases, but equally revealing are the samples of reports and requests sent to superiors, which demonstrate the importance of phrasing in a letter when it is the main form of communication. At times Huang rails against the cumbersome oppressiveness of the bureaucratic machine like a modern line-manager,[7] while at other times he accepts abuse and injustice from higher officials because he knows complaint will bring him no good.[8] Although a local magistrate was a distinguished figure, having reached an enviably high level in the national civil service examinations – the crucial index of status and goal of all ambitious men – he could easily be demoted or have his salary docked, and he would be held responsible for any kind of political disturbance occurring during his tenure, whether or not it was his fault. It was a difficult job to keep an eye on everything, and Huang's three predecessors in Tan Cheng, where he served in the 1670s, had all failed to balance the books. Reduced to poverty and disgrace, they were unable to leave the city until Huang had intervened on their behalf.[9] He wrote his book because he felt that he too had been thrown in at the deep end, and that learning on the job was not enough. In the absence of any legal or practical training he sought to give successors pertinent advice, for the rigorous civil service exams relied mainly on knowledge of the classics and the ability to write commentaries in the correct poetic forms.[10] The skill was that of the scholar, honed over years and through many stages, and its achievement was regarded as a moral education, bringing such wisdom and virtue as would best prepare men for high office. Successful examinees were appointed as magistrates by the Emperor and sent out at random to places chosen by lot, for the law of avoidance stipulated that they should not go where they were known and could therefore be open to favouritism or corruption.

The Yamen and the city

Before further examining the activities of the magistrate, we should consider the form and position of a Yamen, and lacking information about places where Huang served, we can look at others for which we have good documentation. To show a Yamen in its town the translator of Huang's book chose a map of Ping Xiang of 1872 (Figure 4.2). This map is diagrammatic, but it indicates well the focal position of the Yamen at the heart of the walled city on its north–south axis, opening to the south and directly linked to the south gate. This orientation, and the use of a site with mountains to the north and a river surrounding the city to the south, typically conforms with the rules of feng-shui, of which more later. That the Yamen is the building shown in greatest detail accords with its importance, and the graphic

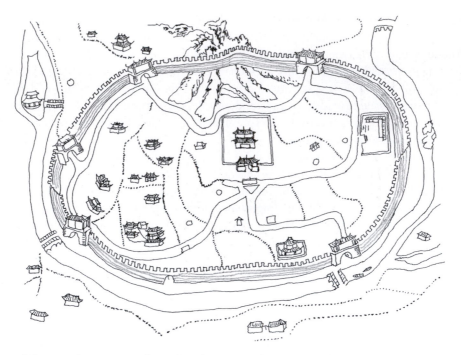

Figure 4.2 Map of Ping Xiang of 1872 based on one in the local records (redrawn by author from Huang 1984).

shorthand presents it as a rectangular walled compound containing a gate and two halls in axial progression with a screen-wall in front. The map also depicts other key public institutions, including the granary, orphanage, guest house, garrison commander's office, temple of the City God, Confucian school, pavilion of the Sacred Edict, and poorhouse. Ordinary houses and commercial premises are too numerous and so are omitted, but the fortifications are shown in detail: they were constantly manned and the city gates were locked at dusk, so the defensive role of the wall was real.[11] The Yamen's wall represented a second barrier, making it a kind of city within the city, like a miniature version of the Emperor's Forbidden City at the heart of Beijing.

To look at a Yamen in detail we shall take that of Neixiang, documented and restored as one of the best surviving examples in China. The buildings in their restored form represent its final state in the Qing Dynasty under Emperor Guang Xu (late nineteenth century), but the initial construction was in 1304, so its layout is representative for Huang's period, as confirmed by a period map.[12] Chinese maps from the local records show it in various stages and in various degrees of accuracy, but the mapping techniques always view the complex from the south end, emphasizing the serial enclosures along the central axis and laying out the buildings in sequence as elevations, with emphasis on the roof. Figure 4.3 shows a map of Neixiang Yamen from the Qing Dynasty Kangxi period (1661–1772). It suggests the surviving layout but with more elaborate roofs. For greater accuracy on the preserved buildings we will use another map redrawn in the traditional style in 1998 by Pengjin Liu (Figure 4.7).

Neixiang Yamen was a walled complex set more or less centrally within the walled and defended city. Its principal contents were the main court for trials and audiences, with the

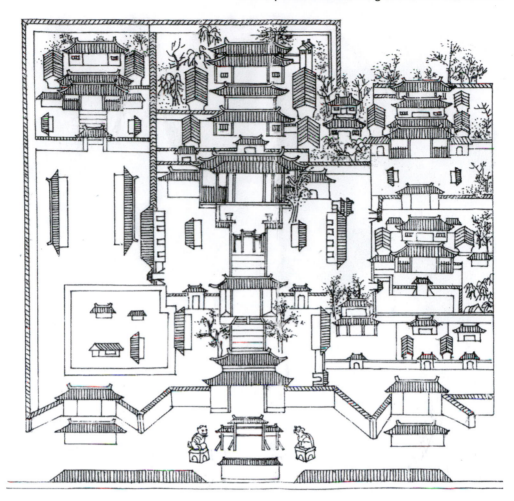

Figure 4.3 Copy of a map of Neixiang Yamen c. 1700 from local records (redrawn by Chen Jianyu from a Chinese source).

magistrate's residence located behind, but it also included the offices of the local administration and police, the prison, the residences of deputies and advisers, and other lesser functions. The word Yamen means flag-gate, and its main gate, always on the south side, was all that most people would usually see. The main gate is always emphasized in graphic presentations, which tend to combine plan and elevation, and generally present the Yamen axially with the gate to the fore, sometimes even in a pseudo-perspective. Within the complex the territory was generally divided laterally into three bands, always with priority to the central south–north axis, and often with dividing walls between centre and side bands. The axial path from the entry gate to the steps to the main hall where the magistrate dispensed power and justice was marked by a raised walk (Figure 4.5). It was symmetrically straddled by the main halls, the largest buildings, in a progressive series, and in more elaborate cases further punctuated by Paifang, purely ceremonial gates which further dramatized the sense of progression. In the case of Neixiang two are shown, one outside the front gate and a second in the middle of the main courtyard (Figure 4.8a).

Figure 4.4 Neixiang Yamen, main entrance in 2009 (author's photograph, May 2009).

Figure 4.5 Neixiang Yamen, first court seen on axis from just within first gate: to left are the posts where horses were tethered (author's photograph).

Figure 4.6 Image of a magistrate at his desk with the accused kneeling before him controlled by two lictors with their bamboo canes (redrawing in Schinz 1996, from a woodblock print of 1628).

The main courtyard, fronted to the north by the main hall where the magistrate sat (Figures 4.12, 4.13 and 4.14), was the public centre of the complex where trials were held, and the long buildings defining its east and west flanks were the main administrative offices divided up between the six departments of Chinese bureaucracy, martial ones to left and west, and liberal ones to right and east.[13] With all this symmetrical framing, nobody could doubt that the central path was the main ceremonial route and hierarchical centre. But as it progressed from south to north, it made the transition from public to private, passing beyond the main hall across an inner court to a second hall used by the magistrate for more restricted business (Figure 4.16).

Crossing yet another court, it arrived at the gate to his residence (Figure 4.17), and after a final one it reached his sleeping quarters (Figure 4.18). A tranquil private garden lay beyond to the rear (Figures 4.19, 4.20 and 4.21). Since there was no break in the outer wall to the north, the magistrate, his family and guests would need to pass back through the entire complex and all its many layers to rejoin the outside world. This must have produced a considerable sense of enclosure. If this public to private progression marks the character of the main axis from south to north, the division into three bands in the east/west direction presented a hierarchy of another kind, highlighting the centre by placing subordinate functions in the side bands, cut off by dividing walls (Figure 4.8c). A loosening of symmetry towards the edges intensified the sense of centre, while allowing contingent adjustment for the diverse accommodation within the side bands. Activities accommodated to the right and east tended to be more positive and propitious than those to the west, so at Neixiang, for example, the prison on the west lies opposite the temples of the local gods in the east. Generally kitchens, stores of grain and silver, and accounting offices tended to be set on the east side as opposed to military quarters and stables placed in the west.

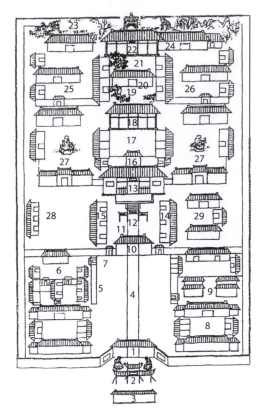

Figure 4.7 Map of Neixiang Yamen with preserved and restored buildings (redrawn by Chen Jianyu after a version drawn in traditional Chinese style by Pengliu in 1998). Key: 1. Main gate; 2. Paifang (a purely ceremonial timber structure); 3. Screen wall at the other side of the street; 4. First court; 5. Place to tie up horses; 6. Prison; 7. Gate of Death; 8. Hostel for eminent guests; 9. Temples of Earth God (right) and of Yamen God; 10. Second gate; 11. Principal court; 12. Paifang; 13. First hall and seat of judgement; 14. Liberal departments: Civil Office, Revenue, and Rites; 15. Martial departments: Punishment, Military, and Works; 16. Gate to second court; 17. Second court; 18. Magistrate's seat; 19. Intermediate court; 20. Gatehouse to residence; 21. Third court; 22. Third Hall and residence; 23. Private garden entered to west of hall; 24. East hall for magistrate's family; 25. Revenue Department; 26. House of the Guards; 27. Houses of Magistrate's Assistants; 28. House of the secretaries; 29. Police Department.

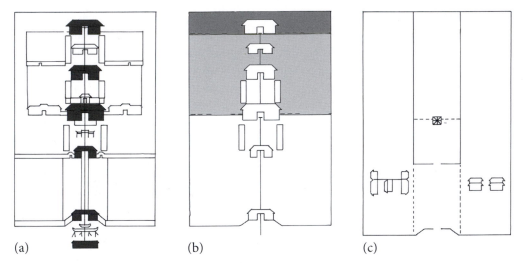

(a) (b) (c)

Figure 4.8 a, b, c Author's diagrams of Neixiang Yamen to be read in conjunction with Figure 4.7. Left (a) shows the south–north progression up the main axis: from bottom to top in black: Screen wall, Paifang, Gate 1, Gate 2, another Paifang, and Halls 1, 2, and 3. Middle (b) shows the progression from public to private with informal garden at the end. Right (c) shows three bands of buildings, the central one strictly symmetrical, outer ones with lesser functions breaking the formality. The asterisk marks the ritual centre, the blocks bottom left are the prison, bottom right the temples of Earth God and Yamen God.

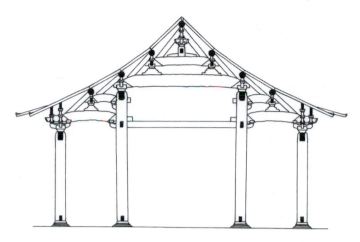

Figure 4.9 Section through a traditional Chinese hall building, showing the interlocking construction of the roof, the curved profile, and bracketing at the overhangs (redrawn by author after Sicheng 1984).

Chinese architecture

Some general points about traditional Chinese architecture are required. Although masonry was important for defensive walls, tombs, and the bases of buildings, the ceremonial architecture for the living was generally of timber, a living material as opposed to the dead stone used for tombs.

Figure 4.10 Neixiang Yamen, second gate with ceremonial Paifang beyond (author's photograph).

Figure 4.11 The Paifang in the main court seen on axis with the Hall of Judgment beyond (author's photograph).

Figure 4.12 Hall of Judgment with Magistrate's desk on axis in the place of honour (author's photograph).

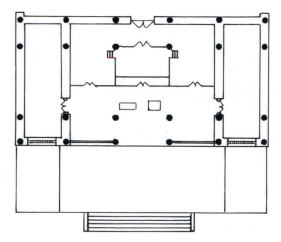

Figure 4.13 Plan of the first hall at Neixiang Yamen, showing the dominance of columns despite walls (redrawn by author from a Chinese source by Chen Jianyu).

The dominating construction discipline was therefore carpentry, which meant modular prefabricated construction with carefully controlled bay dimensions and sophisticated interlocking joints. The plan grid of columns and stacking of beam on beam dictated an orthogonal layout, moving on into hexagonal and octagonal plans when elaboration was sought, as with pagodas.[14] Pagodas also reveal with their multiple layers that the roof was the very essence of Chinese architecture, not only as a vehicle of expression, but because the roof holds the building together, providing necessary bracing and allowing the ground floor columns to stand free. This means that making a traditional Chinese building was first and foremost the making of a roof, to which partitions and outer walls were flimsy additions, summed up in the Chinese phrase *qiang dao wu bu ta*: 'wall destroyed but building remains'.[15] It is therefore no surprise that the favoured site for architectural elaboration is the bracketed joint where columns meet roof structure, and that the complex construction geometry of the hip produces the characteristic curved eaves profile.

The integrity of the roof – as object, as image, and as carpentry process – assured that the major halls of a complex were built freestanding, avoiding collision of roofs and consequent clashes of geometry. But despite this desire to treat the hall as a free-standing entity, the normal layout alternates halls with courtyards which are conceived as outdoor rooms, usually larger and more impressive than the hall interiors. They were formally paved, and halls and courts were equally important for social and ritual purposes. This primacy of courtyards, and use of the halls as relatively shallower dividers between them, meant that the ritual space of the hall was used crosswise rather than lengthwise, the sitting magistrate dominating the axis of the whole complex, but sitting on the cross-axis rather than aligned with the west–east long axis of his hall (Figure 4.13). The courtyard spaces, though sometimes leaking at the corners, could be contained by gates to maintain enclosure, and when the hall blocked the central axis, side routes could provide the way through. But the whole complex also worked as a detached entity, for a palace, temple or Yamen was generally surrounded by a security wall of roofed masonry or mud, which ensured privacy and restricted entry to a limited number of

Figure 4.14 Neixiang Yamen, Magistrate's desk in the central hall (author's photograph).

Figure 4.15 Exit from hall, left, and causeway leading to third court, the gate shown in chapter frontispiece, Figure 4.1. Note the plain lintel on the back of the hall as opposed to the elaborate gate to the second court, and the extreme plainness of the background service wing beyond (author's photograph).

gates. These gates were the main controllers of physical transition as well as sharply defining territory, but as we shall see, practically useless ceremonial gates within complexes also marked significant spatial layers.

From city plans to humble dwellings, Chinese building complexes were generally laid out on a strict south–north axis, the centre-line defining the main ceremonial route from the main entrance which in official buildings should face south. This is the direction connecting the Son of Heaven with the sun, taken for granted even by Confucius's time.[16] The route passed through gates, courtyards and halls, moving from one layer to the next to become hierarchically more important or progressively more private. In the case of Neixiang Yamen, it passed through two sets of gates and a ceremonial stone paifang in the courtyard before arriving at the steps to the main hall. This was the dominant public part of the building, where trials and audiences were held. To understand what this meant in practice we must return to Huang's text.

Arrival of the magistrate

Liuhung Huang describes in detail his arrival at the Yamen, pointing out the need to arrive on an auspicious day and therefore to calculate the travel time in advance. The choice of day, governed by the complex Chinese calendar and a Daoist interpretation of his horoscope, is typical of the need to control order in time as well as space, and of the general belief in the alternating cycles of yin and yang considered to produce good and bad luck. Huang further advises that the arriving magistrate must avoid making his initial entrance to the town by the south and principal gate, as it is associated with the sun, fire, and yang, as is his own role, and excess of the fire element would cause a conflagration in the city during his period of office. Third, he advises that the magistrate should at first avoid all contact with the Yamen, but must instead set himself up in a hostel to prepare a ritual assumption of his territory a couple of days later. He should receive his official seal in the hostel, and undertake an all-night fast at the temple of the City God, making sacrifices and writing an oath to promise his integrity. On the morning chosen for his assumption of office he dons his official robes and returns – at an auspicious hour – to the temple of the City God where he makes further observances, this time in public. This duty completed, he is carried by sedan chair in procession to the Yamen accompanied by playing musicians, and descends inside the main gate. In the space between outer and middle gates he performs two prayers: one to the Earth God, whose shrine is to the side, the other to the God of the Middle Gate. A sample is included verbatim:

> Oh God who controls this gate, thou represent the virtues of yin and yang combined. Neither the virtuous nor the wicked can escape thy scrutiny when they cross thy threshold. I come to officiate in this district with a trembling heart. Only with thy silent help can I fulfill duties on my part.[17]

Then the magistrate enters the main courtyard, walking on the central axis – marked out in special paving – towards a table of burning incense set centrally before the main hall. He kneels before it facing north and kowtows to the Emperor, thanking him for his grace. This accomplished, he turns to salute such colleagues and subordinates as are permitted to enter

Figure 4.16 Neixiang Yamen, third court, used for special cases and meetings (author's photograph).

Figure 4.17 Entrance to the Magistrate's residence across a narrow court (author's photograph).

Figure 4.18 Magistrate's residence, the main hall (author's photograph).

the court, for lesser underlings like constables and runners must remain behind the middle gate. He turns north to ascend the steps centrally into the hall, then faces south again as he takes his axial seat on the raised dais of the main hall, his position of authority at the focal point. A crucial inversion has occurred: at the bottom of the steps he faced north and humbled himself to the absent Emperor, but on assuming office he faces south in his central seat to represent the Emperor. A clerk from the rites department declares the hour auspicious, and the magistrate begins the formalities of his assumption, which include interviewing the heads of the six departments, examining their books and taking their signatures, having the keys of the city presented to him, inspecting the maps, gazetteers and other records, then greeting the constables, runners, lictors, porters, and other assistants. With these formalities complete, his colleagues and subordinates congratulate him from standing positions under the eaves between hall and court. The most senior, the assistant magistrate, then signals the closure of proceedings by descending the central steps from the hall and mounting his horse. As he leaves the courtyard, the chief officers descend the eastern steps to depart, and the middle gate is closed. Having dismissed all underlings except personal attendants, the magistrate can retire northwards into his private quarters, where he may wish to make sacrifices to the God of the Gate of the Inner Quarters and to the Kitchen God, or he may receive private visitors who arrive by the western gate.

Use of the hall and court: Roll call and trial

Three days after taking office, Huang organized a roll call of the court runners at noon, knowing that some of them were corrupt. All were brought into the courtyard and the east and west gates of the Yamen were locked. He had them kneel before him one by one at the bottom of the steps in front of the hall, questioning them to check their identities and to accuse them of their misdemeanours, after which the guilty were summarily punished.[18] The magistrate, occupying his position of power on the axis and sitting in his grand chair on the dais, had not only the advantage of height but also the full enclosure of the hall and the elaborate protection of its main roof, as opposed to the persons brought before him kneeling chairless on the stone flags in the open air.

Everyday court proceedings held primarily in the courtyard were something of an ordeal for both litigants and witnesses, all being expected to kneel for long periods in the open air.[19] For sessions held at noon, after lunch, the magistrate's dais was brought to the front of the hall so that he could more directly overlook the courtyard. Cases were listed strictly in order, and waiting litigants lined up at the front gate, the magistrate having examined the paperwork in advance and marked up for himself the pertinent points. Within the hall he was accompanied by a scribe to document proceedings and two runners standing at attention in the left side of the hall, one of whose duties was to handle tallies, the other to prepare ink. A further runner in the courtyard organized the participants and set labelled tablets on the ground to mark the places where litigants should kneel: plaintiffs at the east corner, defendants at the west, and witnesses centrally inside the inner gate on a raised area of pavement. When a case was to proceed, the runner would report the presence of the parties to the magistrate, and after gaining his approval would call them to their places. Lictors were instructed to stand by and to bring in and display instruments of torture if necessary, as a useful threat against reluctant defendants and lying witnesses.[20] The magistrate himself carried out the interrogation using a series of seven tactics of detection, called the hook, the raid, the attack, intimidation, browbeating, comparison, and compelling. His aim was to determine the truth before imposing judgment, and a substantial portion of the text concerns how to achieve this while disarming the kinds of subterfuges and stratagems regularly attempted by lawbreakers.

The main hall and its court were used for other things besides trials. Tax prompters and payers were made to assemble there, and Huang devised a system of reward and punishment, giving early payers special rosettes and letting them march out accompanied by music, while those in arrears were made to kneel alongside the central path in the court and were even flogged.[21] Taxes were counted in the hall, the silver chests being brought in and set behind the dais, with chest clerks and revenue clerks on hand to weigh contributions and report them in a book, which was finally signed in red by the magistrate himself.[22] The twice monthly roll call of rural police was carried out in the courtyard,[23] and also that of escaped slaves about to be sent elsewhere.[24] The prison where they were kept awaiting deportation was in the corner to the right of the hall, close by.[25] The magistrate could use his hall and court also as the site of munificence, handing out food to the poor on the first day of the month and winter clothing in the tenth month.[26] It was the place where the people met the government, and they were constantly expected to show the magistrate the greatest respect. Huang advises that inter-views of militia heads – locally important people – should be carried out not in the main hall but more tactfully at the entrance gate 'so that the candidates need not kneel before the magistrate'.[27]

Huang's instructions about the magistrate's first entrance to the Yamen show him taking part in an elaborate ritual in a building that he had not yet seen, so we might ask how he knew what to do, and where. Presumably there were assistants on hand to discuss the process beforehand, but the general layout of the building followed a standard pattern easily recog-nized. He would have known it through exposure to the Yamen of his home town, to the spatially similar arrangements of the imperial examination system, and to the limited parts of the Forbidden City experienced during his appointment.[28] Furthermore, not only temples and schools but even large family houses were symmetrically organized around progressive courts on a south–north axis, with the central 'main hall' respectfully dedicated to family ancestors.

Reading of the Sacred Edict[29]

A variant on this general pattern that confirms its general efficacy is the Hall of the Sacred Edict, where moral instruction was delivered on behalf of the Emperor by the reading of sacred texts in sixteen sections, like a Chinese version of the Ten Commandments. Huang explains that when the Sacred Edict is being read, participants should feel 'as if they are in the presence of the Emperor and imagine that he is speaking in person'.[30] This is achieved by making it a highly ordered occasion with dignitaries in official dress and accompanying music, but the axial focus in the main hall is this time the imperial tablet, enclosed in a dragon pavilion. It is set up on a high table like an altar along with an incense burner, a flower vase, and a pair of candlesticks 'arranged in proper order'.[31] The participating gentry and scholars in their robes await the arrival of the magistrate and other senior figures, who descend from their sedan chairs in silence outside the complex without greeting one another 'out of respect for

Figure 4.19 Neixiang Yamen, Magistrate's residence marks the culmination of the axis: the way through to the garden behind is to west, turning the corner past the half-visible moongate to encounter the octagonal gateway and stone stele shown in Figure 4.20, above right (author's photograph).

Figure 4.20 Octagonal gateway and stone stele (author's photograph).

Figure 4.21 The garden with the blank back wall to the Magistrate's residential hall to right (author's photograph).

the imperial tablet'. At ten o'clock they enter the courtyard, officials from the left corner, gentry and scholars from the right corner, and line up to either side of the central path to pay respect to the Emperor by bowing three times and touching the ground with their foreheads nine times. They then enter the hall and stand in order to left and right, again leaving the revered central axis vacant as the absent Emperor's path. Commoners file in at the back in respectful silence, and the appointed lecturer and his assistant place the book on the lectern. The lecturer commands the drum to be sounded three times to open proceedings, and approaches the lectern to read the first verse. This completed, he places the bookmark, bows, retreats, and a sounding board is beaten. His assistant then approaches the lectern to read the second verse, retreating in turn to another boom of the sounding board, and so they continue through all sixteen. Finally the lecturer declares the reading completed and the commoners disperse. The officials, scholars, and gentry return to the courtyard, where their postponed greeting of each other is formally completed under the direction of a master of ceremonies with music playing. In the hall the dragon pavilion containing the tablet is ceremoniously put away. Finally two record books kept in the hall concerning the activities of local people are updated. The red one records good deeds and the black one bad. It is the lecturers' duty later to congratulate or to admonish the persons concerned, and to pass major cases of merit or demerit up to the Yamen for further attention.[32]

Then and now: Cultural relativities

Huang's long and detailed account of the magistrate's life seems sometimes familiar and modern, as for example when he discusses poverty and lack of education as causes of crime,[33] the circumstances of adultery, or when he mentions the advisability of leaving a few small discrepancies in a document for his superior to find, to save him the trouble of raising new errors of his own.[34] One can sympathize with his frequent calls for compassion and understand his strategic use of threats, identifying with his sometimes difficult moral universe. On the other hand the use of torture, the severity and cruelty of the five punishments, which included two kinds of death penalty,[35] and the intimidation of both witnesses and accused without presumption of innocence until proof of guilt, is shocking to the modern reader even if things were little better in Europe at the time. The treatment of women also places a gulf before a modern audience. They were dealt with less severely as criminals, but described as fickle and loose, and when raped they were expected to protest to the last or consent was assumed.[36] It is telling how few women appear in the book, and Huang gives no clue as to whether he is married. The inheritance system is revealed as strictly paternal, tied to surname, and closed to adoptees.[37] On his father's death Huang was obliged to quit his magistracy and mourn for no less than three years, but his mother is unmentioned. There is also gender segregation: a ten-year-old girl, we are told, should not sit at table with her brothers.[38]

If such cultural variations are relatively easy to understand, the religious background is more difficult, and likely to provoke the knee-jerk reaction of 'superstition'. But drawing the line against superstition is a relative matter, and it is evident that Huang, despite indulging in practices strange to us, had defined his own threshold. At one point he dismisses worship of the native dragon and the use of mirrors in controlling water, and at another he dismisses bogus sects.[39] More clearly still, he remarks that one 'must take advantage of people's

Figure 4.22 Neixiang Yamen: the Prison God within his temple (author's photograph).

Figure 4.23 First court at the prison, with the Prison God's south-facing temple to left (author's photograph).

superstitious beliefs' in describing his stratagem of gaining a confession through chaining the accused overnight in the temple of the City God.[40] Although he used the temple in this way, it was a site of religious observance that he took very seriously, the City God being his counterpart in the nether world and a vital agent in the order of things.[41] It was widely believed that the spirits of the dead drifted off to the nether world to be judged by a court that mirrored the earthly Yamen, in which among others the Earth God and City God presided.[42] The prevalence of this idea is evident in the collected stories of Chi Yün, a contemporary of Huang who climbed even higher in the civil service. Several of them include accounts of people who in near-death experiences dreamed of appearing before this ghostly court.[43] That the earthly court became the model for the imaginary one is scarcely surprising, but carrying its order into other realms doubtless helped to legitimate it. Despite an apparently rational and pragmatic stance, Huang also sincerely believed that during his two magistracies he staved off disasters like drought and locusts through special appeals, as well as having kept the world in order by regular observances in temples at the correct times.[44] The idea that the Emperor and his representatives were in touch with the cosmos and could intervene in the order of things was a self-evident and unshakeable truth.[45]

Difficult also for the modern reader to take seriously is the sheer number of Gods, for behind the scientific objection about the possibilities of divine intervention lies a monotheistic prejudice from Christianity and other world religions condemning such promiscuous idolatry as 'primitive'. Most prominent in Huang's book are the City God, the quasi-divine Emperor, and Confucius, but mentioned also are Gods of River and Mountain, of Rain, Wind, and Thunder, of Agriculture, Earth, and Grain, of Literature, of the Horse, of the Military Banner, and of certain specific places, including a Kitchen God present in every house, the Gods of the Middle and Inner Gate at the Yamen, and even a Prison God, whose shrine at the prison entrance must be treated with proper respect (Figures 4.22 and 4.23).[46]

Anyone familiar with Chinese sources will recognize this list as far from exhaustive,[47] but it is a long list nonetheless, and contains many different kinds of things. The Emperor, celebrated in the altar-like presentation of the Sacred Edict, is a living if holy person, and Confucius an historic one, while the City God is a kind of personification of the place that allows the magistrate publicly to develop a relationship with his post and people. The God of the Military Banner is among the more easily understood, since it is paralleled by quasi-religious rituals of 'saluting the flag' worldwide, often including mention of God if not Gods. The Kitchen God as personification of the family home and guarantee of domestic continuity becomes understandable when his role in new year festivities is understood: he has to be dismissed to make his report in heaven, then welcomed back. He has counterparts in the Russian Domovoi and in Thai House Gods still celebrated today.[48]

The most pertinent example for our story is the God of the Middle Gate at the Yamen, addressed in the words on page 79. Defining the edge of the main court space, this gate is a ceremonial rather than a strictly physical barrier. The prayer addressed to the Gate during the magistrate's first entry is heard by all present as a reminder of the territory and power of the court, helping to share and maintain respect. Ritual and object define one another: the prayer adds meaning to the gate, but without the gate's presence there would be nothing to address. The social value is therefore present without any need to propose a supernatural agency or the personification of a God, but a culture attuned to such propositions would naturally attach them.

The prayer to the gate includes mention of yin and yang in close connection with the virtuous and the wicked, suggesting a concept of balance which recurs as a symbol of justice, portrayed in the West in a parallel way by a lady with scales, a rather god-like personification who still reigns over London's Old Bailey.[49] The black and red books of bad and good deeds kept in the Hall of the Sacred Edict also follow the yin/yang principle, as does the idea of balance between propitious and unpropitious dates, good and bad luck. Yin and yang was the foundation of Daoist cosmology, a universal concept applicable to polarities of all kinds, starting with dark/light and female/male. It supported the idea of cycles that swing from one pole to the other and was also the basis of the Chinese binary number system.[50] When Huang, discussing the scientific examination of victims, claims that women have black bones and men white ones, and that drowned women float in the water face up and men face down,[51] he is reflecting a system of knowledge geared to the expectations of yin/yang. Equally typical of traditional Chinese cosmology is his claim that the human body has 365 bones, thus according with the days of the year.[52] Yet more startling to the modern reader is the idea that you could tell if someone was related to an ancestor by letting drops of their blood fall on the ancestor's bone to see whether it was absorbed.[53] In a society obsessed with the blood line of paternal inheritance, it was only logical that living blood should recognize its ancestral source.[54] Either empirical observation had not yet reached the point of undermining such notions, or it was simply ignored in favour of a superior knowledge system presumed to be correct. We tend to see what we are looking for and to construct ideas according to established logical patterns.

The Dao was the essential unity and yin/yang its subdivision into a duality. Three in Daoist cosmology stands for earth, human beings and heaven, four for the cardinal points, and five for the five elements or phases: fire, water, wood, earth, and metal. We need not enter the many complex implications of this system except to note a repeated preference for grouping things in fives and the possibility of mapping the five elements onto the four cardinal points by including centre as the fifth.[55] This profoundly influences the Chinese interpretation of space, both by making orientation generally more significant – hence the almost universal south–north axiality – and by relating it to other fivefold phenomena. The interaction creates a fixed relation between a cardinal point and a colour, for example, a possibility Western readers may never have considered. Blue goes with east, red with south, white with west, and black with north, and these are the colours that Huang reports as distinguishing the caps of the militia on duty in the respective four sides of the city.[56] Huang's text makes frequent reference to fourness. It is implicit in the idea that a piece of land has four boundaries for the cadastral survey,[57] and the ancient Chinese character for a field quarters a rectangle with a cross. He describes the empire as lying 'between four seas', while exiles are banished 'to the four frontiers'.[58] The city has four gates and the surrounding territory over which it holds jurisdiction is divided administratively into four rural areas, each controlled by its own branch of the militia.[59] Huang even finds disorder obedient to the fourfold system when he reports that each of the four districts has its own bandit chief.[60] A small but telling example of fourfold space cited in passing is the mythical story of King Tang. Encountering a trapper who had set four traps to catch all the animals 'from the four directions', the king ordered that those on three sides be opened, which showed both his wisdom and his compassion.[61]

General principles and east–west contrasts

Returning to the general theme of architecture and ritual, what in this example can be considered universal and what specific? The principle established in Chapter 1 that important things happen at the ends of axes is not merely fulfilled but greatly amplified in this highly centralized and hierarchical society, for the magistrate in his central chair sits right at the middle of the Yamen which is also the centre of the city, the symmetrical layout of the complex making its axiality unmistakable. The marking of the central path with special paving, sometimes to define its use by the magistrate, sometimes to leave it vacant in deference to the Emperor, increases the axial definition, and again there is evidence in the *Analects* that ritual passage through space was even 2,000 years ago a pressing concern. This passage specifies correct behaviour while visiting the palace, and without mentioning the axis, gives a compelling idea of sequence:

> On entering the palace gate he seems to shrink into himself, as though there were not room. If he halts, it must never be in the middle of the gate, nor in going through does he ever tread on the threshold. As he passes the Stance, a look of confusion comes over his face, his legs seem to give way under him and words seem to fail him. While holding up the hem of his skirt, he ascends the Audience Hall, he seems to double up and keeps in his breath, so that you would not think he was breathing at all. On coming out, after descending the first step his expression relaxes into one of satisfaction and relief. At the bottom of the steps he quickens his pace, advancing with an air of majestic dignity. On regaining his place he resumes an air of wariness and hesitation.[62]

The Chinese main axis is the crucial defining element, reflected in the written character for centre, 中, and as in examples in earlier chapters, the power of the long axis in defining the main path creates at the same time a cross-axis with balanced polarity of right and left, lending equivalence to plaintiffs and defendants kneeling in opposite corners in a legal case, and setting up a similar balance between officials and scholars as they line up on opposite sides during the reading of the Sacred Edict. In the layout of the Yamen as a whole there is a consistent lateral hierarchy with the main official buildings in the central band and minor functions such as prison, stables, and accommodation for subordinates to the sides. In some examples the magistrate's accommodation at rear centre is flanked to left and right by his immediate deputies.

As in all examples in all chapters of this book so far, relative height is consistently used to define status, typically by elevating the magistrate on his chair, dais, and steps above the courtyard where litigants kneel. The role of the dais had been important during 2,000 years, for among ritual abuses described in the *Analects* is that of making obeisance after mounting the dais instead of before it: this is condemned as presumptuous.[63] Yet another general principle strengthened in the Chinese case is the sense of centre and periphery, the Yamen in the middle of the city with its own gates and sub-enclosures generating a sense of multiple layers of enclosure. All the above matters are relatively easy to appreciate and are arguably universal in principle, if specific in interpretation.

Rather different in relation to earlier Western examples, though, is the greater importance of courtyards as outdoor rooms in the Chinese complexes, and the sense that the halls between them, if not exactly subordinate, are no more than equal. This has often been considered to reflect a specific Chinese appreciation of space which is celebrated in a famous Lao Tzu poem about the space within a pot being more important than its substance.[64] Be that as it may, the buildings seem not thought of as objects, for the progressions of gates, courts, and halls make an integrated series all requiring each other. Although some events happen within halls, others happen between a hall and a court, like a daytime trial, the hall being used like a stage in relation to an auditorium, an arrangement more literally found with Chinese opera. This spatial use accounts for the magistrate taking the cross-axis of the hall rather than the long axis, but it also relies on the hall being open to the court, which is dependent on the columnar nature of Chinese architecture and its floating roof. The open hall with its flimsy partitions and projecting eaves stands in stark contrast with the freestanding masonry enclosing walls used for security and privacy around the complex and between different parts of it, so the inside and outside of the hall enjoy more continuity than that between the inner world of the complex and the outer world of the city. These spatial transitions are of different kinds, softer

Figure 4.24 Main screen wall across street opposite entry of the whole Neixiang complex, as seen from main gate. It is decorated with a symbolic dragon (author's photograph).

Figure 4.25 Entry to storehouse for records at the Neixiang Yamen, placed immediately to the east of the first hall. The axial view into the courtyard is broken by the screen wall (author's photograph).

within and harder without, and there are many more of them. There is arguably a greater tendency in traditional Chinese architecture also to add notional or purely ceremonial gates, which mark thresholds without preventing physical ingress.

A sense of direction

While the rule of compulsory southward orientation may seem ecologically sensible, it has rarely been pursued as consistently as in Imperial China, where it reflected culturally specific Daoist principles of orientation. Such specificity is clear in the associations between cardinal points and colours, which have no natural basis and do not accord with versions found elsewhere in the world.[65] The Chinese orientation system is also not simply solar, but linked with a complex interpretation of the landscape and its natural energy, or *qi*, which is supposed to flow through 'dragon veins'. The practice of feng-shui, respected by Huang and mentioned in two sections of his book,[66] is concerned with interpreting the physical and symbolic features of place. Literally it means 'wind and water', and while it certainly deals with practical issues of water supply and shelter, it also reads the shapes of mountains in relation to mythical beasts of cosmic significance.[67] It must therefore be counted as culturally specific. If its virtue is to convince people that they have placed their settlements in harmony with the Daoist cosmos, and that it will therefore increase their share of good luck, any sense of harmony achieved must surely depend on subscribing to the whole system.

Also related to feng-shui, and unexpected by the Western reader, is the Chinese habit of blocking important axes with screens, such as those outside and opposite the gates of Yamens (Figure 4.24), or those within the gates of houses which prevent a direct view from the street (Figure 4.25).

This practice is very ancient, with archaeological examples dating back to the eighth century BC. Mention in a Chinese dictionary of the third century BC concerns an errant minister who had overstepped his rank by building a screen wall for his house in imitation of the King's.[68] At first the screen wall had only been allowed for official buildings, which was why it became a status symbol, its use and dimensions being strictly regulated across the dynasties. Situated opposite the front gate of low-walled complexes, it played a critical role in advertising their presence, and Yamens tended to have representations of the mythical figures Taotie and Xiezhi, the former a moral reminder to the magistrate not to take bribes, the latter a guardian against disaster. Considered spatially, such external screen walls also defined a public square which could be used for proclamations and public executions, and as yet another threshold space before entering the Yamen,[69] but none of this really explains why the axis was blocked, which stands in contrast with Western Baroque examples, ever keen to show their expansive power. The key to this conundrum seems to be Chinese beliefs in paths of energy which flow about in various forms, again a very ancient notion. One clue to understanding this lies in the extreme centrality of the ancient Chinese kingdom and the mediating link of the King with the Divine:

> The capital, the axis mundi, was also the point of ontological transition at which divine power entered the world and diffused outward through the kingdom ... Supernatural power reaching the earth at the sacred axis of the world was diffused to the four quarters

through cosmo-magically sanctioned channels, so that the pre-ordained dispositions of symbolic space were maintained and harmony prevailed in the realm ... The city gates, where power generated at the axis mundi flowed out from the confines of the ceremonial complex towards the cardinal points of the compass, possessed a heightened symbolic significance which, in virtually all Asian urban traditions, was expressed in massive constructions whose size far exceeded that necessary for performance of their mundane functions.[70]

Though this sounds ancient and even fanciful, we must remember that right up to the end of the imperial system in 1912 the Emperor was considered the Son of Heaven, not in himself divine but acting as an intermediary for the powers of heaven. He was therefore considered imbued with cosmic power which emanated from his person. A screen wall was often required to protect those permitted an audience from his power. A telling detail from the biography of the last Emperor, a mere boy, is that though he was expected to sit facing south during instruction, his tutor was not allowed to sit opposite him facing north – within the stream of his power, as it were – but had instead to face west.[71]

That Huang's Yamen was not the capital does not disconnect it from this system of beliefs, for not only did he represent and distribute the imperial power, the Yamen also imitated at a smaller scale the Forbidden City. One of the strongest clues in Huang's generally pragmatic text that this general belief in flows of energy still applied was the rule prohibiting him from entering the south gate on first arrival lest he cause a fire. The same ideas are reflected in feng-shui practices through conceptions of positive and negative energy (*qi*), both of which had to be controlled.[72] Positive energy was not allowed to become too concentrated or to move too fast, and just as the river in a city site must pass through gracefully and slowly without turbulence so that the life-giving energy is distributed to the place before it leaves,[73] so the *qi* in the air and the wind must be persuaded to meander through a building, distributing its benevolence and not rushing on. This makes it unlucky, for example, to align windows or doors on opposite sides of a house in China without visual obstruction between, lest valuable energy entering on one side passes quickly through and is dissipated. Perhaps it was felt that if the south gate of the Yamen were left unobstructed, the accumulated power of the complex concentrated on the main axis would be too quickly dissipated, but perhaps also for ordinary people the imperial power was too dangerous. Negative energy had to be controlled, and widepread beliefs persist in China to this day that ghosts and evil spirits travel in straight lines and can therefore be thwarted by a screen wall. Without a well-integrated idea of *qi* as a fundamental principle, it is hard to entertain such notions, so this is another case of cultural specificity.

Conclusion

Despite the great cultural differences of a century ago, which made China seem an obscure and exotic place and the Chinese 'inscrutable', Huang's world as understood through a modern translation does not come across as so very strange.[74] One can empathize with his situation and understand his opinions and practical judgements, even if engaging with some of his beliefs requires background study and suspension of one's prejudices. When it comes to the spaces of the Yamen too, there is a surprising familiarity once the nature and distribution of social functions is understood. The importance of the central path and dominance of the magistrate's raised seat on the axis follow hierarchical principles already noted, as does the symmetrical interplay of right and left once the axis is established, though differences of use involve local meanings. The placing of the Yamen within its own wall at the centre of a walled town evokes a sense of centre and periphery that is again familiar and perhaps cross-cultural. Familiar too is the progression through a series of halls and courts found in the Yamen and other Chinese building complexes, traversing layer after layer in increasing exclusion and privacy, even if this universal idea reaches an extreme unknown to the modern West. The southward orientation so universally observed in Imperial China is solar and might be assumed to be a climatic measure, but for the fundamental role of the cardinal points in Chinese cosmology. Cross-connection of the cardinal points with other phenomena makes the sense of direction highly specific, so although the need to locate oneself in relation to earth and cosmos may have been a universal human preoccupation prior to modern times, the way it was done and the values attached to it varied from place to place.

Other things stand out in the Chinese experience as very different. One is the necessary connection of space and time, witnessed in the repeated requirement to do things on propitious dates and to avoid unpropitious ones. This went so far in Chinese life that the Lu Ban Jing (Carpenter's Manual) specifies propitious dates to tile roofs, plaster a house, pave floors, make a cowhouse and make a pigsty – and they are not the same dates.[75] Rather than being rejected out of hand as superstition, it should be seen as the creation of an order in time parallel to that in space, and the manifestation of a shared sense of propriety. Daoist cosmology links time and space through its symbolic numerology, and through its insistence that all things happen in cycles and phases, an empirically observable truth. Also outstanding in the Chinese experience of space is the great proliferation of gates and thresholds, including many present for symbolic or ritual purposes, like the inner gate of the Yamen. This seems to reveal a greater sensitivity among the Chinese to spatial layering, but it may also reflect a widespread cultural preoccupation with separation and reunion.[76]

Notes

1   Huang 1984, first English edition, 655 pages, translated by Djang Chu and subtitled *A Manual for Local Magistrates in Seventeenth-Century China*; it is the source for most of this chapter.

2   Each magistrate was responsible for around 150,000 people: Huang 1984, translator's introduction, p. 17. For a detailed account of the political operation of the Yamen by a modern author see John R. Watt, *The Yamen and Urban Administration*, in Skinner 1977, pp. 353–90.

3   In Jack Goody's view the isolation has been exaggerated. He lists 'Early links between East and West' in an appendix to Goody 1996, pp. 250–62.

4   Waley 1964, p. 64.

5   Ibid., pp. 162–4. (Translation of the *Analects*, Book XII, sections 1 and 5.)

6   He was obliged to burn incense and say prayers on the 1st and 15th of each month in the temple of Confucius and that of the City God, as well as larger seasonal observances, Huang 1984, p. 29.

7   Huang 1984, p. 527.

8   Ibid., pp. 574–6.

9   Ibid., p. 27.

10   For background on the imperial examination system see Miyazaki 1976.

11   Huang 1984, pp. 482–94.

12   It would of course be wrong to see the institution of the Yamen as static, but to trace the changes over dynasties and centuries is beyond the scope of this chapter. An idea of this development taking the city of Quanzhou as case study can be found in Wang 2009.

13   For the functions of the six departments see Watt in Skinner 1977, pp. 367–8.

14   The occasional appearance of circular buildings such as the Temple of Heaven in Beijing is an important exception that proves the Daoist rule: 'heaven is round and earth is square'.

15   Information from Chen Jianyu.

16   In the *Analects* (Waley 1964) there are two references to the ruler being he who faces south – Book VI section 1 and Book XV section 4. For the south–north axis in town-planning see Schinz 1996. In the case of residential complexes the southern axis is also present but the entry is often indirect.

17   Huang 1984, p. 98.

18   Ibid., pp. 114–15.

19   That this was uncomfortable and humiliating is confirmed by further advice to spare the elderly and young women and keep them in a corridor or a secluded place until needed for evidence, Huang 1984, p. 272.

20   Huang 1984 p. 269. He tells of a case where the threat of torture proved effective in producing a confession, but elsewhere admits (p. 278) the reduced value of false confessions.

21   Ibid., pp. 194–8.

22   Ibid., p. 99.

23   Ibid., p. 414.

24   Ibid., p. 430. The slaves were a hangover from the military conquest by the Manchus who had gained power half a century earlier, as explained in the preface, pp. 12–15.

25   Right in this case presumably in relation to the sitting magistrate facing south, as prisons were generally on the west side.

26   Huang 1984, p. 553.

27   Ibid., p. 469.

28   The Yamen of the Board of Civil Office is described in Huang 1984, p. 75, the Court of State Ceremonial, p. 86.

29   For an overview of the political purposes of the Sacred Edict see Watt in Skinner 1977, p. 361.

30   Huang 1984, p. 531.

31   Ibid., p. 533.

32   Ibid., pp. 530–5.

33   Ibid., pp. 315, 378.

34   Ibid., p. 291.

35   Ibid., pp. 251, 283.

36   Ibid., pp. 432, 440, 443, 608.

37   Ibid., p. 451.

38   Ibid., p. 431.

39   Ibid., p. 517.

40   Ibid., pp. 347, 351.

41   Ibid., pp. 114, 514.

42   The classification of the many kinds of Chinese Gods is too complex to summarize here. See Sharar and Weller 1996.

43   Chi Yün 1999. Chi Yün (T. Hsiao-lan 1724–1805) was a high-ranking civil servant who had come first in the metropolitan examinations of 1754 and by the time of compiling his book was president of the Board of Rites, of the Censorate and of the Board of War, as well as having catalogued the imperial library. He collected stories between 1789 and 1798 and put them together for publication in 1800, adding more for a later edition. On the netherworld court see stories 1, 106, 103, and 86; on the roles of the City God and Gate God, see stories 6 and 87.

44   'Who can deny the existence of the influence of the spiritual world over human affairs?', Huang 1984, p. 512; also 'When the rites and ceremonies are properly observed, there will be harmony in nature and a sumptuous crop will be insured' p. 508.

45   For a clear summary of the roles of the 'Sons of Heaven', see Dawson 1978, pp. 3–32.

46   Huang 1984, pp. 43, 96, 97, 127, 205, 168, 481, 516.

47   See, for example, Feuchtwang 1992.

48   For the Domovoi see Sinyavsky 2007, pp. 107–14.

49   If we do not say prayers to her, in court we do still swear on the Bible.

50   For a good summary of Chinese numerology see Crump 1990, pp. 49–57.

51   Huang 1984, p. 372

52   Ibid., p. 375

53   Ibid., p. 372

54   One of my Chinese students tells that it is believed even today that drops of blood from two people falling into water will mingle if they are blood relations.

55   Huang's book mentions besides the Five Punishments, the Five Relationships (p. 551), the Five Confucian Precepts and Five Steps (p. 539), the Five Grains (p. 545), and when discussing horses Five Internal Organs and Five Regulators (p. 588). The *Tao Te Ching* links in three lines Five Colours, Five Tastes, and Five Notes.

56   Huang 1984, p. 476. Note the way this ties in with the red and black books of good and bad behaviour noted earlier: even this has spatial connotations. Good deeds are linked with the colour of fire, south and sun, and the best gate of the city, while bad ones belong to the colour of the unauspicious north. In details like this the system is reinforced.

57   Ibid., p. 243.

58   Ibid., pp. 284, 507.

59   Ibid., p. 111.

60   Ibid., p. 414.

61   Ibid., p. 64, the translator identifies the source of the story as the classic Shih Chi (Historical records).

62   Waley 1964, p. 147 (Book X, section 4).

63   Ibid., (Book IX, section 3).

64   Lao Tzu 1963, book 1 p. 15; 'Thirty spokes / share one hub. / Adapt the nothing therein to the purpose in hand, and you will have the use of the cart. Knead Clay in order to make a vessel. Adapt the nothing to the purpose in hand, and you will have the use of the vessel ...'

65   Among some Native Americans, for example, north was white, south yellow, east red, and west black: see Neihardt 1979.

66   Huang 1984, pp. 127–8, 482–5.

67 Muddy and mystical accounts of feng-shui proliferate. For a clear and relatively short summary see Schinz 1996, pp. 417–19; for the Daoist background see Needham 1956, pp. 33–164. Another summary can be found in Wheatley 1971, pp. 419–23.

68 This information extracted from Chinese sources by Chen Jianyu.

69 Cui Bao, a minister under Emperor Hui in the Jin Dynasty (265–420), described how ministers would stand under the screen wall for some time before going into the Palace, pondering how to handle an audience with the Emperor. Hence the name *Fu-si* for the screen wall, which means thinking again (second section of *Gujin-zhu* (Past and present) entitled *Du-yi* (City and country): information from Chen Jianyu.

70 Wheatley 1971, pp. 434–5.

71 Dawson 1978, p. 21.

72 The best early source on feng-shui, is the *Book of Burial* by Guo Pu (276–324), available in translation by Juwen Zhang (Zhang 2004).

73 Needham 1956, pp. 41, 42.

74 For nineteenth century European views of China and ideas of 'face' and 'inscrutability', see Hevia 2003, pp.174–9.

75 Ruitenbeek 1989, pp. 99–106 also 162,163.

76 Title of an anthropological study by Charles Stafford, Stafford 2000.

CHAPTER 5
THE NUREMBERG RALLY OF 1934

Figure 5.1 March past of uniformed figures through the centre of old Nuremberg during the Parteitag celebrations of 1934 (photograph by Georg Pahl, Bundesarchiv Koblenz no. 102-16190).

Another great pageant tonight. Two hundred thousand party officials packed in the Zeppelin Wiese with their twenty-one thousand flags unfurled in the searchlights like a forest of weird trees. 'We are strong and will get stronger', Hitler shouted at them through the microphone, his words echoing across the hushed field from the loudspeakers. And there, in the flood-lit night, jammed together like sardines, in one mass formation, the little men of Germany who have made Nazism possible achieved the highest state of being the Germanic man knows: the shedding of their individual souls and minds – with the personal responsibilities and doubts and problems – until under the mystic lights and at the sound of the magic words of the Austrian they were merged completely in the Germanic herd. William L. Shirer, eye-witness, 1934[1]

The Nuremberg Rallies began as a celebration and consolidation of the German National Socialist party in 1927 and ended in 1938 as the 'high-mass' for Greater Germany, paving the way for expansion and war.[2] Devised by a political group that had become highly skilled in propaganda, the rally provided a culminating annual rite of definition, renewal, and solidarity, a peak of visible expression for the whole organization and confirmation of faith in its leader. It provided a unique chance for all the party's members, its paramilitary wings, and its subordinate groupings to commune with him, proclaiming *ein Volk, ein Reich, ein Führer!* Commentators have repeatedly noted its quasi-religious character, setting Hitler in a God-like role descending from the skies in his plane, and presenting him as the saviour of the German people.[3] There were altogether ten rallies and they started small, beginning as meetings of the emerging party on a single day. These were held in Munich in 1923, then in Weimar in 1926, since after his failed putsch – an attempt to take power by force in 1923 – Hitler had been banned from speaking in Bavaria. The ban was lifted in 1927, allowing that year's meeting to take place in Bavaria's northern city Nuremberg, and thereafter that city remained the venue.

The choice of Nuremberg was both ideological and pragmatic. The region, according to Ian Kershaw, was *'piously Protestant, fervently nationalist, and stridently anti-semitic'.*[4] The party

Figure 5.2 Albrecht Dürer's house (author's photograph, September 2010).

Figure 5.3 A river scene in modern Nuremberg (author's photograph, September 2010).

Figure 5.4 The Luitpoldhalle, as the Machine Hall for the 1906 Regional Exhibition (Stadtarchiv Nürnberg).

Figure 5.5 The Luitpoldhalle, as decorated for the Party Rally (Stadtarchiv Nürnberg).

found support among the industrial working class, the police were sympathetic,[5] and the local leader was the Nazi extremist Julius Streicher. The city offered facilities for large gatherings at its southern edge: the Luitpoldhalle, a former exhibition hall, could serve for internal meetings; the Zeppelin Wiese (meadow), site of Graf Zeppelin's airship landing in 1909, for open-air events. As a former imperial free city that had hosted the Reichstag, the city's history fulfilled the Nazis' hunger for memory. Its well-preserved walls, castle, and picturesque narrow

Figure 5.6 Hitler walking up the centre of the Luitpoldhalle, from the film *Triumph of the Will by Leni Riefenstahl 1934 (Bundesarchiv film).*

streets met the party's romantic vision of medieval Germany, and Albrecht Dürer, the leading German Renaissance painter and print maker, had lived and worked there.[6] It was also the quasi-mythical setting for Richard Wagner's opera *Die Meistersinger*, which was performed on the opening evening of all the later rallies.[7] Industrial prowess and the Zeppelin added technological development to ancestry, providing a future as well as a past.

Until the end of the 1920s the rally was a minority party affair, the speeches not being taken seriously by outsiders, though the parades were impressive and the event stretched to four days as the choreography developed. Following on from the first rally of 1927, a larger and more ambitious one took place in 1929, but scuffles with other political groups on the streets resulted in two deaths, and the city refused further meetings in 1930 and 1931. They were perhaps less necessary, for the party's interest had by then shifted to the winning of legitimate votes, but once Hitler had obtained power in 1933, a consolidation was needed. The Parteitag of that year grew into a national week-long event, and hosting it became an honour for the city, so opposition was silenced and generous resources became available.[8] Even so, the celebrations disappointed the leadership in their raggedness and imperfections, so every effort was made to assure that in 1934 the whole performance came together.[9] Albert Speer was on hand to organize and to decorate the venues, and the proceedings were skilfully caught in Leni Riefenstahl's propaganda film *Triumph of the Will*, which remains the most vivid record from all the Parteitage. Although further rallies were held in 1935, 1936, 1937 and 1938, and although all involved greater architectural elaboration, they followed essentially the same model, so the week-long rally of 1934 can serve as the significant and convenient example.[10]

The rally of 1934: Tuesday

Hitler flew in on the late afternoon of Tuesday 4 September, greeted by cheering crowds and ringing church bells as he was driven to the hotel Deutscher Hof in the middle of town.[11] It had been suitably decorated, his name up in lights, and SS guards were conspicuous.[12] Swastika flags were deployed and brown and black uniformed presences were ubiquitous. The Führer's first engagement was a reception by the Mayor in the Grosser Saal of the town hall, opening the whole event from the heart of the old city. The *Times*' correspondent found some irony in the ancient inscription over the door which translated reads 'one man's speech is only half: one should hear both sides'.[13] Before an audience of party leaders, local dignitaries, 600 regional party leaders, and the press, the Mayor presented Hitler with a nationalist icon, a book produced by the local Nuremberg bookseller Palm, who had become a German martyr in Napoleonic times.[14] Hitler then made a short speech. The evening's performance of Wagner's *Meistersinger* at the opera house, provided as cultural underpinning for the nationalist ideology, did not prove popular with the lower ranks of the leadership.[15] Later in the evening, crowds thronged in the square outside Hitler's hotel, demanding to see their Führer. He obliged, appearing briefly on his balcony.[16]

Wednesday, 5 September

Next morning, the first full day of the Parteitag, massed party officials gathered in the Luitpoldhalle at the Luitpoldhain (Luitpold's Grove), the main rally site at the southern edge of the city. The great linear steel-framed building had been built as an exhibition hall in 1906 and could hold 16,000 people,[17] but its utilitarian architecture was disguised for this event by a complete internal redecoration, with silk hangings in red, white, and blue (Figure 5.5). A great wreathed swastika terminated the axis behind the speaker's podium, set against a red background. As Hitler arrived the Reich Symphony Orchestra announced his presence with the 'Badenweiler March', a piece commemorating German Victory in the First World War.[18] Slowly he strode down the central axis followed by the other leading figures of the party through a forest of right arms raised in salute (Figure 5.6). The procession was extended as the standard bearers of the SA regions followed on to take their places behind the leaders like a chorus, led by the 'Blood flag' from the failed putsch of 1923, the holiest of Nazi relics.[19] With all in place the orchestra played Beethoven's 'Egmont Overture', another piece connected with heroism and martyrdom,[20] and Rudolf Hess ascended the podium as master of ceremonies. He made a respectful tribute to the recently deceased Hindenburg, war hero and president.[21] Immediately afterwards, to the accompaniment of muffled drumbeats, the SA's new leader Viktor Lutze read out the names of the Nazi 'martyrs' killed in the putsch, implicitly linking Hindenburg with the party's ancestry.

Switching from the dead to the living, Hess made a brief tribute to the Führer, which was followed by a policy speech setting the tone for the congress. Although the content undoubtedly came from Hitler, the honour of reading it fell to Adolf Wagner, Gauleiter of Bavaria. It stated that the party had the power to accomplish all, would brook no criticism or opposition, that the revolution was now closed, and there was to be no other for a thousand years. This event prepared the way for the many subsidiary party meetings, the most immediate being a cultural conference at the Apollo Theatre that afternoon. With Alfred Rosenberg in the chair, Hitler spoke there for an hour about Nazism as a *Weltanschauung* and as a reaction against Jewish intellectualism. He encouraged a return to instinct, intuition, and an 'organic conception of civilisation'. Later there were uniformed parades through the city, reinforcing the links between place and party.

Figure 5.7 The Labour Service marching with spades, from *Triumph of the Will (Bundesarchiv film)*.

Figure 5.8 The Labour Service and flag bearer, from *Triumph of the Will (Bundesarchiv film)*.

Thursday, 6 September

The second day was for the Arbeitsdienst, the Labour Service, who for the first time paraded 52,000 strong[22] on the Zeppelin Wiese, the largest of the party grounds sited south of the Luitpoldhain (Figures 5.7 and 5.8). Since the party included the word *Arbeiter* in its title and sought a levelling down in the name of socialism, acknowledgement of the heroic workers rebuilding the country was an important propaganda event, but their status remained ambiguous. Their uniform and discipline lent them an unmistakably military character, but since the Reich had not yet dared break the international treaty forbidding it to rearm, they carried spades which glinted in the sunlight. Riefenstahl's film concentrates on a dramatic but well-rehearsed moment when chosen individuals step forward one by one, asked rhetorically: 'Where do you come from?' One answers 'From Friesenland', a second 'From Bayern', a third 'From Kaiserstuhl', and so on, laying out orally the geography of the whole country before declaring in unison: 'ein Volk, ein Führer, ein Reich, Heimat!' From the main viewing stand in the centre of the east side, Hitler inspected them as they paraded around in symmetrical formations, the march-past of 10,000 taking at least two-and-a-half hours. In later years they would chant in unison: 'only once a year does the spade rest, once a year we stand before our Führer, in this hour a new belief is kindled'.[23] In the afternoon the whole contingent of the Labour Service marched through the streets of the city, saluting Hitler in the city's central marketplace, recently renamed Adolf Hitler Platz, where temporary stands had been erected for an audience of a thousand. The column took two hours to pass.

Friday, 7 September

On the third day there were parades of police and conferences of party subgroups. Speeches were given at the congress hall about economic affairs by Darré and Reinhardt, but the principal meeting of the party faithful was in the evening at dusk. Gathered on the Zeppelin Wiese were 200,000 party officials with 21,000 flags, to be addressed by Hitler under flood-lights. When he appeared on the platform, flags were carried in long rows through ranks and

Figure 5.9 Night speech by Hitler at the 1934 rally, from *Triumph of the Will (Bundesarchiv film)*.

Figure 5.10 Speer's eagle as backdrop to night speech by Hitler at the 1934 rally, from *Triumph of the Will (Bundesarchiv film)*.

lowered to the music of 'I had a comrade' in homage to the Nazi dead. Hilter then spoke: 'Today our movement stands like a rock and every one of us is ready to fight for it to our last breath. God, who created the German people, has made us strong enough to do this. The Spartan virtues, obedience, modesty, and loyalty, have made us great and only they will keep us great.'[24] More followed about modesty and self-sacrifice. As night fell, fires were lit by the SA on plots of grass outside the embankment, and red and yellow floodlights lit up the smoke. From 1936 onwards, this was to be the occasion to which Albert Speer added military search-lights that turned skyward as the Führer arrived to create a field of giant columns, the so-called 'Cathedral of Ice'.[25] To conclude proceedings 60,000 officers formed a procession with flaming torches through the city, Hitler taking their salute in front of the floodlit main station.

Saturday, 8 September

The fourth day was devoted to the Hitler Youth, who gathered 50,000 strong in the municipal stadium close to the Zeppelin Wiese. This smaller venue saw yet more parades with flags and chanting, but Hitler added a note of intimacy at the end by making a short inspection on foot. Addressing his youth movement he told them to absorb everything that we should one day expect of Germany:

> We want to be one people, and you will become that people. We want no more castes and classes, and you should accept that idea… We want this people to be obedient, and you must practise this obedience. We want you to be peace-loving but at the same time courageous. We don't want these people to be forgiving but to be capable of being hard, and you must steel yourself for this in your youth. You must learn to endure hardships without ever breaking down, for what we create today will pass away, but Germany will live on through you and your hands must carry the flag that we have raised from nothing.[26]

At another meeting before an audience of 2,000 at the Apollo Theatre, Rudolf Hess spoke about the former German colonies, and the country's willingness to reassume their administration.[27]

Figure 5.11 Hitler addresses the Hitler Youth at the stadium, shot of the gathered crowd from *Triumph of the Will (Bundesarchiv film)*.

Figure 5.12 Hitler in the crowd, from *Triumph of the Will (Bundesarchiv film)*.

Figure 5.13 Sunday ceremony at the Luitpold Arena, Hitler arriving at the war memorial after walking the axis from his podium opposite (photograph by Georg Pahl, Bundesarchiv Koblenz no. 102-161966).

Sunday, 9 September

The Lord's day was for Christian Europe the day of rest, quiet and respect, when work ceased, shops were closed, and many of the population attended church. This traditional framing provided the Nazis with an opportunity to create a religious service of their own and a culminating event for the whole week, which *The Times*'s correspondent considered 'the most varied and picturesque spectacle witnessed during the present party rally'.[28] The day was dedicated to the SA and SS, the two paramilitary wings at the heart of the party,[29] whose 120,000 members assembled in the newly cleared and flattened Luitpold Arena. Its tribunes and podium had just been improved by Albert Speer in stone. *The Times* commented:

> The elaborate care shown in the symmetrical grouping of the various formations, their thousands of swastika banners, and the standards of the regional units, made the whole scene impressive even to those foreign visitors who had begun to grow a little weary of the six-day succession of uniformed parades and assemblies. From the platform where Herr Hitler was to speak a paved causeway some 40 yards wide divided two solid phalanxes of brownshirts leading to the War memorial hall at the far end of the stadium, a distance of fully a quarter of a mile.[30]

The Luitpold Arena had developed as a broad rectangular space next to the Luitpoldhalle and had previously served as a park. An exedra on the west side (Figure 5.14) gave a strong sense of focus to the Führer's rostrum, which terminated the 240 metre long central axis

Figure 5.14 Model of the Luitpold Arena, with the war memorial centre bottom and the Luitpoldhalle behind the semicircular viewing stand, top left (Stadtarchiv Nürnberg).

marked by three giant flags. With everyone in order assembled according to rank and region, Hitler mounted his rostrum to address his private armies and praise their loyalty. After a short opening speech came the key moment of the day, which Riefenstahl made the central scene in her film, and which was solemnly carried out every year (Figure 5.13). This was the Führer's submissive act of respect to the party dead and to the German war-dead more generally. Bareheaded, in simple SA uniform, and accompanied by the SA and SS leaders who walked to each side and slightly behind, he left his podium to march down the 240 metre main axis as the crowd stood in solemn silence and a funereal dirge was played by the band.[31] The so-called Führer-strasse was symmetrically paved in large square slabs, but it was most starkly defined by remaining naked and open as a parting in the sea of uniformed figures. It led from the centre of current power to the centre of ancestral power, from the Führer's podium marked by three great swastikas at one end, to the city's war memorial at the other. Attended by his supporting troops, the Führer symbolically crossed from the world of the living to the world of the dead, mounting the steps as he reached the giant squared platform of the memorial with its flaming pylons of eternal fire to either side, and standing in stiff salute as a show of respect along with the SA and SS leaders. This annual duty done, he respectfully backed off, turned, and embarked on the return march, again slowly and respectfully followed by the two underlings. When he regained his podium, it was time for his principal speech.

That year there was a special tension. Scarcely three months earlier Hitler had put down a supposed rebellion by the SA and had had its leader Ernst Röhm murdered. The foreign correspondents had been full of apprehension all week lest there should be some act of retaliation, but Hitler used the occasion to justify himself and to re-establish solidarity:[32]

A few months ago a black shadow gathered over our movement, and many of our opponents cherished the hope that the National Socialist party was on the point of being overthrown ... The SA had no more to do with this disgrace than any other branch of our organisation ... The party will continue to recognise the SA and the SS as the guarantors of the National-Socialist revolution.[33]

Some SA groups had been reorganized and the speech was followed by a blessing of their new standards, accompanied by the sound of gunfire. This was accomplished by the Führer personally touching the cloths of the new banners with that of the holy Blood Flag, thus symbolically passing on the spirit of the party dead to the movement's rising youth. The Sunday ceremony was not just about the party's own memory. It seamlessly fused the party's so-called 'martyrs' with the city's honoured dead from the First World War, not only extending the short-lived movement's past but further legitimizing it as part of a greater and more essential Germanness. Later, in completion of the day's ceremonial, 100,000 SA and SS officers marched through the city, Hitler taking their salute in the market place.

Monday, 10 September, sixth day and last

Following the takeover of power when the party effectively became the state, the army had to be included, and it was given the whole of the Monday for a series of military parades and manoeuvres including sham fights on the Zeppelin Wiese watched from the surrounding stands by a crowd of 300,000 enthusiastic spectators. *The Times* commented that it 'gave the spectator a useful gauge for estimating the degree of military proficiency displayed by the Nazi paramilitary forces'.[34] The day finished with an evening assembly of party officials in the Luitpoldhalle, in form repeating and balancing the opening one of the previous Wednesday morning. This included the same layout and entrance parade, but after a simple introductory address by Hess, Hitler dominated the podium with an impassioned and carefully structured closing speech. He began by remarking that what outsiders might see merely as 'an imposing spectacle of political power' meant infinitely more to the participants, as it had been 'a great reunion of the hearts and minds of old fighters and comrades in battle'. He recalled the heroic early days of the party when it had been 'difficult to be a National Socialist', but went on to claim that even when the party had consisted of just seven men it proclaimed two key aims: 'to be a far-seeing party with a world outlook, and to be the one and only power in Germany'. These it had achieved through struggle and sacrifice, the 'finest characteristics of the German Nation', and in recognition of this, the German people had joined them in increasing numbers. They were happy now that the turmoil of their lives had been calmed by a man 'conscious that the nation's finest blood flowed in his veins, who, having become leader of the state, is determined to use this power for the best and never to give it up'. Appealing to his audience of inner party faithful, Hitler stressed the need for a fighting élite for whom 'it is not enough to affirm "I believe"; they must vow "I will fight"'. At the heart of the speech came a definition of the party: 'For all time the leading elite of the German people ... unchanging in its teaching, steel-hard in its organisation, flexible in its tactics, and in appearance like a monastic order'. The future was engaged by promises that the Reich would last millennia and that 'If the older generation weakens, the young are our power, committed to us body and soul'. Having thus embraced his audience, Hitler dared to stress the need to keep the party pure, rejecting dross, a thinly veiled reference to the SA purge. Towards the end came praise for the army, the main actors of that day, 'the old proud warriors of our race strengthened by tradition' who would henceforth march side by side with party members. The Führer reached a climax declaring that 'the Idea and the Movement live as an expression of the people and are thus a symbol of the eternal. Long live the National Socialist Movement'. To great applause and cries of 'Sieg Heil' Rudolf Hess resumed the platform to announce between cheers: 'The party is Hitler: Hitler is Germany as Germany is Hitler: Hitler, Sieg Heil!'[35]

Relatively short, thin on real information, and lacking in specific statements of policy, this final speech was a crucial element in the party week. It displayed the height of Hitler's rhetorical skill, stressed the power and unity of the party, and made his complete dominance evident. It extended the Nazi movement's chronological scale by strengthening its imagined roots and charting its glorious future. It also extended the party's growing and intentionally exclusive claims on German culture and identity, as so effectively if also nonsensically asserted by Hess during the heat of the applause.

The rally structure and venues

Looking at the rally's whole chronological structure, it had a clear beginning if not two, a Sunday climax for the inner circle, and an end. Specific days were dedicated to different groups with the venues chosen accordingly: Luitpoldhain and Luitpoldhalle for more narrowly party matters, the Zeppelin Wiese for big parades. The stadium was reserved for the Hitler Youth, implying a connection with sport, a cult readopted by the Nazis from the modernists.[36] Smaller internal events used city institutions like the theatre and opera house, while the opening evening crucially used the town hall. But day after day whole performances were routinely tied back to the city by uniformed groups leaving the parade grounds to march through the streets with flags and bands, taking the Königstrasse and Königbrücke to arrive at the central market place (earlier renamed Adolf Hitler Platz) to gain a momentary recognition from the Führer. When larger numbers were involved they used the Station Square, marching through the broader streets of the southern suburbs. The presentation of this spectacle to the city's inhabitants at their windows doubtless invited the interaction of cheering and flag-waving, while the sounds of tramping feet and military music permeated private spaces. The marches also served to define territory with their chosen course through the streets, taking over the public realm, displacing the communal activities of coming and going, the markets, and every other kind of everyday social intercourse.

A larger-scale, more abstract chronological structure was implied through the use of sites and symbols and the frequent exploitation of historical associations. Dürer, Wagner, Beethoven, the Freie Reichstadt, Nuremberg's castle, the German war hero, and the German martyr were all grist to the Nazi mill. The party had to conceal its recent and doubtful origins, instead providing itself with a long and glorious German past and a glorious future, the repeated concerns of Hitler's speeches. Architecture played a significant role in this legitimation through its style, organization, and material. By the time of the 1934 rally, Speer had rebuilt Hitler's rostrum and the surrounding crescent of tribunes in stone with swags and terminal eagles. Claiming in his Sunday speech that the Reich would last a thousand years,

Figure 5.15 Ruin of Speer's tribune at Zeppelin Feld (author's photograph, 2010).

Hitler added: 'just like this stone', gesturing at the podium.[37] That the hard material, vehicle of archaeology and witness to past empires, was intended to propel the Third Reich into the future as well as giving it parity with the past, was further underlined by Speer's concern with how his buildings would appear as ruins, an idea he shared with the leader. They drew on specific examples from the past to establish cultural roots. In designing the tribunes for the Zeppelin Feld, for example, Speer sought inspiration from the Pergamon Altar, one of the prime exhibits of the Pergamon Museum in Berlin, where it exists as a full size reconstruction.[38] Other sources openly admitted were the Baths of Caracalla and the Circus Maximus in Rome, the Champs de Mars in Paris, the stadium of Athens, and the ruins at Delphi,[39] choices reflecting the power and civilization of antique empires as well as the aesthetic art-historical canon. Speer's acute awareness of the relative sizes of the old monuments is shown in the comparative figures he constantly cites, which either remained in his memory or were researched for his memoirs.

The rallies remain monumentalized today in the ruins of Speer's tribunes at the Zeppelin Feld, his best preserved work, and through photographs perhaps the most essential example of Führer architecture: stripped classicism in golden stone, with giant order columns complemented by huge swastika flags, the whole axial, numbingly repetitive and overscaled, presenting impressive perspectives (Figure 5.15). But in 1934 this proud statement did not yet exist, for the rally used the flat grassland of the Zeppelin Wiese on its alternate axis, the Führer's then more provisional wooden stand being placed to the east. It was marked by a huge German Eagle pinned to the flagpoles 'like a butterfly in a collection' as Speer put it in his memoirs (Figure 5.10).[40] He had been put in charge of the rally's architecture in July 1933, but had needed to improvise the setting from what then existed, mainly in temporary forms. The main outdoor gathering spaces all had a prior history, especially the Luitpoldhain, which became and remained the ceremonial centre.

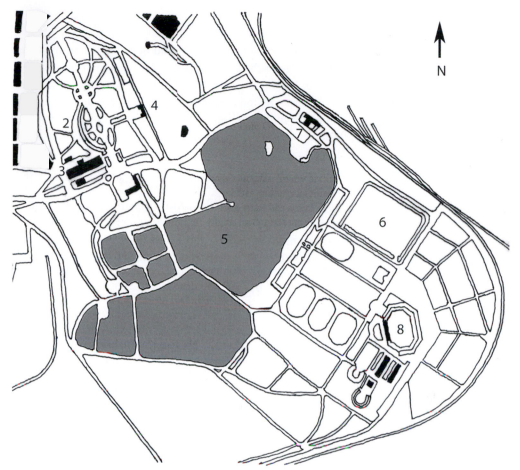

Figure 5.16 Map of 1928 of the recreation area before its use for Nazi rallies, showing the Luitpoldhain top left and the Zeppelin Wiese to right of the Dutzendteich lake. The city of Nuremberg lies above to the north. Key: 1. South end of town; 2. Luitpoldhain; 3. Machine Hall; 4. War memorial; 5. Grosser Dutzendteich; 6. Zeppelin Wiese; 7. Railway Station; 8. Sports stadium (redrawn by author after Fickenscher 1930).

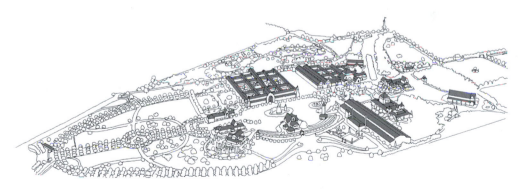

Figure 5.17 Luitpoldhain as laid out for the Bavarian Regional Exhibition in 1906. In the centre the space that was to become the Luitpoldarena, to its right the Machine Hall (redrawn by author after a drawing by W. Kinzinger published in Eichhorn et al. 1992).

Evolution of Luitpoldhain

Until the beginning of the twentieth century the Luitpoldhain had been part of an innocent and relatively virgin landscape on the edge of the city, a mix of forest and man-made lakes. Then in 1906, to mark the centenary of Nuremberg's incorporation into Bavaria, the city was granted the privilege of hosting the Bavarian regional exhibition, which comprised a generous park and a whole sequence of exhibition buildings (Figure 5.17). Designed in the prevalent Jugendstil manner, they housed displays of arts and crafts, while larger industrial objects were shown in the great machine hall, the Luitpoldhalle, named after the Bavarian Prince Regent who opened the exhibition. Between May and October it was visited by 2.5 million people, but after it closed, all buildings apart from the Luitpoldhalle were demolished, the grounds being preserved as a park.[41] The Luitpoldhain originated as the central square of the exhibition, defined by the crossing axes of the principal entry route and the main complex of exhibition halls. As a public open space it was certainly focal, but was much smaller than the version of 1934 because the eastern side was filled with exhibition halls and small courtyards. The exedra of rising terraces to the west was created for the exhibition and persisted as a landform to be re-exploited as the site of the Führer's podium. The exhibition and its park opened up the area as a recreational resort. Although it lay two kilometres from the centre, it was connected by two trams. Its landscape offered walks and picnics, its lakes fishing, boating and bathing. In 1912 a zoo was opened, and in the boom years of the late 1920s sports facilities were added, including a large modernist stadium and an open-air swimming bath.[42] It had already been used for large public meetings before the Nazis, for in 1922, 50,000 social democrat workers gathered there. On 2 September 1923 Hitler and his burgeoning party attended a National Day commemorating the victory of Sedan in the Franco-Prussian war of 1870, which perhaps revealed to them the potential of the place.[43]

A more permanent form of national commemoration began with the decision by the city and its liberal Mayor Hermann Luppe in 1921 to build a war memorial on the east side of the Luitpoldhain.[44] Designed by Fritz Mayer and built between 1928 and 1930, this consisted of a shallow hall fronted by nine tall thin arches in plain stonework. It was flanked by block-like

Figure 5.18 The War Memorial added on the east end of Luitpoldhain's axis in 1928–30, designed by Fritz Mayer and instigated by a social democrat mayor (author's photograph, 2010).

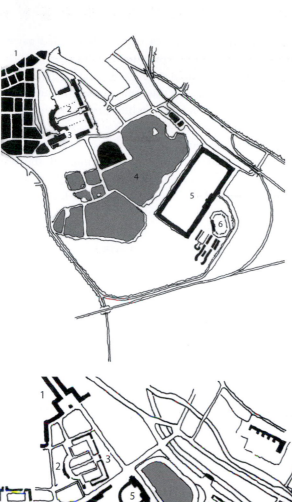

Figure 5.19 Map of rally ground in 1934. At the same scale, this and the map below show how the Luitpold Arena, at first centrepiece, became increasingly marginal, displaced by the axis of the Grosse Strasse. Key: 1. South edge of town; 2. Luitpoldhain now arena; 3. Luitpold halle; 4. Grosser Duzendteich; 5. Zeppelin Feld; 6. Sports Stadium (redrawn by author after a plan in Eichhorn et al. 1992).

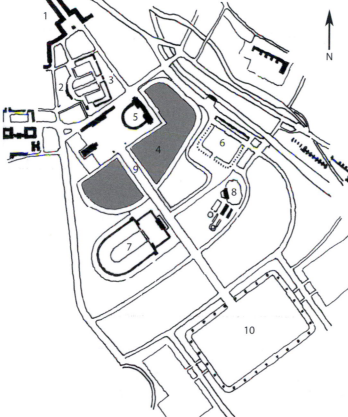

Figure 5.20 Map of rally ground in 1940. Key: 1. Speer's formalized connection with town; 2. Luitpold Arena; 3. War Memorial; 4. Grosser Duzendteich; 5. Congress Hall (built); 6. Zeppelin Feld with revised tribune; 7. Arena for Olympic Games; 8. Stadium; 9. Grosse Strasse; 10. Marching Field (redrawn by author after a plan in Eichhorn et al. 1992).

projections and fronted by a raised forecourt with five bays of large-scale gridded paving and six shoulder-high pylons on each side as bases for flaming torches (Figure 5.18). Its monumental symmetry was dignified, the reduced classical style was typical of the period, and the stress on the outdoor room for ceremonial occasions was appropriate.[45] By no means a proto-Nazi building, it innocently followed the tradition of the architecture of death, yet the Nazis immediately saw its potential, using it unfinished for the Parteitag of 1929. So began their reappropriation, but only in 1933–4 was the Luitpoldhain fully cleared of trees so that the defining 'Führerstrasse' could be laid across it, linking the Führer's rostrum with the War Memorial. This changed the monument's meaning, producing the polar axis between the living Führer and his putative ancestors to accommodate the pinnacle of ritual for the inner circle of SA and SS. It also neatly conflated the noble dead of the First World War with the Nazi 'martyrs', helping the party assert its identity with the nation, consolidating its totality, and implicitly bringing its paramilitary wings into alignment with the army.

Later development

If all the rally sites were somewhat provisional in 1934, there was every intention to consolidate and expand them for grander events in the future, and intensive work went on until 1943, in the later stages using slave labour from concentration camps.[46] From 1934 onwards Albert Speer was chief architect, though local architect Franz Ruff was also involved, charged with building the vast but unfinished Congress Hall. The Zeppelin Wiese was successfully reorganized as the Zeppelin Feld with its famous stone tribunes ready for the last Parteitag in 1938. The Luitpoldhain became the Luitpold Arena with improved and rebuilt podium and viewing stands, and the Luitpoldhalle gained a new and more appropriate monumental stone front by 1935, but all these spaces served more or less the same purposes and rituals in 1938 as they had in 1934, as did the sports stadium and the streets and squares of the city. Hitler and Speer must have had a larger ritual programme in mind when they developed the master-plan of 1940 (Figures 5.20 and 5.21), but it never took place and the buildings remained unfinished. Reminiscing in his Spandau Diaries, Speer saw no parades, but only an object of contemplation like an antique site:

> The party rally terrain was intended, in the course of generations, to grow into a district given over to spiritual ceremony. The rally area itself was only to be the first stage and the nucleus of the whole. Oak groves had already been planted or staked out. All sorts of buildings of a religious nature were to be erected within them: monuments to celebrate the concept of the movement and its victories; memorials to outstanding individuals.[47]

This gentle description belies a plan remarkable mainly for its intended increase in scale, 'gigantomania' as some have called it,[48] and for Speer's clumsy attempt to reorder the locality in a more rational and classical manner. In 1934 the Luitpoldhain set the axial layout for the northern part of the site, while the Zeppelin Wiese, set beyond the ponds on the eastern side, took its cue from road and rail alignments, skewed around by about 30° (Figure 5.19). The ancient ponds in the middle of the site had ended up irregular, even more so the lanes on the causeways between them. Already the plan of 1934 shows the intended congress hall,

Figure 5.21 Model of the rally ground as replanned by Speer, with the Luitpold Arena in the foreground and Zeppelin Feld to the left across the lake. The whole area was intended to be dominated by the central 'grosse Strasse' (Stadtarchiv Nürnberg).

semicircular in form and placed in the middle next to the re-rationalized water's edge. By 1937 this was relocated after Speer had decided his main replanning moves (Figure 5.20 and 5.21). At the southern end of the site he intended a huge Marching Field for parades and exercises, more than four times the area of the Zeppelin Feld. Feeding into this, and leading back towards the town, was the enormous Grosse Strasse which crossed the lake. It was orientated towards the city centre, placing the ancestral silhouette of Nuremberg's castle axially on the skyline. This primary axis was more or less completed before the war brought work to a halt, and as it was sixty metres wide by two kilometres long, it sufficed later as a landing strip for American planes. Looking at the plan north to top (Figure 5.20), the intended Deutsche Stadion lies almost half way down the new Grosse Strasse on the left. This was where, following world domination, the Olympic Games were to take place for ever more.[49] Its position along the Grosse Strasse obeys the diagonal axis from the Zeppelin Feld opposite. At its north end, the Grosse Strasse was to arrive between giant columns headed by eagles at a square about the size of the Zeppelin Feld, with a great columned tribune as entrance opposite. The reorientated congress hall would stand to the right, and a huge cultural building for party events previously held in the Apollo Theatre to the left. Luitpold Arena was to remain beyond, subordinated by the change of axis. At the north end, Speer intended to impose his new planning grid on the edge of the city with a new formal square. The scale of the plan is confusing, especially considering the real sizes of the Luitpold Arena and Zeppelin Feld. For Hitler, it seems, the bigger the better, and quite without limit, lacking all sense of proportion.

Conclusion and contrasts

'Drums, trumpets, patriotic songs, uniforms, parading, goose-stepping, and saluting were such omnipresent features in the week's proceedings that to describe the Nuremberg atmosphere as militaristic is inevitable', remarked the *Times*'s correspondent, impressed also by the laying on of hundreds of special trains, the establishment of camps, and all the rest of the efficient background organization.[50] Certainly a military type of discipline was required to get everybody in the right place at the right time, with uniforms to integrate the individual into the unified mass and to distinguish between the various groups, and military choreography to control the mass-movement of bodies. But military order is also more essential to Fascism, part of the way that people are subordinated and the spectacle is used both to silence and to convince. When the threat was felt from Oswald Mosley's British Fascists in imitation of Hitler, they were thwarted by the simple expedient of banning the black-shirt uniforms, not the first time in English history that the danger of private armies had been curtailed.[51] Uniforms mean power and subordination. Susan Sontag wrote in 1974 that:

> Fascist aesthetics … flow from (and justify) a preoccupation with situations of control, submissive behavior, extravagant effort, and the endurance of pain; they endorse two seemingly opposite states, egomania and servitude. The relations of domination and enslavement take the form of a characteristic pageantry: the massing of groups of people; the turning of people into things; the multiplication or replication of things; and the grouping of people/things around an all-powerful, hypnotic leader-figure or force.[52]

Peter Reichel argues that while democratic systems depend on demonstrating the rationality and visibility of their processes, the totalitarian state has no option but to impose its power by making it as visible as possible and putting it permanently on display.[53] Siegfried Zelnhefer adds that 'Since individuals in the Nazi state were allowed almost no participation in political decisions, the movement's festival was needed as a substitute for the unfulfilled wishes of the year.'[54] The nature of that display had evolved. Starting with a small group of extremists, and using the public meeting as a vehicle for gathering support, the party had discovered the advantage of creating paramilitary groupings and drawing on military notions of honour and obedience, just as Hitler discovered the hypnotic effect of his rhetoric and the sense of control that his performances produced. The political theatre enacted at Nuremberg made party and movement seem omnipresent, rallied the faithful, and left the dissident to slink away. Rather than being just an expression or display of the political process, the rallies were essential in constituting it, in making it real, in maintaining its power. The Sunday service at the rally of 1934, for example, was exploited by Hitler as the key occasion to reunify the party after the 'night of the long knives', to consolidate the military status of the Arbeitsdienst, and to integrate the army. The rally could also override the official political process, for in 1935 the Reichstag was brought to Nuremberg to ratify the change of flag, and the notorious Nuremberg Laws which curtailed the rights of Jews were hurriedly improvised behind the scenes, driven by the need for a premature announcement to satisfy the party's anti-semitic extremists.[55]

What is the same and what different with this set of rituals as compared with the examples in previous chapters? The making of displays and the invention of traditions are undoubtedly present in all the examples, as are the presence of hierarchies and uniforms and a spatial order that sets hierarchical value on the central axis. The place of Hitler's rostrum at the end of the Luitpoldhalle opposite the door, for example, precisely repeats that of the Queen in the House of Lords, while his march during the Sunday service down the central axis of the Luitpold Arena parallels the progress of the Chinese Emperor into the Forbidden City, or that of the magistrate representing him to his seat of office.[56] Furthermore, the marches through city streets by uniformed party members are not dissimilar to the parades, also in various kinds of uniform, of the city companies during Lord Mayor's Day. As patterns of social/spatial activity, all these seem to be cross-cultural and universal in their raw or basic form, though of course loaded in the different cases with very different meanings. Perhaps rather than inventing such patterns, Hitler merely understood and exploited them. In using them, he inevitably imposed on them new and negative connotations.

Different from the other examples are the scale in both time and space. The Nazi rallies were large gatherings by any historic standards, and they lasted a full week rather than the single day taken by the Opening of Parliament or by the Lord Mayor's Show. Furthermore, the contrast in scale between the lone dictator and the mass of his people, visually stressed in the proceedings then recreated in the film showings of the Parteitag presented across Germany, was utterly different from the complex arrangements situating the various layers of politicians and aristocracy in the Palace of Westminster. Black Rod's progress down the axis from Lords to Commons and back was a complex recital of the balance of power, a piece of communal theatre assembled and adjusted over centuries in order to preserve the memory of the political process with all its checks and balances. The axial poles of Queen and Speaker defined the field. In contrast, Hitler's Sunday march to the war memorial was a newly minted event cleverly reappropriating the space and its memorial associations for his own purposes, intentionally blurring the distinction between party and nation. The axial poles this time are the vocal leader and the silent dead. If we have to admit that all nations and political groups invent traditions, this is perhaps only saying that politics and its expression are never static but tend to evolve. In the case of the Nazis, however, there was little time for evolution and hardly any real inheritance or legitimacy. This made the need to construct an identity more urgent, the crudeness of the borrowing more evident, the sense of authenticity more restricted.[57]

The Nuremberg rallies took place in the twentieth century with modern technology, and without trains and lorries the participants could never have gathered, just as without loudspeakers Hitler's speeches could never have been heard. They were also broadcast by radio, a medium then in its heyday, and the party proceedings could be enjoyed in cinemas across the land thanks to Riefenstahl's film. Far more people saw the film than were present in person, and it also suspended the ritual in time, extending its efficacy and memory. As one-way communications, both radio and cinema restricted the recipient to a passive role, which suited the methods of the dictatorship and eased its progress. All this is in stark contrast to the British opening of parliament, which though nowadays partly televised, was originally carried through largely for the edification of its participants, both as a reminder of tradition and as an initiation process for new actors. The Lord Mayor's Show and trials at the Chinese Yamen were likewise rituals held for the attention of participants rather than for spectators elsewhere. Given this shift away from actual location, some have considered *Triumph of the Will* more important than the reality of the 1934 rally, or have seen it as the driver of those events. Great expense and effort undoubtedly went into its making and the choreography was probably readjusted for cinematic purposes, but it would be post-modern to deny the events depicted in favour of the depiction. The reality of the ritual was also needed. Inevitably though, the film now dominates memory, by use of bird's-eye cameras prioritizing aspects of spatial order invisible to the participants at the time, and by suppressing others in the edit.[58]

There was in the rally of 1934 surprisingly little specially contrived architecture, and as we have seen, the most powerful outdoor room, the focal space of the Luitpold Arena, resulted from a series of historical accidents. The stone tribunes of Zeppelin Feld, added by 1938, improved the setting with an architecture suited to the party's grand aspirations. It could work in photographs and it could preserve the memory of the rallies between the times when they were held, but as so often in the history of architecture, the building came late, lingering behind the defining event.[59] The spatial organization of 1934 lay largely in the choreography, which must have been worked out in great detail and have been carefully rehearsed. For just about any kind of parade, spatial layouts must be prescribed in order to set bodies in ordered rows, inevitably indicating ranks, affiliations, and hierarchies, and these arrangements have to mesh with and to define the spatial order of the parade ground.[60] When the bodies start to move, the static spatial order becomes a dynamic one, the parade then seen by spectators as having a beginning, middle, and end passing by. The example of the Lord Mayor's Show indicated the priority of this kind of organization occurring in multi-purpose streets, then giving way to static layouts within ceremonial halls.

Summary to Part One

Comparing the four cases so far presented, the two British ones introduced the concerns of the book and its interpretive method. Each case study revealed a gradual evolution of ritual and setting, involving frequent readjustments. The building of the new Palace of Westminster gave powerful reinforcement and redefinition of the parliamentary process, but without preventing its continuing evolution. On the contrary, the building provided a comforting frame of tradition and constancy while the political reality traversed fundamental changes. The Lord Mayor's Banquet saw an even greater shift as real political power moved away from the proud guilds – no longer makers of anything – and into the financial institutions that dominate the economy. The Lord Mayor was reduced to little more than a figurehead, while the intervention of the Prime Minister, once intrusive, was welcomed as the new focus. His presence guarantees the event's continuing importance, expressing the delicate balance of power between the Government and City as financial hub. The Guildhall building has been added to and readjusted, but without the generosity of reinterpretation enjoyed by Parliament in the mid-nineteenth century. Its architectural additions from the 1970s now seem inept and outdated, and it conspicuously lacks the expenditure lavished not just on more recent monuments like Lloyds and Swiss Re, but even on more ordinary corporate headquarters. The discussion of the Lord Mayor's Show from earlier centuries moved the focus from buildings to streets, raising two crucial issues: first the traditional importance of the street as territory to be claimed and defined as a theatre for displays and processions; second the correspondence and exchange between static spatial settings and the choreography of parades.

The Chinese case, also from the pre-industrial age, moved to a separately founded culture but revealed similarities of principle, including a strong sense of centre and periphery, hierarchical use of the axis, and differentiation between longitudinal and lateral directions. Orientation, based on a sophisticated local cosmology, was taken more seriously. Space was more layered with a more acute hierarchy of public and private in a more centralized and rule-bound society. Limits on behaviour seem to have been stricter than in Europe, with a sense of correctness applied regardless of audience, the Gods knowing all. The spatial structure of the Yamen also seems more tightly defined than almost any European complex, everything positioned according to relative status on the north–south or east–west axis. Chinese streets and town gates were not dissimilar to European examples, and the idea of a citadel (or Yamen) within a city as a nesting series seems to be universal, but the relationship of indoor to outdoor space differed because of the dominant role of the courtyard, separation of boundary walls and the architecture of roofs. Centralized control by the Office of Rites and a sophisticated carpentry tradition meant not only that building types were long established and highly standardized, but that colour, inscriptions, and decoration followed established codes which were widely understood: a veritable 'architecture parlante'. That they remained unreadable to Europeans, and were long denied aesthetic value, pinpoints the specificity of such local meanings, as opposed to the universal principles of hierarchy and axiality discussed earlier. Incidentally, the presentation of the Chinese case as static rather than evolving was merely a limitation of the material, for Chinese rituals and their supporting ideologies were reinterpreted from dynasty to dynasty if not from decade to decade, but this added complexity was beyond the scope of the enquiry.

The final case of the Nazi rallies reintroduced modernity and the effects of mass transport and mass communication, paradoxically allied to parades that took possession of ancient streets and also to an architecture of great scale, classical reference, and apparent monumental permanence. Here the 'invention of tradition' reached a new extreme as Hitler laid claim to everything that suited his purpose, reworking cultural symbols and cultivating the use of the new mass media to recreate reality for the *Volk*. His instinctive understanding of the power of choreography and spectacle, of hierarchies in space and time, paid off, but the talents of Speer and Riefenstahl were needed for the realization. The creation of the Führer's axis as ritual focus drew on universal spatial principles seen in earlier examples if at increased scale, linking an image of universal power with ideas of the eternal. It may have worked better in film than in reality, ushering in a new age of mediated experience.

In the next section we shall examine how people lacking constructed architecture contrived their rituals in relation to place, and organized themselves around the significant movement of their bodies. Perhaps architecture was born of ritual.

Notes

1. Shirer 1941, pp. 26–7, eyewitness account of the 1934 party rally by the US foreign correspondent, later historian.

2. Called the party's high mass by Goebbels in his diaries, quoted in Kershaw 1998, p. 566.

3. Eyewitness Shirer noted of the opening party meeting that 'it was more than a gorgeous show, it had something of the mysticism and religious fervour of an Easter or Christmas Mass in a great Gothic cathedral'. And later: 'every word dropped by Hitler seemed like an inspired Word from on high', Shirer 1941, pp. 24–5. Reichel (2006) deals with this at some length, see pp. 167, 172.

4. Kershaw 1998, p.179

5. Siegfried Zelnhefer claims that the attitude of the police was the decisive factor: see Eichhorn et al., 1992, p. 35.

6   On Nuremberg's history as the party's chosen home see Zelnhefer, 'Bauen als Vorgriff auf den Sieg' in Eichhorn et al., 1992, pp. 31–48, and also Reichel 2006, p. 146.

7   Hitler also gave a special role to the 'Rienzi' overture: on music for the rallies see Speer 1976, p. 88.

8   Hitler gave the city an ultimatum to clear Luitpoldhain of its trees and garden: do so or lose all the advantages that would accrue to the city, see Eichhorn et al., 1992, p. 36.

9   Riefenstahl's film of 1933 was liked by Goebbels but considered inadequate by her, see Reichel 2006, pp. 168–9. See also Speer 1971, pp. 104–5.

10   For the detailed history of the rallies see Zehnhefer in Eichhorn et al., 1992, pp. 31–48 and Reichel 2006, pp. 139–72.

11   Much is made of this arrival by plane in *Triumph of the Will*, and the use of the air was of both practical and symbolic importance for the Nazis, but usually he came by train.

12   Strangers were turned back 100 yards from the entrance, and there was a large squad in a side street. These details and many others in the following descriptions are from daily reports in the London *Times*, 5 to 13 September 1934. These complement descriptions by Shirer as cited above, in Reichel 2006, and in Eichhorn et al., 1992, which though in many aspects more detailed, sometimes fail to distinguish clearly between the rally of 1934 and those of other years. Riefenstahl's film is the main visual source but must be treated with caution, not only because it is highly edited, but because some scenes were reconstructed, as mentioned by Speer (1971, pp. 105–6).

13   *The Times*, 5 September 1934, p. 12.

14   Reported by *The Times*, 5 September 1934, p. 12. Johann Philipp Palm was arrested in 1806 for distributing an anonymous pamphlet about the plight of Germany. Refusing to divulge the author's name, he was arrested by Napoleon's agents in Hitler's home town and sentenced to death. Every year such a symbolic presentation to the Führer was made. In 1933 it was Dürer's copperplate 'Rider, death and devil', in 1936 a copy of the Kaiser's imperial sword, the original in possession of the city. In 1938 after the annexation of Austria Hitler returned the compliment by retrieving the imperial treasure from the Wiener Hofburg after 123 years. Reichel 2006, p. 154.

15   Albert Speer reported that in 1933 the opera house was 'empty' and after failing, even after instructions from Hitler, to get an adequate attendance from the party faithful who preferred their beer, tickets were sold off to the local bourgeoisie, Speer 1971, p. 103.

16   Shirer 1941, pp. 23–8.

17   Shirer (1941) says 30,000, perhaps relying on Nazi propaganda of the time, as does *The Times*. Eichhorn et al. (1992) state 15,000. *The Times* (6 September, pp. 13–14) identifies them as 'mostly uniformed party functionaries and SS, army troops and navy, representatives from 14,000 party branches'.

18   Composed by Georg Furst in commemoration of the first German victory against the French in 1914. It became Hitler's habitual entry theme.

19   It had served as the party standard during the failed bid for power in Munich in November 1923, where a gun battle in the streets had left fourteen of the nascent party and four policemen dead, and it was supposedly soaked with the party members' blood, see Kershaw 1998, pp. 200–12.

20   Count Egmont was executed by the Spaniards in 1568, but paved the way for the liberation of the Netherlands. Beethoven, composing in 1810 to accompany a play by Goethe, intended to celebrate his heroism. Reichel, writing about this opening ceremony in the Nuremberg party rallies more generally, also refers to the use of pieces by Wagner and the playing on the organ of the 'Niederländische Dankgebet', the Chorale of Leuthen associated with Frederick the Great's victory over the Austrians in 1757, Reichel 2006, p. 157.

21   Paul von Hindenburg (1847–1934) who had been a war hero and then from 1925 president. He

played a decisive role in Hitler's rise to power, although he was not a party sympathizer. For a clear political summary of the Nazi takeover see Paxton 2004, pp. 91–6.

22 A perhaps elevated figure reported in *The Times*, 7 September 1934, p. 12.

23 Reichel 2006, p. 158.

24 As reported in *The Times*, 8 September 1934, p. 12.

25 So-called by the British Ambassador Nevile Henderson, recorded in his memoirs, quoted (proudly) by Speer, and in Reichel 2006, p. 163.

26 Elements of the speech as presented in Riefenstahl's film *Triumph of the Will* and largely following its translated subtitles.

27 *The Times*, 10 September 1934, p. 12.

28 Ibid.

29 The SA (Sturmabteilung) and SS (Schutzstaffel) were the two paramilitary organizations invented by the Nazi party in 1921 and 1923 respectively. The SA, so-called storm-troopers and brown-shirts, were created not only to show solidarity but also to fight in the street battles of the early years. The black-uniformed SS was a kind of praetorian guard for the leader created in 1923. It gradually became the senior organization, closer to the heart of the party cult and ruthless in executing the party's dirty work.

30 *The Times* 10 September 1934, p. 12.

31 According to *The Times*, composed by Dr Hanfstaengl. It is unclear whether the music in Riefenstahl's film was the original or recorded later, but with the technology of the time it would have been necessary to construct the soundtrack and easier to record its elements separately.

32 Several times mentioned by *The Times*' correspondent, but even more dramatically revealed in Shirer's diary: 'There was considerable tension in the stadium … We wondered if just one of those fifty thousand brown-shirts wouldn't pull a revolver, but not one did', Shirer 1941, p. 27.

33 *The Times* 10 September 1934, p. 12.

34 *The Times* 11 September 1934, p. 11.

35 Based on the speech as recorded and presented in Riefenstahl's film *Triumph of the Will* and largely following its translated subtitles.

36 Reichel 2006 has a whole chapter on this, pp. 327–50, but see especially pp. 329–30.

37 Shown in Riefenstahl's film *Triumph of the Will*.

38 Speer 1971, pp. 96–7.

39 Ibid., pp. 96, 106, 113.

40 Ibid., p. 61.

41 Eichhorn et al., 1992, pp. 7–29.

42 Alfred Hensel was the landscape architect from 1922, Otto Schweizer as Oberbaurat planned the stadium and baths from 1925, which won an international prize as a modernist work, Zelnhefer in Eichhorn et al., 1992, pp. 33–4.

43 Reichel 2006, p. 146.

44 As the main political opponent of Julius Streicher and modernizer of Nuremberg, Luppe was in no way a Nazi sympathizer. A lawyer by training, he was a founder member of the DDP (German Democrats) and held the mayorship of Nuremberg from 1920 until deposed by the Nazis in 1933. He worked in coalition with the SPD to push through his social reforms of the 1920s, and stood for the national elections as an SPD member in 1933. After the Nazis took power he was arrested, forced to resign, and made to leave the city. He died in an air raid at the end of the war.

45 Comparable for example with the simple interior of Heinrich Tessenow's Neue Wache in Berlin.

46   Jaskot 2000, pp. 47–79.

47   Speer 1976, p. 322.

48   Reichel 2006 quotes H. Brenner 'Bau-fanatismus', p. 374, and gives the statistics of the proposed Berlin buildings on p. 372. The Berlin triumphal arch would have been 120 metres high, as opposed to 50 metres of the one in Paris.

49   Speer 1971, p. 129.

50   *The Times* 12 September 1934, p. 11.

51   Blackshirts and London meetings of the British Union of Fascists were banned by the 1936 Public Order Act. Following the Wars of the Roses Henry VII passed laws in 1487 and 1504 to regulate uniforms and liveries, and fined the Earl of Oxford heavily after a welcome that had involved too many retainers.

52   Sontag, 'Fascinating Fascism', in Sontag 1980.

53   'The acceptance of authoritarian use of power depends primarily on making that power visible, as opposed to democratic power systems whose legitimation rests in the rationality and visibility of their proceedings. The totalitarian power-state has no alternative but to fall back on its order of foundation and the power of its forms. It is therefore forced into making a permanent display of its power', Reichel 2006, p. 10, my translation.

54   'Rituale und Bekentnisse', in Eichhorn et al., 2002, p. 90, my translation.

55   Kershaw 1998, pp. 566–70. On page 539, discussing Hitler's divide and rule, fostering of confusion and disinterest in political structures, Kershaw notes: 'Hitler's approach to the State was exploitative and opportunistic… he gave no consideration to forms and structures, only to effect.'

56   It was made stronger in the Chinese case by the reservation of the central axis for the 'Son of Heaven' alone.

57   In his book on politics and ritual, David Kertzer claims that it is the lack of ability to answer back that makes ritual so effective as an instrument of power. He also comments that: 'Many of the most powerful symbols of legitimacy are of religious origin. It should come as no surprise, then, that new political forces eagerly rummage through the preexisting body of religious rituals and symbols to find those that will enrich their own ritual forms… even when a new political regime is the sworn enemy of the previously dominant religion, it may make more sense to try to appropriate the church-linked ritual than to destroy it', Kertzer 1988, p. 45.

58   The events are too long to make a real time record practicable, even from the static viewpoint of the spectator, and it is hard to resist the temptation of merging views from several camera positions. Film lends itself to the creation of virtual space by editing together these multiple viewpoints, while actual spatial relations are limited to those visible within the single take. In addition, film imposes a frame, restricts the viewpoint, removes binocular vision, and cuts out the other senses, most importantly the haptic.

59   Barry and Pugin's Palace of Westminster, reinterpreting the accumulated history, is typical. Other examples are the 'perfect' Greek theatre of Epidaurus, built long after the peak of the Greek drama, or the enclosed and specialized English theatre which long post-dated Shakespeare's Globe.

60   Considered in militaristic terms for persons like soldiers with relatively simple body skills. Dance, theatre, and acrobatics do not usually involve so many people and the movements can be much more complex, but they still need to be worked out in advance.

PART 2
PEOPLE AND THEIR TERRITORIES

Figure 6.1 Arrernte elders in front of a bough shelter, Alice Springs, Central Australia, c. 1896 (Spencer and Gillen Archive XP14285; photograph by F. J. Gillen, titled 'Group of old men at Wurley').

CHAPTER 6
HUNTER-GATHERER ARCHITECTURE:
THE AUSTRALIAN ABORIGINAL PEOPLE

As an example of the practical and spiritual life of the hunter-gatherer, the rich anthropological literature on the Australian Aboriginal People provides a suitable case to engage the question of whether and in what sense such technologically limited peoples can be said to have architecture. The impossibility of establishing institutions in permanent buildings raises two crucial questions about how what we regard as architecture's normal role can be fulfilled: what is the minimum degree of spatial definition required for public events, and how is the communal memory to be recorded?

Before the 'discovery' of Australia by Europeans the Aboriginal People occupied the whole country, including the inhospitable central desert regions, but at an extremely low density. Baldwin Spencer and F. J. Gillen, writing in 1899, gave the example of a group of forty people occupying an area of 100 square miles.[1] Their ancestors have probably been there for more than 40,000 years, the result of the human expansion out of Africa around 100,000 years ago that populated the whole world.[2] At that time the ocean gap was smaller, but they would nonetheless have arrived from the north by sea. Continental drift and rising sea levels increased their isolation, ensuring a development relatively separated from other groups of humanity, though there were sporadic contacts with Indonesia and Melanesia.

A hunter-gatherer existence was universal among humankind at the time of their arrival, and seems to have persisted across the world until only around 10,000 years ago when agriculture developed. The old prejudice that hunting and gathering was inefficient, taking so much time that there was little left to do anything else has been undermined both by theory and experience, for Marshall Sahlins demonstrated that primitive agriculture was comparatively far more labour intensive,[3] and anthropologists working with hunter-gatherers have reported a fairly relaxed way of life.[4] But this can only work under two limitations: a low population density in relation to sources of food and a mobile existence in order to exploit a relatively large area. The latter means travelling light, especially in the absence of domesticated load-carriers such as horses or camels, which were absent from Australia until introduced by Europeans.

It is enough to have to carry knives, spears and boomerangs, pouches of small objects, food or raw materials and minimal clothing declaring status and identity, without also trying to drag along the materials for a house. The Aboriginal People therefore recreated shelters at each location from materials on the spot as the group moved on in pursuit of game or to exploit fruit as it came into season. These have not attracted much attention as architecture, but Richard Gould, who lived with the Yiwara in the 1960s, has left a reasonably full description of making one, a process that takes about two hours.[5] Semicircular in plan and 5 to 6 feet in diameter (1.6–1.8 m), the family shelter consists of a series of branches whose stems are stuck into the ground and arched together, then given a grass covering. The ground within is dug out by about 3 or 4 inches (75–100mm) and the hemispherical back set against the prevailing

Figure 6.2 Arrernte family with possessions in front of a bough shelter, Alice Springs, Central Australia, 1896 (Spencer and Gillen Archive XP9552; photograph by Baldwin Spencer c. 1896, titled 'Arrente family with possessions in front of a bough shelter, Alice Springs').

wind, while a small fire is lit at the focus in front and carefully controlled all night as source of heat and light. This basic and economical arrangement allowed near naked people to rest in comfort while the temperature descended to around freezing.[6] The same economy of design applied to personal possessions, leading to some ingenious items of equipment serving several purposes, such as the 'pitchis' of women, wooden vessels that served as spades or as bowls in which to gather and transport edible matter. Similarly, the men's spear-thrower was primarily devised to give more impetus in hurling a spear at game animals, but also had a built-in flint for use as a knife, and by generating friction on a shield it could even become a fire-lighter. Furthermore, the linear pattern incised on at least some examples represented a kind of plan of the landscape.[7]

In Western society it is assumed that land is owned by a householder, a farmer or the nation (the roads, for example), and signs of ownership or cultivation are visible everywhere, with routes paved or at least cleared, and the marking of boundaries with hedges or fences or curbs. Even in 'the country', which is supposed to be the product of nature, we rely on paths and signs. Conversely, having 'no fixed address' makes you something of a non-person, creating difficulties about your right to vote, to have schooling, or to receive other social services, so travellers and gypsies have suffered prejudice and have found it increasingly difficult to maintain an itinerant existence. No wonder then, that Europeans arriving in Australia considered it an 'empty' country open to claims. Captain Cook had been given the duty of setting up 'proper marks and inscriptions'[8] beforehand, and such assumption of ownership for colonizers persisted legally until as late as 1976.[9] In European eyes possession of land meant occupation and use, all the signs of modification by cultivation and setting up artificial boundaries, and owners were expected to attempt defence of their territory. Because the Aboriginal People occupied it so thinly, left so little trace and seldom turned up to defend it, their occupation was considered insignificant. Even sympathetic Europeans saw only rights to fruits in season or 'religious sites' to be respected as a kind of equivalent to our churches and cemeteries, not rights to the landscape as a whole.

Yet the landscape as a whole was possessed by the Aboriginal People with a sensitivity all the more admirable for their lightness of touch. Even in seemingly barren parts of the interior where European explorers starved to death, they could sustain a satisfactory existence, knowing exactly how to make the most of local plants and animals for food, sucking water from roots when no waterhole was nearby, knowing which plants to use for making tools or equipment, and able to navigate safely across deserts. Their ability to track animals was so far in advance of Europeans' that they were even sometimes attributed with a 'sixth sense'.[10] It was normal for them to be able to recognize any member of the tribe merely from a set of footprints, while mothers would tease their children by mimicking with fingers the tracks of animals.[11] Such perceptual and practical skills were absorbed from an early age, but they were reinforced by a great body of shared knowledge gathered together in the tribal mythology: the story of the dreamtime.[12] Expressed in an immense series of tales, songs, dances, plays and other ritual events, this linked people, time and landscape, allowing them to make sense of the world and then to act upon it. As an explanation of tribal history, it was also the key to relations with other groups who in great measure shared it, and to a larger network of

Figure 6.3 Extract from map of dreaming tracks in Central Australia around Alice Springs. Emily Gap is Unthurqua written vertically upwards in the middle (from Spencer and Gillen 1899).

territories stretching right across the continent. This social network allowed conflicts to be settled and contacts to be made for purposes of marriage and trade.[13]

The dreamtime

In a mythical time before memorable history, people were supposed to have evolved from a number of ancestors, mostly animals or plants, that had made journeys across the earth, committed various significant deeds, then returned to the ground at special places which therefore became landmarks. Each mythical ancestor was the subject of a cult to which some members of the tribe belonged, so a person would regard him or herself, for example, as a kangaroo man or an emu woman, having supposedly been conceived by the spirit of this ancestor. They would feel kinship with others and take on duties related to the perpetuation of that part of the myth. The mythical structure therefore linked classification of people with classification of plants, animals and heavenly bodies, tying these in turn to features in the landscape. Combining practical knowledge with spiritual, this 'cosmology' gave a place and origin to everything. Enrico Guidoni has gone so far as to call it scientific, on the basis that: 'it proceeds by way of social necessities to an examination of analogies within the natural world and goes on to appropriate them for itself, instituting a relationship of cause and effect, which, precisely because it cannot be verified, is said to have taken place in the mythical dreamtime'.[14]

Figure 6.4 Emily Gap, MacDonnell Ranges, Central Australia, from the south side, a sacred place dedicated to the witchetty grub (Spencer and Gillen Archive XP9932; photograph by Baldwin Spencer, titled 'Emily Gap from S. side MacDonnell Ranges').

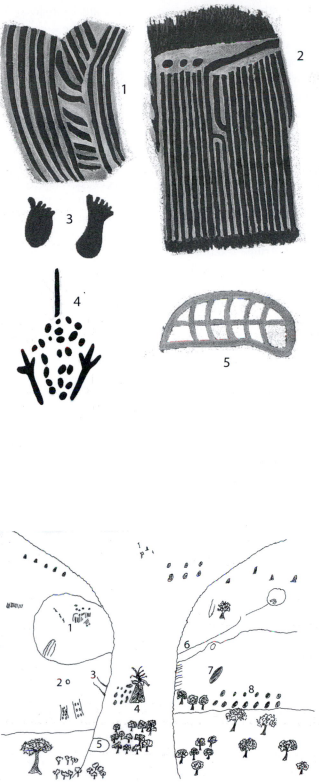

Figure 6.5 Sacred paintings adapted from versions in Spencer and Gillen's book (1899), the first two representing the Witchetty Grub Totem and identifiable in the photograph in Fig. 6.7 on p. 126. Key: 1. Slanting lines represent shoulders of the ancestors; 2. Line slanting to right represents a woman looking upwards and the circles represent eggs; 3. Footprints of ancestral women; 4. Representation of an emu and its eggs (taken from another set of drawings); 5. A witchetty grub in the chrysalis stage. Drawings 1, 2, and 3 are red and white, drawing 4 is black, drawing 5 yellow.

Figure 6.6 Sketch map of Emily Gap identifying the various sites of memory and ritual, north to top, from F. J. Gillen's notebook. Key: 1. Ilkinya at spot where women painted themselves and watched men opposite in the Ilthura making Intitchiuma faint imprint of hands where women rested their hands on rock; 2. Hole in rock face represents man's navel chilapachila; 3. Deep cleft in rock made by a grub who came under the range from Jessie Gap and emerged here; 4. Central dead tree with oval stone female grub of alcheringa. Stones beneath represent men who sat down close by him; 5. Big stone indicates spot where the oknirabata Ilporewuna sat down; 6. Steep rock up and down which men run and alartunja casts uchaaquaa 2nd act Intitchiuma. Alknalinta; 7. Pitcher-shaped stone jammed in cleft. Pitcher of Intwailiuka deposited in this spot by him when Ulathirka mob coming; 8. Great black stones sprung up where Ulathirka mob were stopped by Intwailiuka who subsequently led them to the Ithura (redrawn by the author after F. J. Gillen's notebook in the Barr Smith Library, unnumbered doc. 18, accessed via Spencer and Gillen Archive website).

Unable to locate themselves permanently through residence, the Aboriginal People could locate their spirits instead at sacred sites, places of spiritual power given by the dreamtime ancestors whose invisible presence remained there. This belief was reinforced by the Aboriginal idea of human conception according to which a foetus receives its spirit not from its human father but from spiritual impregnation by a dreamtime ancestor as the pregnant mother passes by its site. To live the mobile life required a particular direction and seasonal rhythm, moving from waterhole to waterhole and taking advantage of fruits and vegetables in season while also respecting the rights of neighbouring groups. Ideas of ownership more commonly associated with residence were therefore applied instead to places along a route, and paths taken across the landscape were mapped according to the structure of paths taken by the dreamtime heroes who formed it, leaving signs of their occupation. At large scale the very hills and valleys were interpreted as enlarged versions of animal tracks, the course of a river being produced by the snake, for example, while at a smaller scale even the placing of a single rock or tree could be charged with spiritual significance. The following example from Spencer and Gillen, who spent several months studying the Arunta tribe in 1896, gives an idea of how densely packed with significant features an area of landscape could become. The description concerns Emily Gap (Figures 6.4 to 6.7), a cult centre of the Witchetty Grub Men near Alice Springs (a witchetty grub is the large and edible caterpillar of an Australian moth):

> Emily Gap is probably, owing to its central position, the most important spot in the Witchetty country. It is a narrow gorge not more than a hundred yards from end to

Figure 6.7 Drawing of Utnerrengatye caterpillar on rocks at Emily Gap, Northern Territory, Australia, 1896 (Spencer and Gillen Archive XP9776; photograph by Spencer or Gillen, titled 'Drawing of Utnerrengatye caterpillar on rocks at Emily Gap 1896').

end and about thirty feet in width, hemmed in by precipitous rocks of red quartzite, and runs from north to south right across the long ridge, which, for some 200 miles, bounds the Horn or Mercenie valley on its southern side. Within a radius of two miles of this gap there are eight or ten holes, varying from three to five feet in depth, which are supposed to have been sunk by the dreamtime men. They are strictly tabu to women and children, who must not on any pretence go near them, and their exact locality is well known to all members of the local group. Each hole contains, carefully covered over, one large stone which represents the witchetty in its chrysalis stage, and a smaller more rounded stone which represents the egg stage. It was just within the northern entrance to the gorge, at a spot marked now by a large stone, close to which stands the trunk of an old and long since dead gum tree, that the great dreamtime leader of the witchetties sprang into existence. With him and with the people whose leader he was many of the natural features of the gorge are associated in tradition. The stone has since been associated not only with the spirit of the original hero, but also with men regarded as his successive reincarnations, the last of whom was the father of the present headman. A number of smaller stones close by represent men who sat there with him, for during his life he spent much time in this spot, which he chose because, owing to its position, he could easily guard the approach to the gap and keep guard on the storehouse of the sacred churinga [stones imbued with dreamtime power], which was always located in one of the many clefts which he made in the rocks for this purpose. In the western wall of the gap is the sacred cave where he performed the ceremony intended to increase the number of the witchetty grub on which he and his companions fed. Directly opposite, but low down on the eastern wall of the gap, is the sacred drawing on the rocks that it is believed sprang up spontaneously to mark the spot where the dreamtime women painted themselves, and stood peering up to watch the ancestral leader and his men perform the ceremony. This spot is called the Dreamtime Women's Camp and one of the drawings is said to represent a woman leaning on her elbow and gazing upwards… About 200 feet beneath the sacred cave is a steep broad band of quartzite which stands out and dips steeply into the bed of the creek. Called 'eyes painted around', this marks the spot where the dreamtime leader stood in the base of the creek and threw numbers of sacred stones or eggs up the face of the rock, as is still done today. Here also he used to sit while he pounded up large quantities of the grub. On the northern edge of the rock is a long deep ridge-shaped depression, which looks as if the stone had been cut with a great knife, and this marks the spot where the dreamtime leader's special pitchi [bowl] rested while he poured in the pulverised grubs. Above the ridge called 'eyes painted around' rises abruptly a high precipitous wall of rock, and in line with this an old pine tree stands marking the spot where certain churinga were stored by the dreamtime leader and are still stored by his successors. These represent the eggs that the dreamtime people carried in their bodies and at the present day every man belonging to the cult lodge has a few which he believes were carried by his dreamtime ancestors, and when he dies they are buried with him. Any round pebble found in the vicinity of the gap may be one of these churinga, but only the old men can tell whether it is genuine or not.[15]

Spencer and Gillen go on to describe the locations where representatives of the various dreamtime groups are said to have arrived and sat down. These consist of 'a group of stones', 'a great jumble of quartzite boulders, much weather-worn', 'a group of gum trees', 'a large boulder standing in the bed' and 'a group of gum trees and acacia scrub', all precisely located (Figure 6.6).[16] This example shows the extent to which the landscape could be 'read' through the mythical narrative, each lending the other self-evident validity. The landscape became a series of special places, each commemorating a particular set of ideas. A cave, a clear enclosure, becomes a site of primary ritual, but mostly it is a question of taking cognitive possession by attaching meanings to existing natural features. More actively, there are pits dug in which sacred objects are stored, and highly visible paintings made on cliff walls, both of which add artificial mnemonics of the myth.[17] The painted markings arguably serve the same kind of memorial purpose as architectural embellishments in settled societies, employing a symbolic vocabulary that was widely understood. Stencil-painted hands as a kind of signature adjoin conventionalized representations of plants and animals from the dreamtime stories. Often it is the tracks of animals that are represented rather than their bodily appearance, giving rise to something like a plan view (Figures 6.5 and 6.6). These tracks in themselves are also in a sense architectural, being the visible modifications of form in the ground that record creatures' activities. According to the myth, of course, in exaggerated form they actually constitute the landscape. The sacred stones or pieces of wood described by Spencer and Gillen as 'churinga' and sometimes inscribed with dreamtime drawings are mnemonic objects of critical importance to ritual occasions, with powers that make them dangerous to the uninitiated. The spirit of each person is supposed to be represented by one, and they are kept in secret storehouses at cult sites like the pits described in the quotation above. Removed only temporarily for ritual purposes and later respectfully replaced, these objects have a far more permanent home than their itinerant owners, and remain the physical evidence for the people's fundamental sense of location. There are several ritual occasions when the direction of the person's ancestral home has to be acknowledged, suggesting that their relation to its location is always known.[18] This sense of belonging to place must be greatly reinforced by the knowledge that one's ancestral spirit entered one's mother as she passed through this ancestor's area of the landscape which, charged with the spirit of the dreamtime, conferred one's identity as an emu, kangaroo, witchetty grub, or whatever.[19]

Renewal of cult sites

The relationship between the landscape and dreamtime events depended on reinforcement through several kinds of rituals that played a dominant role in Aboriginal life. The rituals concerned with the celebration and renewal of cult sites were undertaken by members of the cult lodge of the dreamtime hero who had made the site, under the guidance of the local cult lodge's headman. The overt purpose of these rites, as applied to the dreamtime figures that take the form of animals and plants, was to ensure the health and multiplication of the species,[20] but clearly they also served to reinforce the brotherhood of the cult lodge members, to initiate new members into its practices, to perpetuate familiarity with the site, and to maintain it in good condition. Although the timing of each was under the control of the headman, it had also to relate to the seasons, tending to anticipate the period of fertility and growth that follows the rainy season. The witchetty grub ceremony at Emily Gap is a convenient opening example, since it applies to the site already described.[21]

According to Spencer and Gillen, men of the cult, led by the witchetty headman, leave the village quietly and unobtrusively. They carry no weapons nor even the usual personal decorations, and are under obligation to fast. In silent single file they make their way to the site at Emily Gap, where they camp for the night. At daylight each picks two twigs from the gum trees at the mouth of the gap, one to be held in each hand throughout the ritual, while the headman carries a 'pitchi' or bowl that he has brought with him. In single file they follow the ancestral route to the cave in the western wall of the gap, where the first ritual takes place. The focus is a large block of quartzite surrounded by several smaller ones on the cave floor, which represent the mature grub and its eggs. Gathering around, the cult group chant witchetty grub songs that encourage the laying of eggs, while tapping the stones rhythmically with their sticks. The headman then picks up an egg stone and taps each man in turn on the stomach saying 'you have eaten much food', after which he strikes each on the stomach with his forehead. They then leave and descend to the creek, stopping under the cliff painted with 'decorated eyes', where the dreamtime hero is said to have prepared and eaten the grub, and more tapping of stones and invocations to lay eggs take place. At the base of the rock there is supposed to be a big stone buried representing the mature moth, and here the hero stood to throw up eggs, an action repeated by the headman with egg-like 'churinga', while other cult lodge members run to and fro on the ledge chanting. Next the group marches in single file to one of the secret store holes, where the headman digs up stones representing the animal and its eggs, which are carefully examined and cleaned. Here the headman again strikes each man in the stomach, declaring 'you have eaten much food', and again butts them with his forehead. This ceremony is repeated at each of the other store holes which are solemnly visited in turn, after which all return to the camp, but not before stopping to decorate themselves elaborately for a second set of ceremonies.

Such bodily decorations were important for all major rituals, carefully and elaborately made following conventions specific to the cult. Usually preparation took considerably more time than the performance. In this case, materials such as feathers and down and paints had been carefully assembled at an agreed place beforehand so that the cult group could appear immediately in role, ready to act out their parts. The ceremonies near the camp, consisting of many more singing and dancing performances about the witchetty grub, will be described in due course. They are a way of reincorporating the cult lodge members and sharing in the power of the witchetty spirit, but they also express and reinforce the structural relationships of the whole social group by giving them spatial form. Something must therefore be added here about Aboriginal kinship.

Quite apart from the fifty or so cult lodges associated with the dreamtime ancestors, Aboriginal society was also divided into moieties, each with subsections.[22] Moieties (from the French *moitié*, half) are intermarrying groups with reciprocal obligations: you are obliged to marry someone from the other half of the society, a practice we shall meet again in later chapters. But among the Aboriginal People this is only the start of the system, for each moiety is further divided into two or more subsections, each with special names, which again involve specific intermarrying rules. Complicating the issue yet further, the children of a marriage belong neither to the mother's nor to the father's subsection, but to a specific other subsection, and so the structure rotates from generation to generation.[23] Memberships of cult lodges tend also to be moiety-specific, applying a further layer to the marriage rules.[24] The system is hard to describe without recourse to diagrams, and the precise structure varies from tribe to tribe even though they intermarry. Furthermore, the terms for kinship relations describe groupings unfamiliar to a Western reader, the word for 'mother', for example, covering not just the actual mother but the whole group of women to whom the mother belongs.[25] Richard Gould suggested that this marriage system was an advantageous adaptation to the difficult environment, since it meant that marriage partners often had to be sought from afar, establishing networks of kin-sharing ties that would cooperate, building mutual dependency, and reducing risk of conflict.[26] Returning to the Arunta as described by Spencer and Gillen, the moieties each divide into two subsections, the Purula and Kumara who marry the Bulthara and Panunga, and it is significant for our study that precisely these groups appear as identifiable spatial entities on ritual occasions.

The witchetty grub cult belonged to the moiety of the Bulthara and Panunga.[27] Men of the opposing moiety, the Purula and the Kumara, were supposed to be quite unaware of the departure of the cult group, but were obliged to be present when they returned to take an essential if largely passive role in the second set of rites. While the ceremonies at the cult site described above were being enacted, an elder left behind, whom we shall call the camp leader, was organizing things at home.[28] His primary duty was the preparation of a ceremonial ground outside the main camp, where he made a special elongated shelter intended to represent the witchetty in its chrysalis stage. This building had to be large enough to accommodate all the returning cult lodge members and have a cleared dancing space before its entrance. He also had to organize the decoration of all the women, whose bodies were painted in alternate red and white lines for the active moiety and in white lines tinged with red for the passive one. Having arranged this and other details, he had to assemble the whole tribe to wait on the ceremonial ground to welcome the returning cult lodge. The men of the opposite moiety would sit on the ground in a line 40–50 yards behind the chrysalis shelter with the women of both moieties behind them, those of the active moiety standing and the others sitting. Presumably there was a secret runner to coordinate the timing.

The cult lodge members, painted with the appropriate dreaming patterns, arrive formally at the ceremonial ground in single file behind their leader, who stops every few paces with his hand shading his eyes, to 'look for the women'. As the cult lodge members appear, the camp leader sings a formal greeting, then they enter the chrysalis shelter, at which point all the men and women of the opposing moiety lie face down on the ground where they must remain in silence for many hours. Sitting within the chrysalis, the cult group sing witchetty songs, and at the appropriate moment they shuffle out in single file behind the cult leader, representing the emergence of the mature moth. Now they can break their fast, as indeed the insect does, being brought food and drink by the camp leader. They return to the chrysalis and continue the song sequence until dusk, when they emerge once again to resume their singing grouped around a fire placed on the side away from the 'audience'. Singing continues all night, and women of the cult moiety must stand on watch, both to assure that all the opposed moiety retain their prone position, and to watch the cult celebrants 'as the women did in the dreamtime'. As dawn nears the fire is extinguished, and all are released to return to the main camp except the cult group, who repair to a private men's camp to remove their body decorations. Feathers and other valued materials are awarded to men of the opposite moiety, and communally provided food is brought by the camp leader. The cult group maintain seclusion until the end of the day, when they obliterate their body paint with ochre rubbings and resume their normal body ornaments before returning to the main camp.[29]

To summarize, the ceremony has two more or less equal parts and two contrasting sites. In the first the cult group seek spiritual reunion with their spirit at the sacred site, while in the second they share the spirit power with the rest of the tribe at a specially prepared ceremonial site. This is centred on a temporary building which represents the chrysalis, with cleared ground in front of its entrance for the ceremonial emergence and a focal fire for night singing. With its relation of stage to audience, this arrangement is not unlike a theatre. Spencer and Gillen do not comment on its placing, orientation, or relationship with the main camp, but we can infer from the examples below that all are probably significant. When the tribe gathers, the active moiety stands while the passive one sits, then prostrates itself in utter subjection. Witchetty markings are reserved for the cult group, but all women are painted in moiety colours, so the structure of society is made doubly manifest. The asymmetry between active and passive roles between moieties applies only to this particular cult, for roles are reversed when a cult lodge belongs to the opposite moiety. The restriction of cult lodge membership to initiated men, on the other hand, is an asymmetry widely found among Aboriginal Peoples, though we should note that the presence of women in the second ceremony is absolutely essential.[30]

Initiation rituals

Although they involve much time and effort, the seasonal rituals connected with cult sites are simple in comparison with the Aboriginal rituals of initiation. These are concerned with the passage from boyhood to manhood and they culminate in the act of circumcision which removes a female element of the body to make the boy a man, while also implying his symbolic death and rebirth.[31] Since the tribe's spiritual knowledge is restricted to initiated men, these rituals are also the occasions on which this essential knowledge is passed down from one generation to the next, a process that involves the whole tribe, even if the role for women and children remains more limited. Among the descriptions by anthropologists who have witnessed such events, Richard Gould's of a Yiwara ritual in 1966 is particularly vivid:

On most evenings nightfall comes quietly in the desert, but not now. Big fires are lighted as the women and children assemble ... The men walk over from the dance ground and stand waiting. About 200 people are present. There is an air of excitement, with shouting and laughter as everyone waits for darkness to fall ... At long last the initiated men form into two tight bunches, [the two moieties], and start for the dance ground. The men in each group alternately run and walk towards the dance ground, grunting or shouting in unison as they go. When they arrive, each group runs back and forth across the large clearing where the ceremony will take place, then sits down in a circle and starts singing. The women and children follow the men and sit together at one end of the clearing. As the singing continues, several women get up and perform a simple dance, hopping stiffly with their heads and arms hanging limp. As soon as they finish, about a dozen men assemble at the opposite end of the clearing about 100 feet away. The women and men all pick up burning sticks from the fires and, with much shouting and histrionics, hurl the firebrands through the air at each other. This causes a brilliant effect, like fireworks. After a few minutes, the women send some young boys running across the clearing to the men, who toss them in the air and make them run back in a line. Finally the men sit down and return to their singing.

One man remains at each end of the clearing to build up an enormous bonfire, then these men too, return to their song circles. For a while the gathering becomes quiet, except for the singing which grows less excited and more carefully cadenced. There is real tension at this point, with the women and children straining to see past the bonfires. Suddenly the three naked novices emerge from between the two fires, running in a line in perfect step with one another and with the rhythm of the singers. From a choreographic point of view this is a brilliantly engineered dramatic climax which would delight the most jaded ballet-goer. As the boys appear, the women and children begin to wail loudly, and before the boys reach the end of the clearing where everyone is seated, another electrifying sound is heard above the cries. A carved sacred board of medium size, called a bullroarer, is rotated rapidly through the air and as it spins it emits a weird, heart-stopping noise which is said to be the voice of the totemic Kangaroo. Even after I had seen this ceremony several times, the whir of the bullroarer always brought shivers up my spine. The effect on the women and children is dramatic – in a screaming mob they all run away from the dance ground and away from the camp, back to their temporary camp in the bush.

Singing continues for a while as several men get up and perform a rapid backward dance with wildly vibrating knees. After they sit down, the two bonfires are built up, and again there is an air of expectancy. The bright glare of the fires acts as a curtain across the far end of the clearing. While the singing continues, a pair of unpainted naked men emerge, weaving back and forth across the clearing in a rapid, high-stepping dance. They skilfully control their movements in exact unison, and between them in an upright position is suspended a magnificent string cross constructed on an eight foot spear. This piece of sacred paraphernalia is called waniki, and it is, for the duration of the ceremony, the actual body of the dreamtime Kangaroo. The novices see this exceedingly sacred item for the first time as they sit upright between the song circles. The dancers pass swiftly in front of them, then zigzag their way back across the clearing and disappear behind the fires. Everything is done so expertly and happens so quickly that it hardly seems real. My subjective reaction to this episode was that at no other time I could recall did I feel more as if I had been in a dream while still awake, and I think this is exactly the dramatic intent of the performance. The action flowed silently, in perfect time with the rhythm of the singers, emerging out of the blackness between the fires at the end of the clearing and returning there, all in the space of perhaps thirty seconds. The absolute perfection of this presentation of the waniki was talked about among the men for weeks afterward.

Abruptly, the singing stops. A group of young men run forward and build a large bonfire, then settle themselves next to one another on their hands and knees to form a 'human table' in front of it. One of the novices is picked up and carried by several of his elder brothers to the table. They lay him across it on his back. Another brother grips the boy's penis to keep it steady, and the operator [the novice's maternal uncle and potential father-in-law] steps forward. Still another brother draws the foreskin forward as far as he can. The operator then takes a stone knife and, either by slicing directly through or by cutting around a few times, removes the foreskin … It is passed to the boy's older brothers, who take it away and place it by the fire. If it wiggles while drying it is a sign that the boy will be unruly and a possible troublemaker (in the sexual sense) as an adult. Then the dried foreskin is shared and eaten by the brothers … The boy is congratulated and led to the fire where he sits, letting the heat dry the wound.[32]

The initiation process can involve several boys at once and take altogether many months. According to Mervyn Meggitt, who lived with the Walbiri in the mid-1950s, it consisted traditionally of four stages: a two-day rite of separation, a two-month grand tour of surrounding country under the protection of an elder brother, the central ceremony, and finally some rites of reincorporation.[33] The central ceremony as he describes it goes on day and night for around a week, the bulk of it consisting of narrative enactments of the deeds of the dreamtime heroes from tribal mythology. These concentrate particularly on the figure to which the boy's cult lodge is dedicated: kangaroo, emu or other. They are presented in traditional order through long periods of rhythmic singing and dancing interspersed with brief actings out of moments from the dreamtime by suitably decorated figures.[34] The degree of involvement and endurance far surpasses attendance at a Wagner Ring Cycle, for everyone has a part to play and there is no periodic leaving of the theatre to resume ordinary life. As the essential transmission medium for an oral culture, the performance is no mere cultural superstructure but the very essence of life and being. Throughout the process, roles are allotted according to cult lodge and moiety, so the whole kinship structure is put on display. This clarifies the network of relations in which the boy finds himself and which he must perpetuate, including those with his prospective in-laws, the group within which he is obliged to find a wife.[35]

The central set of ceremonies takes place on a specially prepared ceremonial ground with a specific name.[36] The most detailed description we have is that of Meggitt, who has provided the most detailed plan available (Figure 6.8).[37] This marks not only the various points at which actions took place but also where fires were lit, important symbolically as well as providing illumination at night. Meggitt's plan concurs in essentials with descriptions by other

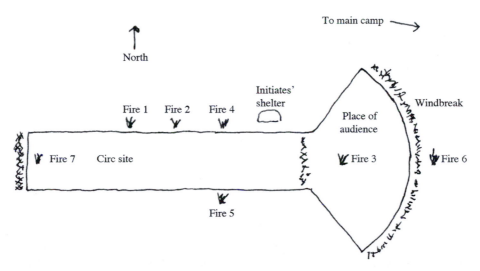

Figure 6.8 Plan of circumcision ground (redrawn by author after Meggitt 1962).

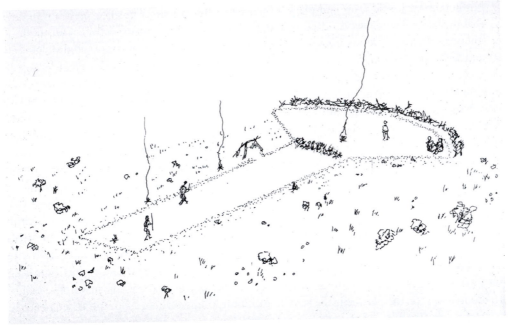

Figure 6.9 Author's isometric drawing to give a sense of scale and based on Meggitt's plan.

anthropologists who give less spatial detail but tell of similar events.[38] Physically, it consists of a funnel-shaped clearing made by scraping the desert floor with boomerangs to leave a slight mound along the edges, then adding windbreaks of tree branches at various crucial points. The design is supposed to have been passed down by dreamtime heroes, and the myths include stories about such grounds created as rain pans,[39] which would be models in being both flat and clear of scrub. It is clear, though, that quite apart from having a suitable topography, the site must have a carefully chosen location. It must remain within earshot of the main camp and also be to the west of it, for the created groundwork has to be strictly orientated east–west, and the larger east end is for the women and uninitiated who participate mainly as spectators. They must be able to come and go without witnessing the secret inner rites and preparations taking place to the west – the 'backstage' as it were. In contrast with this free access from the east, the novice in his dangerous state of transition is kept hidden for his secret lessons in a shelter to the south and west, which women and children must scrupulously avoid.

The ground is used in various ways in the course of the rituals, but the circumcision proper is the definitive event. This occurs on the linear part of the ground three-quarters towards the west end, with the assembled audience gathered at the east. The linear element of the ground is also in effect the stage for most of the dreamtime presentations, with actors emerging at the west end, dancing their way down towards the audience at the east, then working their way back up again. Possessed by dreamtime spirits, decorated to make their everyday selves unrecognizable, and carrying sacred emblems which must never otherwise be seen by the uninitiated, they remain mysterious visitors from another world, and must come and go without direct contact, but in contrast the groups of chanting men and dancing women who provide the essential continuity between these sudden events remain at the east end as the visible community of this world.

The total ritual is so long and complicated that even Meggitt's detailed description fails fully to reveal its spatial and chronological structure.[40] A few key instances, however, can draw attention to the ways in which the ground is used. Soon after it is first made some kangaroo rituals are performed largely for the benefit of the novice, involving only a small group of actors and his guardians. These take place suitably scaled-down on the linear part of the ground alone (Figure 6.8), with the initiate and his guardians to the east and the action to the west illuminated by a fire to the right (at Fire 1), in other words the event respects the central axis and westward orientation of the spectacle, but on a reduced scale.[41] Later in the series, when events have been heavily concentrated around the social east end, the boy is removed to the west to be decorated with a powerful design that is potentially dangerous: again the west is explicitly associated with the spiritual.[42] At dawn on the last day, all those sitting at the east end are told to turn west, whereupon they see men appearing in turn dancing with Jarandalba boards, running in diagonally from the north-west, then south-west, then west, then north, and so on in turn until twenty or thirty of them are circling the group.[43] These boards, which Meggitt calls 'the title deeds to the territory' have incised drawings depicting dreaming tracks, and in this way they are formally presented. The runners make a radial formation as if arriving from all directions, but the first two come symmetrically from either side of the western axis.

Despite all the foregoing events, it is the actual circumcision for which the ground is primarily prepared, and which gives it the starkest spatial definition. The chain of events starts at sunset, which strikes along the axis of the ground and is presumably the basis of its orientation, for the dying sun symbolizes the death of the novice as a boy, who by sunrise must be reborn as a man. As the sun sets a pair of symmetrical fires is lit, one either side of the axis (Fire 4, Fire 5), then an elder brother of the novice marks out the ground by running to one end, banging a shield on the ground, then running down the axis to the other and repeating the gesture. This is the signal for the widi dancers, each equipped with leafy poles about 9 ft long tied to the ankles and sticking up in the air. They appear alternately from the sides of the east end, arriving one by one at the centre to dance singly before moving to stand and face west. While gathered at the north-east and south-east corners they represent the opposed moieties, which during the preparations have reciprocal obligations, but they become united when they assemble on the axis. When all are present, they turn and dance towards the assembled audience in various groups, and the circumcisers join them. At this stage an elder brother of the novice lights a fire at the west end of the axis to reveal a Wanigi cross stuck axially in the ground.[44] Made of two Jarandalba boards lashed together, this is the most powerful item of symbolic equipment. The widi dancers now stand along the axis in single file and the cross is made to travel axially west–east through the channel above their heads defined by their pairs of upright sticks. It stops at the end facing the audience, where the initiate is raised to touch it with his chest, whereupon the spirit of the lodge enters him. Passing on eastwards down the remainder of the axis, the cross is set up to mark its east end, and must be placed straight or the circumcision would go askew. After more events, including nightjar figures and kangaroo men who dance backwards down the clearing, it is time for the circumcision proper. The group of men involved moves to the central axis near the west end, at point marked 'circ site' illuminated by fire (Fire 7), and several of them crouch to make a human table. The circumcision takes place much as in Gould's description. Then the successful initiation is announced by a brother nearby with a burning widi pole, who dashes it to the ground as a signal, and the boy's mother at the other end of the ground puts out her firestick which she has kept alight throughout the proceedings to symbolize his life. As a child he has died.[45]

Once the ceremony is over, the symbolic trappings are swiftly destroyed or disassembled, and just as the human circumcision table which showed the solidarity of the brothers and their cult lodge collapses and disperses, so the circumcision ground itself soon returns to desert scrub, though for the uninitiated it remains a dangerous and forbidden place,[46] and presumably for all involved the location will be remembered along with other special places in the landscape. The next ceremony will occur somewhere else, the ground being made anew, perhaps by another group but again by elder brothers of the novice under guidance of an older man who remembers how things should be done according to sacred instructions issued in the dreamtime.

Location and direction

The circumcision ground has a curious status. It has none of the long-term memorial significance of the cult sites described in previous chapters, yet it is the most complex piece of spatial organization produced by the Aboriginal People. It acts as a locating and coordinating device for the great number of ritual events associated with initiation, giving them somewhere to 'take place' and relating them to each other, while defining spatially the role of all participants. Without it the process could not occur, and even with it everybody has to understand its meaning and the implied rules of its use. Just as with the narrative of the myth, every repetition allows some young people to experience it for the first time. Others consolidate the lesson of last time around, and the mature pick up refinements to prepare for their role as guides in making it when they become elders. The ground is thus both a statement of spatial information and a means of sharing it. Like the myth, and indeed the language, it may be altered or reinterpreted each time as old ideas are forgotten and new ones introduced. But each time it is made, it re-forges a social agreement about the use and meaning of space.

The first thing it offers is a special location. Some lesser rituals happen within the normal camp, but the ceremonial ground is a space set aside. Second, it must be chosen in relation to the main camp and other places in the landscape, both the sacred sites and the places nearby used as preparatory spaces, like the shelter where the boy is coached to the south-west of it, and a women's camp where they bid him farewell to the east. Third, it is orientated and thus related to the cosmos. Not only the motions of the sun but the position of the stars are the only clock available,[47] and the east–west placing establishes a linear principle by which the main motions of the ceremony (from west to east) oppose the motion in the sky. Fourth, this orientation creates an axis that is immediately recognizable as the primary space-defining gesture, involving symmetry and centrality, defined unambiguously by the parallel banks of earth at the edge. The axis serves to differentiate between the direction of movement along it and the static left–right symmetry across it, as in nearly all earlier examples. Its length gives rise to a polarity of opposed ends: the west as the stage for spiritual events, a sacred space, and the east as a profane auditorium for the spectators. Again we are reminded of axial polarities such as the Queen's throne and the Speaker's chair, the Chinese screen wall and Magistrate's desk, Hitler's podium and the war memorial. The culminating event, the circumcision proper, takes place near the end of the axis, just as the altar is placed in a church. The symmetrical fires, the repeated placing of the sacred Wanigi at various points along the axis, and its dramatic progress down the passage formed by the widi dancers, all reinforce perception of the axis as the defining element. At the profane end where the whole of society gathers are a number of events of social consolidation which take circular or semicircular form, following the centre and periphery principle. At times the novice is brought back reassuringly to sit in the centre of society, while at other times he sits alone with his guardians exposed to dangerous spiritual forces further up the axis. The axis is reinforced by two preparatory rituals that must be accomplished before it is used: the progressive women's dancing down the clearing for several days beforehand, and the ceremonial definition of the brother banging his shield at each end in turn before the main ceremony.[48] The bilateral symmetry around the axis gives rise to a completely different kind of polarity in the other direction – between left and right as one stands at the centre. This is used at some points to define the two moieties, such as when the widi dancers run in alternately from left and right. At times there are also two singing circles in symmetrical competition with each other, equidistant from the axis.

The choreography of events on the ground follows the same kind of pattern as rituals made less formally elsewhere, such as in the main camp, in which central and linear principles evidently apply. People assemble in circles and half-circles, in single file, in opposed rows facing each other, in alternating diagonal or zigzag formation, and so on. These geometries of activity may be of ancient origin and presumably existed prior to the invention of the ceremonial ground, but the ground brings them all together in more coordinated form, causing their patterns to intersect and lending them a cosmic dimension through imposition of the east–west axis. The ground also marks out, by its very appearance and disappearance, the time period occupied by the whole chain of ceremonies.

The Engwura ceremony

Although the circumcision ceremony is by far the most important in Aboriginal life, it is only the first stage of initiation. As men penetrate further into the arcane realms of tribal secrets they are expected to undergo an even worse operation, subincision, which may be performed as an adjunct to a later circumcision ceremony. Progress in seniority among the Arunta studied by Spencer and Gillen culminates in the Engwura ceremony, a kind of ordeal by fire, which they describe as particularly important in bringing distant branches of the tribe together to share the enactments of the dreamtime. The one they witnessed lasted four months with at least one ceremony each day,[49] and readers interested in the ceremonial structure and detail of performances must seek their very full description.[50] Here we need concern ourselves only with the ceremonial ground, which repeats certain aspects of that discussed above but also differs from it in important respects. Spencer and Gillen provide a location map (Figure 6.10) which shows the placing of the ground in a flat spot of a river valley with hills to either side. The orientation is again effectively west–east, with sites for keeping the sacred churinga on the west side and camps to the east, divided into moiety groups. The dry riverbed is used ceremonially to accentuate the transition between sacred and profane, and the bed of a small tributary behind the ground is used as cover to allow the actors to approach unseen. As for the ground itself, it lacks the defining west–east channel between earth banks of the circumcision ground: instead there is a single bank of earth about 30 ft (10 metres) long, 2 ft (60 cm) wide

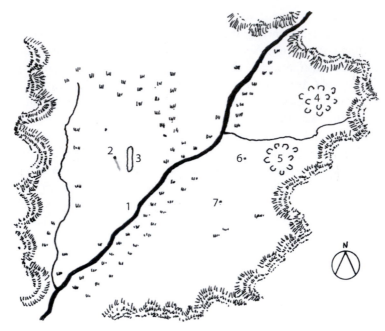

Figure 6.10 Map of the Engwura ceremony. Key: 1. Todd River bed running south-west with two small tributaries; 2. Kauaua pole and its shadow; 3. Parra: the bank of earth; 4. Camp of the Purula and Kumara; 5. Camp of the Panunga and Bulthara; 6. Spot where the Purula and Kumara women stood when throwing fire; 7. Spot where the Panunga and Bulthara women stood when throwing fire (redrawn by author after Spencer and Gillen 1899).

Figure 6.11 The Engwura ceremony, with participants standing in front of the parra with the kauaua erect (drawing by Claire Blundell Jones after photograph in Spencer and Gillen 1899).

Figure 6.12 The Engwura ceremony, participants lying down with their heads on the parra (drawing by Claire Blundell Jones after photograph in Spencer and Gillen 1899).

and 1 ft (30 cm) high called the parra.[51] This is placed north–south to define the eastern edge of the ground, and is given more visible substance and efficacy as a screen by sticking branches into it. For the most important part of the ritual series it combines with a 20 ft (6 m) high ceremonial pole, the kauaua, which is placed about 30 ft (10 m) axially to west of it to define the ritual centre.[52] In this series of rites much more of the ceremonial seems to take a circular rather than a linear form, revolving around either the kauaua or the parra. The latter acts as the primary marker of the site and as a barrier between the sacred ground and profanity beyond. Doubtless it also helps restrict the view of the uninitiated from across the river. But it has one direct and important ceremonial use, for the novices under instruction repeatedly lie down to the west side of it, their heads on it like a pillow, their bodies projecting into the sacred ground (Figure 6.12).[53] Its importance as a symbolic barrier is underlined again at the end of the chain of ceremonies when its centre is ceremonially broken through by the headman, thus opening the west–east axis between the sacred kauaua to west and the profane camps to east.[54] The novices and guardians follow the headman through this symbolic gateway in single file with linked hands and in total silence, before joining the women for rites of reincorporation across the river.

Conclusion

Most theories of architecture assume shelter as their starting point, yet the Aboriginal family house as described by Gould is a pretty simple affair. Houses taken together seem even less architectural, for plans of Aboriginal camps tend to look somewhat random. Even so, they are not devoid of structure. At ceremonial times at least groupings of shelters follow moiety lines, and there have to be peripheral places reserved respectfully for exclusively male and female use.[55] Furthermore, Gould reports that the distance between clusters of shelters directly expressed the friendly or hostile relationships between extended family groups.[56] This is scarcely surprising when one considers that the camp must frequently be made and remade, lending itself as an ideal vehicle for demonstrations of cosiness or enmity.

If the Aboriginal assemblage of brushwood can be interpreted as a minimal house, their cult sites can equally be read as minimal temples maintained by initiated 'priests' of the cult lodge, and the circumcision ground as a minimal theatre. For a people without doorways and with no threshing to hold, the gap broken through the parra at the end of the Engwura ritual could also be regarded as a first gateway. The importance attached to that low mound parallels that in the myth of Rome, according to which Romulus killed his brother Remus merely for jumping over and making fun of the furrow representing the city wall.[57] Marks in the ground are also tracks, traces of things that have happened, whether they mean that a prey animal has recently passed by, or that a hill was made by a dreamtime ancestor. Such marked places are even produced by the very activity of a ritual, as with the singing of the kangaroo songs and thumping of shields on the ground, which produces a ring of depressions as a short-term record of the event, a kind of sculptural representation.[58] In every case with the Aboriginal People, spatial definition is at a bare minimum, and their 'buildings' would barely be perceptible to an outsider, let alone be constraining or coercive by their presence, as fully developed buildings are. 'Buildings' such as the earth banks on the ritual ground operate primarily as signs to identify places and settings for action, giving not only the location and orientation but also important hints about the choreography, and allowing the social structure to display itself, defining who's who. But for such meanings to be attached and used appropriately, all must be read and understood within the particular cultural system.

Minimal though they are, the presence of these 'buildings' is vital for the Aboriginal People, for without marking out the territory in some way it would be impossible to coordinate their shared events. Space can thus be understood as the temporary mediator that carries the shared understanding of spatial values during the period when the purpose-made ritual ground meshes with the choreography of the performance. This, arguably, is the true beginning of architecture: which serves not the purpose of shelter but that of sharing knowledge and defining relationships. It may also be considered an aesthetic experience through the way it provides an appropriate location for each person within the cosmos as it is understood, giving him or her a role that rhymes with the order of things. All of this grows out of the active process of recognizing and memorizing the landscape by connecting practical everyday activities with the mythical events of the dreamtime.

Highly noticeable in the Aboriginal Peoples' ceremonial arrangements is a geometry and axiality that repeats, or perhaps rather anticipates, the kind of arrangements seen in this book's Part 1. Still far from a developed building technology or the making of cities, we see here an ordering based on the juxtaposition of bodies and their relationship with the cosmos, and this supports well Pierre Bourdieu's theory of the body as geometer. He argued that the three primary directions of space, long before becoming dimensions, or for that matter Cartesian coordinates, were projected out from the body, so that our experience of polarities is founded in bodily movements forward and back, left and right, up and down, which supply the very basis of our spatial understanding.

An analysis of the universe of mythically or ritually defined objects, starting with the circumstances, instruments and agents of ritual action, makes it clear that the countless oppositions observed in every area of existence can all be brought down to a small number of couples which appear as fundamental, since, being linked to one another only by weak analogies, they cannot be reduced to one another except in a forced and artificial way. And almost all prove to be based on movements or postures of the human body, such as going up and coming down (or going forwards and going backwards), going to the left and going to the right, going in and coming out (or filling and emptying), sitting and standing (etc.).[59]

Practice, he argued, should therefore not be considered as subordinate to an underlying theory, text or instruction, nor is it merely the exemplification of hidden structures, be they symbolic, linguistic or mythical: it is enacted, remembered and understood in its own right. This potentially puts architectural space back at the centre of experience, as the site at which understanding is generated, rather than being supplied later as a metaphorical superstructure. It also reinstalls the human being as agent. The person engages the environment by means of his or her *habitus*, the compilation of perceptions, ideas and habits through which sense is made of the world: the *habitus* engages with the space in which he or she finds themself.

Notes

1   The witchetty grub people of Alice Springs, see Spencer and Gillen 1899, p. 9.

2   On both genetic and linguistic evidence the estimate of their establishment in the continent is 40,000–60,000 years, see Luigi Luca Cavalli-Sforza, *Genes, People and Languages*, London: Penguin, 2001, pp. 92–6.

3   Sahlins 1972, *Stone-age Economics*.

4   For example Gould 1969 on the Yiwara Aboriginal tribe, see pp. 3–36.

5   Gould 1969, p. 19.

6   This detail added from Spencer and Gillen 1899, pp. 17–19.

7   Spear throwers 'serve as mnemonic devices for recalling the sacred tradition in its correct sequence by calling to mind the particular songs which evoke the mythological events occurring at each place' Gould 1969, p. 81, but he never saw them used practically as a map.

8   Hiatt 1996, p. 17.

9   Ending with the Aboriginal Land Rights Act (Northern Territories) of that year: Hiatt 1996, p. 31. His chapter 'Real estates and phantom hordes', pp. 13–35, is a fascinating history of the struggle to reconcile Aboriginal ideas about land ownership with those of the Europeans.

10   Gould 1969.

11   Gould (1969) describes this ability in great detail, and also in Gould (1980, p. 8), where a two year old walks for the first time and it is her footprints that are the focus of attention.

12   Dreamtime is the now generally accepted term, but anthropologists report that words like Alcheringa (Arunta – Spencer and Gillen) and illingwurra (Yirawa – Gould) are essentially untranslatable. Gould offers 'a word denoting an idea of time and human destiny', Gould 1969, p. 66.

13   Different tribes specialized in different types of implements and had access to different raw materials, so there was considerable exchange: see Gould 1969, p. 56.

14 Guidoni 1975, p. 22.

15 Spencer and Gillen 1899, pp. 424–8. This quotation has been shortened without marking small cuts, and Aboriginal words that make little sense taken out of context are omitted. The word 'Alcheringa' meaning the mythical era has been changed to the modern 'Dreamtime', the now generally accepted term, and 'totem' is changed to 'cult lodge' for consistency.

16 Ibid., pp. 428–9.

17 At some of these sacred sites there are or were ritual renewals of the paintings as part of the annual cult: see Gould 1969, pp. 121–7.

18 In the initiation ceremony, a boomerang is thrown in the direction of the initiate's mother's dreamtime camp: Spencer and Gillen 1899, p. 259. Similarly, malevolent magic with pointing sticks and spears is done in the direction of the victim, even if he is far away, and the magic may be accomplished by a shooting star; pp. 534 and 549.

19 Since the identity of the child depended on it, perhaps visits to an appropriate spot were arranged during pregnancy. If a pregnant woman passing by one of these charged places wanted to avoid impregnation by the spirit, she would pretend to be old: Spencer and Gillen p. 337.

20 Spencer and Gillen 1899, p. 169.

21 Ibid., pp. 170–9.

22 Durkheim and Mauss (1963, p. 35) counted fifty-four 'totems' in Spencer and Gillen.

23 Spencer and Gillen 1899, pp. 55–76.

24 Variable from one tribe to the next, but see Spencer and Gillen 1899, p. 60. Durkheim and Mauss (1963, pp. 36–7) claim that the cult lodge system among the Arunta had once precisely interlocked with the moiety structure and sub-structure, but the system had 'crumbled'.

25 Spencer and Gillen 1899, p. 58.

26 Gould 1980, p. 85.

27 By a majority of thirty-five to five, see Spencer and Gillen 1899, p. 120.

28 Spencer and Gillen seem to imply that he belonged to the active moiety, but do not explicitly say so. Meggitt's account of the Walbiri shows that actors and preparers or decorators consistently belonged to opposed moieties, making the reciprocal nature of the relationship even more apparent: Meggitt 1962, p. 224.

29 Spencer and Gillen 1899, pp. 175–8.

30 I have been relying here on old fieldwork by male anthropologists collecting data from other males, and therefore presumably biased in that direction. Anthropologists who have worked as couples – Gould (1969) frequently cites 'my wife' – have managed to produce more balanced accounts allowing the women larger roles. More recently, in *Daughters of the Dreaming*, Diane Bell has shown that the women also had their cults and there was more of a balance, see Bell 1983.

31 For the three stage division of a rite of passage into rite of separation, liminal rite and rite of reincorporation see the classic text Van Gennep 1908.

32 Gould 1969, pp. 113–16, with small cuts. This ceremony of the Yiwara is clearly different in detail from the one below described by Meggitt for the Walbiri tribe, but shares many of the same principles.

33 Meggitt 1962, pp. 281–316.

34 Gould above (observing 1966) described the actors as 'naked' though equipped with the 'sacred paraphernalia' but Meggitt describes decorated actors (1950s), and Spencer and Gillen (1896) even more so, with many accompanying photographs. Whether the elaboration of costume varies by tribe or has merely deteriorated through loss of tradition is not clear.

35 Meggitt (1962) is very detailed and consistent on these roles, which were for him a major interest; Spencer and Gillen (1899) are vague.

36 'Apulla' among the Arunta, see Spencer and Gillen 1899, p. 219, who also provide a basic plan.

37 Meggitt 1962, p. 286.

38 Meggitt (1962) describes it as funnel-shaped, east–west orientated, widest at the eastern end, 30–40 yds long (90–120 ft), 12 yds at widest extremity and 5 yds at narrowest. Gould (1969) reports it as 100 ft long (30 m), Spencer and Gillen (1899) report it as 40–50 ft long, also east–west but placed 40 ft from the eastern brake at which the men assembled and a further 40 ft from the east end and the novice, i.e. 120–130 ft (36–40 m) in all. They describe it as only 5 ft wide (1.5 m) inside the earthbanks, which including them would make it 10 ft (3 m) to Meggitt's 15 (4.5 m). Only Meggitt positively positions the fires: Gould reports two bonfires at opposite ends, which could be Meggitt's f4 and f5, since actors appear between them.

39 Spencer and Gillen 1899, pp. 433 and 438.

40 Meggitt 1962, pp. 281–316.

41 Ibid., p. 287.

42 Ibid., p. 294.

43 Ibid., p. 296.

44 Evidently the same ceremonial object described by Gould as a 'waniki' above.

45 Meggitt 1962, pp. 301–4.

46 Spencer and Gillen p. 380, reported for the Engwura ceremony, but this was presumably a general principle.

47 'At about 2.a.m., when Orion is overhead', is noted by Gould (1969).

48 Gould, in the description quoted above, notes that the men traverse the ground prior to the ceremony. Spencer and Gillen describe 'singing the ground' to validate it (1899, pp. 293 and 298).

49 Spencer and Gillen 1899, p. 271.

50 Ibid., pp. 271–386.

51 Ibid., p. 281.

52 For construction of the kauaua see Spencer and Gillen 1899, p. 364.

53 Ibid., p. 351.

54 Ibid., p. 378.

55 Ibid., p.178, footnote.

56 Gould 1980, p. 117. Earlier in the book (p. 17) he discusses friendship as the main motive for camping close together.

57 Rykwert 1976.

58 Gould 1969, p. 106.

59 Bourdieu 1977, pp. 118–19.

CHAPTER 7
THE OGLALA SIOUX AND THE FOUR DIRECTIONS

Figure 7.1 Photo of Black Elk about to make a prayer, 1947 (National Anthropological Archives, Smithsonian Institution, USA).

Figure 7.2 Projected reconstruction of the lamentation ceremony (drawing by Claire Blundell Jones after author's sketch).

Figure 7.3 Projected reconstruction of the Heyoka ceremony (drawing by Claire Blundell Jones after author's sketch).

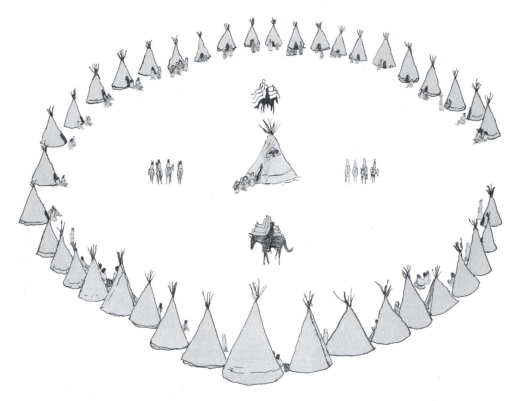

Figure 7.4 Projected reconstruction of the horse dance (drawing by Claire Blundell Jones after author's sketch).

The sun was almost setting when we came to the hill, and the old man [the mentor Few Tails] helped me to make the place where I was to stand. We went to the highest point of the hill and made the ground there sacred by spreading sage upon it. Then Few Tails set a flowering stick in the middle of the place, and on the west, the north, the east and the south sides of it he placed offerings of red willow bark tied into little bundles with scarlet cloth. Few Tails now told me what I was to do so that the spirits would hear me and make clear my next duty. I was to stand in the middle, crying and praying for understanding. Then I was to advance from the center to the quarter of the west and mourn there awhile. Then I was to back up to the center, and from there approach the quarter of the north, wailing and praying there, and so on all around the circle. This I had to do all night long.[1]

So begins the description by Black Elk of a lamentation ceremony carried out by him in 1881 at the age of eighteen.[2] Black Elk was an Oglala Sioux Holy man who had witnessed the Battle of Little Bighorn as a thirteen-year-old boy and grew up with the tragedy of his people's dispossession and cultural destruction. He was one of the last Native Americans to accept the calling of a holy man while the tradition persisted, and he survived long enough to be able to give a rich oral account of his beliefs and experiences to John Neihardt in 1931.[3] The lamentation ceremony, bemoaning the fate of the Oglala Sioux people and seeking guidance from the spirits, took place at the beginning of spring, just as the new grass was beginning to shoot, for this time also marked the revival of the spirits. It was preceded by four days of fasting, the smoking of a pipe, and a ritual purification in the sweat lodge, a kind of steam bath. Black Elk and Few Tails then travelled some distance to arrive at the top of the holy hill, a special place where the spirits would present themselves.[4]

After the initial preparation, which consisted of the denuding of a square of ground before placing the offerings,[5] Black Elk was left alone to experience his vision (Figure 7.2):

> Standing in the center of the sacred place and facing the sunset, I began to cry, and while crying I had to say: "O Great Spirit, accept my offerings! O make me understand!" As I was crying and saying this, there soared a spotted eagle from the west and whistled shrill and sat upon a pine tree east of me. I walked backwards to the center, and from there approached the north, crying and saying: "O Great Spirit accept my offerings and make me understand!" Then a chicken hawk came hovering and stopped upon a bush towards the south. I walked backwards to the center once again, and from there approached the east, crying and asking the Great Spirit to help me understand, and there came a black swallow flying all around me, singing, and stopped upon a bush not far away. Walking backwards to the center, I advanced upon the south. Until now I had only been trying to weep, but now I really wept, and tears ran down my face; for as I looked yonder towards the place whence come the life of things, the nation's hoop and the flowering tree, I thought of the days when my relatives, now dead, were living and young … And while I was crying, something was coming from the south. It looked like dust afar off, but when it came closer I saw that it was a cloud of butterflies. They swarmed around me so thick that I could see nothing else. I walked backwards to the flowering stick again, and the spotted eagle on the pine tree spoke and said: "Behold these! They are your people. They are in great difficulty and you shall help them".[6]

The vision now began in earnest. The butterflies were whimpering, then flew back to the south. The chicken hawk announced that the grandfathers were coming, and a great storm arose from the west, the 'thunder being nation'. Two men appeared, then the heads of two dogs, around which butterflies danced. The men mounted horses and charged on the dogs, applauded by the thunder beings, and the butterflies turned into swallows, which also attacked the dogs and drew blood. The dogs were then revealed as white men. As the vision receded, the storm grew fiercer. Black Elk lay down in the centre and offered the sacred pipe, then drew his robe around him and slept. The hail fell all around him and water trickled in the gullies, but the centre remained dry. He dreamed of his people and how he could help them, and coloured lights from the sky blazed, eventually revealing a special herb. As dawn was beginning to break, he saw the happy faces of the unborn amid scenes of rejoicing and harmony. The sun rose, and Few Tails reappeared to conduct him back to his village, where another pipe was offered to the Six Powers and there was a further session in the sweat lodge. Black Elk then described his vision to the elders, who assured him of its validity, and instructed him to perform it twenty days later as a theatrical presentation in front of all the people. He was to do it with the help of Heyokas, the sacred fools who have had thunder visions, and who do everything in reverse.[7] The conversion of the vision into a performance took some organization. A special site was chosen where the people could gather in a circle around a sacred tipi and a fire, in which stones were heated and placed in a water pot to make it boil (Figure 7.3). The Heyoka in charge began the ceremony with an offering on the fire of sweet grass to the powers of the west, then a dog was ceremonially sacrificed by two of his assistants who broke its neck with a rope. The dog's hair was singed away then it was cleaned and butchered, and its head and spine were given to the leader of the ceremony. Taking six steps away from the water pot each time, he offered it with suitable incantations to the spirits of the west, then to those of the north, east and south, and finally to the spirits above and to mother earth. Still standing six paces from the pot, he swung the dog's body three times, on the fourth letting it fly into the pot, then he did the same thing with its heart. While the dog cooked, the Heyokas, thirty of them representing the days of the moon (month), entertained the crowd with comic antics. They were dressed in red with streaks of black lightning, the hair on the right side shaved while that on the left remained long, and they carried parody versions of bows and arrows. Meanwhile the ceremonial leader repaired to his sacred tipi, where he sang holy songs twelve times over in reverence for the twelve moons. When the meat was cooked, Black Elk and another Heyoka, representing the men who vanquished the dogs in the vision, mounted horses. First they faced west side by side and chanted a song about half the universe having sent voices. Then they brought proceedings to a dramatic climax by charging towards the pot and deftly extracting the dog meat, spearing it with arrows. Black Elk took the head and his companion the heart. This was taken as a general invitation for all to descend upon the pot and grab some meat which, owing to the ritual, was supposed to have gained powerful curative properties. According to Black Elk, the ceremony made everyone feel better:

> for it had been a day of fun. They were better able to see the greenness of the world, the wideness of the sacred day, the colours of the earth and to set these in their minds. The Six Grandfathers have placed in this world many things, all of which should be happy. Every little thing is sent for something, and in that thing there should be happiness and the power to make happy.[8]

As with the Australian Aboriginal Peoples' wichetty grub ceremony described in the previous chapter, the ritual process had two stages: first of all the communing of an initiated group with supernatural powers, then the sharing of the knowledge and power so gained with the rest of the tribe through a theatre-like display. Different from the Australian case however is the great emphasis on the four cardinal points, which are heavily loaded with symbolic associations and addressed in the sequence west/north/east/south, ending with the direction of the 'nations hoop' and the 'flowering tree', an evident embrace of sunlight and fertility. The site chosen for the first ceremony was the top of a hill, following a worldwide convention not only about the hierarchy of height but also getting closer to the sky.[9] But this holy elevated place was adapted for the ceremony by Few Tails with just a handful of gestures: the flowering stick added for the centre linking earth and sky, and the four small bundles marking west, north, east and south: the orientation must already have been known from observation of the sun's path, but was reinforced by commencing the ritual in alignment with the setting sun.[10] The second ceremony is by contrast primarily circular and concentric, with a circumference of spectators surrounding a central sacred tipi along with its associated fire and boiling pot. Once the action starts, though, the cardinal orientations are again strictly observed, with special deference to west and south.

The Horse Dance

Later in Black Elk's account comes a ritual loaded with even more symbolic associations: the setting up and operation of a sacred tipi as part of the Horse Dance inspired by his vision. His elaborate description may have been perfected in memory and seems idealized,[11] particularly when his vision of a parallel event enacted by spirits in the clouds is taken as 'a greater reality', but the spatial symbolism is again strong and consistent. It begins with a sacred tipi set up to mark the middle of a large circular camp:

> First they sent a crier around in the morning who told the people to camp in a circle at a certain place … They did this, and in the middle of the circle Bear Sings and Black Road set up a sacred tipi of bison hide, and on it they painted pictures from my vision. On the west side they painted a bow and a cup of water; on the north, white geese and the herb; on the east, the daybreak star and the pipe; on the south, the flowering stick and the nation's hoop. Also they painted horses, elk and bison. Then over the door of the sacred tipi, they painted the flaming rainbow. It took them all day to do this, and it was beautiful … Right in the middle of the tipi the Grandfathers made a circle in the ground with a little trench, and across this they painted two roads – the red one running north and south, the black one east and west. On the west side of this they placed a cup of water with a little bow and arrow laid across it; and on the east they painted the daybreak star.[12]

Elaborate preparations were made for the ceremony, including fasting, a spell in the sweat lodge and a long rehearsal of songs. Four young women and six old men were chosen as actors, 'virgins' representing the vitality of the tribe and 'grandfathers' its ancestry. The four virgins were given symbolic tokens representing the four directions: a healing herb and a goose wing representing the cleansing wind for the north, a holy pipe for the east, the flowering stick for the south and the nation's hoop for the west: 'thus the four maidens, good and beautiful, held in their hands the life of the nation'.[13] Sixteen horses were selected by colour, four representing each cardinal point: black for west, white for north, sorrels for east and buckskins for south. Their riders were also coloured: black with streaks of blue representing lightning for west, white with red streaks for north, red with black streaks for east and yellow with black streaks for south. Black Elk, as the central figure, represented the thunder beings of the west, the source of his vision. He was given a bay horse and was painted red with black streaks. He wore a black mask with an eagle's feather.

The ritual began with Black Elk, the six grandfathers and four virgins all concealed in the sacred tipi (Figure 7.4). The grandfathers began singing to announce the arrival of the horses and their riders, who lined up in turn to face their respective cardinal points: west, north, east and south. After a song announced his arrival, Black Elk left the tipi preceded by the four virgins, who stood facing west as he mounted his horse behind them. The grandfathers then emerged and lined up abreast facing west behind Black Elk, announcing and regulating the performance with their singing and drumming. As they sang: 'the horse-nation of the west is dancing, they are coming to behold', the four horsemen of the west wheeled around to line up behind them, the other three groups following in turn. After a brief silence, Black Elk sang a prayer to the west, addressed to a cloud which represented the thunder spirit. The cry was made four times. Next the grandfathers addressed a song to the horses, which responded with gestures and neighing, and Black Elk saw in the cloud a repetition of his vision. Seemingly in response to the ritual, a storm now broke: 'the thunder beings were glad and had come in a great crowd to see the dance'.[14] At this point the four virgins held up their symbols of office and sick people came to be blessed. Then the music began again and the horse dance started. The group of black horses first moved forward to the west, and the others followed in turn, but on reaching the west end, the blacks wheeled around to follow the buckskins, while the whites took the lead, prancing towards the north side. Then the sorrels led until they reached the east, and the buckskins took over for the south. Finally the blacks took over again to return to the west. Whenever a cardinal point was reached, the centrally placed grandfathers sang of the powers of that quarter, and sitting astride his standing horse, Black Elk respectfully faced that direction, singing his own response. This procedure was repeated four times, an increasing number of riders joining in. On reaching the west for the fourth time, the whole troop turned inward to address the centre, the four virgins at the front before Black Elk on his horse. Behind him stood the six grandfathers with eight horses to each side: sorrels and buckskins on their right, blacks and whites on their left. Black Elk had to call out four times, then all rushed to 'coup' the sacred tipi, for the one to strike it first would gain special power.[15] The main actors then re-entered the tipi to light a sacred pipe which was passed around the whole village to mark the end of proceedings. Black Elk claimed that on re-entering the tipi, they discovered that the sand in the model at its centre had been disturbed by tiny hoof prints, proof of a miniature magic horse dance that had taken place simultaneously. This microcosm version related to the world of the Oglala Sioux as their world related to the spirit world beyond.

The circle and centrality

Two ideas about spatial organization stand out repeatedly in Black Elk's account: the circle and the four directions. The circle was powerfully symbolized in the nation's hoop, but was also spatially the pattern both of the dwelling – the tipi –and of the encampment. The camp's form of a ring was not only a convenient enclosure against hostile tribes and predatory animals, but also defined shared social space in contrast with wild nature beyond. The ceremonies gathered in this chapter all have a markedly centred character, most dramatically demonstrated by the idea of a microcosm in the focal tipi of the horse dance which included imagined movements of miniature horses. Black Elk had this to say of circular thinking:

> You have noticed that everything an Indian does is in a circle, and that is because the power of the world always works in circles, and everything tries to be round. In the old days when we were a strong and happy people, all our power came to us from the sacred hoop of the nation, and so long as the hoop was unbroken, the people flourished. The flowering tree was the living centre of the hoop, and the circle of the four quarters nourished it … Everything the Power of the World does is done in a circle. The sky is round, and I have heard that the earth is round like a ball, and so are all the stars. The wind, in its greatest power, whirls. Birds make their nests in circles, for theirs is the same religion as ours. The sun comes forth and goes down again in a circle. The moon does the same and both are round.[16]

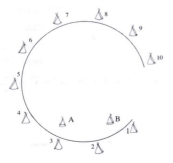

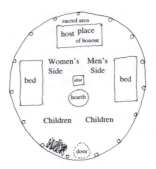

Figure 7.5 Cheyenne camp circle with north to top and entrance to east redrawn after George Grinnell. The centre would be the position for the temporary dance lodge or council lodge, A and B are cult lodges of the Sacred Arrow and Sacred Hat (redrawn by author after version reproduced in Fraser 1976).

Figure 7.6 Plan of a tipi, normally set up with the door at bottom facing east (redrawn by author after Faegre 1979).

Figure 7.7 Cheyenne engraving on a silver water cup depicting a peyote meeting in plan. In the centre is the crescent-shaped altar with firewood ready to light, and more wood is piled outside the eastern door. Small circles are ordinary celebrants, stars the ritual officials (redrawn by author after Nabokov and Easton 1989, p. 171).

Figure 7.8 Dorsey's plan of Cheyenne camp circle showing the coming together of two groups (Dorsey reproduced in Fraser 1968).

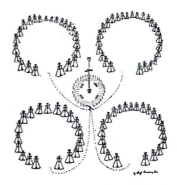

Figure 7.9 A Sioux camp arrangement drawn by Luther Standing Bear showing four separate groups around a central ceremonial ground (from Standing Bear 1933, p. 121).

By contrast, at the end of his account, when his people have been herded into a reservation, the disaster is epitomized by the imposition of the square and the loss of centre:

> All our people now were settling down in square houses, scattered here and there across this hungry land, and around them the Wasichus [white men] had drawn a line to keep them in. The nation's hoop was broken, there was no center any longer for the flowering tree. The people were in despair.[17]

The most important Sioux ritual of all, the sundance, was circular in form and powerfully concentric (Figure 7.10). This was a celebration of fertility and vitality associated with high summer and was linked in myth with the fecundity of the buffalo. A circular enclosure was built of brushwood at the centre of the village, with a special tree incorporating a token living branch installed as the ritual focus. To it were fixed the lines to which young men attached themselves through the skin of the chest or back, leaning out on them as they danced in pain as a protracted test of their manhood and endurance. The tree-trunk to be used for this sacred purpose had to be identified in the forest by a holy man, who prayed over it in private. It was then visited by people bedecked with flowers, danced around by pregnant women, and struck by a brave warrior before being cut down by a group of virgins. It had to be carried back to the village by chiefs, stopping four times in deference to the four seasons.[18] A hole had to be prepared for it in the centre of the ceremonial ground. Before it was set in place there was a general competition among the mounted warriors to 'count coup', rushing in to touch the sacred central spot, for the first to do so supposedly gained immunity from violent death that year. This event was followed by a feast for all, and the next day the tree was set up with appropriate solemnity and prayers. Before being used for the two-day sundance it was visited by mothers with young children for a blessing, so that 'the sons would be brave men and the daughters the mothers of brave men'.[19] Long after the ritual was over, the place and its tree trunk were treated with awe and respect as sacred.[20]

The camp and its east–west axis

Whenever formal encampments were made, and particularly for ceremonial events, the tipis of the Sioux, the Cheyenne (Figures 7.5 and 7.8), and other plains tribes were pitched in a circle, sometimes in a single band, sometimes two or three dwellings deep.[21] Normally the ring of tipis had its entrance gap to east, direction of the rising sun, though for some special occasions involving death, such as war parties, it could instead face west, a ritual inversion that only serves to confirm the power of the symbolic intent.[22] The gap to the east produced an implied axis that made the middle of the western side the most significant location in the ring and the place of chiefs, so Little Wound could proudly report that 'in a camp of all the Oglalas I am entitled to place my tipi at the chief place opposite to the entrance to the camp circle'.[23] In the plan of the tipi also (Figure 7.6) the place diametrically opposite the (normally east-facing)[24] entrance was the place of the host and of the honoured guest, who sat on the host's left because this was the side of his heart, an inversion of the European convention that favours the right hand. In a diagrammatic plan engraved as an emblem on a Cheyenne ritual vessel (Figure 7.7) three stars representing ritual leaders are set opposite the entrance and one to the left of the door, the male or honourable side, while ordinary celebrants are depicted as small circles. In the middle is the fire shown as crossed sticks, while between it and the officiants lies the crescent-shaped altar. Diagrams by James Walker following his early twentieth century discussions with Native Americans confirm the same arrangement for other rituals set within the tipi, always with the principal celebrant on axis.[25]

At this point we might hazard as a general principle that in circular arrangements the making of an entrance implies an axis that privileges the point on the opposite side as the hierarchical culmination of the progress of entry. This logically also becomes the main direction of bodily movement, setting up a potential division of the contained space into right and left halves. This left/right division is present for both camp and tipi, reflecting the ordering of society at different scales. Considering the camp, during major rituals such as the sundance the enclosed space could be half a mile wide. The central lodge was the dominant focus, but the tribes assembled segmentally in groups with the most important on the west side, a special tipi for the chief of chiefs being set up in front of it. James Dorsey recorded various layouts including a central sacred tipi of the forty-four chiefs used on the day of appointing new chiefs by the Cheyenne, suggesting that the hierarchy of centrality applied in a political as well as a

Figure 7.10 Depiction of a sundance ceremony painted on a tipi cover (redrawn by Claire Blundell Jones after an image in Josephy 1995, p. 389).

religious sense.[26] He also recorded an arrangement in which two interrelated Cheyenne tribes camped on opposite sides of the east–west axis, each with its own medicine lodge (Figure 7.8). Luther Standing Bear, on the other hand, reports that four groups of Sioux camped in separate circles around their ceremonial ground (Figure 7.9).[27] The common factor seems to be that camp circles were divided by clan in a strict order, and since clans were traditionally matrilinial and exogamous (i.e. you took your mother's name and had to marry outside your own clan) the camp circles were direct displays of kinship structure. Not all sources agree, some suggesting that such ordering was only followed on formal occasions,[28] but even if the arrangement was sometimes looser – and doubtless it was also adjusted to the terrain – there seems to have been always a sense of appropriate order in setting up camp.[29]

Reginald and Gladys Laubin, tipi experts who frequently visited and camped with Native American tribes in the mid-twentieth century, reported that they were allotted a position next to a particular Crow family and told 'this is your place for ever'.[30] Far from the Native Americans' sense of location being eroded by frequent moves, it seems rather to have been intensified by the need to retain and recreate the tribe's spatial order. The Laubins also reveal the conduct of a move. When the Omaha tribe – another branch of the Sioux – travelled, they retained the social sequence in which they camped (Figure 7.11), so on arrival the caravan leaders would cross the chosen campsite, then, dividing to left and right, would set up their tipis either side of the entry gap while other families followed suit, pairing off to left and right to complete the rest of the circle behind them. The entry gap therefore faced the direction of travel. When the party moved on, they would set off precisely in reverse order, the gatekeepers being the last to leave. The spatial order of the camp was thereby automatically preserved from place to place, while it also generated the structure of the caravan on the move, keeping the social order constantly visible.[31]

The circular tipi

Like the camp, the tipi was a circular structure, sometimes regarded as a smaller version of the same thing. Materially, it consisted of a series of crossed poles bound together at the top then clad in a cover made of buffalo hides sewn together (Figures 7.12, 17.13 and 17.14). The Sioux tipi had three primary poles which were set up first to establish the structure, while a fourth special pole was added for lifting the cover into place after the twenty or so subsidiary ones had been added.[32] The cover was buttoned together on the line of the door, an oval shaped hole just large enough to step through. It normally faced east, the structure leaning back in the opposite direction against the prevailing wind. A small fire burned near the centre, the passage of smoke being controlled by a pair of flaps, each moved by its own pole. With careful control of this hearth, comfort could be maintained with sub-zero external temperatures. The lower part of the tipi's volume was isolated from the cold outer skin by a hanging lining, and the floor was covered in skins. Basic beds were made of boughs or pallets of hides, and backrests with wooden props allowed relaxed sitting with legs stretched out on the floor. Belongings were kept in hide boxes that doubled as saddlebags, and everything was set up in the same place each time camp was pitched. Tipis belonged to women, who made, erected, and maintained them, and according to one report, no man was allowed to enter a new tipi until it had been completed and subjected to a dedication ritual by a brave warrior.[33] The tipi for a newly

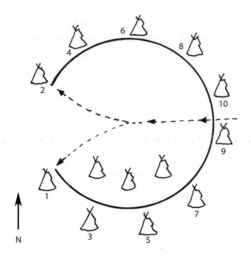

Figure 7.11 Drawing of an Omaha camp circle, indicating the pattern of establishment. Caravan leaders arrive from the right and east, divide to define the entrance, and pitch their tents in order back around the circle (redrawn by author after Laubin and Laubin 1957/89).

Figure 7.12 Elevation of Black Elk's tipi (redrawn by author after Laubin and Laubin 1957/89).

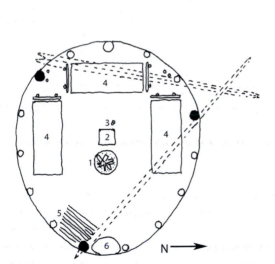

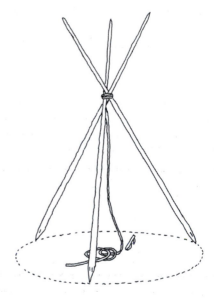

Figure 7.13 Tipi plan showing the primary three-pole structure, tie, and internal layout. The blacked poles are the primary structure and the dotted lines show erection positions. Key: 1. Fireplace; 2. Altar; 3. Securing peg; 4. Beds; 5. firewood store; 6. entrance, east-facing (redrawn by author after Laubin and Laubin 1957/89).

Figure 7.14 The basic three-pole structure of the Sioux tipi, lashed at the top and with a tie-down rope (redrawn by author after Laubin and Laubin 1957/89).

married couple was provided by the bride's family, and they were expected to camp with her family. The bridegroom's father and father's brothers would reciprocally be responsible for the provision of horses, the essential means of transport.[34] Before these animals were introduced by Europeans, the cover and poles had been dragged from site to site by harnessed dogs, and everything had been relatively smaller and lighter.

Just as the Australian Aboriginal 'Wurley' combined a semicircular shelter with a focal fire, so the Native American tipi in its more severe environment threw a full shelter around a central fire used for light, heat and cooking. Before the provision of flints or matches, the fire was kept continuously alight, and an official fire-keeper was appointed to carry live coals in a buffalo horn from one site to the next, rekindling the same shared fire in every tipi. With its column of smoke, the fire made an axis rising to the heavens, but contact with mother earth was underlined by the presence of a family altar: a small square patch of cleared ground close by the fire and beneath the crossing of the poles. Here on the naked earth sweet grass, cedar, or sage were burned as incense carrying prayers to the 'Ones Above'.[35] The altar was used in every domestic ceremony and for a kind of grace before meals, an offering being made by burning or burying a small sample of food.

As noted earlier, the place of the father and honoured guest was on the west, axially opposite the door (Figure 7.6). They would be closest to the altar, which lay between them and the fire. Possessions were laid out with a hierarchical sense that those furthest inside were most important or sacred, while those closest to the door were most profane. The east–west axis of the tipi also marked a potential division between north and south sides, for traditionally men occupied the north and women the south.[36] This was the case with many Native American tribes, for example the Navajo.[37] It was strictly observed in the case of the Mistassini Cree, who not only divided between sides according to gender, but also slept in order of seniority. The anthropologist Adrian Tanner reported that sisters were quite unnerved when a brother intruded on their side of the tent merely in jest.[38] When entering the tipi, a Sioux man moved to the right and a woman to the left, each walking around behind the backs of those already present, for it was rude to pass between them and the fire. The worst breach of etiquette was to step into the altar, which it was believed would enrage the spirits and cause a storm.[39] Many customs reflected and supported this hierarchical reading of space: when a pipe was smoked – always an activity with deeply spiritual associations – it was lit by the head man at the back then passed round to his left (north side), being smoked by each person in turn as far as the door, then it was passed back to the head man unsmoked. In the case of a full meeting of men who also occupied the south side of the tipi, it was passed unsmoked round to the man nearest the door then smoked on the way back, so that again it moved always to the left.[40]

The four directions

A constant respect for orientation has been noted, suggesting that awareness of it was habitual. For an itinerant people living in a trackless uncultivated country it was essential to maintain a sense of position and to be able to follow the migration paths of prey, and it was also important to understand as far as possible the vagaries of the weather. The choice of south as the propitious direction undoubtedly relates to the life-giving sun as experienced within the northern hemisphere, but the west is almost its equal as the source of the prevailing weather, bringing both threatening storms and life-giving rain. In the absence of clocks the measure of time was given entirely by heavenly bodies.[41] This was not just a case of following the sun: confined half the time by the starry sky, they must also have counted the passage of the night by the progress of constellations, as we already saw with the Australian Aboriginal People. Setting up a ritual site on a hilltop required only observation of sunrise or sunset, moments which tended anyway to be involved in staging the ritual and were predictable by prior observation. Without knowledge of distant seas and continents, of an outer world beyond, and finding themselves at the mercy of seasons and weather, it was only logical to conceive an outer cosmos filled with spirits both beneficent and malevolent, and to propose this as an other spirit reality impinging on the practical everyday one. The four directions marked the human interaction with this outer spirit world while maintaining the sense of centre, but it belonged to no compass, the directions' phenomenological basis being rooted simply in observation of the heavens. A mythical story establishes the four directions spatially as being the work of Tate, the wind spirit, who placed his lodge in the middle of the world and sent his four sons out to the edges, establishing the four directions and thereby dividing the circle into quarters.[42] From them come the four winds, and the four associated eagles: 'the golden eagle of the east, symbol of the sun from which comes life; the spotted eagle of the south which carries the souls of the dead to the land of happiness; the black eagle of the west, denoting sunset or darkness; and the bald eagle of the north, which brought the winds and snows of winter'.[43] Besides the four seasons there were also four divisions of time: day, night, moon and year, and four major losses or tragedies were supposed to occur in human life.[44] Overseeing all this in the heavens were four primary spirits and four groups of four lesser ones, making sixteen in all,[45] and as we have seen in the examples above, ritual practices tended almost invariably to number things by fours and use sequences of four. Sixes also occur, which is achieved spatially by adding the vertical directions of earth and sky, appropriate to the grandfathers of the horse dance because of their closeness to the spirit world. But most commonly and explicitly, the four directions were acknowledged one by one in correct order every day when the sacred pipe, which makes the connection with the spirits, was lit and pointed at each of them in turn.[46]

With this in mind, a final example from Black Elk conveniently ties space, number, and ritual irrevocably together. A man whose son was dangerously ill came to the holy man for help, and was sent home to fetch a pipe with an eagle feather. When he returned he was told to pass around to the left, place it at the back of the tipi, then leave by the right. Black Elk gathered assistants, then went to the sick boy's tipi. He offered the pipe to the six powers and passed it round, then beat a drum in imitation of thunder, because: 'when the power of the west comes to the two-leggeds, it comes with rumbling, and when it has passed, everything lifts up its head and is glad and there is greenness'.[47] The tipi was pitched with the entrance south, and the sick boy lay to the north-east, 'so we went around from left to right, stopping on the west side when we had made a circle'. There followed a prayer uttered while facing west, then Black Elk addressed north, east and south in turn, 'stopping there where the source of all life is and where the good red road begins'. He addressed the west again, this time lighting the pipe which was passed around. Next, he approached the boy and stamped the earth four times, then sucked at his stomach, 'drawing through the cleansing wind of the north'. He chewed a sacred herb, put it in water, blew some on the boy and some to the four quarters. Next day the boy recovered. The first prayer given referred to the four quarters and two roads crossing each other, which the Great Spirit had made:

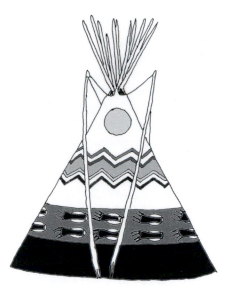

Figure 7.15 Blackfeet tipi symbolism. The dark part at the top represents the sky with stars, and the stripes immediately below the rainbow. The dark skirt at the bottom represents the earth, also decorated with stars, and on the surface is a ring of U-shaped mounds which are places of prayer. The light middle carries the vision painting of an animal, and the arrow down its throat represents its lifeline or source of spiritual power (redrawn by author after Nabokov and Easton 1989, p. 164).

Figure 7.16 Bear Medicine tipi: the circle at the top is the bear's den. The zigzag pattern lightning and storm and rainbow, on the ground are the bear's paw marks (redrawn by author after Laubin and Laubin 1957/89, p. 250).

You have set a power where the sun goes down… In vision you have taken me to the center of the world and there you have shown me the power… From where we are always facing (the south) a virgin shall appear, walking the good red road, offering the pipe as she walks, and hers is also the power of the flowering tree. From where the Giant lives (the north), you have given me a sacred cleansing wind, and where this wind passes the weak shall have strength.[48]

In a short digression from his account of this event, Black Elk offers an explanation of 'why we always go around from left to right', turning a spatial metaphor into a temporal one:

Is not the south the source of life, and does not the flowering stick truly come from there? And does not man advance from there toward the setting sun of his life? Then does he not approach the colder north where the white hairs are? And does he not then arrive, if he lives, at the source of light and understanding, which is the east? Then does not he return to where he began, to his second childhood, there to give back his life to all life, and his flesh to the earth whence it came? The more you think about this, the more meaning you will see in it.[49]

Decorating the tipi

Native American tipis were of more or less standard design for each tribe, but while most were used as ordinary dwellings, a few were used as 'medicine tipis'.[50] Only these and the tipis of the specially honoured were decorated, but such decoration was considered highly significant (Figures 7.15 and 7.16). It became the means by which the sacred buildings of the community, and the dwellings of chiefs or shamans, could be picked out from the others. The designs on medicine tipis had a specific symbolic content, and when the tipi cover of a particular cult wore out, it was replaced by an identically painted new one. The sewing of the cover from several hides was a communal task for many women, and its completion was marked by a feast.[51] The hide of the old one retained some sacred character, so it could not simply be disposed of by recycling as bags or moccasins like that of ordinary tipis: instead it had to be destroyed.[52] Similarly, when ownership of a medicine tipi changed hands, the new proprietor had to be initiated into the rituals, vowing to conduct them as required. New designs were also made, the results of dreams or visions that had been received by the owner and validated by the tribal elders. The painting was carried out by a specialist artist on the dreamer's instruction. So charged was the power of the design that a new cover for a medicine tipi was pegged to the ground and walked upon by tribal members before being used, as this was supposed to bring them health and good luck. The symbolism varied from tribe to tribe, but colours and patterns were related to those used for ritual body painting and for the decoration of other artefacts. In contrast with the handed-down styles of European architecture about which we still argue, the intended meanings seem to have been widely understood. Convention divided the cover into three horizontal bands: the red-painted bottom represented the earth, the top the sky, typically with white discs as stars, while the middle represented the world of men, with depictions of animals and birds or pageants of battle or the hunt. Narrative themes could commemorate real historic events or the imaginary world of the vision. Black Elk described one in the quotation cited above in relation to the horse dance:

> on the west side they painted a bow and a cup of water; on the north, white geese and the herb; on the east, the daybreak star and the pipe; on the south, the flowering stick and the nation's hoop.[53]

The hoop represented many things: 'the unity of the tribe, the world, complete and perfect life, return of the seasons, the sun, moon and so on'.[54] Many tipi designs reflected the symbolism of the four directions in some way. A Cheyenne design described by the Laubins shows a trail from each of the four quarters ascending from the earth to the sky:

> On this trail are dragonflies bearing messages to the Thunder. The black band at the bottom of the tipi represents the earth. Above it are the puff balls that grow on the prairie and the red road, the good road of life. The puff balls are sometimes called 'dusty stars' for they appeared so quickly and grew so fast they were thought to be stars fallen from the sky.[55]

If not actually depicted on the cover, the four directions could instead be picked out in applied rosettes hung around the outside. These had to be made and fixed in precisely the right order, for a mistake would necessitate a serious rite to propitiate the spirits:

Four old men who had counted coup in battle were called. The faulty rosette was removed: one of the men took the sewer's awl and counted coup on the place where it had been; he then returned the awl, and the rosette was resewn.[56]

Four heroes had to be present even if only one had to act: each direction was represented.

Conclusion: Centre, two roads, four quarters

Like the Australian Aboriginal People, the Native Americans relied on an oral culture, carrying a mythology that combined practical actions with spiritual ideas, engaging the weather and the landscape, that was interpreted to include sacred places where people could commune with their ancestors. More sedentary peoples like the Navajo even related these places directly to events in their tribal myths.[57] Again as with the Australians, the Native Americans also engaged with the fauna and flora. As hunters they needed an understanding of their prey, but other creatures on this earth were also regarded as brothers to be respected, each with its particular characteristics. A hierarchical description of animal spirits by the Native American Thomas Tyon starts as might be expected with the Buffalo, the greatest prize as prey but also the general symbol of fecundity, virtue, and industry. His skull is the ritual focus for the sundance, and he is the protector of women during pregnancy. He is followed by the Bear, whose mischievous spirit means love and hate and bravery. Then comes the Coyote, who stands for thieving, cowardliness and a more malevolent mischief. The spirits of Wolf, Dog and Elk follow, and then that of the dam-building Beaver, who is the patron of work and domesticity. Birds come next, and then the Snake, who is sly and a liar. Fish is the spirit of ablution and the Frog the patron of occult powers.[58] This consciousness of animals was also manifested in the cult groups specializing in animal powers such as the Bear Society, and in the personal naming of people.[59] The powers above had to be thanked for their bounty, and animal bodies had to be cut up and distributed in an appropriate manner, not only to assure that all parts were put to good use, but also because the organs carried specific spiritual values and social associations.[60] Animals also had ceremonial roles to play and were the bearers of omens, like the birds and butterflies of the second quotation in this chapter, or the eagles supposed to carry away the spirits of the dead.

A further parallel is that the tipi, as a dwelling surrounding a fire, followed the same basic principle as the Aboriginal shelter, and in southern parts of the United States shelters once existed that were markedly similar to those of the Australians.[61] The use of pack dogs and, after their introduction, of horses meant that the hunters of the plains could drag their camp of tipis with them rather than remaking it like the Australians, and that they could possess many more tools and belongings. These could be set up in a much more ordered way, the space becoming at the same time more definitively gendered, including feminine ownership of the tipi and uxorilocal marriage. The encampments also embodied social order, set up as a circle or combination of circles. The circle offers no direction, only centre and periphery, but the camps gain an implied dividing axis from the entrance, normally east-facing in deference to the rising sun. So emerges the linear principle and the notional cross-axis giving four directions. Ritual observances always refer to the four, centrally symbolized by the crossroads in the sacred tipi. The two crossing roads are the 'good red' one and the difficult black one, and they divide the world into quarters dedicated to particular spirits.[62] The four directions receive an elaborate symbolic load, apparently greater than with the Australian Aboriginal People, and with an added number symbolism of four and six (adding the earth–sky axis) that occurs repeatedly in the time and space of Native American cultures.[63] The association of the cardinal points with particular spirits, colours, animals and so on is surprisingly similar to that found in ancient China,[64] while the idea of locating centre at the intersection of north–south and east–west roads has much in common with the founding of cities in rectangular form around a central cross-roads, most famously in the Roman town with its decumanus and cardo. As Joseph Rykwert demonstrated, this phenomenon is worldwide, suggesting either early cultural dissemination or reinvention in different times and places.[65] If the coincidence between Chinese culture and those of Native Americans is the result of cultural dissemination, it presumably dates back 17,000 years to the crossing of the northern land-bridge, long before the making of cities.

The Sioux use of crossroads, number, and calendar points to a culture that has engaged with agriculture, and their history as far as is known suggests that the pursuit of the buffalo was a late specialization encouraged by the introduction of the horse. A closely related tribe, the Crow, practised an elaborate fertility ritual involving tobacco, considered the primal plant that produced visions by its narcotic effect. The elaborate Crow tobacco ceremony involved the laying out of a primal field or garden in the form of a rectangle 60 yards by 6 yards with the plants arranged in rows, then marking the process of growth from seeds to harvest with chronologically structured ritual observances.[66] The site of the primal field was supposedly dictated by a vision given to a member of the Tobacco Society, and the choreography of parades to this ground was elaborate, but its position and orientation are not given in the otherwise rich account.[67] It seems the ritual cycle encapsulated the memory of an earlier agricultural stage in the Crows' existence rather than the birth of a new agriculture, but it is striking nonetheless. The relation of agriculture to geometry will be further considered in later chapters, and a further aspect of this case study anticipates studies to come: the ritual felling, carrying, and erection of the sundance tree for the most important of group celebrations has striking parallels with the treatment of trees for building, particularly in East Asia, indicating a nascent ritualization of the building process.

Notes

1   John G. Neihardt, *Black Elk Speaks, Being the Life Story of a Holy Man of the Oglala Sioux*. Lincoln, NB and London: University of Nebraska Press, 1932/79, p. 182.

2   Neihardt 1979, pp. 105–30.

3   For the story of their meeting see Neihardt's Preface of 1960, and the later independent account by Raymond J. DeMallie which outlines Black Elk's whole biography (DeMallie 1984).

4   The ritual practice and preparation behind Black Elk's description was fairly standardized, and the vision was both personally sought and socially expected, prepared for by fasting and a sweat bath. The vision was also a universal experience sought by every individual during the rite of passage at puberty. For details on this and on Sioux beliefs and customs more generally see James Walker, *Lakota Belief and Ritual* (1980), a valuable compendium of Native American material containing numerous first-hand accounts recorded in the late nineteenth and early twentieth centuries. On the idea of the vision see particularly *Seeking a vision* by George Sword pp. 84–6, and *Instructing a vision quester* by James Walker on pp. 132–4.

5   Walker's (1980) sources speak of a piece of ground ten feet square which is prepared by complete clearing of vegetation, giving contact with the earth, as with the altar in the tipi.

6   Neihardt 1979, pp. 182–4

7   Ibid., pp. 184–7. For an independent but corroborative description of the Heyoka ceremony by Thomas Tyon see Walker 1980, p. 156.

8   Neihardt 1979, p. 193.

9   See Eliade 1958, p. 111; Lethaby 1956, pp. 40–53; mentions of vision sites in the different personal accounts in Walker 1980 consistently refer to hilltops.

10 In the absence of the compass, the sun's position was the defining observation. In an account by James Walker about the Buffalo Ceremony, the special ceremonial lodge is described as set up with its door to the east 'so that the rising sun might fall on the catku or place of honour in the tipi', Walker 1980, p. 245.

11 Not for the last time in this book, the source is someone who had been responsible for the tribal ideology, deeply versed in its secrets and keen to read it into every situation. He was also relying on his memory over a long period, which gave him further reason to reinterpret events in the light of his own understanding. Even if this is an exaggerated reading of what actually happened, it usefully exposes the underlying ideas. It also shows the mnemonic value in an oral culture of possessing some key structural concepts with which to order narratives and events.

12 Neihardt 1979, pp. 162 and 165.

13 Ibid., p. 166. Note that the nation's hoop, which normally belongs to the south, is temporarily relocated in the west, presumably because the whole ritual is dedicated to the thunder beings.

14 Ibid., p. 171.

15 This action symbolic of taking life, related to hunting and war, also appears as part of the sundance ritual, see p. 97.

16 Neihardt 1979, pp. 194–5.

17 Ibid., pp. 213–14.

18 Walker 1980, 176–83 for transcribed oral accounts by Native Americans.

19 This and the preceding, Neihardt 1979, pp. 96–8.

20 'The Sun Dance poles which were allowed to stand from year to year were never desecrated. Children coming upon a pole would at once become quiet and respectful, while older people often stood in silent reverence for a moment or two', Standing Bear 1933, p. 156.

21 Fraser 1968, pp. 19–22; Laubin 1989, pp. 293–300.

22 Laubin and Laubin 1989, pp. 293–300.

23 Walker 1980, p. 67.

24 Laubin and Laubin 1989, p. 295.

25 See plans in Walker 1980: ceremonial lodge of the Hunka Lowanpi, p. 240, ceremonial lodge of the Tatanka Lowanpi, p. 254.

26 Fraser 1968, fig. 22.

27 Standing Bear 1978 (1933), p. 121.

28 Lowie 1983 (1935), p. 12.

29 On moving camp see Standing Bear 1975 (1928), pp. 23–5.

30 Laubin and Laubin 1989, p. 294.

31 Ibid., p. 299. George Sword's account, recorded in 1896, notes that a move of camp was controlled by a *wakiconze*, translated by James Walker as a magistrate, who was appointed by the elders and

settled disputes. For the keeping of law and order there were also *akicita*, translated as marshalls: see Walker 1980, pp. 80–1.

32 For full and practical detail on all of this, see Laubin and Laubin 1989, *passim*.

33 Laubin and Laubin 1989, p. 104.

34 Ibid.

35 Ibid., p. 109.

36 Ibid., p.110

37 See Nabokov and Easton 1989, p. 327.

38 Tanner 1979, p. 80.

39 Laubin and Laubin 1989, p. 112

40 Ibid., pp. 113–14.

41 For a summary of time and number see Standing Bear 1933, pp. 156–7.

42 Walker 1980, p. 54. This is part of James Walker's summary of Oglala mythology, taken from a lecture text. His fieldwork dated from before 1914 and he died in 1926.

43 Standing Bear 1933, p. 122.

44 Ibid.

45 Walker 1980, pp. 50–4.

46 On daily use of the pipe see Standing Bear 1933, p. 156; on the meaning of the pipe as a connection with the spirits see George Sword *Consecrating a pipe* in Walker 1980, pp. 87–90.

47 This and the following quotations are from Neihardt 1979, pp. 199–203.

48 Ibid., p. 201.

49 Ibid., pp. 200–1.

50 Laubin and Laubin 1989, pp. 241–65.

51 Faegre 1979, p. 158.

52 All this and more below from Laubin and Laubin 1989, pp. 241–73.

53 Neihardt 1979, p. 162.

54 Laubin and Laubin 1989, p. 252.

55 Ibid., p. 257.

56 Ibid., p. 258.

57 Kelley and Francis 1994.

58 Walker 1980, pp. 119–20.

59 On the Bear Society see Thomas Tyon, *Bears are Wakan* in Walker 1980, pp. 157–9.

60 Tanner 1979, pp.178–80.

61 See for example the photograph taken by Powell's expedition in Utah 1873, reproduced in Nabokov and Easton 1989, p. 303.

62 Of course this is a society that did not have roads in our sense, so they might be better described as paths or tracks, except that when symbolically represented and coloured they are artificial and precisely intended as roads.

63 A parallel and closely related case to the Sioux is the Cheyenne, as reported in detail by George Bird Grinnell in the 1920s (Grinnell 2008). In their myth of origin, p. 1, woman goes north and man south, connected respectively with winter and with thunder which brings fire, so showing an essential connection between gender, direction, and season. The Cheyenne village circle is open to the east, p. 17, and the orders of the day are given serially to east, south, west and north. Medicine

pipes, p. 187, are also smoked to the four directions, and etiquette in the tipi, p. 36, is similar to that of the Sioux. Places of chiefs at a meeting, p. 125, are marked by forty-four sticks, four first placed at the cardinal points and 4 × 10 between them, each stick being removed as the occupant arrives. When a decision is made, the crier goes to announce it to the four directions.

64　The striking structural similarity between the Sioux classification system and that of the ancient Chinese was pointed out a century ago by Durkheim and Mauss (1901–2, 1963): the values ascribed to the cardinal points are different, but the structuring process is much the same.

65　Rykwert 1976, pp. 163ff.

66　Lowie 1983 (1935), p. 291.

67　Ibid., pp. 274–96. The observations were made in 1910.

CHAPTER 8
THE TUKANOAN MALOCA

Figure 8.1 Barasana man painting the front of a Tukanoan maloca (photograph by Stephen Hugh-Jones).

Figure 8.2 Maloca and its clearing or plaza seen from the air, showing the gabled front and rounded rear (photograph by Brian Moser, courtesy of Stephen Hugh-Jones).

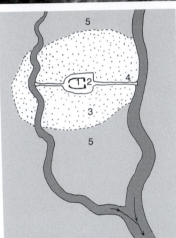

Figure 8.3 Maloca setting with main river to right and minor tributary to left: 1. The maloca; 2. The cleared space around it; 3. The manioc gardens; 4. The port; 5. The rainforest (redrawn by author after Christine Hugh-Jones 1979).

Figure 8.4 Maloca front with central door and decorated lower panels, the upper part made of woven palm leaves like the roof (photograph by Brian Moser, courtesy of Stephen Hugh-Jones).

With this chapter we move on to a permanent house, the sole home of a particular group and centre of their world. Tukanoans are Native South Americans living in the Amazonian rainforest, and this case study draws largely on the accounts of anthropologists Stephen and Christine Hugh-Jones, who lived with a subgroup called the Barasana between 1968 and 1970.[1] Although for convenience I have set much of the description below in the present tense, it accepts the situation of forty years ago as a brief window onto another world, without considering how the people live now or how they have been affected by globalization.[2] It also accepts the structuralist basis of the Hugh-Joneses' analysis, which provides an exceptionally rich array of data.[3] The Barasana were then living in groups of about thirty in a longhouse called a maloca (Figures 8.2–8.4), each within an hour or two of the next by canoe or on foot. Despite this isolation, relations with adjacent groups were essential for intermarriage and other kinds of social interaction, so the malocas and their residents, while in some ways autonomous, were in others interdependent, which are reflected both in their architecture and in its ritual use. Food production was gender-divided between male hunting in the forest and female cultivation of the staple manioc, from the tubers of which a bread is made. The manioc was grown in prepared gardens cleared in the forest around or close to the maloca. The tropical climate with its dry and wet seasons produced annual cycles in foods such as fruit and fish which were acknowledged and celebrated, but the abundant flora and fauna provided year-round food without significant storage, and as it remained relatively warm, fires were mainly for cooking. The longhouse with its wooden skeleton and woven roof provided protection from sun and rain as well as a retreat from the forest. Though physically a light, short-lived and flimsy structure, it carried a great symbolic load. Seen from the air, a maloca is powerfully concentric (Figure 8.2). The house stands on naked and constantly weeded ground called the *maka*, within an area of rainforest burned to form the garden where the women's manioc is the main crop, but where small quantities of tobacco, maize, coca and fish-poisons may also be grown by men.[4] In some cases planted fruit trees line the perimeter of the *maka*, adding a further intermediate layer. According to the Desana, an adjacent tribe who also inhabit malocas, these trees are the perches of imaginary protective eagles. The Desana also consider that the maloca has an imaginary cloak like a placenta, and that a further imaginary woven fence protects the clearing against marauding animals and evil influences.[5] However many layers real or imaginary are envisaged, the sense of human centre (culture) versus wild periphery (nature), could scarcely be clearer, and the layering continues within the maloca. It is found again in the contrast between the peripheral family compartments around the edge and the ritual focus, site of the sacred paraphernalia, which occupies the tallest central space lying within the innermost four columns encircled by the ritual dance path (Figures 8.7 and 8.10).

Despite its spatial concentricity the maloca is not circular, though it presumably could have been, as the region is not without round houses and round villages.[6] Added to its centrality is an obvious linear principle which differentiates front from back, left from right, and implies an unmistakable primary axis. This axiality is embedded in the very concept of the building, for construction starts with the five pairs of central columns, their lashed-on cross-beams, and the three sets of longitudinal purlins that form the primary support for the roof (Figures 8.5, 8.6 and 8.8). Starting with the placing of the columns, the maloca must be laid out initially along its centre line, and the first decision concerning the number and spacing of columns also determines the layout of its ritual centre. The five pairs of columns are regarded as male, and identified with the men who build the maloca. They also reflect the five specialist roles

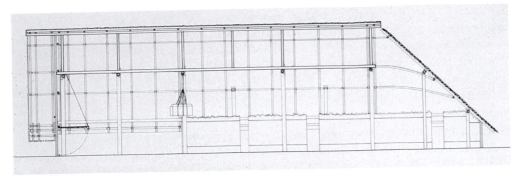

Figure 8.5 Long section of a maloca showing main structure, compartments, lifting door, and hanging feather box (drawn by Pascale Scheurer after data from Stephen Hugh-Jones).

of chief, chanter/dancer, warrior, shaman and servant, which myth applies to five brothers in order of age.[7] Reconstruction drawings by Scheurer from Hugh-Jones's data indicate that the bay spacing varies, and that each larger bay of the ritual centre matches two standard bays of peripheral columns: this must have been taken into account during the preliminary setting out.

Considering the whole enclosed envelope, the 42° double pitched roof drops from an eight metre ridge to eaves at just over a metre each side, producing the triangular section that lets the interior space rise to a central climax of ritual importance.[8] This triangle shows itself externally in the gable front, while the potential for façades elsewhere is denied, particularly if the rear end of the building is rounded as it is ideally supposed to be,[9] forming the rear roof as a

Figure 8.6 A maloca under construction showing primary columns and beams, purlins and rafters (photograph by Stephen Hugh-Jones).

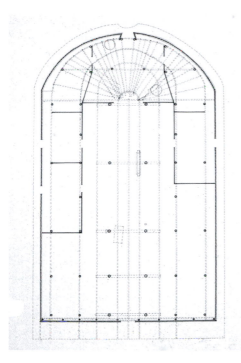

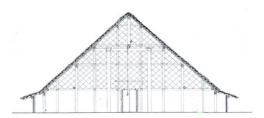

Figure 8.8 Cross-section of a maloca showing the primary structure (drawn by Pascale Scheurer after data from Stephen Hugh-Jones).

Figure 8.7 Plan of maloca showing the family compartments gathered around the rear end, with outlines of the feather box and anaconda canoe in the central bay. The circle just right of the axis in the rear is the communal hearth (drawn by Pascale Scheurer after data from Stephen Hugh-Jones).

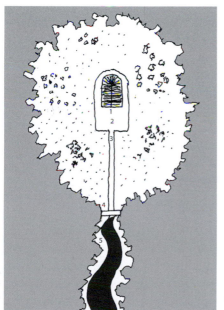

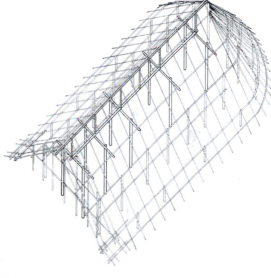

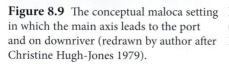

Figure 8.9 The conceptual maloca setting in which the main axis leads to the port and on downriver (redrawn by author after Christine Hugh-Jones 1979).

Figure 8.10 Axonometric projection of structure (drawn by Pascale Scheurer after data from Stephen Hugh-Jones).

half cone and letting it slope to the ground on three sides. The lower part of the symmetrical front is often clad in sheets of bark, as opposed to the woven palm used elsewhere, to accept decoration with symbolic figures, and it is the main part of the building to receive such treatment.[10] As the face to the outside world, it is the side encountered by approaching visitors, and it combines with the space before it to define an outdoor room for public exchange – the Hugh-Joneses call it a plaza. As the aerial view in Figure 8.2 shows, a larger proportion of the cleared *maka* lies to the front than to the sides or rear. This external space has great ritual significance in inter-house events, and it is also the place where possessions must be brought out of the house and deposited at times of ritual purification, such as during the dangerous lunar eclipse.[11] This confirms its role as the definitive 'outside' as opposed to 'inside', linked and divided by the key threshold of the main doorway. The maloca's approach normally links it to the local river, the axial path connecting its door directly with the landing stage (Figure 8.3). In the dense and relatively trackless forest, rivers are the principal landmarks as well as the main means of communication, and ideally the building should face east, as the continent's rivers generally flow west–east. Tukanoan myth has it that the various tribal groups arrived progressively upriver, forming a family tree which branches out as it departs from the river mouth, and which defines a group's place within the ancestral hierarchy. We shall revisit the significance of this, but first we must address the social essence of the maloca and the way it defines and frames everyday relationships.

The maloca is a house for a group of related families, normally brothers with their wives and children, the eldest brother being the headman and founder of the house, which therefore bears his name. Its life begins when he and his brothers decide to set up on their own, identifying the area of forest in which they intend to live, then clearing it and starting to assemble the frame, beginning with the definitive paired central hardwood columns. Later the rest of the group, including the women and neighbours, help with the finishing, which consists largely of the woven cladding.[12] The manioc gardens are started before the house is complete, and may continue in cultivation beyond it, for everything has a limited timescale. The forest soil can be depleted after as little as two or three years, causing the gardens to be moved or extended, and the maloca itself may be rebuilt after as few as ten years due to the deterioration of its fabric, but even if reclad it is unlikely to last more than thirty years, for it changes with the community. When the leader dies, the maloca dies with him, and he is buried under its centre, and a new one is founded elsewhere by the reconstituted community.[13] The burned site may later be reused as a garden, in which case the plots for planting are set out in ways that remember the house's former layout, the combination of pepper and tobacco – which are regarded respectively as female and male crops – being distributed with respect to the house's original spatial gender divisions.[14]

The maloca's gable door is the front door mainly used by the men, while the door in the rounded end leading to the manioc gardens belongs to the women, most roles and duties being assigned by gender. Men occupy the front end both literally and metaphorically as protectors, ritual leaders, and officiators at public events involving outsiders, while women and children are situated protectively and more privately behind, each nuclear family living, sleeping, cooking food, and keeping its possessions in a compartment on the rear periphery. These compartments have doors to the outside connecting to the manioc gardens and are the domain of mothers, young children, and unmarried girls. Fathers come and go, sleeping in a hammock in the compartment, but spending the daytime out hunting, or in the company

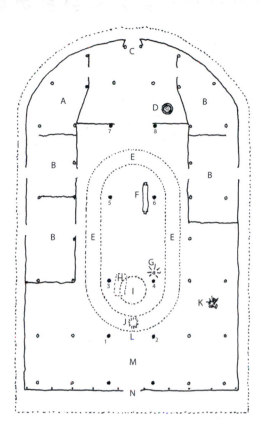

Figure 8.11 Maloca plan with sites of ritual use. Key: 1 to 8 central lines of columns which define ritual space. A. Headman's compartment; B. Other family compartments; C. Women's door; D. Griddle – womb of house; E. Dance path; F. Anaconda canoe; G. Light post; H. Feather box above; I. Men's circle; J. Ash-burning for coca; K. Coca-toasting fire; L. Men's chanting place; M. Coming-in-standing-place; N. Men's door (redrawn by author after Christine Hugh-Jones 1979).

Figure 8.12 Maloca interior with everyday activities: the front had not yet been added (photograph by Stephen Hugh-Jones 1979).

Figure 8.13 Anaconda canoe in which ritual beer is brewed by the women for communal rituals (photograph by Stephen Hugh-Jones).

of other men in the male front of the house. Boys, on reaching initiation, join the world of men, and though allowed to visit the family compartment in the day, are expected to sleep in the middle of the house. Only when married and expecting a child do they again occupy a peripheral compartment which is built for or allotted to them.[15]

Family compartments tend to be laid out hierarchically with the leader's hindmost, so from the front door the whole length of the maloca must be traversed to reach his, providing the greatest spatial depth. Since visitors are admitted gradually from the front and to a limited extent, the leader's implied command of the entire space from the back end reflects his dominance. Regarding him as presiding at the back also justifies the siting of his compartment on the left, for it lies to his right hand when he looks towards the front. The leader's compartment adjoins the central part of the end space which in daily use serves as a gathering area for women and contains the site of the griddle used when cooking is communal. To divide the half-round women's space from the columned male centre, a temporary woven screen can be installed just behind the last pair of main posts on ritual occasions (Figure 8.15). When this is in place, the male front part is secluded from the female rear, preventing women and children seeing the parade of sacred musical instruments during male initiation, and so protecting them from malign powers. Spatially this screen identifies the principal internal threshold between male public ritual space and female private dwellings. Also significantly placed on the main axis is the men's circle. Set between the front pair of the four central columns in significant contrast with the rear pair where women grate manioc, this is the part of the house where men gather at dusk to smoke and chew coca, sitting on stools telling stories and joking together. They sit

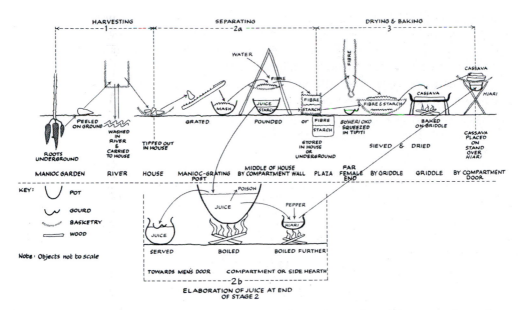

Figure 8.14 The manioc production cycle summed up diagrammatically with locations. The staple food that is turned into bread and beer, is poisonous in its raw form (Christine Hugh-Jones 1979).

in a line, coca and snuff being passed down by the headman. Women may occupy an outer circle, but they usually retreat to bed before the men.[16]

Eating rituals and sharing of food are indicative of social relationships, and the Tukanoans' gender division in food production has far-reaching consequences. As noted earlier, men bring meat and fish from the forest, and sometimes also grubs and insects or fruit, while women grow and prepare the staple manioc for bread and beer in their gardens, taking on all the work apart from initial clearing of the forest. The preparation of the initially poisonous manioc tubers through stages of peeling, grating, and cooking is laborious and time-consuming, but the supply is more constant and predictable than the men's hunting, and can be relied on when hunger threatens.[17] The men lead a predominantly communal life with other men, but the women when not in their compartments are busy in their manioc gardens, which are owned and worked strictly by family. Cooking and preparation of meals, all by women, operates at a family level within separate compartments, but eating is ideally a communal affair in the centre of the house, men being served before women and children. The meal combines male fish or meat with female manioc bread, spiced with chilli pepper which has explicitly sexual connotations. The sharing of food thus unites male and female principles, hunting and agriculture, combining their economic production from periphery to centre, and uniting the community. Everyone must contribute, and family piles of cooked bread are laid out in public space outside compartment doors. Everyone knows who contributed what to the communal meal, and excessive private consumption is disapproved of.[18]

It being forbidden to marry within the maloca community, wives are found from other malocas which may be some distance away and even speak a different language, so women relocate to join their husbands.[19] There can also be a reciprocal arrangement involving the double marriage of brother and sister, in which case a compartment loses a daughter as it gains a daughter-in-law. Just as nuclear families come together in a maloca, so malocas come together in intermarrying sets to define a larger territory and social network. Although minor informal visits occur often between community members, more essential formal interactions are organized every few weeks. The commonest type is a ritual dance called 'Food-giving House', in which the territory of the maloca is reinterpreted to frame relations between residents and outsiders. The use of the word 'house' in the naming of such rituals shows the degree to which building, group and event are identified, just as in European life we talk about schools and clubs doing things.

Without a calendar or a defined week, the dance is usually arranged at three or four days' notice starting with a decision by the host leader and the delivery of an oral invitation to the guests at one or more other malocas. This defines a named sequence of days for host women to brew manioc beer and for their guests to prepare the offerings of male food that they must bring: hunted meat or fish. The ritual beer is fermented in a hollowed-out log at the centre of the house called a 'beer canoe', (Figure 8.13) that symbolizes not only the means of transport between communities but also mythical transitions such as the arrival of the ancestors and the departure of the dead, buried in canoe coffins.[20] The guests arrive in the late afternoon, and after dark they chant and dance with the hosts on the plaza in front of the house. They do not enter, but sleep in temporary shelters nearby. The next morning they are allowed to enter the house and do so with much ceremony, presenting the food they have brought to the hosts. Dancing begins within the house, and continues all day and night, only ending at dawn, so the normal daily cycle of time is broken.[21] The guests remain towards the front, while the hosts move to and from the rear to serve them, symbolically taking the female role. As beer is drunk the initial formality breaks down amid hilarity:

> Initially only guests dance, but, by the end, hosts and guests sit together, dance together and progress from formal chanting between opposed groups to informal banter and raucous laughter between undifferentiated individuals. This progressive effacement of formality and separation between hosts and guests, kin and affines, culminates in a communal meal. The smoked meat or fish is served up with home-baked manioc bread to everyone present so that the territorial group, made up of neighbouring houses, now presents itself as a single commensal 'family', the guests acting like a meat-providing 'husband' and the hosts as a bread-baking 'wife' … Not surprisingly, the house itself is sometimes spoken about as a woman: the rounded rear end is her head, the front entrance is her vagina, and the cavernous interior is her womb.[22]

He House

If Food-giving House is the most frequent type of social ritual, it is also part of a whole cycle of such rituals which take place across the year, culminating in the annual initiation cult called *He* House, which is timed by the occurrence of certain fruits and the presence of the Pleiades star cluster on the horizon.[23] This is essentially a male ritual, so use of the male third person singular would be appropriate, but the name *He* follows the local language and refers particularly to the set of sacred musical instruments which are the main cult objects. These are made of paxiuba palm and consist of flutes and trumpets of various sizes named after birds, animals, or stars in accordance with myth. Regarded as eternal heirlooms, they are kept hidden in the river mud near the landing stage when not in use. Being male, columnar, phallic and homologous with the house's main columns, they are dangerous to women and children, who must never see them, even if they cannot help hearing the music. The *He* instruments represent the ancestors and the world of myth, resurrected to speak once a year when they are withdrawn from the river, prepared, played, and shown to the initiates as bearers of the essential secret knowledge.[24]

The whole ritual takes four days and nights, including initial phases of separation and final rites of reincorporation, though for the initiates the assumption of their new role takes much longer. Typically boys from several malocas are transported into manhood together, and the process is led by a powerful and experienced shaman who makes contact with the world of spirits and ancestors. He is supported by elders, who don feather ornaments and lead parts of the dance, and by senior chanters, who choreograph and control the sung unfolding of myth. Before the ritual, the maloca is prepared by scrupulous checking of compartment screens, sealing of potential peepholes, and installation of the screen door to close the female end. A special enclosure is constructed for the shamans at the front end just inside the door, placed on the right with respect to the headman as he looks back across the space. At the end of the ritual, another enclosure is created on the opposite side for the initiates. The male front end of the maloca during *He* House is regarded as the realm of the ancestors, and most if not all ritual activities depend on the central axis, ordered by relative position between the male and female ends and according to whether they are inward or outward facing.

On the first day visitors arrive from other malocas and the home group make preparations, the men gathering with their guests on the plaza while the women behind are busy making beer. In the afternoon the men visit the waterside to retrieve and prepare the *He* instruments, replacing their soft sounding parts to make them work again. Within the maloca shamans prepare sacred coca and red paint. Ritual proceedings begin at dusk, when the young men arrive from the river playing the *He* instruments, and women and children must flee, but are later confined in the back of the house. The instruments are played round and round the maloca all night while a senior flute called Old Macaw is sounded in front of the façade. As a preparatory rite against disease, a shaman appears on the plaza with burning beeswax, fanning the spiritually powerful smoke in the four cardinal directions. Only the elders may enter the house, chanted in by the shamans, and there they carry on chanting, while the rest of the men chant all night long outside.

At dawn on the second day the *He* instruments are played into the house, and the women flee from the back. Players march twice around the circular dance path clockwise before parading down the central axis towards the door. Emerging outside, they circle the maloca again before turning back in, again circling twice around the dance path, and returning on axis to stop as the leader reaches the door. They put down the instruments on the right side edge of dance path, then sit as a group outside the shamans' enclosure. The elders sit in two groups on either side of the men's door. As morning wears on, a shaman hands round a sacred cigar and places sacred gourds of snuff and red paint in the middle of the house, materials used to anoint and decorate bodies. Once this is done, all go to bathe in the stream in the late morning and the *He* instruments are dipped in water to give them a drink. The party returns to the maloca and much beer is drunk while a chanting session is held. Two elders with crowns and

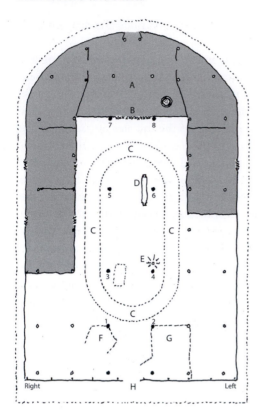

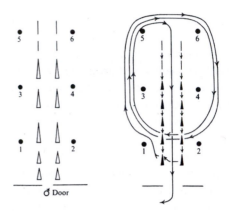

Figure 8.16 Choreographic plans relating movement of musicians to the principal columns of the maloca during *He* House: right shows the path taken by the parade of trumpets, and left the positions in which the instruments are laid down in pairs beside the axis. Column numbers are as in the adjacent plan (from Stephen Hugh-Jones 1979, appendix).

Figure 8.15 Plan of the house during *He* House, showing screen in place, and the added compartments for shamans and initiates. Key to plan: 1 to 8 numbered columns as in drawings above. A. Family compartments temporarily screened off; B. Main screen and gender divider; C. Dance path; D. Anaconda canoe with ritual beer; E. Light post; F. Shaman's enclosure; G. Initiates compartment; H. Men's door (redrawn by author after Stephen Hugh-Jones 1979).

Figure 8.17 The sign of the yagé mother figure marked on the threshold by a shaman during *He* House (Stephen Hugh-Jones 1979).

ornaments dance the senior Old Macaw flutes up and down the middle of house: only flute players are allowed the centre path.

Not until dusk on the second day are the initiates brought in. Their hair is cut, they are painted black, and they are carried in on elders' shoulders. Once inside, they are made to stand in front of the door, fingers linked, and are given shamanized berries to fortify them. They then crouch in a foetal position in front of the shaman's enclosure to receive tobacco and coca. A shaman prepares yagé, the most powerful hallucinogenic, outside the house. When he has finished he draws a yagé figure on the threshold (Figure 8.17) using the yagé bark pulp, and throws the remainder onto the roof. The *He* instruments are paraded again in front of the initiates, with much chanting. Women and children leave the house as the dangerous *He* power approaches its climax.

At midnight on the second day the leading shaman establishes himself on the centre line of the house between posts 5 and 6 (Figure 8.15) towards the female end, facing back towards the door, in order to distribute yagé and coca to all the men. They come forward to receive it then act out aggressive spearing as they return to their places. There is another parade of the *He* instruments. In the small hours of the morning of the third day two shamans chant, while the guardian of the initiates burns beeswax around the house followed by the *He* instruments, the small ones now played by initiates. The wax burning is a climax, and the women must leave the house to avoid inhaling the dangerous male smoke: as with the Sioux of the previous chapter, it is a link with the world beyond. Next two decorated elders play old flutes and the men line up in two groups with staves and whips. The flutes are played in the middle of the house, while others run in the side aisles acting out spearing and shouting 'I will kill you'. Two gourds filled with coca and snuff are placed between posts 1 and 2 (Figure 8.15) at the front of the house. A shaman takes whips to the female end, and all participants run up the side aisles making spearing gestures and stand in line before the shaman. They step forward to be ceremoniously whipped from foot to head, their hands aloft bearing a staff. All are whipped and yagé is served. Black paint is taken to the female end, where initiates paint each other. There is another parade of *He* instruments, which are played sporadically all morning. Some men sleep, but the young must remain awake.

At midday on the third day there is a further parade of *He* instruments around the house, and special ones called Old Callicebus Monkeys are played by shamans for the only time. Snuff is served. Just before dark the *He* instruments are paraded around the house in a routine called 'ending the dance' and 'going to make the tree bark low'. They go around the outside of the house twice, then enter the door on axis, the leaders halting just beyond the third set of posts. The pairs of players then form two lines facing each other. They swing their trumpets to the left, to the right, then straight out, blowing them in each position close to the ground. The whole line then walks to the men's end with the rearmost leading to repeat the swing action, then back to the female end and a repeat. Dividing into pairs they go around column 6 then twice clockwise round the dance path and back down the middle after circling column 5. As the leaders arrive at the men's door they do another triple swing in inverted form, starting with left, right, then centre. It is now dusk of the third day and once the *He* instruments have been removed from the house the exhausted participants are allowed to sleep. They move to the female end, since the male end is still dangerously occupied by *He* spirits. They lie on mats on the ground rather than in the usual hammocks, consistent with the prohibition of stools during *He* House for all apart from shamans.

At dawn on the fourth day the *He* instruments are brought out for the last time, the flutes being played up and down the house and the trumpets round and round the outside. Initiates are anointed with snuff and water, then in late morning all men go to the river to bathe, taking the *He* instruments with them. They consume emetic leaves and vomit to purge *He* material. At midday the women move all contents of the house temporarily to the front outside space for purification. The house is swept. Small fires of burning leaves are made outside its doorways. Bark wrappings are taken off the *He* instruments and they are returned and hidden. The shamans construct the compartment just left of the men's door (Figure 8.15) where the initiates will sleep as their rite of passage continues. It is placed at the extreme male end, and the boys are now allowed to sleep in hammocks. At dusk the long fast of the participants is broken with a small meal of female manioc. The use of stools is again permitted and the removal of the dividing screen reconnects the female end of the house, marking the point at which normal life is resumed.[25]

Symbolic context of the ritual: House as universe

This chronicle of events omits the content of the teaching and of the enactment of myth, as well as the complex symbolic attributes of the many artefacts and substances involved. The whole procedure concerns the passage of boys to manhood, symbolizing death as a child and rebirth as an adult, and involving the transmission of oral knowledge about the workings of the world, the origins of human beings and their technologies, the qualities and uses of plants and animals, the rules of morality and conduct and so on. The central role of the *He* instruments lies not only in providing the music for the ordered performance but that they represent in presence and in voice specific named ancestors, maintaining their power and temporarily bringing them to life, so providing evidence to validate the mythical knowledge. The instruments are regarded as physical survivals from a mythic past rather than as human artefacts, and they cannot be remade.[26] For the initiates, their presentation is an awesome exposure to the most holy of relics, and the sealing of the rear of the house to make sure that women cannot see them, as well as the regular flights of women and children out of the house during key stages of the ritual, are responses to the danger of their power. The house columns, male and homologous with the *He* instruments, also act as symbolic objects helping to sustain the ritual, defining the field in which dancing occurs. The maloca as a whole serves to locate all aspects of the ritual, which would be unthinkable without it. Furthermore, the house carries ideas about the organization of space which are universal for the Barasana. Their everyday world revolves entirely around a maloca. Neighbours also reside in malocas, spirits and ancestors in imaginary ones. The building type supplies a generic idea of house reapplicable to the world of myth and ancestors, and almost all the myths recorded by Stephen Hugh-Jones include mention of a house or manioc garden.[27] By the same token, ideas about mythical houses inform real ones, so much so that during ritual the two become magically entwined. As Stephen Hugh-Jones puts it:

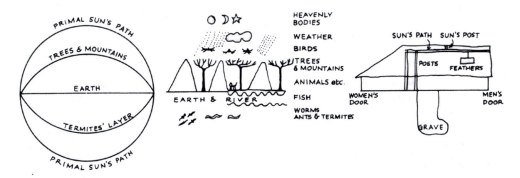

Figure 8.18 Diagrams of the vertical dimension as conceived by the Barasana, with the sun's reversed path through the underworld on the left, layers of sky events in the middle, and key vertical elements of the maloca on the right (Christine Hugh-Jones 1979).

The Barasana maloca is a microcosm of the universe itself: the roof is the sky, the house posts are the mountains that support the sky, and the floor-space is the earth. Malocas are conceptually, though not always actually, orientated along an east-west axis so that the men's door represents the Water Door in the east where the sun rises, and the women's door is the door in the west; the centre of the house is the Pirá-paraná area, the centre of the world. The earth is thought of as being bisected by a river running from west to east and conceptually the house, as a microcosm of the universe, is also bisected by a river. Thus, on a cosmic scale, there is only one house, the universe itself … In the beginning, this universe–house had no people inside. The anaconda ancestors … were the sons of the Primal Sun … The anaconda entered the World through the water door in the east, and from there swam upriver towards the west. He travelled up the Milk River to the Apaporis and thence to the Pirá paraná, the middle of the world. Undifferentiated and as yet not human, the head of the anaconda represented the top-ranking sib [brother] and its tail represented the lowest sib: the head was towards the west, the tail towards the east. On arrival at the centre of the earth the anaconda reversed its position so that its head now faced the east and its tail the west, and then it gave rise to human beings… These human beings were the *He*-people, whose names are those of the *He* instruments, and their order of emergence gave rise to the ranking of the different sibs.[28]

Conflation of the Amazon with the anaconda unites the main local landmark with the most impressive waterbound predator, and the meanderings of the river are like the movements of the giant snake. The leading mythical hero 'Manioc-stick Anaconda' adds the main food plant on which the Tukanoans depend both for their staple diet and for their ceremonial beer. The beer is brewed in an 'anaconda canoe' kept at the centre of the house and aligned with the imaginary river (Figure 8.13). Even more compellingly, the actions of the anaconda ancestor, who gave birth to the original *He* People, are acted out in time and space to bring the maloca to life. Stephen Hugh-Jones again:

The journey of the ancestor anaconda and its subsequent division into sons, the apical ancestors of the different sibs, is paralleled by the sequence of events at *He* House where, through the powers of the shamans, hallucinogenic drugs and contact with sacred ritual objects, the maloca becomes the universe and the people inside become the *He* People or first ancestors. The *He* instruments are taken from their hiding places under water in the forest. They are inert (dead), and outside the house and thus outside the world. The women and children are confined to the rear of the house so that an exclusively male society is brought about, just as in ancestral times there were no women. As the *He* enter the house they are played by a column of men, walking two abreast, the front of the column representing the head of the anaconda and the rear its tail. They enter through the men's door, equivalent to the Water Door in the east through which the anaconda ancestor entered the world. The column proceeds from the men's door towards the women's door, from east to west, as the anaconda swam upriver from the east. Once inside, the column goes around the edge of the house and then comes down the middle from the rear end, stopping as the head reaches the men's door. The men then put their instruments down on the floor in two parallel rows lying end to end up the middle of the house and representing the anaconda lying on the middle of the earth. The head of the column now faces east with its tail to the west, as did the anaconda at the end of its journey. Then the column is broken up and the instruments dispersed, just as the anaconda's body was divided into the component sib ancestors or sons.[29]

The choreography of the dance, if one might so call it, enacts the idea of the myth, but mainly in the two dimensions of forward and back, left and right, using the maloca's flat floor and recordable in a plan (Figure 8.16)[30] But after so much consideration of the main axis and of centre versus periphery, there remains the conception of the vertical dimension: up and down, above and below, and the way spatial organization reflects Tukanoan ideas about the cosmos. Phenomenal experience suggests various layers above the ground (Figure 8.18), starting with animals on the surface then looking up to trees and mountains. Next come birds possessing the freedom of the air, then clouds and winds, and finally the heavenly bodies. Beneath ground level are the fish in the river and the termites and worms, then the graves of the dead, but deeper layers can be imagined. Living in a boundless forest on a seemingly flat earth, it seems that the sun vanishes in the west to rise after the same interval in the east, so it must travel west–east in the underworld. In myth underground layers are imagined symmetrical with those above, and mythical ancestors engage with the sun's reverse journey. Thus in the story of Manioc-stick Anaconda, which Tukanoans cite as the authority about the layers of their universe, the hero falls into a pit trap and on through to the underworld landing on the bank of a river where Moon and Morning Star pass by, followed by Sun in his canoe. Manioc-stick Anaconda joins Sun in his canoe at midday in the underworld, while it is midnight in the earth above. They travel together to a landing stage in the east, where Sun alights to begin his daily journey across the sky, his canoe being rowed back downstream by animal attendants to collect him from the west at dusk. Manioc-stick Anaconda vaults up to the next layer up to join the Termite People's dance, and is helped across the underworld river by Tapir shaman, returning to the earth's surface with the help of flying termites.[31]

Shamans, as the ritual experts in contact with the cosmos, can traverse the vertical layers of this imagined cosmos. Associated with the sun, they are said to traverse the central beam of the house from east to west during the *He* House ritual.[32] In doing so they pass the sun post, a short vertical post in the centre of the house above the spine beam, which celebrates the moment when the sun is vertically ahead. They wear feather crowns associated with birds, which are kept with other ceremonial equipment in a feather box, suspended in the middle of the house over the right front male corner of the space between the four central columns. In periods of inter-group warfare this object was considered the key prize. In contrast with it, the *He* instruments hidden underwater are beneath ground level, buried ancestors linked with the river and the anaconda. The jaguar, the largest land predator, is also prominent in myth, and in the maloca of the neighbouring Desana the three pairs of main columns and cross-beams are called the three red jaguars and decorated as such, while the central ridge beam represents the Sun Shaman, and is thought of as a ladder interpenetrating cosmic levels.[33] The variation in mythical reference here is no surprise, but the concept of verticality remains, as does the emphasis on the phallic bones of the primary structure.

Verticality of house and cosmos in theory is linked with relative height in practice. Passage from low to high comes with maturity, and the word for initiates during *He* House means people from another level. The initiates are carried across the threshold on the shoulders of elders, emphasizing the cosmic connection between physical passage into the house and their rite of passage, the last journey as a child through the most important door between outside and inside worlds. Once inside, they crouch close to the ground in a foetal position. This reading of the vertical dimension explains why only shamans can sit on stools during the ritual while others sit on the ground, and why when finally allowed to rest, everybody lies on a mat rather than occupying the usual hammocks, though once the ritual is over the initiates are immediately allowed hammocks again. Stephen Hugh-Jones claims that even foods are height related, for the ants and termites first given to initiates come from the ground, as do manioc tubers. They progress to small fish from beneath the river surface, to small land animals, and finally to larger ones.[34]

Conclusions and comparison

Barasana mythology is loaded with reference to plants and animals, which serve as prey, food, and medicine, establishing a body of knowledge as well geared to sustainable life in the rainforest as that of the Aboriginal People to the Australian desert.[35] At the same time the women's manioc gardens exhibit both the burgeoning order of an agriculture and a sophisticated exploitation of food crops. The maloca provides a remarkably pure example of the house that is at once habitation, temple and meeting place, a visible concentration of human culture within a wild world.[36] It clearly articulates social relations, gender roles, and the relativity of public relationships with outsiders. It also defines a relation to the outside world through its orientation and deference to the river, and although there is less reference to the four directions than with the Sioux of the previous chapter, this idea does emerge at certain crucial moments, as does the implicitly triaxial system of six directions present in both peoples' cosmologies.[37]

Once the complexity of the maloca's spatial order is understood, it seems so specific that it could hardly be otherwise. The public side is strongly differentiated by the river link, plaza, and decorated façade, whose iconography reflects the anaconda myth. Principles of centre and periphery and of linear axial development, already discussed in earlier chapters, are not merely present but dominant and definitive. The gabled section produces not only a weatherproof roof but the central climax essential to all ritual. This depends in turn on the dominance of the five pairs of primary columns,[38] which mark the founding of the maloca and then define its sacred centre. Gable, roof and columns together produce the bilateral symmetry that gives the maloca both its front and its creature-like identity, which can take a varying androgynous form.

If traditional architectural history has tended to pursue single definitive readings of form and iconography as if that were the end of the matter, the Hugh-Joneses show that the maloca sustains contrasting readings in which it may be predominantly female, predominantly male, or a representation of the cosmos, depending on the ritual context. This multiple reading is no surprise considering the dominance of the house in Barasana experience, the lack of alternative spatial types, and the need for an oral culture to find mnemonics within buildings and everyday artefacts.[39] Humans are strongly disposed towards metaphorical thinking, seeing one thing in terms of another, and developing classification systems that readily adapt the order of one field to reapplication within another.[40] We learn the world through homology and analogy, so local buildings and objects are ready reference points in exchanging ideas and explaining to children the way things are. In the absence of texts and other media they have a relatively greater importance.

Study of the ritual process has further shown how movement patterns of parades and dances mesh with the organization of spaces, reinforcing territorial definitions and marking thresholds. Dance sequences underline the difference of inside from outside, and even enact through their choreography some significant spatial movements which are remembered and understood in relation to myth. As with the Aboriginal circumcision rites of Chapter 6, the representations in dance are no mere secondary repetitions of mythical material vested in other forms or records, but constitute the primary form, learned, remembered and repeated by participants as bodily practices. The dances must have somewhere to 'take place' because actions and positions must be coordinated, and as new players are initiated into the process, so every spatial demonstration becomes an exchange of ideas. The organization of the building sets the stage, while the performance supplies a reading of the building's meaning. Since neither dance nor maloca conform to written rules or records, the dancer/chanter in charge or the new maloca headman is free to reinterpret the form of the dance or building each time, and even if variations are not consciously sought, the selective and reconstructive nature of human memory will produce them. The common fund of knowledge is in continuous evolution, without anchor in a permanent memory store, so the longevity of buildings and artefacts such as the *He* instruments has a special role in providing temporal continuity, as well as in helping to define and share ideas about the nature of things.

A new topic that emerges with the maloca to be pursued in more detail in later studies is the matter of building rituals. Information is scarce, but we know that the building process is organized by the headman and his brothers, and starts with the six pairs of male columns which define the axis and central sacred space. The wider community is then involved in the cladding, and the new house is inaugurated with a feast. The meanings of house elements are thus established during the construction process and associated with particular groups.

Notes

1   Stephen Hugh-Jones 1979, Christine Hugh-Jones 1979.

2   That it has some historical depth is shown by the quotation from A. R. Wallace describing an almost identical maloca in 1889: see Carsten and Hugh-Jones 1995, pp. 227–8.

3   Theories and fashions in interpretation change, but so do the people studied and their culture. This means that we are always dealing with narratives about narratives and cannot eliminate the bias of interpretation. I have necessarily selected from the Hugh-Joneses' rich account the things that I find spatially significant without attempting to re-theorize their position.

4   Stephen Hugh-Jones 1979, pp. 29–30.

5   Reichel-Dolmatoff 1971, pp. 106–7.

6   There are both circular villages and circular houses in the region, for example the village of the Bororo and round house of the Waiwai.

7   Carsten and Hugh-Jones 1995, pp. 238–9.

8   That is to say that a flat ceiling is unthinkable, for without the added central height many avian aspects of the rituals could not be played out, and the cosmological readings of the house, explained later, would be insupportable. The 42° is deduced from photographic evidence and reflects our way of understanding, not theirs, lacking geometry and instruments. Presumably the

house is measured out in paces on the ground and the heights with paces along the constituent tree trunks.

9   Wallace's description of 1889 quoted in Carsten and Hugh-Jones 1995, p. 227 specifically mentions this, but the malocas of the adjacent Desana, equally differentiated between front and rear, are reported as square both ends, see plan in Reichel-Dolmatoff 1971, p. 105.

10   The main columns may also be decorated, typically with Anaconda motifs, see Carsten and Hugh-Jones 1995, p. 242. On the painting of façades among the adjacent Desana see Reichel-Dolmatoff 1971, plate 3, and the numerous text references to body painting.

11   The red moon is said to bleed, and this blood will contaminate everything in the house that is not removed during the danger and replaced later. Similar ritual purification applies to family compartments at childbirth, see Christine Hugh-Jones 1979, pp. 123–5.

12   This would have been a wonderful example to support Gottfried Semper's theory of cladding had he known of it.

13   Family members who die are all buried beneath the house in coffins made from canoes, a woman next to the door of her compartment, but the leader is the one buried on axis in the centre, reflecting the social hierarchy, see Christine Hugh-Jones 1979, pp. 109–10.

14   Christine Hugh-Jones 1979, p. 228.

15   For detail on the compartment see Christine Hugh-Jones 1979, p .48.

16   Ibid., p. 204.

17   For a full description of manioc growing and processing see Christine Hugh-Jones 1979, pp. 174–92.

18   Christine Hugh-Jones 1979, pp. 50–2. Stephen Hugh-Jones 1979, pp. 30–1.

19   Kinship structures and marriage rules are a complex technical aspect of anthropology, the pursuit of which would overburden this presentation. For a detailed exposition see Christine Hugh-Jones 1979, pp. 76–106.

20   Christine Hugh-Jones 1979, pp. 206 and 207.

21   Stephen Hugh-Jones 1979, p. 34.

22   Carsten and Hugh-Jones 1995, pp. 232–3.

23   Stephen Hugh-Jones 1979, pp. 65–7.

24   Ibid., pp. 134–62.

25   This very reduced account is derived from chapters 4, 5 and 6 of Stephen Hugh-Jones 1979, selecting for spatial aspects. Hugh-Jones gives much more detail both of the practices and of the roles of the participants, also the meanings of the different *He* instruments. He includes a chronological chart of the ritual on pp. 74–5.

26   Stephen Hugh-Jones 1979, p. 143.

27   Ibid., pp. 262–308. Among thirty-three translated narratives only eight stories fail to mention a maloca or its manioc garden, though most of these houses are the abodes of mythical characters.

28   Ibid., pp. 151–2.

29   Ibid., p. 153.

30   The words we are obliged to use can be deceptive. Choreography as a taught skill requires some form of notation which then seems to remove its essence to paper, and the same can be said of the drawn plan. While these are powerful aids to our understanding, we must not forget that a dance can be learned, remembered, and repeated as a dance, pure practice.

31   Christine Hugh-Jones 1979, pp. 257–66.

32   Stephen Hugh-Jones 1979, p. 220.

33   Reichel-Dolmatoff, 1971, p. 106.

34   Stephen Hugh-Jones 1979, p. 221–2.

35   Oscar Forero of the University of London produced an enlightening conference paper in 1999 about Tukanoan agroforestry practices and their link to myth and ritual from a sustainability viewpoint: see *The March of the Manikins* on the Yale website: http://research.yale.edu/CCR/environment/papers/forero.pdf

      Forero O. A. (2001), 'The March of the Manikins: Agroforestry practices and spiritual dancing in Northwest Amazonia' in Conference Proceedings, Conservation and Sustainable Development: Comparative Perspectives, Center for Comparative Research, University of Yale, New Haven http://research.yale.edu/CCR/environment/papers/forero.pdf (accessed30 January 2016).

36   The maloca is also imagined as a house for spirits, for example the death house described in Christine Hugh-Jones 1979, p. 112.

37   The most explicit reference to fourness in ritual is the occasion in *He* House when the shaman on the plaza 'fans the smoke in the four cardinal directions to send away illness, disease and shamanic attack'. Stephen Hugh-Jones 1979, p. 73. The idea of a triaxial system is explored in detail in Christine Hugh-Jones 1979, pp. 238–74 with diagrams.

38   Six if you count those within the round end, but they are beyond the ritual space and behind the women's partition.

39   Reference to a recent Hugh-Jones paper and the significance of baskets for mythology and counting. The male initiates are taught how to weave circular baskets at the same time as learning the tribal mythology, and are obliged by the technique of the process to count the threads.

40   See Lakoff and Johnson 1980.

CHAPTER 9
THE DOGON OF MALI

Figure 9.1 Dogon man sitting outside a *ginna*, the patriarchal house (photograph by Peter Hübner 2005).

Figure 9.2 Dogon village (Songo) from above, showing typical distribution of flat-roofed houses and thatched granaries (photograph by Peter Hübner 2005).

The Dogon of Mali remained in relative obscurity until the twentieth century, living in a remote and arid inland area of West Africa that was eventually colonized by the French. Once discovered, they won early fame among African peoples for their carvings and dancing masks, which influenced early twentieth century artists, and their organic-looking mud-built buildings have long been enjoyed by enthusiasts of vernacular architecture, given a particular boost in mid-twentieth century by the Dutch modernist architect Aldo van Eyck.[1] Understanding of its significance was aided by the detailed account of their culture by the anthropologist Marcel Griaule, who worked with his student and companion Germaine Dieterlen and various other assistants from the 1930s, visiting the Dogon, observing them, questioning them, and recording their way of life. Not until 1947 did the elders of the villages of Ogol permit exposure of their religious secrets, deputing the task to the old blind hunter and sage Ogotemmêli, who agreed in what turned out to be the last year of his life, to tell Griaule what he knew. Interviews took place over thirty-three days, which transcribed and translated became the basis of Griaule's famous book *Dieu d'Eau* published in 1948, and released in English as *Conversations with Ogotemmêli* in 1965.[2] Griaule made bold claims for the status of the Dogon cosmology and its ethical and philosophical sophistication, which, if questionable in places, at least helped dislodge earlier patronizing assumptions about 'the primitive' and the limitations of oral cultures.[3] The physical and symbolic descriptions of house and village given by Ogotemmêli and recorded by Griaule are the starting point for this chapter, setting physical

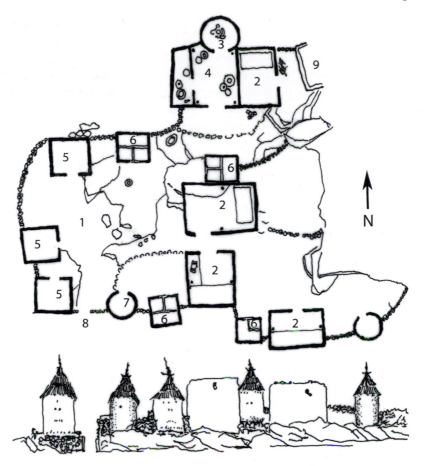

Figure 9.3 Group of buildings in Ireli after a measured survey by Wolfgang Lauber. Key: 1. Main courtyard; 2. Dwelling with bed; 3. Kitchen; 4. Storage; 5. Maize store; 6. Granary; 7. Ritual objects store; 8. Entrance; 9. Neighbour (author's redrawing after published plan and elevation in Lauber 1998).

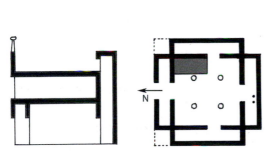

Figure 9.4 *Ginna* or patriarchal house as presented by Griaule 1947. It has the formal front with ancestral niches shown in Figures 9.6–9.9, and the section shows the columns on the parapet which once received libations. The grey object is the marital bed (author's drawing after Griaule 1965).

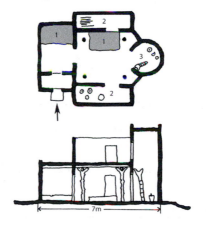

Figure 9.5 Normal family house. Key: 1. Bed; 2. Storage; 3. Kitchen (author's drawing after Fritz Morgenthaler in Jencks and Baird 1970, p. 198).

space within a more general account of the order of things as sustained by Dogon myth. Let us start with the family house.

Built by hand using mud or mud bricks, often on irregular escarpments so as to leave the good land below free for agriculture, Dogon houses can appear at first merely amorphous clusters of rooms and courtyards following the contingencies of the terrain and a serial addition of cells. Each house generally has a courtyard as the main outdoor room and workspace, enclosed by a string of granaries, and narrow streets wind between them in a fairly dense conglomeration. But despite the irregularity a recognizable house type emerges – at least in the eastern part of the Bandiagara escarpment – whose repeated form is recognizable in high-level photographs.[4] The relatively recent plan and photo of Ireli from Wolfgang Lauber show three such houses, each with a central square room surrounded by narrower flanking rooms, the one at the far end being circular (Figures 9.2, 9.3 and 9.5). These are the standard family houses, but there are also larger ones called *ginna* with two storeys and a ceremonial front, which belong to the patriarch of a family group. This is the type described by Ogotemmêli as it applies to his own house, and because the ancestral house is the model for the other. His description is somewhat ideal, and Griaule idealizes it further with a reductive plan and section drawings (Figure 9.4) which show a square main room surrounded by four narrower roomlets. The north is the entrance lobby and the south the kitchen, with a pair of stones marking the hearth. The side roomlets are mainly used as stores, but all four roomlets add insulation and thermal mass as buffer zones to protect the living space from afternoon heat and early morning cold.[5] As the mud is weak, the walls and flat roof are built around a supporting structure of wooden beams held up by four internal columns. The upper floor, accessible via a notched tree trunk ladder in the kitchen, is a walled and mud-floored terrace surrounded on three sides by further roomlets, the front one being the primary granary. The open terrace is used for sleeping in hot periods and for drying crops safely in the sun. Symbolically associated with the sky, it also figures in funeral ceremonies, when the householder's relatives climb up in mock battles, firing guns into the air.[6] The central room downstairs is the focus of family life, with a built-in bed on the east side where children should be conceived, for the house is above all a vessel of procreation. The child must be born in the centre of the house, delivered from its mother who is seated on a stool facing south. It takes possession of its soul as its four limbs first touch the earth of the ground floor.[7] For Ogotemmêli, the whole house symbolizes the union of the couple:

> Inside the house, the several rooms represent caves of this world inhabited by men. The vestibule, which belongs to the master of the house, represents the male partner of the couple, the outside door being his sexual organ. The big central room is the domain and symbol of the woman; the store rooms each side are her arms, and the communicating door her sexual parts. The central room and the store rooms together represent the woman lying on her back with outstretched arms, the door open and the woman ready for intercourse. The room at the back which contains the hearth and looks out onto the flat roof, shows the breathing of the woman, who lies in the central room under the ceiling which is the symbol of a man, its beams representing his skeleton: their breath finds its outlet through the opening above. The four upright poles (feminine number) are the couple's arms, those of the woman supporting the man who rests his own on the ground.[8]

Figure 9.6 Ogotemmêli's own house (drawing by Claire Blundell Jones after a photograph by in Griaule 1948).

Figure 9.7 Another *ginna* with offerings to ancestors (photograph by Peter Hübner 2005).

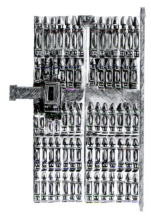

Figure 9.9 Upper door from a *ginna* leading to a primary granary where seeds are kept for resowing. The figures on the latch represent the original human couple and the others the ancestors (drawing by Claire Blundell Jones after example in the Musée de l'Homme, Paris).

Figure 9.10 Plan of a typical courtyard with 1. Family house; 2. Granaries; 3. Storage building and 4. Adjacent house (author's drawing after Fritz Morgenthaler in Jencks and Baird 1969).

Figure 9.8 A surviving but badly eroded *ginna* (photograph by Peter Hübner in 2005).

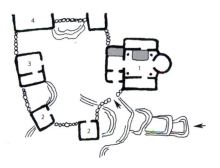

Ogotemmêli's instructions for the use of the conjugal bed within the house are surprisingly explicit. The couple must lie on their sides with their heads to the north, the man facing west and the woman facing east, which is also the convention for burials, and 'they never lie in any other position'.[9] Under the bed are kept the seeds for next year's crop except for the cotton seeds, which are placed on the lintel of the inner door, the threshold representative of the woman's vagina. Human fertility is linked with the fertility of the fields:

> In sexual intercourse the man is sowing: he is like a Water Spirit causing fertilising rain to fall on the earth and on the woman, on the sown seeds.[10]

Symmetrical about its central axis, which is also the way in and out, the *ginna* has a front which, in contrast with its plain back and sides, is loaded with symbolic value (Figures 9.6–9.8). Ogotemmêli's threshold was his customary sitting place during Griaule's interviews, and above it on axis lay the door to the family's primary granary on the first floor, where the seeds of the *ginna's* primary field were kept, the granary 'acting as the depository of the spiritual principles of sex of the grains from the harvest until the sowing of the following year'.[11] To either side were open niches arranged repetitively in vertical lines, and rising from the parapet were the remains of columns which had been constructed as altars to the ancestors on which libations could be poured. Ogotemmêli again presents an idealized version:

> The front wall with its eight rows of ten niches represents the eight ancestors and their descendants, numerous as the fingers on their hands. The ancestors occupy the niches in order of birth beginning with the highest row. The niches should never be closed, for the ancestors need to breathe the outdoor air … The circular holes in the pediment, ten in number like the fingers of the hand, are occupied by swallows' nests, the poultry yard of the ancestors … The eight small columns on the top of the wall are the altars of the ancestors, beginning with the first ancestors on the left. In a narrow house with only two or three vertical rows of niches the columns are fewer. In a wider house there may be ten or more but the traditional number is eight, one for each ancestor.[12]

Monserrat Marti's Dogon ethnography of 1957 confirms the importance of the altars to the ancestors, one of which should theoretically be provided for each male forebear. They were places where offerings could be placed in pots or libations be poured, and there were also shrines inside the house. Ritual respect for the ancestors was shown twice a year, but offerings were also made in cases of illness, war, quarrel, a coming journey, or even to assure a good hunt.[13] The emphasis of the number eight in the façade description reflects the identification in Dogon myth of eight ancestral groups stretching back to the primordial couple, and the use of eight as a general classifier. The ancestors are further represented on the carved surface of the wooden granary door, ideally as eight rows of eighty figures, while the door latch carries carved figures of the guardian and his wife, sometimes with the primordial couple added above. Again the number given is ideal, for surviving examples usually show a smaller number of figures, such as the ten rows of seven shown in Figure 9.9. The ordinary houses as shown in Figures 9.5 and 9.10 follow essentially the same plan form as the *ginna* except that the kitchen at the rear end is round – therefore more head-like – and that they lack a ceremonial front, often having side entrances to the vestibule instead of the axial one. This makes good sense once the hierarchy is understood. The patriarchal extended Dogon family led by the senior male could possess several houses in a group, so that for example one lower Ogol family in 1935 had sixteen houses in which lived fifty persons,[14] but it centred on a single *ginna* regarded as the ancestral seat, and all the structures were linked with the family by inalienable right.[15] It was therefore appropriate for the senior house to be the site of memory, worship, and celebration, declared by its façade and axial layout. Rising further in the hierarchy, a yet more elaborate version is found in the house of the Hogon, local chief priest and leader (Figures 9.11 and 9.12), which is equally axial and symmetrical with an additional wide bedroom behind instead of the kitchen, adding to the spatial layers. Its plan symbolism 'is the image of a man who is seated with his arms at his sides, thus representative of [the God] Amma himself in his stability and permanence',[16] and the principal altar within the house lies in the position of the right hand. The Hogon's house has a more elaborate façade than the standard *ginna*, with special kinds of mural painting, and faces a courtyard with an external altar and 'primordial pond'. In sum, all these house-types have an axial, symmetrical and orientated form based on a central room, but the *ginna* and the Hogon's house heading the hierarchy have elaborated fronts, further stressing the axis and main threshold.

Architectural surveys of Dogon villages show that almost every house has a courtyard where most of the daytime work is done and much life is lived. The conversations with Ogotemmêli hardly mention these courtyards, though they obtrude into descriptions of how the meetings take place. The courtyard is family space, and in Griaule and Dieterlen's later work *The Pale*

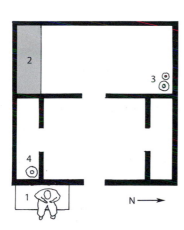

Figure 9.11 Plan of the Hogon's house. Key: 1. Bench where the Hogon presides; 2. His bed; 3. His water supply; 4. Main altar to Amma (author's drawing after Griaule and Dieterlen 1986).

Figure 9.12 Façade of the Hogon's house (drawing by Claire Blundell Jones after a photograph in Griaule 1948).

Fox it is even called 'the meeting place of souls and forces'.[17] Its outline is defined by mud walls and a chain of granaries, which though smaller than the houses are more distinctive with their domed or conical thatched roofs, so that the positive forms of a village seen from above are its houses and granaries, the negatives its streets and courtyards. Surprisingly little is said in Griaule's books about thresholds, but Marti notes that at times of death and birth the main doorway to the house is marked respectively by an added pair of branches leaning together or a pair of faggot bundles, both signs that the house is in transition.[18]

The granary

Before substantial contact with the outside world, Dogon life depended on grain, which would grow quickly in the wet season to be eaten in the dry, so the safe preservation of a good harvest was paramount. It was attended by ritual procedures too numerous to list, and the eight different kinds of seed involved figure prominently throughout Dogon myth.[19] There were several granaries to a household (Figure 9.13), enclosing its courtyard like towers on a town wall, their small high access doors reached by ladder and facing inward. They often belonged to different family members, for traditionally each man or woman had their own, and polygyny was practised.[20] Lifted clear of the ground on mud-coated wooden bases against damp and vermin, they were bowl-like containers, much smaller than the house and accurately square or sometimes round, but their detached forms and conical thatched roofs made them visually prominent, and they often had added decoration with moulded reliefs. Stored grain signified health and wealth, and Griaule reports that even looking into someone else's granary was considered grossly intrusive. Granaries were internally partitioned, traditionally in eight sections: four quarters in the base and another four shelves around the upper part (Figure 9.14). This was to accommodate the eight crops given by the God Amma to the eight Dogon ancestors: in the base little millet, white millet, dark millet, and female millet; in the upper part beans, sorrel, rice and digitaria. The fourfold division suggests a connection of grain with the cardinal points, which is further demonstrated in the practice reported by Griaule of the priest throwing millet seeds towards the four cardinal points during rituals connected with sowing.[21] In the centre of the base of each granary between the deposits of grain was placed a large spherical pot containing oil from another crop, the fruit of the lannea acida tree, surmounted by two smaller pots (Figure 9.15). The large pot, according to Ogotemmêli, represented the womb of the granary, reading the whole thing as a woman lying on her back with her legs in the air, the compartments of grain being her eight internal organs. During the conversations, Ogotemmêli also described an ideal 'flying granary' which represents the Dogon world system, and Griaule sketched it for his book (Figure 9.14). Like an inverted basket – the physical model offered by Ogotemmêli to explain it – it rises from a circular base to a square top, the circle representing the sun and the square the sky. Running up the middle of each side is a stair. It faces a cardinal point, is associated with a planet or a star(s), and contains a group of earthly creatures. North couples the Pleiades with men and fishes, south Orion's belt with domestic animals, east Venus with the birds, west the 'Long-tailed star' with insects, plants, and wild animals.

Each step of each stair is allotted some particular species or group in an orderly series, so the imagined flying granary (in the later book also called an ark) becomes a taxonomy

Figure 9.13 Two granaries with traditional decorations (drawing by Claire Blundell Jones after a photograph in Griaule 1948).

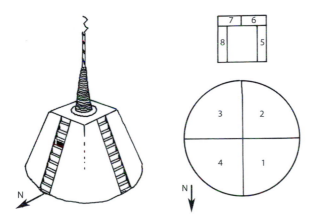

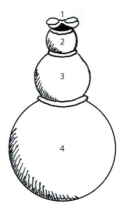

Figure 9.14 Redrawn versions of Griaule's diagrams of the mythical flying granary and its eight internal plan divisions with the places for the eight varieties of grain (author's drawing after diagrams in Griaule 1965).

Figure 9.15 Arrangement of triple vessels placed at the centre of a granary, symbolizing: 1. Twins; 2. Purity; 3. Fetus; 4. Mother (author's drawing after diagram in Griaule 1965).

identifying the creatures of the world, including man. The lower steps of the north and human side are occupied by Bozo, the earlier inhabitants of the region whose livelihood was fishing: the sixth step is the granary's entrance, and the ones above it remain empty.[22] The interior, like a real granary, is divided in two fourfold layers to bear the eight seeds. Like the first chapter of Genesis, the story of the flying granary offers a mythical system that divides groups and assigns an order of progression, while relating them to cardinal directions.[23] Uncertain of some details, Ogotemmêli consulted other elders to fill in the gaps, and when asked by Griaule where animals yet unmentioned could be, he replied that they shared steps with those already ascribed, lining up behind them. Griaule asked how there could be space enough for all, and Ogotemmêli replied that of course they were symbolic, so any number could be accommodated: this despite the fact that he had given the celestial granary dimensions in cubits: twenty in diameter, eight at the top of each side, ten for the height.[24] Being blind and lacking recourse to texts or drawings, the old man could only use a battered basket to explain the basic geometry, but the imagined granary was for him a mnemonic for the world order, defined by its geometry in imaginary space, and populated systematically according to direction and numerical order. The imagined space parallels the tricks used by modern performers of memory feats, who associate items for recall with particular progressions in buildings. But perhaps it works both ways, for imaginary architecture can generate a symbolic loading to be reapplied to real buildings.

The village

Maps and aerial photographs of Dogon villages seem organic and disorderly, even if certain building types and public spaces can be discerned, and even though there is an evident 'grain' repeating the same kinds of shapes at the same kinds of sizes. Hardly evident at all, though, is the idealized concept of village claimed by Ogotemmêli, drawn by Griaule, and much reproduced since (Figure 9.17). Had it been invented by the anthropologist it would indeed be a tall order, but as a reading supplied by Ogotemmêli, it joins the ideal house and flying granary as another exemplar and mnemonic of how things should be.

> The village should extend from north to south like the body of a man lying on his back. Lower Ogol is almost correct. The head is the council house, built on the chief square, which is the symbol of the primal field. On the north side of the square is the smithy, as was that of the bringer of civilization. To the east and west are houses for menstruating women; they are round like wombs and represent the hands of the village. The large family houses are its chest and belly; the communal altars at the south of the village are its feet. The stones on which the fruit of the Lannea acida is crushed, placed in the centre of the village, represent its female sexual parts. Beside them should be set the foundation altar, which is its male sex organ, but out of respect for the women this altar is erected outside the walls.[25]

The chief square (*place principale* in French) was the main place for social events, including the cycles of masked dances which marked the turn of the seasons, demonstrated the agricultural calendar, and even celebrated the Sigui, the sixty-year religious cycle dedicated to the God Amma that was shared from village to village. Ogotemmêli claims that:

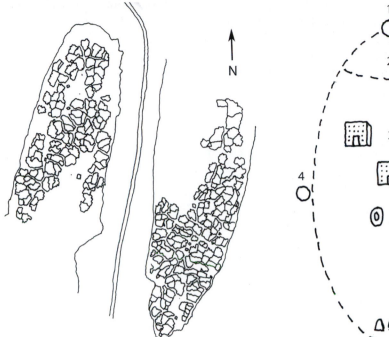

Figure 9.16 Map of Upper (left) and Lower Ogol (author's drawing after Griaule and Dieterlen 1986).

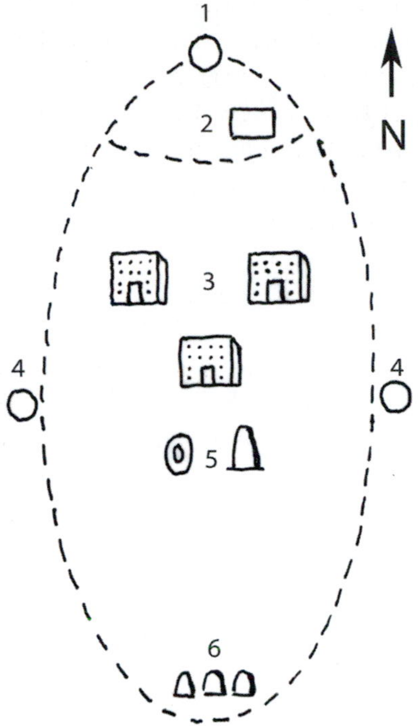

Figure 9.17 Ideal village plan symbolic of a body, as reported by Griaule 1948, Griaule and Dieterlen 1986. Key to above: 1. Abode and workshop of the smithy and mythical bringer of fire set at the northern margin; 2. *Toguna* or men's meeting house as the head; 3. Family houses as the chest; 4. Women's menstrual houses as the hands; 5. Oil-crushing stone and village altar as the female and male genitals; 6. Altars as the village's feet (author's drawing after Griaule 1965).

Dances first took place on the primal field in front of the smithy, which provided the music for them. The primal field was the first main square. Nowadays the dance floor is the main square of the village, situated on the north with the smithy at the edge of it.[26]

The chief square was also the focus of funerary rites, the corpse of the deceased being brought from the house on a specially constructed frame by four male relatives, who ran ahead of a great crowd of mourners firing guns, beating drums, and wailing. They deposited their burden at the centre of the square, then sacrifices were made and a funerary oration given, intended to advise the departed about the journey to be made. This social event was an essential part of a five-day ceremony involving the whole village, all normal activities being suspended.[27] Although on plans and aerial photographs the 'square' has little definition (and is not square, despite its symbolic link to the first field),[28] its use and existence were crucial to social life and belief, along with its essential relationship to the nearby council house and smithy.

Figure 9.18 *Toguna* at Ireli with its nine columns (photograph by Peter Hübner 2005).

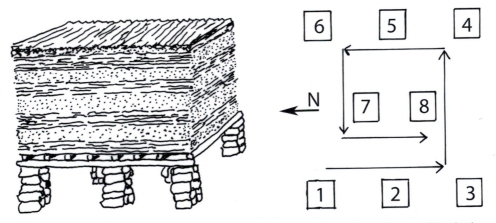

Figure 9.19 Order of the columns: there are also eight layers of straw, alternately placed (author's drawing after Griaule 1948).

The council house or *toguna* (Figure 9.18) is in contrast with most other Dogon structures a free-standing building, a low open structure on columns with a flat thatch roof piled up in alternating horizontal layers. According to Ogotemmêli it was the first thing built when a village was founded, along with the houses for menstruating women, both being gender-exclusive.[29] The *toguna* is the nearest the Dogon have to a public building, a kind of parliament for the village elders, providing them with shelter from the heat of the day. The interior being insufficiently high for standing participants, they had to sit or crouch, which discouraged physical altercation. The supporting columns, sometimes carved in wood, sometimes of stone stuccoed in mud, mimicked human figures representing the ancestors, who by this means seemed to take part. Ogotemmêli claims that there should be eight columns representing the eight ancestral lines, and he states that the *toguna* should be orientated north–south with three columns to each side and two in the middle (Figure 9.19).[30] The columns have a prescribed order starting in the north-west, which traces out a spiral pattern representing a serpent coiled along a broken line, the imagined presence of the mythical ancestor Lébé. The pile of millet stalks on top, by-product of the life-sustaining agriculture, is immensely thicker than its sheltering role would demand, evidently serving for display, while its layering in alternate directions reinforces the discipline of the right angle and mimics the process of weaving.

The smith and laying out the first field

The smith with his quasi-magical powers had the honour of residing to the north of the village at its head, yet was considered an outsider, along with his wife the potter, because of his special role and a mythical ancestry that rendered him impure.[31] His ancestor supposedly guided the sacred granary down to earth, and the spindle projecting from its centre (Figure 9.14) represents the arrow with which he caught it. The sense of secrecy and prestige surrounding the smith is common to blacksmiths in many African cultures, and the exclusiveness of quasi-magical craft skills handed down within the family also fitted them for the roles of healer and

Figure 9.20 A Dogon field system, divided into squares with earth banks between plots (drawing by Claire Blundell Jones after Griaule 1948).

sorcerer. In terms of cultural evolution the smith is among the first specialists supported by the whole social group, for instead of cultivating fields of his own he produces tools for others, for which he is eventually paid in produce.[32] As well as forging tools in iron, he also served as the village's worker in wood, producing the carved doors and shutters for houses and granaries, and the sacred masks for ceremonial occasions. These had to be carved in complete secrecy at the command of the mask society, and the smith had to fell the tree branches. In myth he is the bringer of fire, for he stole a piece of the sun, concealing it in the roof of the granary in order to smuggle it down to earth. Heaven retaliated with thunder and lightning, but the smith stood firm, and after things had calmed down he descended from the granary to take possession of the earth, imposing a first geometry:

> He came down the north stairway and marked out a square field, ten times eight cubits on each side, oriented in the same way as the flat roof on which he had descended, and on which the unit measurement of land-holdings was to be based. The field was divided into eighty times eighty squares of one cubit a side, which were distributed among the eight families descended from the ancestors whose destiny it was to remain on earth. Along the median line of the square from north to south eight dwelling houses were built, in which the earth was mixed with mud taken from the granary. The smithy was set up to the north of this line.[33]

Because of the need to break the earth and because of the linear progress of plough or hoe, a field becomes rectangular, emerging from a geometrical practice. Dogon cultivation relies on small square plots divided by shallow upstanding ridges on which people can walk (Figure 9.20). The sunken squares retain the rain and allow it to soak in, likewise containing irrigation.[34] Ogotemmêli claimed that the plots followed the size set by the celestial granary, were orientated to the cardinal points, and furthermore that cultivation activities – sowing and weeding with the hoe – took place in a given direction, beginning on the north side and moving from east to west, then back again to the east. The cultivator advances first on one foot and then on the other, changing his hoe to the other side with each step,[35] so the rhythm of practical work follows and confirms the primary geometry. Agricultural work is therefore like weaving, the technical process that is for the Dogon the most direct practical expression of geometry, bringing together the warp and the weft at right angles, and giving rise to a mat or piece of cloth that is necessarily flat and rectangular, a quintessentially geometric product. The loom produces clothing and bedding, but its most important product is the funeral pall, which should consist of eighty alternating black and white squares sewn together in a chequerboard pattern. This is explicitly linked by Ogotemmêli with the house façade, the field pattern, the pattern of houses and courtyards as seen from above, the layout of the village, and squared patterns repeated in dancing masks, decoration on buildings, and many other cultural products. These were brought together in a single illustration by Griaule (Figure 9.21).

A significant addition to the list is the table of divination, a rectangle traced out in sand on flat ground at the edge of the village and divided into a regular grid. Its squares were given significance by the inscription of signs, the addition of small pots containing liquids, and other ritual paraphernalia, prior to questions being asked. If during the night a fox came and left his footprints, the pattern was interpreted by the ritual specialist as the mark of the mythical fox Yurugu, symbol of night, death and disorder: an answer had been given.[36]

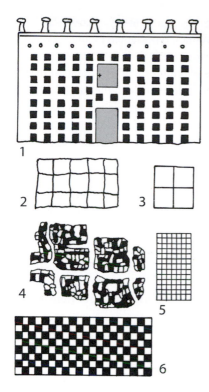

Figure 9.21 Homology of the *ginna* façade, plans of field and village and woven funeral pall (author's drawing after Griaule 1948).

Figure 9.22 A Dogon loom (photograph by Peter Hübner 2005).

The loom in mythology

The Dogon loom is a symbol of procreation, not only because it unites the warp and the weft, but because it brings together women's work of spinning with men's work of weaving. Weaving is connected with language, for the plaiting of a fibre skirt by the Nummo, the pre-human twin ancestors who needed to cover the shame of their mother earth, was the 'first word' and imposition of order.[37] The 'second word', built on the primitive language of the first, was the work of the seventh ancestor, whose name joined the male number three and female number four in a perfect combination. According to Ogotemmêli, he spat out eighty cotton threads then distributed them between his upper teeth which acted as the teeth of a weaver's reed to make the uneven threads of the warp. Doing the same with his lower teeth made the even threads, and by opening and shutting his mouth he created the movements needed for weaving, using the tips of his forked tongue to propel the shuttle and add the weft, so that the web emerged from his mouth 'in the breath of the second revealed word'.[38]

> The cooperation of man and woman, in storing the seeds, sowing and growing the cotton, has the same meaning as spinning and weaving, symbols of love. Spinning cotton and weaving clothing is exactly the same as a man and a woman entering the

house to sleep together and produce children. The weaver, representing a dead man, is also the male who opens and closes the womb of the woman, represented by the heddle. The stretched threads represent the act of procreation. The cotton threads of the weavers and the numerous men in the world are all one. The making of cloth symbolises the multiplication of mankind ... The Word is in the sound of the block and the shuttle. The name of the block means 'creaking of the word'. Everybody understands what is meant by 'the word' in that connection. It is interwoven with the threads: it fills the interstices in the fabric. It belongs to the eight ancestors; the first seven possess it: the seventh is the master of it; it is itself the eighth.[39]

The loom consists physically of four vertical stakes connected by four horizontal bars and is read as a symbolic and numerical body, echoing the structure both of the flying granary and of the house:

> The craft of weaving, in which the craftsman works facing south, is the house of the seventh nummo, and the structure of the loom is composed of all the eight ancestors. The four vertical stakes (male) mark the bedroom; the four horizontal bars (female) represent the flat roof.[40]

Dogon numerology

In his exposition of Dogon ideas, Ogotemmêli returns repeatedly to the number eight, which besides being the number of ancestors and of the holy kinds of grain given by Amma, also applies to the family groups and their rules for intermarriage, a matter of crucial importance to any society, and perhaps supportive of Emile Durkheim's theory that collective representations act to justify the order of society by making it seem self-evident.[41] In the conversations, the old man explained the social order with the help of an anthropomorphic figure (Figure 9.23). The human figure lying on its back is decked out with eight special totemic stones which are reflected in real life by priestly covenant-stones. Added to these are numerous smaller cowry shells, the original form of currency and therefore the practical method of counting beyond the fingers.[42] The totemic stones mark the body's eight joints, reflecting the advance in mythical evolution from stiff limbs to bendable ones.[43]

An additional stone was added for the head, which designates the number nine and chieftainship. Placed to left and right in upper and lower limbs, the totemic stones indicate the relations within which families are allowed to marry. The same interaction could be indicated on the fingers of one hand (Figure 9.24) by applying the eight in four combinations, each of which add up to nine, the number of chieftainship.[44] Ogotemmêli described this system by pointing to his own limbs and fingers, therefore taking for granted the symbolic relations between numbers and bodies. Ten he acknowledged as originating from the ten fingers, a widely accepted explanation for this worldwide phenomenon.[45] Four repeatedly refers to limbs as well as to cardinal points. The doubling of four to make the ideal eight not only allows the coupling of male and female, but also reflects the importance of twins in Dogon mythology: the Nummo water spirits who were the first legitimate offspring of the sky and the earth, representing perfection. Twins represent equality, and are the symbol of exchange

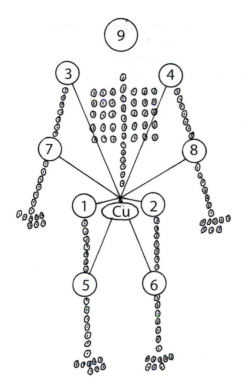

Figure 9.23 Numbers and the body, Cu is copper with its generative connotation (author's drawing after Griaule 1965).

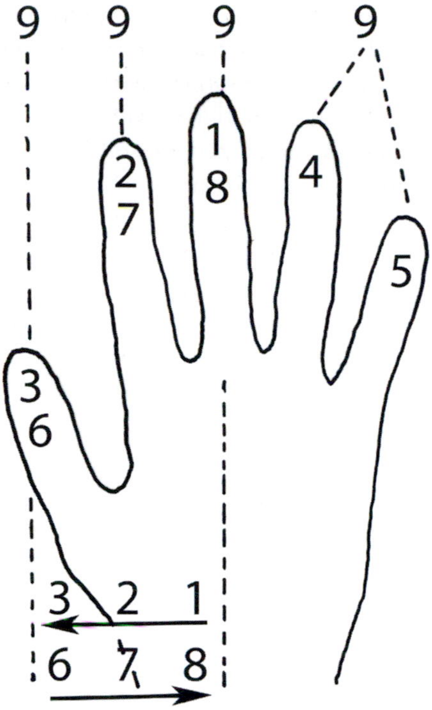

Figure 9.24 Number system applied to the fingers indicating marriageable combinations (author's drawing after Griaule 1965).

which should be on equal terms, guarding the morality of the market.[46] Summarizing his conversations with Ogotemmêli, Griaule listed eightfold phenomena in a table which includes languages, crafts, constellations, animals, drums, wind instruments, and several other kinds of things.[47] The Dogon tended to think in eights.

Territory and landscape: Altars, trees and shrines

In contrast with Ogotemmêli's idealized version, real Dogon villages seem to have been more dictated by the rocky terrain and topography, its particularities and limitations, its bluffs and caves.[48] Yet irregular as it was, every part of the land seems to have been known and owned, criss-crossed by paths sanctified by mythical ancestors, every baobab tree named and respected. Some places were forbidden and to be avoided, others revered and respected, renewed at intervals by offerings and worship. Griaule concluded that it was:

> as if the inhabitants had organised it rock by rock and mound by mound, impregnating it with their life, giving their names to it, and laying out each settlement, symbolically, after the pattern in which the earth had first been organised around the spot where the heavenly granary had come to rest.[49]

He reported one short walk of 200 metres that passed through several village quarters, including the bare uncultivated patch that is the tomb of the god/ancestor Lébé, the slippery track along which his serpentine form is said to pass nightly into the town, the entrance to the cave in which he lives visible in the cliff beyond, and a heap of stones that is one of his principal altars.[50] Much more is found in the later book by Griaule and his student Germaine Dieterlen *Le Renard Pâle* published in 1965.[51] There is a detailed description of the 'Cave of the Fox', a mythical ancestor's first dwelling on earth, with added stone structures and paintings to exemplify a mythical reading, a ritual site strikingly similar to those of the Australian Aboriginal People (see p. 126). This later book also includes numerous photographs of altars to Amma, Lébé, and other deities. There is even a plan of Upper and Lower Ogol which sets the altars in a series called the 'blood route', delimiting a 'mythical territory' to be followed during seasonal rituals (Figure 9.16), and this is considered to be connected with the order of the stars.[52] Detailed descriptions of altars and holy places are accompanied by elaborate narratives of their symbolic content, backed up by presentation of symbolic drawings, some of which are painted on rocks or façades, others made ritually on the ground as an act of foundation before an altar is set up. If the presented data are insufficient to allow a full understanding of the ritual paths of the many Dogon ceremonies, there is at least a systematic typology of altars, with their shapes, positions, and materials. Their seasonal celebrations geared to the calendar and to rites of passage evidently involved theatrical presentations and dances presenting the famous Dogon masks, whose symbolism echoes that already discussed. These celebrations must have had prescribed routes both to ensure the coherence of the choreography and to assure that appropriate altars were acknowledged in the right order. The BBC film *Tribal Eye* of 1975 presented by David Attenborough permits a glimpse of several dance sequences, parts of a genuine funeral ritual, and even the carving of a new mask by the smith, noting in his commentary the presence of places both sacred and prohibited, ritual avoidances between groups, and a clear choreographic order.[53]

The sanctuary

Returning to Ogotemmêli's narrative, Griaule relays a detailed description of a particular sanctuary dedicated to the cult of Binu which is represented in the pages of the original *Dieu d'Eau* both by a photograph captioned *Sangabilou de Do* and a drawing that more closely follows Ogotemmêli's description of how it should be (Figure 9.25). Located in a village quarter but distant from the dwellings, it is a diminutive house described as a cube measuring six cubits per side (3.6 m). A single room entered by double doors contains cult objects and altars private to the priest. The striking feature is the front façade, decorated with symbols, flanked with conical turrets, and with a parapet protecting the flat roof behind. On the right is a seat for the incumbent priest, and above the door two window-like holes. At top centre is an iron hook, and to either side mound-like altars over which, at appropriate moments, libations of millet gruel or the sacrificial blood of a dying animal are poured and allowed to run down. Like a theatre set, the building focuses a space for an audience in front as they attend rituals of agricultural renewal at sowing and at harvest. Griaule stresses the importance of the sacrifice:

> On the altar, the virtue of new, fresh, blood combines with what has been left there by a
> long series of ritual murders: for the altar is a store-house of forces, on which man draws

at the appropriate time, and which he keeps constantly fed. It is also the point of contact between man and the Invisible. So long as the altar is fed, and its power is renewed by fresh offerings, the Nummo, when he hears the Word, comes to drink, to draw strength and maintain his life.[54]

Ogotemmêli describes the sanctuary as an ancestral tomb, claiming it to be a primal building more ancient than the family house but similar in form, and obeying the same principle of orientation. Just as the interior represents the tomb of the god-like ancestor Lébé, the roof represents the primal field in which he was buried, and the iron hook at the centre of the parapet is the smith's anvil. Set on the centre line between roof and façade, this piece of iron – with multiple associations too complex to address here – is where the eight ears of corn gathered at the harvest must be hung, while the adjacent roof is the place where the seed corn is spread out to absorb real and spiritual moisture before being sown. Griaule's redrawn image of the building shows the whole set of symbols on the front as described by Ogotemmêli: footprints of the priest, stars, the ram, the serpent, the moon, the priest's forked staff, throwing sticks, and the robber's crook. The two holes above the door allow the painted serpent Lébé to pass in and out, but also recall a past practice of removing soil from the ancestor's tomb to transfer it to a new village foundation. Above the holes is a chequerboard of white squares contrasting with empty ones, symbols of 'things of this world', echoing the fields, the village, the house-front, and the funeral pall, as discussed earlier.[55] The paintings on the façade, renewed for the agricultural rituals each year, were not just thought of in terms of their passive symbolic import but were considered actively to promote germination, while the sacrifices of animal blood or millet gruel poured down the façade were but painting in another form, visibly transforming the appearance of the building as they performed their life-giving work. The materials used as a paint carried their own magic significance.

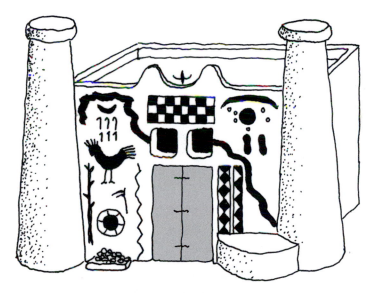

Figure 9.25 The shrine of *Sangabilou de Do (author's drawing* after Griaule 1965).

Iconography and *The Pale Fox*

In our modern condition there is much uncertainty about the symbolism of buildings and doubt about their value as signs, for we have lost the coherence of our inherited building traditions and gained many alternative forms of communication. In contrast, the iconography of the Dogon sanctuary is clear and vivid. In Ogotemmêli's time it still supported shared mythical structures, was revalidated by ritual use, and remained present as a reference point for explanation. In the absence of written texts, it served as a common visual language, its spatial order and signs playing an essential role in the sharing and transmission of ideas, as well as in establishing identity of place. In their later book *The Pale Fox*, Griaule and Dieterlen give much more attention not only to mythology but to the drawn and painted signs associated with it, which may be displayed on a façade, ritually applied under the foundation of an altar, or even drawn in the air. When they were publicly enacted, the material with which a depiction was made added to its magic efficacy, for example millet gruel from the holy grain if white, and blood if red. An extreme instance is a figure drawn on the Hogon's façade at the time of his ordination made with the faeces of a snake, echo of Lébé, a material far from easy to collect.[56] Numerous geometrical signs represent the cardinal points and the four elements: there are depictions of plants and animals, including their footprints and traces. There are patterns of stars, and complex spirals depicting processes of growth. Combinations of curving tapered lines without obvious reference to the visual world seem more like gestures, but are attributed precise significance as so-called master signs. Griaule and Dieterlen claimed there were 266, and identified four kinds of depiction applied to the same object, representing different phases of its existence. The master sign of a house, for example (Figure 9.26) represents neither plan nor elevation, and lacks pictorial significance even when the strokes composing it have been explained, but the *yala* and *tonu* of the house (Figure 9.27) are geometric diagrams of its plan, the *yala* representing the foundational outline and the *tonu* the perimeter wall.[57] These diagrams support Ogotemmêli's reading, but his explanations have often been doubted, both for their accuracy and their elaboration. Repeatedly he speaks of what should be rather than what is: we seem never to find the ideal ten rows of eight but something less, not the ideal northern orientation but avoidance of the prevailing wind and rain, not a village laid out to a grid-like woven cloth but one subject to the vagaries of topography. Into every structure is read a maximum of significance, sometimes requiring very protracted connections. If invented by

Figure 9.26 Master sign of house (author's drawing after Griaule and Dieterlen 1986).

Figure 9.27 *Yala* and *tonu* of a house (author's drawing after Griaule and Dieterlen 1986).

the anthropologist, all this would have little credibility, but Griaule followed Ogotemmêli's words even if his translation coloured them, and taken as a whole, the 'conversations' have a wonderful consistency, with returning themes that mesh and resonate with each other. It may be a mere reflection of Ogotemmêli's personal world, but he was the one chosen by his fellows as the possessor of a shared narrative. Other elders might have offered alternative accounts, but it is the nature of oral culture that ideas condense in the heads of individuals, to be transmitted by conversation and signs. As the essential becomes consolidated and the unnecessary details drop out the message changes, but the knowledge-base is carried forward and renewed at the same scale. This is both efficient and economical, carrying its history within it rather than setting it out as a cumulative external body. For the modern reader living in an increasingly complex, contradictory and fragmented world, the degree to which Ogotemmêli's cosmology obeys an interlocking pattern is striking. One kind of phenomenon is always understood in terms of another, which reflects both metaphorical thinking and the associative nature of memory.[58] Dogon knowledge is at once practical and religious, providing a rationale about what to do next as well as answers to the eternal questions: how we come to be on this earth, how we relate to the heavens, what it means to be man or woman, who are the ancestors, whom can one marry, what happens after death?

Conclusion

Like Aboriginal People and Tukanoans in earlier chapters, the Dogon classify the features of the land and its human and animal inhabitants, but we see also in Dogon myth overriding concerns with agriculture and the gift of grain, with the arrival of knowledge through language and the acquisition of technologies like spinning and weaving, pottery and blacksmithing. All receive mythological origins and cosmic meanings, not in the manner of museum labels, but in a way that charges each activity with current significance. We also see signs beginning to become a form of writing, and a development in the use of number, which while still first counted on the fingers or the limbs, nonetheless allows the possibility of continuing into the hundreds. Order in space is connected with order in time, so the development of a coherent calendar is essential to allow synchronization with the seasons, and necessary worship for successful crops. The Dogon calendar has a five day week and thirteen months of twenty-eight days each. There are four seasons, two dry and two wet, the latter allowing the most intensive cultivation from May to October.[59] Awareness of a longer timescale is evident in the sixty-year cycle of the Sigui shared across the region, so that although in each village it occurs only once in a lifetime, adjacent ones hold it in between. This longer timescale is also reflected in the ten generations of ancestors leading back to the first human beings, although the slide into mythical time rather than adding further generations seems not to have bothered the Dogon. Numbers are quantities when measuring or paying for produce, but they also serve as symbols, at least the integers. Griaule's table of correspondences assigns numbers to life-roles, constellations, internal organs, colours, languages and many other categories of phenomena, so that for example the number one links the smith, the Pleiades, the stomach, yellow, and the Toro 1 dialect.[60] We shall see in the next chapter a similar process within Dong culture, but more elaborated, and with a quite different set of number references. People require classification systems in order to identify and discuss phenomena, and it is easiest to assemble new classes in accordance with existing ones. The correspondences so created become incorporated into the perceived structure of reality.

Number is deeply lodged in Dogon architecture, and Ogotemmêli's idealization in terms of fours, tens and eights may appear at first merely an attempt to tie buildings conveniently to other aspects of life, but it is more than that. His ideal conceptions of buildings and village become the essential medium for understanding and transmitting spatial relations, for linking geometry and number with the organization of practical life. Pierre Bourdieu's 'body as geometer' with its three directional movements, already mentioned at the end of Chapter 6, is surely the starting point, and dimensions in hands breadths, cubits or days' walk are bodily measures. The cardinal points, which resound throughout the mythology, refer to the visible rotation of the sky and are identified with constellations. The ancestral groups are supposed to have come from them, the mythical sign of the egg of the world represents them,[61] the order of the seeds follows them, and the Hogon or chief priest is supposed to divide his day between them, moving around his house to follow the sun.[62] The idea of the flying granary connects heaven and earth, symbolically combining spinning, the smith, the first field, fire, and the sun. Foursquare, orientated, and linking circle with square, that granary was never built and has an impossible scale, but serves as an essential model. It even has dimensions evoking the numbers and relating to human measures.

When it came to actual construction, the Dogon had no specialist builders beyond the smith whose job it was to make windows and doors, and building was carried out as a communal activity.[63] But the ownership of land and the decision as to where and how to construct remained with the family patriarch, head of the particular *ginna*, in other words with an elder like Ogotemmêli. Such men had to know what a house was supposed to be like, and to advise like an architect on its construction. The imaginary house and village were therefore not mere retrospective interpretations, but models for potential future prescription. The already noted diagrams depicting the foundation and perimeter of a house were accompanied by drawing of specific figures on or under the site, many of which are described and discussed in *The Pale Fox*. There is a foundation stone laying with suitable oaths and the placing of a symbolic bulb, and at the corners of the house a series of drawings is made on the ground related to the joints of the body, so giving it a bodily order. In the upper floor granary more special figures are drawn in each corner related to the mythology of the four main crops, the seeds of which will be reverently stored there, while in the side gallery as close as possible to the granary and front is built a family altar.[64] More will be said of building rituals in the next chapter, and of the way they reinforce both the definition of space and the symbolic meaning of the building before the fact.

In comparison with peoples of earlier chapters, the Dogon are more permanently settled, existing in the same place for generations in houses that see births and deaths, and stand for the continuity of the family. That is why such houses could never be sold, but only reoccupied or rebuilt by permission of the patriarch. The Dogon's sedentary existence also encouraged the emergence of distinct building types: patriarchal houses with facades, smaller subordinate houses, decorated granaries, and the network of streets and alleys of the village, leading through to its ceremonial main square. On it lies the most distinctive building of all, the *toguna*, a parliament marking the beginning of specialized politics, which had become necessary due to the size of the settlement. The highest concentration of symbolic signs is found at the sanctuary, a temple-like building for communion with god-like ancestors.

Notes

1 Van Eyck wrote chapters in the Dutch periodical *Forum* of which he was editor and contributed a chapter to Jencks and Baird, *Meaning in Architecture,* 1970.

2 Griaule 1965.

3 Griaule has been subjected to the customary parricide, particularly from Walter van Beek in the early 1990s whose revisits failed to unearth the same mythology, but he has also been defended, and his Dogon material remains a rich source if in need of some reinterpretation. Andrew Apter's criticism of Griaule's search for an 'urtext' and his plea for multiple versions is a hopeful basis for reconstruction: see Apter 2007.

4 For the most abundant and accurate set of drawings see Lauber, *Architektur der Dogon,* 1998, which has surveys of several households in Ireli. Lauber's book also shows the considerable difference between the Dogon architecture of the eastern and western cliffs, the latter being much more rounded and organic, and not discussed here.

5 Observation by Wolfgang Lauber, see Lauber 1998, p. 39.

6 Marti 1957, pp. 44–7.

7 For a description of the birth customs see Marti 1957, p. 39.

8 Griaule 1965, pp. 94–5.

9 This image of a man lying on his side is imposed on the plan of an asymmetrical house in a revised interpretation by Griaule and Germaine Dieterlen in their essay 'The Dogon' which is included in Forde 1954, pp. 83–110. The spatial sequence is essentially the same, the anthropomorphic reference somewhat adjusted.

10 Griaule 1965, p. 96.

11 Griaule and Dieterlen, *The Pale Fox,* 1986, p. 378.

12 Griaule 1965, pp. 92–3.

13 Marti 1957, pp. 77–9.

14 Ibid., p. 37.

15 Houses were never sold, even when disused and collapsing, and it was up to the patriarch to permit family members to reoccupy and repair them, Marti 1957, p. 37.

16 Griaule and Dieterlen 1986, p. 532.

17 Ibid., p. 88: mentioned in discussion of signs depicting the house.

18 Marti 1957, pp. 44–5.

19 A much repeated theme in *The Pale Fox.*

20 The bride, coming from a different family, brought with her a token set of seeds from her father's house, and was then given an annual share of the husband's seeds to put in her granary. On her death these would be collected by members of her family to pass on to her daughters. In this way aspects of her family identity were preserved in the granary, see Griaule and Dieterlen 1986, p. 282.

21 Forde 1954, p. 87.

22 Griaule 1965, pp. 30–40.

23 The parallel with Genesis may of course reflect missionary influence, or indeed Griaule's conscious or unconscious recourse to his own culture in making the interpretation.

24 Griaule 1965, p. 31.

25 Ibid., pp. 96–7.

26 Ogotemmêli quoted in Griaule 1965, p. 189. The mention of music is not fanciful, as the rhythmic operation of hammer and bellows was the sound signature of the smith, see McNaughton 1988, p. 30.

27   Marti 1957, p. 49.

28   In a later description by Griaule and Germaine Dieterlen the square is actually described as being round 'like the sky which it represents': see 'The Dogon' in Forde 1954, p. 96.

29   Not equality but almost the opposite. Men were in charge of tribal secrets, women regarded as dangerous during menstruation, but the women's huts as the 'hands' of the village were also the places for female initiation rites.

30   Lauber 1998 claims that for structural reasons this is generally six or nine, but some photographed versions also have many more columns. The idealizing tendency of Ogotemmêli's version is discussed below.

31   Griaule 1965, p. 87. His place in myth has deprived him of life-force and meant that he does not work like others. The smith is anomalous which makes him at once sacred and dangerous, but he is also powerful and can work magic: for a detailed examination of these paradoxes in his role see McNaughton 1988.

32   Griaule 1965, p. 88.

33   Ibid., p. 44.

34   For details of agricultural practices see Marti 1957, pp. 21–3.

35   Griaule 1965, p. 77. More on this in the chapter 'The Dogon' by Griaule and Dieterlen in Forde 1954, including the myth of a spiral layout of the first fields.

36   Yurugu the jackal or 'pale fox' is a rogue in mythology, born of a first violent encounter between the God Amma and the earth, who came before the perfection of the Nummo twins and remains their opposite, a lonely wanderer, powerful and anomalous. For a summary of his position see Marti 1957, p. 56; and for details of the divining table, p. 81. The rectangle set out is described as around 70 cm wide and between one and five metres long. For details see Griaule and Dieterlen 1986, p. 294ff.

37   Griaule 1965, p. 20.

38   Ibid., p. 28.

39   Ibid., p. 73.

40   Ibid., p. 72.

41   Durkheim and Mauss 1963 pp. 82–3.

42   Also used as bride wealth, see Griaule and Dieterlen 1986, p. 264.

43   When the flying granary crashed to earth the smith's limbs were broken, and so he gained joints.

44   Griaule 1965, pp. 50–5.

45   Crump 1990, p. 41.

46   Marti 1957, p. 30.

47   See table in Griaule 1965, pp. 222–3.

48   Numerous photographed and drawn examples can be seen in Lauber *Architektur der Dogon*, 1998.

49   Griaule 1965, p. 76.

50   Ibid., p. 75, see also pp. 116–18.

51   Griaule and Dieterlen 1986.

52   Ibid., pp. 250, 252, 348.

53   *The Tribal Eye*, BBC 1975, available on DVD.

54   Griaule 1965, p. 131.

55   Ibid., p. 111: the original text carries far too many symbolic readings to engage with here.

56   Griaule and Dieterlen 1986, p. 356.

57   Ibid., pp. 88, 95.

58   Lakoff and Johnson 1980, Bartlett 1932.

59   Marti 1957, p. 21.

60   Griaule 1965, pp. 222–3.

61   Forde 1954, p. 88.

62   Ibid., p. 101.

63   Marti 1957, p. 33. On the details of construction techniques see Lauber 1998.

64   Griaule and Dieterlen 1986, pp. 373–9.

CHAPTER 10
THE DONG, BUILDING TYPES, AND BUILDING RITUALS

Figure 10.1 Drum tower in Tang'an, Guizhou Province, the centre of a Dong hill village (author's photograph 2014).

Figure 10.2 Tang'an village seen from below, from the wind and rain bridge at E on the plan opposite, and with rice paddies in the foreground (author's photograph 2014).

The Dong people are a minority group living in South West China, a mountainous area shared between the provinces of Guizhou, Hunan and Guangxi, and they number around 3 million. The original migration patterns of their arrival are ancient and obscure, though DNA and linguistic evidence allow some speculation about westward links to the area of Vietnam, Laos and Thailand, cultures that also build houses on wooden posts.[1] At the same time there is long-standing cultural influence from the Han, including a Daoist world view. Before the late twentieth century the difficult geography rendered communications with the rest of China severely limited, there was little impulse to travel, and places as near as 5 km could be regarded as remote. The Dong were therefore more or less self-sufficient, producing the staple rice, textiles, tools, buildings and most other necessities within their wooded valleys, intermarrying with other local villages, and carrying on their own orally-based culture.[2] Unusually, they had no written language until the 1950s, and had developed instead a strong tradition of communal singing, which gives structure to their rituals while preserving knowledge, mythology and practices.[3] In the absence of written rules and written histories,[4] material culture has served a greater mnemonic role for them in carrying the order of things at every level, and the making of artefacts, necessarily local and hand-based, has provided an opportunity for the reinforcement of meaning that has been well exploited and maintained.[5] The Dong village (Figure 10.2) consists mainly of houses, but the Dong have developed public and ceremonial buildings which explicitly express their political structure, and their building rituals have become especially elaborate. Even for an ordinary house there is a multi-stage communal narrative that begins with the cutting of the first tree and only ends with the

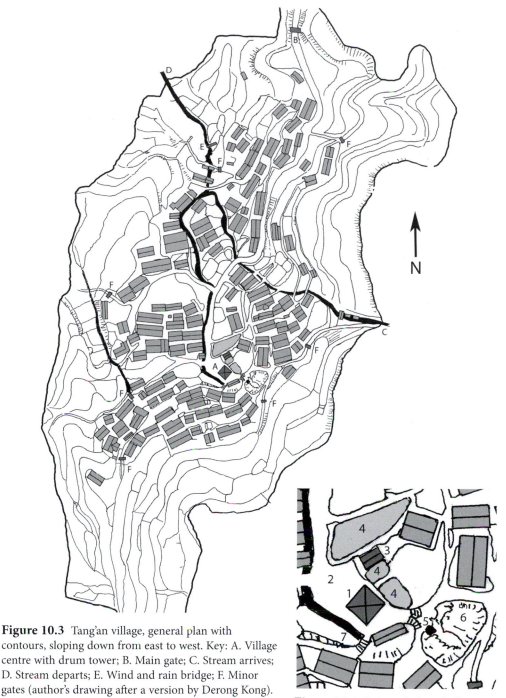

Figure 10.3 Tang'an village, general plan with contours, sloping down from east to west. Key: A. Village centre with drum tower; B. Main gate; C. Stream arrives; D. Stream departs; E. Wind and rain bridge; F. Minor gates (author's drawing after a version by Derong Kong).

Figure 10.4 Enlarged plan of village centre, same orientation. Key: 1. Drum tower; 2. Village square; 3. Drama stage; 4. Ponds; 5. Water source; 6. Sa-Sui shrine; 7. Earth God shrine (author's drawing after a version by Derong Kong).

lighting of the first fire. But more of that later: let us first look at the structure of a typical Dong village and its component parts.[6]

The small village of Tang'an provides a relatively simple and unspoiled example, though it is far from the valley bottom and watered only by a couple of small streams (Figure 10.3). It occupies a fold in the hills facing down to the north-west with peaks behind to the east, and the topography is crucial, not only because roads and houses largely follow the contours, but because rice cultivation requires floodable terraces that force them to be physically expressed. The self-evidently life-giving water is believed to flow from 'dragon veins' in the mountains, and brings with it essential *qi*, the energy driving all life.[7] Water is also one of the five elements (better called phases because regarded as transitory) in the Daoist philosophy that was universal in China and is still prevalent in the Dong region, so in the siting of a village the river always plays a dominant role, and the practice of feng-shui (wind and water), already mentioned briefly in Chapter 4, page 69, is employed as a matter of course to ensure propitious conditions. The main tool is the magnetic compass, an early Chinese invention, which before the arrival of Western theories could be regarded as an indicator of earthly *qi*. For use in feng-shui it accumulated multiple concentric scales allowing different kinds of reading. Of primary importance are the direction of the river and its tributaries and the positions and shapes of local mountains, read symbolically as types named after mythical animals such as 'white tiger' and 'azure dragon'. A feng-shui master, who may be a village elder or a Daoist priest,[8] checks local landscape features against the compass to assess the auspiciousness of a site for dwelling, cultivation, or most importantly a graveyard where ancestors will sleep soundly and not return to haunt their descendents.[9] All this underlines a general Dong sensitivity to questions of direction and orientation. As everywhere in China, the direction of the sun is also crucial, and the preferred orientation for a dwelling is southwards, but local topography may preclude it as in this case. In Tang'an, the most visible feng-shui move is the construction of a roofed 'wind and rain' bridge at the lower end of the village (Figure 10.8). Not providing a significant crossing, it has little practical function, but it sets the village boundary, frames impressive views, and marks the water mouth.

A Dong village interior consists very largely of family houses, normally permanently inhabited by just two generations since care for grandparents tends to be shared between brothers. The houses are of *ganlan* type, visible rectangles of consistent size on the Tang'an plan, the few larger ones being rice barns. Houses are timber framed with China fir, and stand on wooden poles which usually rest on short stone pads. They are built by local carpenters with the help of the whole local population to assemble the frame. The houses are constructed in bays of about 3.5 metres, and gather along streets and alleys in a meandering form. The separate construction of each makes its layout orthogonal despite slight shifts of angle between them, but layouts also reflect the sequence of construction and local feng-shui readings related to site or neighbours – the avoidance of a door or a ridge being placed directly opposite that of a neighbour, for example. Most houses have open galleries facing south or the valley view.

The public buildings

In contrast with the relatively even grain of houses, the plan of Tang'an village (Figure 10.3) includes six kinds of public building. At the village centre is the drum tower A with its square

Figure 10.5 Drum tower at village centre and drama stage to right (author's photograph 2014).

Figure 10.6 The community fireplace within the drum tower, which is the social and political centre (author's photograph 2014).

Figure 10.7 Wind and rain bridge in Di'ping, celebrating a necessary river crossing. Such bridges were paid for by the community, thought propitious, and marked the peak of carpentry performance (author's photograph 2014).

plan, and immediately to its north the drama stage B where sung performances take place (Figure 10.5). Close by on the edge of the village square but at smaller scale are shrines to the earth God C and to Sa-Sui D, the village's divine grandmother: there also is found the village well. To north-west and down-valley on the village edge is the aforementioned wind and rain bridge E (Figure 10.8), and in other peripheral locations outgoing paths have roofed and lockable gates F, G (Figures 10.9. 10.12 and 10.13). The drum tower (Figures 10.1, 10.5 and 10.6) with its impressive stack of roofs is the tallest and most important building in the village, the founding gesture that establishes the village centre along with the paved square, which it dominates. It is freestanding, supposed to be visible from every house and traditionally was audible too, for the drum after which it is named was struck to gather people together for meetings and in emergencies. Square or sometimes polygonal in plan, the drum tower is purer in concept than the Dong house, although its frame construction follows the same principles. Its polygonal geometry requires more skill in execution and remains proudly on display within its hollow interior. The external form of multiple eaves is clearly rhetorical and intended to impress, but its elaboration also exemplifies the Chinese principle that a building is first and foremost a roof, not just for its real or symbolic shelter but because the structure remains open between posts, needing an intersecting network of beams to lock everything together. Symbolically the drum tower is said to represent a tree, but it is also covered with carved and painted decorations: those at Tang'an (Figure 10.1) include carved fish on the external angles, which because of their association with water are supposed to protect against fire. In the centre are carved dragons, and on the eaves many painted narratives in a scroll-like order.[10]

Figure 10.8 Wind and rain bridge at Tang'an, marking the water mouth of the small stream and the edge of the village, but not providing a significant crossing: the view from it back towards the village is shown in Figure 10.2 (author's photograph 2014).

Figure 10.9 The lower village gate, rice paddy, and wind and rain bridge beyond (author's photograph 2014).

Figure 10.10 Village water supply with gargoyle and drinking cup (author's photograph 2014).

Figure 10.11 Shrine to Sa-Sui, the village's divine grandmother (photograph by Derong Kong).

Socially, the drum tower represents a clan, and each village used to be exclusively occupied by people of the same surname.[11] Villages were exogamous, the men obliged to find wives from other villages and the women to marry out.[12] The drum tower therefore marked the social and administrative centre of each extended family group, and was the place where the village head-man and elders of the *dou* or clan met to take decisions and resolve disputes, sitting around a circular hearth in the centre of its base where a fire was kept constantly burning, a larger communal version of the domestic fireplace (Figure 10.6). The traditional practice during periodic rites of renewal of taking a light from this fire to relight each house hearth was an active demonstration of this hierarchy of centre over periphery.[13] The drum tower is always placed next to the main open square where people gather to eat, drink, sing and dance, which is called 'drum tower square' (Figure 10.5). To one side at Tang'an, across a pond, is the second type of public building, the singing stage where performers gain an advantageous position overlooking the crowd, and where antiphonal rituals of sung questions and answers are enacted. Next to the drum tower is a village pond, which is both a water source in case of fire and a place for farming fish, connected with the river and the irrigation system. In Tang'an, owing to the steep slope it is double.

The third specialist building type is the 'wind and rain' bridge. In valley locations such as Di'ping it can be much more prominent (Figure 10.7), but even a small place away from a main river like Tang'an was felt to need one (Figures 10.8 and 10.9). Such bridges are not only fully roofed but often also equipped with multiple pavilions, sometimes bearing shrines to Chinese gods.[14] This presence of shrines echoes the provision of Western medieval chapels on bridges as sites of gratitude for a successful crossing and marker of a significant stage on

Figure 10.12 One of Tang'an's upper gates from inside (author's photograph 2014).

Figure 10.13 The other upper gate from outside (author's photograph 2014).

Figure 10.14 Tang'an main gate in 2010 which has since been demolished (photograph by Derong Kong).

Figure 10.15 Dong house under construction in Jitang, 2014 (photograph by Derong Kong).

a journey, but there is more. A bridge brings together two kinds of movement, and since the Dong regard a river as bearer of life-giving *qi*, the bridge is the controller of the water-mouth and adjuster of feng-shui. The river is also the bringer of souls returning for reincarnation, which is why women wishing to conceive a child go to pray there. Bridges were also connected with other rites of passage, believed both to bring life and to take it: Xuemei Li interviewed a carpenter who believed he had gained a son in reward for his work on a bridge. On the other hand, people strove to keep their young men away from bridges under construction lest they collapse and die, being turned into the bridge's guardian spirit.[15] A river forms a natural boundary between social groups, and in valley sites a bridge is required at least in the wet season for safe crossing, if also facilitating contacts and commerce. Where villages are separated by a river, the bridge becomes the frontier and place of arrival, which helps explain why so much money raised within the local community was spent on building and repairing them. Given sometimes wide spans and a need to construct piers and abutments, a bridge could be the carpenter's riskiest structural task, but it was also his best chance to show off his skills in structural geometry and in making the elaborate multiple roofs. The bridge in its ceremonial role stands as equal and opposite of the drum tower, marking the limit of the village as opposed to its centre.

Tang'an also possesses numerous road gates (Figures 10.9 and 10.12–10.14) marking the edge of village territory. These count as a fourth kind of Dong public building. They are hardly defensive as they could easily be circumvented, but they can be closed at night to mark a curfew. The local importance even of minor gates as definers of territory was traditionally assured by the performance of the Blocking Ceremony as a prelude to inter-village festivities and courting.[16] This took place at certain pre-assigned dates when the people of one village would visit another by formal invitation for festivities lasting two or three days. During these visits eligible young people could get to know one another, and the progress of the ritual followed a pattern from formal introduction to increasing intimacy, a kind of communal courtship. The first stage of the interaction was a contrived confrontation at the village gate, or at a bridge which became a gate when acting as the socially relevant boundary. Beforehand it was temporarily blocked by the residents with feminine paraphernalia such as looms and spinning wheels, since the host company were acting the feminine role to male outsiders. At the appointed time the guests would arrive in procession before the gate and in formal song demand the right to enter. The residents would reply in kind, refusing them for well-rehearsed reasons, and the visitors would repeat their demand, adding details of gifts they were bringing, how much trouble they had taken, and so forth. Eventually the residents would give way, guiding the visitors to the village square for feasting, dancing and more antiphonal singing (Figure 10.22), and in the evening visitors would be paired off with host families for the night. By the next day everyone had become more familiar and informal. When these festivities came to an end the village gate or bridge was the site for 'sending off', a custom by which hosts beg their guests to stay while the guests insist they must leave, but are delayed with more attractions and distractions before being accompanied to the gate.[17] For both welcome and departure a defined frontier was evidently needed, and it took the form of a village gate, which, like the decorated gates in Chinatowns across the world, is more marker and symbol than real barrier.

The Dong family house

It was Alberti who originally wrote that a city should be like a large house and a house like a small city, even if Aldo van Eyck repeated it so effectively in the middle of the last century.[18] In the case of the Dong village the homology could scarcely be stronger, for the drum tower represents the clan as the house represents the family, each with its hearth, like a nesting series, macrocosm and microcosm. Closer study of the house and its connected rituals will allow a deeper glimpse into this microcosm. Dong houses are mostly of two or three storeys with an overhanging double-pitched roof and subsidiary short roofs at the ends (Figures 10.16–10.18). Plans vary across the region, but the raw earth ground floor is normally used for subordinate functions like animal pens, storage, firewood, and workspace, though it can also serve mercantile purposes. It can be left totally or partially open, and may absorb changes in ground level. This allows the suspended timber-planked first floor to become the main platform for living, usually with a long open gallery on the south side for food preparation and other daytime work (Figure 10.19). This gallery is often also circulation space, serving as the landing from the floor below and the point of departure for the ladder to the floor above. Generally central to the plan and more enclosed is a hearth room centred on a stone-lined clay fireplace set in a raised section of the wooden floor, with a smoke hole in the floor above (Figure 10.21). The fire was traditionally kept alight for cooking and heating by the women night and day, becoming in winter and early spring the focus of family life.[19] Emitting not only warmth but light, it was the place for many activities, from spinning, weaving, and embroidery by the women, to basket-making and repair work by the men. It was a place for children to play, for family gatherings, for the ceremony of 'oiled tea' and for singing and playing the pipa, but most crucially of all it was the place for offerings to ancestors:

Figure 10.16 A pair of Dong houses with the galleries on different floors and differently orientated (author's photograph 2014).

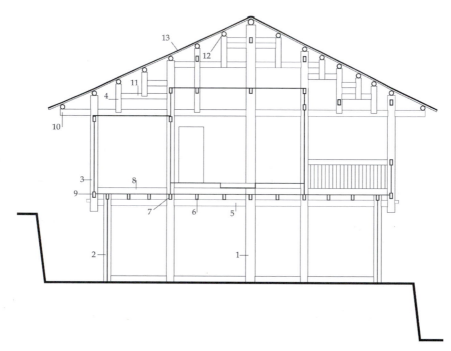

Figure 10.17 Section of a Dong house showing the carpentry system, with open gallery to right and hearth room in centre: it runs vertically. The plans are shown in Figure 10.18 (drawn by Derong Kong).

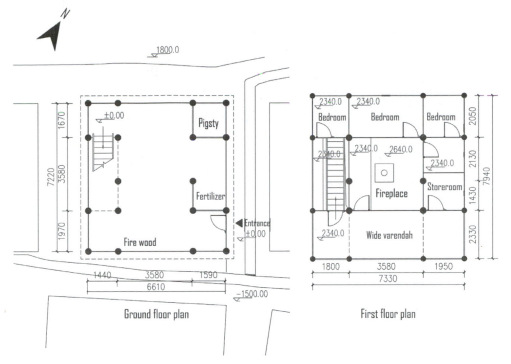

Figure 10.18 Ground and first floor plans of the same house built in the 1950s, showing the column layout, stair and central hearth room (drawn by Derong Kong).

> The Dong believe that the fire pit itself is the memorial tablet of the family's ancestor: if the fire were to die out, the family would have no progeny, so nothing is more devastating than destroying a Dong fire pit.[20]

In the simple example shown in plan in Figure 10.18, the hearth room is part of a south-to-north progression that begins with the open gallery where visitors arrive and ends with the principal bedroom to north, a sequence of spaces increasingly enclosed as it becomes more private. Surrounding rooms, relatively dark and enclosed, double as storerooms and bedrooms. Some Dong houses have two hearth rooms, often reflecting habitation by two brothers, each with his family. In some regions the first floor of the house also has a central hall as distributor where large family rituals take place, but the hearth room has been the essential focal point of family life, as shown by many customs (Figure 10.21). Whether there is a hall or just a hearth room, the door from the gallery is of ritual importance as an inner threshold, but it does not compete with the ground floor outer door which remains the principal threshold of family territory.

Constructionally, the Dong house exists first of all as a wooden frame, celebrated as complete when the ridge pole is added, and often left naked before being roofed and clad by the owner (Figure 10.15). As in all traditional Chinese architecture, members are horizontal and vertical without diagonal bracing, so stability depends on the interlocking joints and the stiffening effect of roof members. The frame is the carpenter's work and represents his discipline. It requires initial decisions with the owner and Daoist adviser about position, roof, direction

Figure 10.19 Woman weaving on the first floor gallery of a house (author's photograph 2014).

Figure 10.20 Mark-ink craftsman marking out columns (photograph by Derong Kong 2010).

Figure 10.21 Men gathered around the smouldering hearth (author's photograph 2014).

of gable, and number of bays. Then trees must be obtained, timber members be cut to size, complete with mortise and tenon joints appropriately numbered. The system is by its nature orthogonal, even if corners sometimes have to be irregular. The carpenter must also think sequentially, from erection of main posts to placing of the ridge beam, aware of precisely how many of each component are needed and their sizes, while maintaining an order of assembly that maintains stability at every stage. This is no dry technical process but ideologically loaded, for numbers and dimensions, questions of odd versus even, choices of direction, and even the timing of operations have to fit in with Daoist calculations about what is propitious. The timber frame system dictates the basic plan order that is visible in the patterns of columns, but it also lends itself to flexibility and variations in the way it is completed and clad. The southern gallery can remain open to air and view between freestanding columns almost like a modernist building (Figure 10.19), while the north may in contrast be solidly clad with only the tiniest of windows, typically about 40 cm square. Partitions within the house can be flimsy additions, removable to reorganize the spaces, or even to enlarge them temporarily for social occasions. In the vertical direction, the frame allows jettying out floor by floor, the inner columns maintaining continuity, while outer ones cantilever off the edge of each floor. Where extensions are made, shallow roofs are added to assure shelter from sun and rain. Further variations are produced in the façades by projection of whole bays and smaller cupboards beyond the line of the frame. Many houses have an added half-bay to one side with its own lean-to roof.

Figure 10.22 Courting ritual with traditional antiphonal singing, but now performed for the benefit of tourists (author's photograph 2014).

The house during rites of passage

The Dong house is primarily the abode of two generations, but it is understood as the permanent family seat and abode of ancestors, and is expected to be the site of birth, marriage and death, along with the rituals that accompany them. The symbolism of transition and crossing of thresholds both literal and imagined is therefore strongly reflected in the spaces of the house and the meanings assigned to them during periods of transition. Marriage among the Dong was traditionally a protracted process marking an alliance of households if not villages, and therefore needing to be socially sanctioned. The process of inter-village festivals for singing and courting has already been mentioned in connection with the Blocking Ceremony. This allowed eligible partners to get to know one another within a controlled community context (Figure 10.22). The next stage was for secret meetings, the boy visiting the girl's house of an evening to serenade her in song and play the pipa, climbing a ladder to encounter her at a rear bedroom window, but not being allowed to enter the house. She would sing in return, so although the parents undoubtedly knew what was going on, they and the suitor had scrupulously to avoid one another. After a few such meetings and the establishment of an agreement between the couple and their parents, their engagement could be announced, which was called 'stepping into ash' in reference to the family fireplace.[21] There were specific dates regarded as propitious for this, including 7 February, 6 March, 8 April and 8 August, and it involved some ceremony. First the couple would go to the boy's house to burn incense and

Figure 10.23 Two small girls playing at a house threshold: note the inscribed cill. The couplets posted either side of the opening are elegiac couplets written on white paper to mourn a recently deceased family member, and one of the grass marks over the opening is of bamboo, related to the funeral and intended to dispel bad luck (author's photograph 2014).

paper money and to make offerings of meat and wine to his ancestors at his fireplace, then they would proceed to the girl's house to make offerings to her ancestors at her fireplace, letting off fireworks on the way as a public announcement. After this the girl could visit the boy's house and join in with family tasks, but only entering as far as the gallery, for to intrude into the hearth room would be considered presumptuous.

Marriage

After a due period the couple would marry on a carefully chosen day with much preparation by both families. Details vary across the region, but the basic pattern is that a group from the groom's family, ranging from one elderly couple to twenty people, go to the bride's home to collect her on the afternoon before the wedding day. They arrive with gifts at the appointed hour, setting off fireworks, to find the door blocked with tables and benches. Members of the bride's family demand in song to know who they are, why they come, and so on; and the groom's group must sing replies in what is evidently a reduced version of the village Blocking Ceremony. In due course they are admitted, but only after paying symbolic 'opening gate money'. The visitors are then conducted to the hearth room where a feast is held and offerings are made to the ancestors. It can be quite elaborate. In Sanbao villages, the bride's family place the loom and spinning wheel in the central room, hang a duck on the beam, and place a bowl of wine with floating glutinous rice grass on the table in front of the ancestral shrine. Placed there also is a special doll made of dried grass, dressed with a wooden comb, silver earrings, necklace, ring, new clothing and loincloth. It is the duty of the singing master from the groom's group to sing about the origin of all these objects before the bride's family serves them with a meal and wine, and they must continue with songs about worship of the ancestors, the creation story, and so on. If they cannot remember the words, they are embarrassed.[22] Late in the evening the groom's party depart accompanied by the bride, who thanks her parents for their care of her and weeps in reluctance to leave. She is led to the door by an old woman reciting auspicious words, and sometimes furnished with red bride shoes and a red umbrella. Seemingly universal is the custom that the bride is carried out of the main door by her brother and must not touch the threshold or jambs, lest she bring catastrophe to the household.

The group then process with lanterns to the groom's house where the bride makes an elaborate entry in the absence of the groom and his family, who stay out of the way until the propitious moment arrives to meet her. In Hekou and Wendou, Jingping County, the bride is carried over the threshold by an old woman who has a son and daughter, and they step over the 'seven stars light' beside the gate.[23] In Nine Villages, Xiaojiang area, the Ghost master is present when the bride arrives, and lights a fire in front of the door, making incantations against evil spirits.[24] A person acting the role of Fengchuan, a kind of honorary uncle,[25] who has a son and a daughter, holds the bride's hand as she steps over the fire and gives her a pig feeding bucket. As she enters the house, she treads on the threshold to indicate her reluctance, and places the bucket in a corner, which is supposed to mean the pigs will grow fast and big. While the bride is in the ground floor, her feet are washed by the Fengchuan, who puts on them a pair of new shoes, then accompanied by the bridesmaid she enters the bridal chamber.[26] When it is time to drink 'six conjunction wine', a reference to the six directions,[27] the groom and his parents emerge to greet her and there is another party. At dawn the bride's female companions return home. The next afternoon they bring more gifts to the groom's house, and the groom's companions set up a barrier in front of the gate in yet another version of the Blocking Ceremony. After a few exchanges of song the bride's party are admitted and presented with the wedding feast.

A variant of this arrival found in Xingdi Township, Congjiang County, is that instead of the pig feeding bucket, a bowl of rice is left in front of the house, which the bride must take in and place by the fireplace to show that she brings fertility and abundance. Then the man and woman who escorted her enter the house, followed by the Ghost master. He chooses a place for her to sit facing an auspicious direction and the others sit beside her.[28] He places salted fish, sticky rice, and wine beside the fireplace, then burns paper money and incense to worship the ancestors. He invites the bride and her escorts to eat some of the offering, consumes a token sample himself, then announces that the rite is finished. The groom's family now enter the house and the bride joins in family activity as a family member. On the second day she returns to her parents with a gift of sticky rice and salted fish, escorted by three women. The bride may stay at her parents' home or go to her husband's home as she wishes.[29] Despite the elaboration of these ritual interactions between families, the couple remains subject to a kind of probation, for although she is permitted to meet and sleep with her husband from time to time, the bride is expected to remain resident at her mother's house and the marriage is not regarded as permanent, being dissoluble by either party until she becomes pregnant. It is the first child that effectively consummates the marriage, and in many Dong regions only at its birth was the full dowry paid.

Birth of the first child

The bride is expected to live in her mother's home until she is pregnant, but as her state becomes evident she is taken to her husband's house so that their first child can be born there, the confinement taking place in the inner room. After the birth, the midwife encloses the placenta in a specially prepared kind of yellow mud, and buries it in the ground beside the house's central column. The placenta of each following birth is added in line away from the column. As the yellow mud seals the placenta, it is called the baby's house, with the belief that as long as this 'house' remains within the family home, the baby's soul will not stray, and the baby will be healthy.[30] Various limits and prohibitions apply for the first three days of the baby's life, so that although relatives can visit, it is dangerous for a stranger to enter and bring 'strange air (qi)' which could harm the infant. As a warning a special 'grass mark' is hung on the door, which not only indicates the arrival of a baby, but also its gender[31] (a grass mark is shown in Figure 10.23). The father of a newly born child is also considered potentially dangerous during this period, and should not enter other people's houses or even walk under their eaves, lest he pollute them with 'bloody air'. On the other hand, the first visitor to enter a house after a birth is called the 'stepping over the threshold person'. It should not be a woman: a lucky person is a man who has sired both a son and a daughter, who is well-off in food and clothing, clever, and strong, or is an official: then he is welcomed. The Dong believe this person will influence the new infant's future personality, temperament, and status.[32] Whoever it is, he is treated as the guest of honour, and the host offers a bowl of sweet fermented rice with eggs, then entertains him to a banquet.[33] On the third day after the birth, the family conduct a ceremony. The Ghost

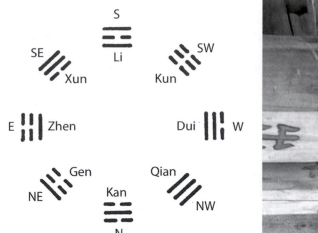

Figure 10.24 The Daoist ring of trigrams, 'later heaven' version (author's drawing).

Figure 10.25 The ring of trigrams on a main beam of a wind and rain bridge in Xiaohuang (author's photograph 2014).

master places a long branch covered with newly woven Dong cloth in the central room, one end facing towards the inner room, the other towards the door. The father stands at the end closest to the inner room, while the Ghost master and others take up positions on both sides. The Ghost master burns incense and paper money while reciting congratulatory words, then picks up the child from the inner room, takes him to the far end of the branch, and hands him to the people standing on each side. Praising the health of the infant, they pass the baby forward, letting him seem to walk along the whole length of the cloth before being received by his father. They believe that 'walking the cloth' will make the baby grow smooth like new cloth, and that life on the road will be smooth and less bumpy.[34] A further rite is to allow the baby to be held by a child of the same gender but from another clan and a healthy family. In recompense the host must give that child three eggs, a roll of sticky rice, and a box of salted fish. These ceremonies having been completed, other people can freely enter the house. In Xiaohuang village, when the baby is one month old, the family cut white paper in the shape of a human figure. They place this paper figure in the middle of the central room or beside the fireplace, and set up bamboos on both sides and three bundles of rice grass in the middle as a model of a door. This manner of honouring the child is said to ensure good health and ease of upbringing. During the first month, the baby is supposed to live at its grandmother's house. In Wujia village, the grandmother gives the baby a first haircut and throws the hair into the ash of the fireplace, which is believed to prevent the child from being frightened. These customs may reflect past matriarchal rights. Although the daughter has married into another clan, her blood relationship comes from the mother's side, so when a baby is born, it must be cared for by the maternal kin, as an indication that the daughter originally belonged to them.[35]

Death

The Dong do what they can to counteract the unpredictability of death and to define a place for it both physically and symbolically. People who die away from the village must not be brought back into the house, and those who have suffered unfortunate deaths should be cremated elsewhere. A person dying of old age or illness at home is considered unlucky simply to die in bed, so as he or she nears the end they are placed in a chair with their feet on a rice box. Once death has occurred, the tripod in the kitchen is inverted, money is thrown in the well to pay for the water to wash the corpse, the relatives put on special clothes, and a grass mark is hung on the outside door to inform the village (Figure 10.23). Care is taken to avoid even numbers: for example if two buckets were brought from the well, someone else might die. The corpse is then washed and laid out on the 'dream bed', contrived of three planks set on benches and covered with a length of cloth. It is set up in the central room which for the northern Dong is the hall, for the southern Dong the fireplace room, temporarily renamed 'mourning hall'. The deceased's head should face the family shrine or fireplace, the feet the outside door.[36] At the foot end are placed a bowl of rice with burning incense, and an oil lamp to light the deceased's way on his or her journey.[37]

The appropriate date for burial must be calculated by a Daoist priest, and it must match the person's birth date. The Daoist is also the adviser in the making of the grave, its site and orientation being more important in feng-shui terms than the location of a house, since ancestors need to sleep in peace and must not return to disturb the living.[38] People choose their own graves, dug by male relatives who euphemistically refer to it as a well. On the day chosen for the funeral the Daoist priest officiates at a ceremony in the house attended by the whole family. He chants invocations about the afterlife and the need for the deceased to take the correct road. Offerings include the sacrifice of a red cock. To start the journey to the grave, the priest smashes a water bowl, and as the corpse is taken out, relatives weep to emphasize the pain of separation.[39] The coffin must not touch the ground along the way. The deceased's departure and consequent change in the house's state is promptly signalled at the house door by changing the white antithetical couplet for red, and hanging a length of red cloth from the lintel, to indicate that bad luck is fading away and good luck is coming.[40] In some places smoke is blown through the house to eliminate bad air.[41] In Lingping County, every house along the road or lane where the coffin passes is hung with leaves or white cloth as a protection from evil spirits.[42]

Further celebrations occur at the grave, where any footprints remaining from the grave-diggers must first be expunged. The Daoist priest uses a compass 'to check the lie of the land', then sacrifices a chicken and lowers it into the grave with incantations. He may draw within the grave the diagram of the eight trigrams, primary scale of the compass and encapsulation of Daoist cosmology (Figure 10.24).[43] Back at the house, a lavish funeral reception follows. Mourners may be welcomed at the gate with a vessel of water in which to wash their hands, followed by a bowl of rice flavoured with the chicken sacrificed at the grave, as a breakfast before the feasting within.[44] In a gesture of extravagance, people are encouraged to take empty bowls away with them for luck.[45] In some regions funerary celebrations are further extended. In Liping County two days after the burial relatives and friends are invited for dinner. After they have eaten, the host makes a small cooking stove of yellow clay and brick, and erects a memory tablet on a base of rice. One month later, a relative visits the grave in the middle of the night and sweeps it three times with three clumps of Bamang grass. He brings the clumps of grass home and places them in front of the memory tablet beside the fireplace, cooking some rice over offerings of paper money then distributing it to everyone. This marks the end of their funeral process, for they believe that by eating the rice cooked in this way, a hopeful future is assured.[46] In Rongjiang County the feast for the dead occurs three days after burial and centres on the ancestors. Family members lay out food and wine in the central room, but before the appointed hour all are obliged to leave except an old lady who lights a small oil lamp and stands at the main door proclaiming a roll-call of ancestors. She leaves the door ajar and retreats to a safe hiding place, then waits an hour before emerging to clear the table, which marks the end of the funeral.[47] The ancestors have visited, but nobody saw them.

Perhaps because of their predominantly oral discourse, the Dong seem to have remained close to the origin of metaphors as physical acts in space, and symbolic actions are seen by them as having a real efficacy in their animist world of spirits. This must be effective in terms of conveying meaning and sharing beliefs, as well as applying shared values to physical space, even if the spirits addressed have no real existence or agency. We should not too readily dismiss such things as 'superstition', nor think that under a scientific world view we have lost them for ever. The lack of belief in the soul persisting after death in modern life, for example, and the denial of heaven as a credible destination, do not eliminate the 'feeling' of the presence of dead relatives whom we know are no longer physically present, but which is so common an experience of grieving. Our dead parents and siblings live on in our memories, and when we share the experience of loss by discussing them with others, even by praying, it is at least an aid to social solidarity and a confirmation of family continuity as well as a reassurance that we are not alone in missing them. In this sense the world of ghosts and spirits remains, as indeed does Santa Claus, a fantasy we still share with our children though many if not most participants know full well that it is an act of the imagination.

Order in time and space

In all of the family rituals the space of the house figures strongly, with its shrine and/or fireplace as centre and its main door as periphery, each decorated with offerings and markings appropriate to the occasion. In the case of marriage, the to and fro between bride and groom's households shows that it is not just the individuals but the whole lineage that is coupling. The homology between the house's fireplace and that in the base of the drum tower, which marks the identity of the community at larger scale, is paralleled by the relationship between house door and village gate, microcosm and macrocosm in a nesting series. In the parallel of door and gate, the holding of blocking rites during the betrothal process directly echoes the larger blocking ceremony between village clan groups, and dramatizes the significance of crossing the threshold. Comparing the rituals of birth and death, there is a marked similarity between the site of the child's first symbolic walk and the dream bed of the deceased, both linear bridge-like constructions set up in the centre of the house and orientated between fireplace or shrine and outside door. They construe life and death respectively as journeys from inside to outside. The direction in which things are contrived to happen is frequently significant, reflected in many aspects of Dong culture. The compass of the Daoist priest, for example, emerges not only during feng-shui investigations concerned with building, siting, and burials, but also ceremonially during passage from one village to another, held by the leader as if in a guiding role, even though everyone already knows the way.[48]

The compass's talismanic role reflects the fundamental importance of the four cardinal points in the ancient Daoist numerology, a system inherited from Han China in which each integer carries special symbolic value.[49] This was briefly discussed in Chapter 4, page 86, but the basic principles are worth recapitulating. The number four represents the four directions, becoming five with addition of centre, eight if intermediate points are included. The progression starts with one, the Dao or original unity. It divides into two as Yin and Yang, female and male, dark and light, even and odd, which is also the general principle for polarities and cycles of all kinds.[50] Three is the realms of heaven, earth, and the human beings caught in between. It can be represented by the trigram, a symbol of three horizontal bars, each of which is either full or broken. Full bars represent yang or male, while broken ones represent yin, and a cycle of eight trigrams (Figure 10.24) includes all possible combinations, rotating in a cycle from full yang to full yin to represent a world where everything works in cycles, thereby combining time and space. The diagram is tied to the space of bodily experience by representing the cardinal points and sub-points, so it is directly transposable onto the compass. It contains further secrets, implicitly incorporating the five elements (or phases, because they change) of wood, metal, fire, earth and water. These can exist in a constructive or destructive sequence, and provide the basis for a fivefold classification of other phenomena, such as colours, tastes, sounds, planets, musical notes, body parts, and so on, with the implication that all are connected with the cardinal points.[51] The eight trigrams figure also represents time, geared to both hour and season. It tacitly embraces the numerical phenomenon of the nine-part magic square centred on five, so that all in all, it provides a compact summary of the order of things which can be learned and redrawn relatively easily. Eight cardinal points, each with its own name, can surround a ninth imaginary point as centre, and nine was the most honourable number in Imperial China, the country regarded by its leaders as the centre of the world.[52]

The use of number was essential in the work of carpenters, and since in pre-modern China numbers were never empty instruments but always carried their symbolic baggage, both the single trigrams and the cycle of eight are frequently represented in carpenters' work (Figure 10.25). The same consciousness is reflected in the everyday rituals and practices among the Dong, which reinforce the meanings given by the carpenters. Arguably, all this reflects a general sensitivity to questions of direction. For example, in the early stage of courting between couples meeting at the supposedly square flower garden, there are ritual exchanges in song about whether they should sit in the north, south, east, or west, enumerating the advantages of each.[53] Traditionally Dong law was supposed to operate in the six directions, that is the four cardinal points combined with up and down, which led logically to a classification of crimes by six major kinds and six minor, with appropriate punishments.[54] Overtly directional in another way was a practice carried out by the parents of a baby who cried too much at night: they put up a signpost at a crossroads somewhere, which by helping others to find their way was supposed to let the baby find his.[55] A disturbed older child was considered to have lost his soul, and his mother could try to restore it with a ceremony at the house threshold facing the outside world and involving rice and an egg, which was believed to help the soul return.[56] Spatial in another sense was the ritual inversion practised by a man claiming to have been falsely accused. He had to stick paper money on his clothes, put the cooking tripod on his head upside down with incense sticks on its legs, put on his rain cape inside out, and go out to a wild place to make his appeal to the spirit of sky and earth.[57] This is strikingly similar to the Russian formula against the Leschi spirit whose trickery causes one to become lost in the woods: take off all one's clothes then put them on inside out.[58] One kind of broken order is counteracted by another, and however blind or deaf the spirits, the actor at least feels able to regain control over the order of his or her world.

The order in space discussed above was accompanied by an order in time, reflecting the sophisticated Chinese calendar with its numerology based on twelve earthly stems and ten heavenly branches, and its success in reconciling the motions of the earth with those of the moon by recognizing a recurrent sixty-year cycle. There had to be correct times not only for religious observances or social rituals like marriages and funerals, and the birth date of a person had to be considered in relation to anticipated activities in much the same way as with Western astrology, but there were also lucky and unlucky days for many other kinds of activities. For example, among the Dong travel was considered risky, but especially to be avoided were the dates 7, 17 or 27 of the month. Even at home evil spirits could be rampant, and the fourteenth day of the seventh month was an especially unlucky time when everyone locked their doors against them.[59] Essentially practical tasks were also computed for luck according to the calendar. The ancient Chinese carpentry manual, the 'Lu Ban Jing', which was known and followed by Dong carpenters, includes numerous tables about the appropriate times for undertaking particular construction tasks or starting to assemble certain building types.[60]

Building rituals

Although most building work among the Dong has long been carried out by specialist carpenters, and although the chronological sequence of the building process necessarily follows the discipline of frame construction, the whole local population of kin and neighbours is needed to assemble a house, and the obligations of the 'kuan' political organization dictate the duty of all to help, in a reciprocal fashion. As the house is the seat of a family and expected to bridge generations, its construction is believed powerfully to influence the family's fortune, and therefore the building process includes numerous rites both to propitiate harmful spirits and to bring blessings and prosperity.[61] These include not only feasts with specific kinds of offerings, but also theatrical enactments, with people cast in roles to recite songs and poems loaded with Dong mythology. The building rituals can be divided into eight stages. The first is for the house owner to select a carpenter, who is normally invited for a meal. They visit the site together and discuss the functional requirements, the appropriate number of bays, and the choice of propitious dimensions, already taking into account the rules of 'Lu Ban'.

The second stage involves purifying the site and determining the orientation of the fireplace room or main hall, for which the feng-shui master must be present. He makes a detailed reading of the site with the compass, but only after offerings have been made to the local spirits and the site has been sprinkled with holy water. The compass is set up on a special table on a bed of rice – always stressing fertility – and a reading is marked with a thread that will determine the centre line of the hearth room or main hall. Not only must the local topography and mountains be read symbolically and taken into account, but also the positions of the neighbouring houses and the potential influence of the owner's birth date.

Figure 10.26 Pre-assembling a house structure at Xiaohuang (photograph by Derong Kong, 2010).

Figure 10.27 Erecting a house structure at Xiaohuang (photograph by Derong Kong 2010).

The third stage is the acquisition of timber for the frame, which is mainly cut in a forest area belonging to the owner's family, and must not be done without propitiating the mountain and tree spirits and choosing an auspicious day. However, the very first tree to be cut, and subject of the most ceremony, is the ridge beam, also called the golden beam. It is the key member, since adding it tops out the house and completes the frame, and unlike the other timbers it must be 'stolen' from the forest of another clan or village. This is done in the middle of the night but with due ceremony, including begging the spirits' permission, letting off fireworks, and leaving a gift of money for the land owner.[62] The tree must fall in a specified direction and then be carried to the village without being set down, before being placed carefully in a propitious direction. After it has been obtained the other timbers can be collected and stacked.

The fourth stage is the inviting of the trees onto the trestle for processing by the carpenters, another occasion for offerings and fireworks, and with controlled orientation. Now the mark-ink craftsman, leader of the carpenters, assumes the dominant role, but as they start on the golden beam, it is the house owner who holds the other end of the string as the first ink line is snapped. A general feast follows. Over the subsequent fortnight or so the team of carpenters marks up and cuts all members of the frame, along with all mortise holes and projecting tenons. The sizes are coordinated by a special bamboo ruler prepared for the job by the mark-ink craftsman (Figure 10.20), and in the absence of drawings he must remember how many components of each size are needed and how they will fit. This stage requires a high degree of skill and accuracy, since the communal construction that follows must be achieved quickly without revision or adjustment.

The setting up of the frame comprising the fifth and sixth stages is the most dramatic, for it rises in two days, with the help of the whole local population (Figures 10.26 and 10.27). On the first day the flat gable-like sub-frames are assembled and moved into place ready for the final erection. Offerings are made, and there is a ceremony of 'starting the hammer'. Early the next morning starting at around 4 am more offerings are made and a cock is sacrificed. The frames are joined with intermediate members, intending that the entire house frame be complete by sunrise except for the ridge beam, which is added later in a separate ceremony as the climactic gesture. This is the seventh stage, which should take place on a particularly propitious day soon after the frame is complete. The mark-ink craftsman is the main actor, playing the part of the legendary carpenter Lu Ban, while two of his assistants play Wenqu Xing and Wuqu Xing,

Figure 10.28 Conflicts of modern life: people watching television by the communal hearth and under the dragon in Yin'tan drum tower (author's photograph).

civil spirits. An elaborate table of offerings is set up, a handful of symbolic objects is packed into a slot in the beam, and after preliminary prayers the assistants who act as civil spirits climb to the top of the frame and throw down ropes to lift the golden beam. Playing Lu Ban, the mark-ink craftsman ascends the ladder making a continuous recitation step by step, and when he reaches the top supervises the placing of the beam, then walks along it from end to end wearing brand new shoes. The assistants throw ceremonial cakes to the gathered villagers below, and a general feast follows funded by the householder. The house frame being complete and ready for finishing, everyone celebrates.[63]

The eighth and last stage after the filling out of the frame marks the handover and occupation of the house, with the mark-ink craftsman again playing Lu Ban, and a healthy, wealthy, middle-aged man who has sired male and female children playing the 'Wealthy Spirit'. In a house with a hall the ritual takes place at the inner door, the threshold to the hall, and begins with the two players declaring their roles, the Wealthy Spirit on the outside bringing gifts of rice and gold, Lu Ban on the inside declaring the excellence of the door and enumerating its propitious dimensions. After some altercation similar to that performed at the Blocking Ceremony, the Wealthy Spirit is admitted and presents a money bag to the house owner. He then proceeds to light the fire in the hearth for the first time, using glowing coals from another of the family fireplaces. All is done with poetry and song to reinforce the meaning of their actions.

Conclusion

To integrate the material of this chapter into the general themes of this book, some comparisons are needed. Following on from the Dogon, the Dong demonstrate even more clearly developed building types, and the family house is again the focus of the family. In the same way, the drum tower echoes the political role of the Toguna, though with a broader public purpose. Decorative and representational work is again reserved for public buildings, more elaborately than with the Dogon, making the communal buildings stand out even more from the houses. Less has been noted of Dong shrines, but they are present in many forms, omitted only to avoid making this chapter too long.[64] Just as the Dogon village has a focal square, so too does the Dong, showing a powerful sense of community and group identity, but the contrast between centre and periphery is perhaps stronger, especially with the addition of wind and rain bridges and frequent celebrations involving the threshold. The Dong seem to possess a heightened sense of the significance of crossing thresholds, stressed by the theatre of their blocking ceremonies at varied scales which tell of separation and reunion, clarifying group identities and territory. Decoration of thresholds is reported among the Sioux and the Dogon, but seems more marked among the Dong, with added markings to celebrate birth, death, seasonal festivals, and even personal misfortunes. The Dong building process, persisting still,[65] is based on skilled carpentry with local wood but requires the aid of the whole community, so the stages in creating a house become a local spectacle, during which all witness what a house consists of and how it is made. Like other social rituals, the building rituals transmit shared knowledge and mythology, but more particularly they define what a house is. Experience of them confirms people's expectations and consolidates the house as family seat and place of spiritual being, not just a commodity as in the modern world. The carpenters' geometry is no empty technical exercise but carries a Daoist-based cosmology paralleled by ordering in time, for all operations must be completed at auspicious moments. That a compass can also be read as a clock sheds interesting light on the perceived connection between time and direction, and on Henri Bergson's observation that we can hardly avoid representing time in terms of space.[66]

Looking back over the middle section of this book, we see a progression from hunter-gatherers living almost naked in the landscape to a specialized agricultural community in a permanent village with many craft technologies, considerable specialization, elaborate political organization and developed building types. I have presented it like an evolutionary series, which was admittedly part of the aim, but the observations all belong to the last century or so, and the people are all modern even if their technologies seem outdated. Cultures evolve quickly, so we can by no means assume they represent past stages, only that they show us ways people *can* or *could* live, people we know to be biologically much the same as ourselves. Looking across this rich display of cultural representation through artefacts as well as myths, we find familiar human themes celebrated again and again: the discovery of fire and cooked food which we have had for the best part of a million years, language which we have shared for at least the past 100,000, representation in art, now pushed back to at least 40,000, and tools for agriculture and technologies like weaving and smithing which are more recent, but still prior to cities and writing. The handed-down memories have a vivid character, as we see social institutions and mythologies displayed through architecture along with relations to gods and cosmos, and the development of sign and number.

It has not been my concern to examine the current predicament of the Dong under the influence of tourism and globalization, and readers will have noticed some ambivalent alternation of past and present tenses (Figures 10.22 and 10.28).[67] My purpose has been rather to document how their relationship with their architecture still worked in the late twentieth century, and particularly to look at their building rituals, which may represent a persistence of practices once much more widespread.

Notes

1   For summaries of theories about their origin see Geary et al. 2003, pp. 2–3 and Ruan 2006 pp. 14, 15, 20–3.

2   For detail on their language see Geary et al. 2003, pp. 26–42.

3   Geary et al., 2003, p. 214. Written literature started in 1958, songs were remembered by rhyme and repetition, and could be 1,700 lines long. Drama had been transcribed since the 1830s in Chinese.

4   As elsewhere in China government reports and gazetteers were compiled and retained at regional centres, without being available locally.

5   For Dong architecture the best general source is Ruan 2006.

6   My reading of the Dong would not have been possible without the researches and translations of two of my PhD students at the University of Sheffield, Xuemei Li 2008 and Derong Kong 2016, both of whom I gratefully acknowledge.

7   *Qi*, sometimes written *chi* or *chii*, is manifested in the wind and the breath, linking rhythms of the earth and the body, and exists in yang and yin forms. It lies behind the cycle of the five phases, and the six *qi* play a major role in Chinese medicine. For further information on this puzzling and untranslatable concept see Needham 1956, pp. 216ff.

8   Before the revolution and consequent repression there were Daoist temples with monks, and a handed-down Daoist expertise has persisted among an elite who can read and write Mandarin, and are therefore regarded by the illiterate as having special powers.

9   See Ruan 2006, pp. 78–80. A concise general summary of Han feng-shui is given in Schinz 1996, pp. 416–17.

10   For a more general discussion of iconography see Ruan 2006, p. 96.

11   Large villages may have more than one drum tower, each still representing a specific social group with recognizable territory. Dimen has five.

12   Many areas used to favour cross-cousin alliances, but legal adjustments have been made over the last half-century to allow more flexibility, diluting these customs.

13   Ruan 2006, p. 94.

14   Bridge gods are depicted and described in Xuemei Li's PhD thesis *The Life Bridge: An Anthropology of the Origins of the Dong 'Wind and Rain' Bridge in Southern China*, University of Sheffield, 2008.

15   Ibid.

16   Geary et al. 2003, pp. 205–9.

17   In a more general sense these rituals of arrival and departure in China are fruitfully analysed by Charles Stafford in Stafford 2000.

18   Alberti 1986, p. 13 (Book I, Ch. IX).

19   Ruan 2006, p. 90.

20 Ibid., p. 162.

21 Derong Kong's research from Zhang 2008.

22 Ibid.

23 Derong Kong's research from Yang 1999.

24 The Ghost master acts on behalf of the individual family, to dispel ghosts and pray to gods. When villagers are ill or have suffered loss, they come to him for an appropriate ritual. He also performs some rituals connected with rites of passage, such as determining the day and time of the ritual, as well as organizing it. He is also involved when people construct a new house. Villagers both respect and fear him, for his magic arts and spells apply not only to ghosts but can also be implemented on people. Information from Derong Kong.

25 Fengchuan is a temporary title for a middle-aged man with a son and daughter whose success in life and fertility bestow good luck. It is an honour for him, but he must be familiar with the rules and procedures of the marriage ritual, as his job is to manage it.

26 Derong Kong's research from Yang 1999.

27 Cardinal points plus up and down, so a symbol of the universal.

28 In Leli Seventy-two villages' area, the bride sits against the central column and faces east (Derong Kong's research from Yang 1999).

29 Derong Kong's research from Zhang 2008.

30 Derong Kong's research from Wu 1989 (B), p. 98.

31 In Liping County the grass mark for a boy is made of one chilli and rice grass, while for a girl it is a cruciform grass mark and egg shell. The Orange leaves means blessing the infant in an auspicious way, making it easy to bring up (Wu 1989 (B)). In Xiaohuang village, if the infant is boy, the grass mark should be made of chill and rice grass, if the infant is girl, it should be made of eggshell, red cloth and rice grass.

32 Derong Kong's research from Wu 1989 (B).

33 Geary et al. 2003, p. 96.

34 Ibid., p. 106.

35 Derong Kong's research from Zhang 2008.

36 Derong Kong's field survey.

37 Geary et al., 2003, p. 106.

38 Ibid., p. 111.

39 Ibid., pp 102–11.

40 Derong Kong's research from Xiao 2010.

41 Derong Kong's research from Yang 1999.

42 Derong Kong's research from Wu 1989 (A).

43 Geary et al., 2003, p. 109.

44 Derong Kong's research from Yang 1999.

45 Geary et al., 2003, p. 110.

46 Derong Kong's research from Wu 1989 (A).

47 Derong Kong's research from Yang 1999.

48 Geary et al. 2003, p. 207.

49 On the essentials of Daoism see Needham 1956, pp. 33–164, pp. 216ff.

50 Female/male and dark/light have no automatic relationship, the first depending on sexual reproduction and the second on the rotation of the earth, but sun and moon are the most

prominent heavenly bodies, and women's menses have usually been related to the latter. In a patriarchal culture run by an emperor called 'Son of Heaven' and sitting on the solar axis, the association of gender with sun and moon was a powerful supporting assumption and taken as self-evident truth.

51 See the table of symbolic correlations in Needham 1956, pp. 262–3.

52 Alfred Schinz (1996) named his encyclopaedic book about Chinese town planning *The Magic Square* as he considered this the key concept.

53 Geary et al. 2003, pp. 78–9.

54 Ibid., p. 66.

55 Ibid., p. 99.

56 Ibid., p. 171.

57 Ibid., p. 159.

58 Sinyavsky 2007, p. 119.

59 Geary et al. 2003, pp. 170 and 178.

60 Ruitenbeek 1989: translation of the 'Lu Ban Jing' with commentary in which he claims (p. 138) that almanac sections comprise over 30 per cent of the first of the two books, and he gives a list of activities so regulated.

61 There seems to be a yin–yang balance between lucky and unlucky events, so that for example in the 'Lu Ban Jing' the positive and negative prescriptions are about equal; see Ruitenbeek 1989.

62 Yu 2001 pp. 108–10, text obtained and translated by Xuemei Li for her doctoral thesis at Sheffield that I supervised.

63 Fu and Yu, 1997, pp. 181–2.

64 Xing Ruan deals with them in some detail, see Ruan 2006, pp. 60–5, and his long text on the Sax ritual pp. 70–8.

65 A visit to several Dong villages in May 2014 revealed recent wooden buildings as well as the creeping takeover by block and concrete, and we were able to interview carpenters at work.

66 Bergson 1910, pp. 124–5.

67 Their predicament in the modern world has been extensively discussed both by Norman Geary (2003) and Xing Ruan (2006).

PART 3
MODERNITIES

Figure 11.1. A woman preparing the ground for vegetables in the old way, near Cologne (author's photograph 2014, sanctioned by LVR-Freilichtmuseum Kommern).

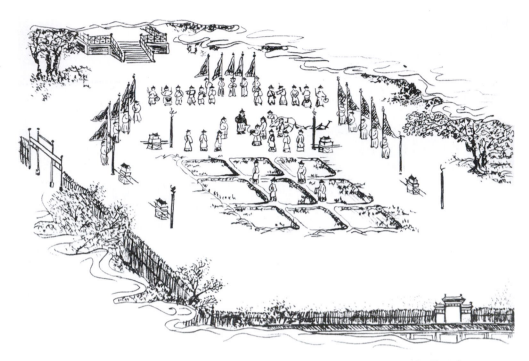

Figure 11.2. The Chinese Emperor ritually ploughing the first field in spring at the Temple to Agriculture, with plots laid out according to the Magic Square (from Schinz 1996, p. 70, his redrawing after a seventeenth century print).

Figure 11.3. European village scene, for mixed production and with free-range chickens (author's photograph, sanctioned by LVR-Freilichtmuseum Kommern).

CHAPTER 11
THE EUROPEAN FARMSTEAD

As we saw in the last chapter with the Dong and their irrigated rice paddies, agriculture requires manipulation of the landscape, from choice of suitable sites for growing particular crops to meticulous hard toil in preparing the ground and caring for them. It requires a deep consciousness of topography and climate, careful observation of what will grow where, of how much sun and water a site obtains, how well protected it is from storms or frost. Also staple crops must be perpetuated, the seed being gathered and preserved for the next season, with an eye to the largest best yielding specimens to improve the genetic line. Not only are grasses like wheat and rice the result of long selection for larger grain, but fruits have been enlarged and sweetened to be edible without cooking. Textile plants like flax and cotton were chosen for their pliability and strength of fibre. Maize was developed for its large cob by indigenous people in South America around 3,000 years ago, and we know it particularly to be the result of human manipulation because it is not self-propagating without human agency.[1] Most cultivated plants, then, were a vital stock, among the most precious things one could own. Numerous rituals from across Europe have been reported about gathering and protecting the last sheaf of grain in which the crop's spirit is supposedly retained, the origin of the corn dolly, noted as 'Mother Earth' by George Ewart Evans, collector of oral history in rural East Anglia.[2] We have witnessed the importance of Dogon granaries and their mythical role in the making of the world, built with separate compartments dedicated to the holy seeds. Nearer home, the widespread use of the term threshold, in both the literal and metaphorical sense, testifies to the importance of the gathered harvest as the essential foundation for modern life.

The ten-thousand-year history of the spread of agriculture does not allow identification of a clear beginning,[3] for Aboriginal peoples modified the landscape by staging regular fires, and may well also have developed orchards by spreading the crop of fruit-bearing trees or groves of nuts.[4] The manioc gardens of the Tukanoans seen in Chapter 8 were clearly agriculture, if carried out alongside hunting, even though they lasted but a few of years and left little long-term trace. The equatorial climate did not require much designation of seasons, but in cooler parts of the world the need to sow and reap at the right times prompted the ordering of the year and the development of a strict calendar, along with anxiety about predicting and controlling the weather. Agriculture therefore brought with it not only a reordering of space and taking possession of land, but also a definitive ordering of time. Life depended on choice of the right moment for sowing and reaping, and a bad harvest could mean starvation. Evans summed it up as follows:

> The harvest was the climax of the rural year … The whole village was involved and there was a carefully laid down ritual which had long roots far back in medieval times. The first step was known as *Taking the Harvest*. This meant that the men on each farm, with the addition of certain seasonal workers … agreed with the farmer to bring in the harvest on 'piecework' … The harvest worker certainly earned his double pay as he started working at five o clock in the morning and finished at dusk.[5]

The harvest festival still exists in the church calendar as a moment for the display of the earth's bounty and the giving of thanks to divine forces, but such ritual structures used to be much more dominant and occurred across the world. In Imperial China the Emperor, as Son of Heaven, was obliged to lead a series of annual rituals in temples attached to the capital (Figure 11.2), including the ritual ploughing of the first furrow of the holy field in spring to open national agricultural production, which was accompanied by a personal ordeal of fasting.[6] Should this observance not be made, disaster was sure to follow. The holy field, accompanied by the altar to the Earth God, was orientated and divided into nine squares, following the ancient numerological system of the magic square, the cosmological structure taken also as the basis of Chinese city planning. Right up to the end of the nineteenth century, therefore, the intimate connection between agriculture, the city, and the calendar was regularly celebrated as a universal order, and in rural China shrines to the Earth God still exist.

Agriculture was at first a chancy occupation, leaving people subject to starvation after a bad harvest, but it meant that human beings could settle and build to accumulate specialist skills, so that villages, then towns and cities, could develop. With the Dogon the making of cloth was prominent, and also the quasi-magical role of the smith; there were also priests or holy men. Later came craftsmen and builders, eventually scribes and teachers, and finally violins and violinists along with philosophers. There was simultaneously the market, a move from barter to money, and finally banks leading to globalization. Staying in one place and harvesting crops meant long-term commitment, at least a season to cover sowing to harvest, but many years to develop reliably fertile fields and irrigation systems, centuries to improve techniques and refine crops. The investment was enormous, gratification delayed, and in climates beyond tropical zones overwintering entailed storing of produce. Caring for the land came to mean investment far beyond a generation, and so brought the necessity of handing down to children and inheriting family projects from ancestors, sowing trees you would not live to fell, or putting extensive work into a small rice paddy that would yield little immediately but extended a growing system.

If the farm is an enormous investment, it is also everywhere an expression of a way of life and the processes of work. In Europe it made good sense until only a century ago to plant a wide range of crops and raise a variety of animals, for the first object was to feed the family; there was need for a mixed diet, and before the advent of refrigeration most crops were perishable so had to be eaten in season. Therefore food on the table varied with the time of year and it was necessary to grow things to mature at different times. Also there was a need for reserves, so if one thing failed another would provide. This rational explanation omits the aesthetic delight of the cornucopia and the culinary development and tastes that went with it, all the more affecting when it is the product of your own work. Taking excess crop to market or bartering with neighbours would allow you increasingly to have things made by others, but developed eventually into the monoculture of modern mass-farming, which converts the entire crop into money and the farmer into another anonymous consumer at the supermarket. But only three or so generations ago all that a farming family owned was bound up in the farm and its equipment, the stored bounty of the harvest, and the stock of animals. It was their wealth, their source of pride and expression of aesthetic pleasure, exemplified both in the farm buildings and the way the land was treated. It was readable not only in the size and elaborate construction of the barn but also in the extent of the manure heap, not only in the decorated front of the farmhouse but also in the making of gates and fences, and in the cultivation of

HOME AND COUNTRY ARTS

By W. R. LETHABY

Figure 11.4 Iconic haystack in Lethaby's book (author's scan of Lethaby 1923).

Figure 11.5. Wooden handmade fence, Guizhou Province, China (author's photograph 2014).

Figure 11.6. Farmhouse interior with traditional handmade furniture (author's photograph 2014, sanctioned by LVR-Freilichtmuseum Kommern).

247

the kitchen garden, with lettuces and beans set out in ordered patterns alongside carnations (Figures 11.1 and 11.3). The layout of a vegetable patch is the record of months of orderly work which can be accomplished with rhythm and skill, involving a degree of close visual and physical contact with the soil that has now become rare, since the average field feels no footfall but only the occasional pass of a tractor wheel.

That William Lethaby noted the rituals of agriculture and admired the skill with which a good hayrick was stacked has already been mentioned in the introduction. He even included a small drawing of one on the title page of his book *Home and Country Arts* (Figure 11.4). It was a temporary building for storing fodder for the winter, topped with its own thatched roof made of the same material. The appearance and disappearance of such structures followed the progress of the year, revealing both the extent of hay production and the farmer's skill in preserving the material. Writing in the 1920s, Lethaby defined a good many further country crafts and rituals, but the list could be almost endless.[7] The making of a fence (Figure 11.5), a gate, a cart, a basket, let alone a pie or a loaf of bread, could be done with skill and pride, revealing the essence of a craft tradition in a handmade world. In the same way the farm buildings in the countryside naturally reflected the agricultural process and its changes with the seasons.

> Study of old work of all kinds shows us that a play element was maintained in it all as necessary to its very self and being – an element which we may call variously pleasure or quality or poetry or art … Of old time, farming, while as it always has been mighty hard work, was organised to include a series of festivals.[8]

That it was hard work is not in doubt. The cutting of the wheat by hand at the right moment, binding it into sheaves, then getting it into the barn required enormous effort, and then there was the need to extract the grain. Nowadays this is done instantly in the field by the combine harvester, but traditionally it was done in the barn with a flail on the threshing floor, an activity spread throughout the winter that took hours daily.[9] The museum guide for the Cloppenburg open-air museum, the oldest in Germany, reports that until the end of the nineteenth century the farmer and his assistants would flail together from about three in the morning for several hours, at a rate of thirty strokes a minute wielding a flail weighing two kilos, followed by the gathering of the precious grain and the rebundling of the straw for other purposes.[10] After that the grain still had to pass through the local mill before it became flour: the staple bread was hard won. Social conditions could be feudal. Farm labourers were generally paid little because they were given board and lodging, but poverty was never far away. Reporting about rural Suffolk as late as 1900, Evans describes the practice of gleaning, the search for spilled grain among the wheat stubble after the harvest was cut. Children were kept from school for a whole week to help, for only this precious salvaged grain would keep hunger at bay during the following winter. People competed for access to the field, so the farmer had to guard it until he could declare it open, leaving a last sheaf standing as a symbolic 'policeman'. In some villages bells were rung to regulate the hours of gleaning.[11]

If there was poverty, there was also prosperity, and evidence can still be found across Europe of wealthy well-equipped farms whose buildings can hardly be dismissed as utilitarian, being on the contrary highly elaborated. Until the end of the nineteenth century the lowland landscape at least was mainly devoted to agriculture, operated from villages formed largely of groups of farms, but usually also equipped with a church and a whole village economy of millers, smiths, wheelwrights, saddlers, potters, weavers, masons, carpenters, thatchers and other such specialists to fulfil local needs using locally available materials. There were not only beautiful buildings made to last but also a legible language of building types, differentiating one purpose from another and each region from the next. They have been slow to enter the canon of architectural history, relegated largely under 'vernacular', but examples have been gathered in open-air museums, starting with Skansen in Stockholm of 1891, which had a crucial influence on the development of Scandinavian modern architecture.[12] For the purposes of this book, farms are a wonderful example of a way of life strongly expressed, with an ordered landscape and calendar, ritual activities, hard work yielding physical results, and close relationships with plants and animals.

The Lower Saxon Hall House

This is a type remarkably consistent in its basic arrangement, found all the way from the Netherlands to Pomerania. There are impressive German examples dating from around 1600, but few persist in original form outside open-air museums. The main source for this chapter is the life work of Gerhard Eitzen, who started to record and draw them in the 1930s and helped with the moving and reconstruction in museums.[13] His collected work includes hundreds of plans showing both the consistency of the essential type and the endless small variations that make each unique. The hall house is a great linear building (Figure 11.7) culminating in a central hearth, where originally an open fire burned continuously on the floor, giving out heat and light, and cooking food in iron pots slung over it on a kind of crane. There was originally no chimney but only a spark hood, so the smoke drifted upwards through the loft to escape at the ends of the ridge. In front of the hearth was a long central space stretching back axially towards the main entrance, spatially continuous but divided into two areas called *Flett* and *Deele*. The *Flett* was the area around the hearth, extending into side bays with a dining table one side and a washing area on the other.[14] This was the domestic centre and realm of the farmer's wife, where the cooking was done and all would gather to eat and relax. The *Deele* (earlier form of *Diele*, modern German hall or entry space) was by contrast the long floor area beyond used for agricultural purposes. It had to be accessible through double doors by horse-drawn wagons in order to bring in and unload the harvest, which was stored in sheaves on the floor above. Later it became the threshing floor where every winter morning grain was beaten out of the ear. Eitzen also claims that it was used along with the *Flett* for festive purposes, but does not give further detail.[15] On either side of the *Deele* in bays projecting beyond the main structural frame were stalls for cattle, which in winter could be fed with hay directly from the *Deele*. To contain dung and urine, these side areas were set considerably lower, and rather than clearing them daily, straw was added to produce a deep layer of well-trodden manure. Horses were kept in loose stalls at the front of the building to either side of the main doors, ready to be saddled up or harnessed. Thus in its basic arrangement the building brought people, their animals and the stored harvest together under one great roof. Archaeological remains of prehistoric versions suggest that this arrangement is ancient, along with the form of timber construction that it requires.[16] Essentially this consists of a line of columns on each side supporting the ties of a triangular roof pitched at 45° or more (Figure 11.7). It was originally

(a)

(b)

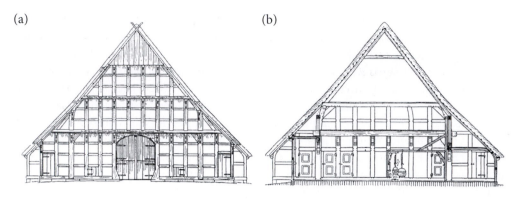

(c)

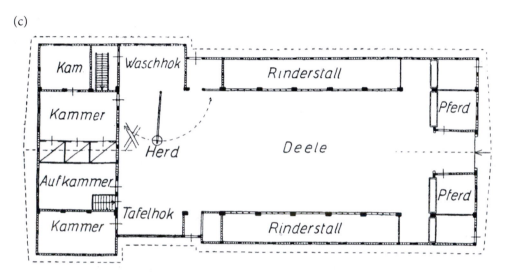

(d)

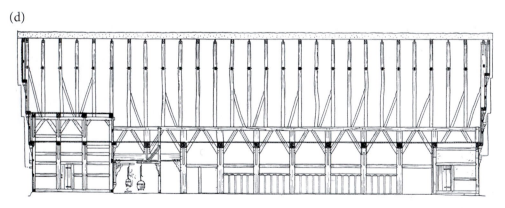

Figure 11.7 Lower Saxon Hall House at Emsland, North Germany, a. Front with jettied levels, b. Cross-section, c. Ground floor plan; key: Deele = hall, Herd = hearth, Rinderstall = cow stalls, Pferd = horse, Kammer = bedroom, Aufkammer = reception room, Tafelhock = table corner, Waschhock = washing corner. d. Long section (Drawings by Gerhard Eitzen, Archive Museumsdorf Hösseringen).

clad in thatch, by-product of the harvest, which covered most of the external surface, was renewable, and provided good insulation, but it also defined the gable end as main front and place of display, set if possible to face the village street.

From surviving records it seems a dozen or more people lived in such buildings and the social structure could be quite complicated. Before the late nineteenth century political power in Germany was divided between the aristocracy, the church and the burghers, excluding the rural population. Farmers, though in charge of the *Hof*, mostly suffered some degree of bondage, varying from protection payments and rents to much harsher restrictions limiting inheritance, requiring permission for marriage, and yielding children into service.[17] Under the farmer's control in turn were the farmhands, who ate at his table and were therefore well-nourished, but gave their lives to service on the farm. They were accommodated in lofts above the horses if they were male, in side rooms at the hearth end of the *Deele* if female, both groups spatially assigned to the working part. By contrast the farmer and his family occupied separate apartments behind the hearth beyond the *Flett*, where there were cupboard beds in the wall for warmth, separate quarters for the generations, and special lofts above for stored grain and other produce of value. As the technology developed, this room-group came to include a *Stube* or clean living room with a stove fed and flued from the *Flett* behind. Some historic reports by eighteenth- and nineteenth-century visitors, including Voltaire, claim that the *Flett* was dirty and smoky, but another author comments positively on how perfectly placed the farmer's wife was at the hearth to oversee all domestic and agricultural operations. The fact that her name was often inscribed alongside his on the gable front underlines the significance of the role, in charge of everything at home while he was in the fields.[18] It is difficult to gauge the impact of the open central fire, but it was retained even in noble architecture long after the chimney was known and understood.[19] Careful tending and skilful handling of fuel could presumably reduce the smoke, but it also had its uses in curing meats, drying out the stored harvest, and deterring insects. Eitzen was convinced that the smoke had served a major role in preserving structural carpentry, helping some buildings to last in good condition for 400 years.[20] In the case of the *Zweiständer*, the basic type, the whole building was assembled around two lines of columns, each the heart of an oak tree around 50 cm thick, tenoned into a thick plate (see Figure 11.7 sections).[21] These were linked with a line of longitudinal lintels, and to cross the broader *Flett* at the end, two pairs of columns were omitted in favour of deeper lintels, the largest timbers of the building. On this basic structure the cross-beams of the upper floor were placed, and the roof trusses could be assembled without further ties or collars, leaving a great triangular volume for the storage of the harvest. All this was specialist work by a *Zimmermann*, local carpenter, doubtless with the farmer's and his hands' help. Surviving examples from the late sixteenth century were built to last with evident pride, most vigorously expressed in the front gable (Figure 11.8) by constructive elaboration through serial jettying out, exposed frame, half hip, or added decoration. Here also long inscriptions were carved, recording the name of the farmer and sometimes his wife, the name of the carpenter, the date, and the blessing of Lord Jesus Christ.[22] As with earlier examples in this book, there is no doubt that this was the front and place of arrival, of all sides that treated most formally, and most richly decorated. Generally the fenestration of the private rear end remained asymmetrical in accordance with the inner layout, unstressed by any need for spectacle.

Although the great hall house encompassed much of the farm, it seldom stood on its own. An arrangement sketched by Eitzen (Figure 11.9) shows the farmhouse on its plot next to

Figure 11.8. Quatmannshof in Cloppenburg Freilichtmuseum near Bremen (author's photograph 1983).

Figure 11.9. Farmstead in Damnatz with village street bottom right and thatched hall house set back. The building on the street was a later added barn (drawing by Gerhard Eitzen, Archiv Museumsdorf Hösseringen).

another, flanked by three other buildings and a well. On the street with an outer entrance is a hay barn, defending the farm from the growing village. Hay was kept separately to avoid the smoke which would spoil the fodder for the animals, and the central entrance bay allowed for protracted unloading as well as adding a layered entry sequence for visitors. Beyond this barn was the pigsty, kept separate against the odour, and at the back of the plot was the bakehouse separated on grounds of fire. The well is recognizable by its counterweighted lever. Eitzen dates these subordinate buildings as more recent than the house of 1650, and the entrance barn follows a practice not current until the eighteenth century, but all constructions follow the same technology of exposed timber frame and thatched roof.[23] Looking beyond the farm at the village, one might find a row of farms side by side on the main street, and Eitzen mentions the presence of a timber-framed church opposite the farm he drew. There might also be workshops of smiths and wheelwrights, brewhouses, and wind- or watermills. The Cloppenburg open-air museum includes an inn built on the same pattern as a farmhouse.

Comparisons

Eitzen's 750-page book includes endless plans of the same type with subtle variations, and the type was followed for centuries. It is not just formal and structural, but above all a layout that sets persons, animals and tasks in an expected order, defining space in terms of centre and periphery, oppositions and adjacencies, so that anyone local visiting a farm for the first time would recognize more or less how it worked and regulate their behaviour accordingly. Comparing it with examples in earlier chapters, we see again both an increasing hierarchy of privacy from front to back as in the Chinese Yamen, and a combination of centrality in the hearth with linearity in the building as a whole. Moving to a larger scale, we note that the village possessed a clear set of building types befitting different functions, each with its own special features and hierarchy. The village church served as a social focus like the Dong drum tower, but in Germany, as in most of Europe, time has moved on faster, most old buildings have now gone, and such ancient farmhouses as persist are no longer used as originally. Only in the open-air museum do you get an integrated sense of how it was, for in the course of the twentieth century farms became mechanized, fields larger, and the need for a large workforce evaporated. Nor was there further need for large-scale local storage, so barns have fallen into disuse along with the granary. The preciousness of the seed for resowing, so vital to the Dogon, is all but forgotten. There is a curious similarity between the Lower Saxon Hall House and the Tukanoan maloca, despite the latter's much shorter lifespan and lack of a specialist builder. Both are linear structures with a celebrated gable, primary columns as starting point of both spatial definition and construction, domestic rear with central hearth, and a great sheltering roof. As there was no path for cultural diffusion, the similarities must reflect independent invention, if also the limited size and span of trees as a building material, the need for manhandling, and the aim to produce as much shelter as possible. The only thing that might truly count as cultural diffusion is the central hearth, essential for warmth as well as cooking in the German farmhouse, but regarded in the maloca also as the house's womb. This sets up in both buildings a fundamental sense of centre and periphery. We might also consider the linear progress from the *Hof* or plaza, the confrontation with the decorated gable, and subsequent progression through the axial interior space towards the hearth, as a type of spatial layering potentially present in the habitus over a very long period, and always ready for reinvention.

The farm as a functionalist proposition

The idea 'form follows function', usually attributed to Louis Sullivan, became a rallying cry for the Modern Movement at the turn of the twentieth century, driven on by a biological notion of fitness for purpose and by a recognition that the proliferation of applied styles was becoming increasingly meaningless.[24] The arts and crafts philosophies of William Morris and Lethaby paved the way with their concentration on the elegance of things simple and direct, following their own logic. Silos and industrial buildings were admired by Le Corbusier and others, and when the Modern Movement was in full spate were ascribed to something called 'The Functional Tradition'.[25] As I have argued elsewhere, however, most buildings of the early Modern Movement are functional only in a somewhat limited sense, often shaped more by a logic of construction and assembly than by disciplines of use,[26] or driven by an abstract aesthetic system borrowed from the other visual arts. In some key cases too, an ideal of open-ended flexibility precluded any kind of direct response to intended usage.[27] But some early modernists were more serious and sincere in their functionalism, particularly Hugo Häring (1882–1958), whose masterpiece of 1924–5 was a farm complex (Figures 11.10 and 11.11). After an early career in Hamburg, Häring arrived in Berlin around 1920, became acquainted with Ludwig Mies van der Rohe, and was given space in his office. There the two architects

Figure 11.10. Farmstead at Garkau, near Lübeck, designed by Hugo Häring for Otto Birtner, 1925, seen from approach lane with cowhouse to left and barn behind to right (author's photograph c. 1990).

convened an avant-garde group, the Ring, which had key roles in the modernist architectural politics of Berlin and the founding of Congrès International d'Architecture Moderne (CIAM).[28] Under the desperate economic conditions following the First World War hardly anything was being built, but revolutionary change had ignited hope, so this group dreamed and speculated about where architecture was going, made propaganda, and took part in exhibitions.

It was during this period of hope and ferment that Häring found his new direction, and it so happened that his most promising client was a farmer, Otto Birtner, who seems to have started with the idea of a modest extension to his farmhouse, but went on with Häring to plan an entire new farm engaging the latest methods. In the end only barn, cowhouse and implement sheds were built, but these became the test cases for the new functionalist architecture and have remained key examples. Built at Garkau, near Lübeck, in Schleswig-Holstein, Häring's farm lay within the general area in which the kind of hall house examined above is found, and in the 1920s many ancient examples were still extant. Häring ignored the traditional combination of farm and dwelling, planning a separate L-shaped farmhouse with living and sleeping wings, but he did attempt to produce a series of building types each dedicated to its particular purpose. He differentiated, for example, between the housing of cows, pigs and horses, so that the whole building group (Figure 11.11b) was not dissimilar to that depicted by Eitzen (Figure 11.9), and revolved equally around a farmyard for outdoor work. That he was interested in a harmonious relationship with the setting is reflected in the final words of his essay about the building, in which he claimed it 'seems to belong more essentially to its site and landscape than older structures nearby'.[29] He claimed also that there was 'no room for influences of another kind, such as folk art, earthy traditions, Saxon gables surmounted by horses' heads'. For the time it was far from traditional since he employed modern materials and methods, including flat roofs and concrete frames, and on the cowhouse even a ribbon of horizontal windows. The largest building was the great storage barn, still required in that era to retain produce for winter, and instead of building it with a trussed roof, Häring chose a lamella structure achieved with short intersecting planks (Figure 11.11d). This was justified on the basis that the lack of ties made the internal volume more usable, but he must have been pleased also that the lamella structure had to follow the line of thrust, so producing a pointed arch, a case of form follows structure. The base was concrete, with a storage cellar beneath.

Most remarkable of all was the cowhouse (Figure 11.11a, e, f, which echoed the traditional hall house in two main ways. One was the sectional arrangement with storage above, producing a hayloft from which fodder could be dropped onto the feeding floor below. The other was ranking of cattle in two lines, though they entered their stalls from behind with the feeding floor in front, as opposed to the open *Flett* of the traditional building. With this arrangement it was easier for the farmer to drop the hay from the trapdoor into the middle of the semicircular end and to fork it along the food floor to the cows. It was also easier with the good clerestory lighting to inspect the cows from the rear and to approach them for milking. Their dung was not turned into solid manure with straw in the traditional way but immediately evacuated and washed down a drain behind the stalls, which because of the round end made a loop. A further similarity with the hall house was the central structure of regular columns, now in concrete rather than timber and cast with limbs tapered following load. This supported the entire perimeter so horizontal windows could admit maximum daylight. Unlike the traditional hall house the ceilings sloped up towards the edge, justified on the basis

Figure 11.11a. Garkau farm, cowhouse (author's photograph c. 1990).

Figure 11.11d. Garkau farm, barn end (author's photograph c. 1973).

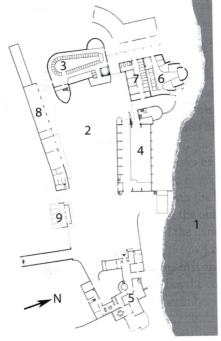

Figure 11.11b. Garkau farm, site plan. Key: 1. Pönitz lake; 2. Farmyard; 3. Cowhouse; 4. Barn; 5. Farmhouse; 6. Pigsty; 7. Stables; 8. Implement sheds; 9. Henhouse (redrawn by author after Joedicke 1965).

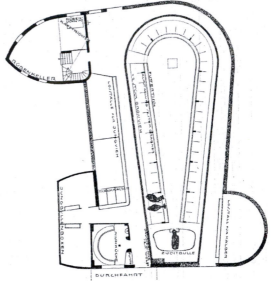

Figure 11.11e. Garkau farm, cowhouse plan (modified by author after Häring's original published in *Die Form* 1925).

Figure 11.11c. Garkau farm, cowhouse interior (author's photograph c. 1973).

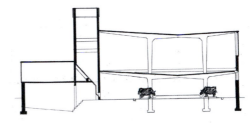

Figure 11.11f. Garkau farm, cowhouse section (redrawn by author after Joedicke 1965).

of good ventilation, the cows' warm breath being guided to ventilators around the perimeter instead of their breathing on each other and spreading disease.[30] In plan the cowhouse was pear-shaped, partly to accommodate the movement of the cattle in and out of the pointed end, swinging around the round end, but the main reason was the accommodation of the bull, father of the herd and most valuable animal, at the pointed end of the plan and on the major axis of the whole.[31] The cowhouse had added to it subordinate extensions, each of recognizable shape. At the northern corner was added a semicircular pen for calves, at the eastern corner the dairy, and in the southern corner a combination of silo and root cellar, which has always been the favourite view used in publications. The silo worked by gravity feed, with an inverted pyramidal base to gather the fermented grass towards the trap door, but for the same reason it also had a triangular head rising above the rest of the building, to which a pipe could be attached, allowing the cut grass to be blown in. The root cellar had a sloping floor for drainage and low side doors through which turnips could be off-loaded from a cart. The practical arrangements were sincere and credible, and Garkau was visited in its early years by farmers to see its progressive arrangements as well as by architects. For Häring, though, it was a test case for a self-generating architecture and a manifesto of functionalism, published with one of the most detailed explanations of the period.[32]

Equally important for its historical reputation was the display of materials and textures, which prompted its rediscovery around 1960 as an exemplary anticipation of the New Brutalism,[33] but here too Häring was drawing on vernacular tradition. The focus of Eitzen's interest in the Lower Saxon Hall House was the oak frame along with its jointing and detailing, as this carpentry work constituted the primary construction involving the most palpable skills. In most recorded examples the frame is seen in the principal gable end, usually the main front, and set in contrast with infill panels of wattle or brick. In the most extravagant ones upper layers are jettied out with decorated joints, an unnecessary but impressive elaboration. When brick infill was used, panels between frame members were often assembled in contrasting brick bonds (Figure 11.8), both to make a lively pattern and to demonstrate that since they were not load-bearing they could be played with. Häring played with brick bonds even more extravagantly, using soldier course to get around tight corners, building in projecting horizontal courses to fend off passing carts, and adding vertical stops for sliding doors. On the barn end (Figure 11.11d) such a doorstop combines with a series of declining horizontal courses in a manner far beyond necessity, both making an exciting composition and declaring architect and bricklayer at play. Häring also made the most of weatherboarding, vertical on the cowhouse where it had to turn corners and horizontal on the barn ends. In few twentieth century buildings is there a greater sense of contrasted texture, and there would have been even more if the pigsty designed in 1926 had been added, with its thatched roof and a wall of rounded boulders. As in the vernacular examples, each material has its place and rational way of being worked, so they are not in the least interchangeable, unlike the thin claddings intended for purely visual impact that surround us today.

A revised farm project 1943

Häring's stated aim was to discover the forces impinging on the building in order to give it the form 'discovered as that which expresses the claims of performance fulfilment in the simplest

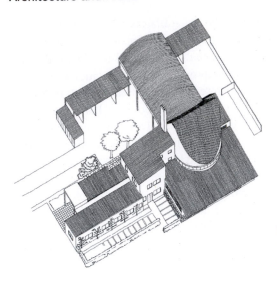

Figure 11.12a. Hugo Häring, unexecuted design for a farmstead 1943, location unknown, axonometric projection (author's drawing),

Figure 11.12b. Farmstead section. Again the organizational relationships and operations of the farm are the inspiration and the orientation is crucial (redrawn from pencil originals in Häring Archive, Akademie der Künste, Berlin, photographed 1983).

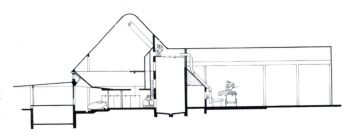

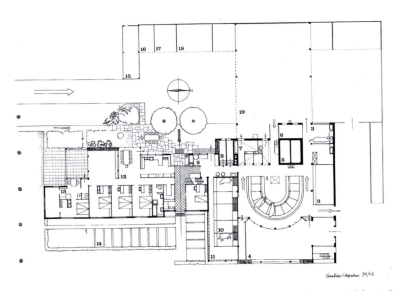

Figure 11.12c. Farmstead plan. Key: 1. Cowhouse with 12 cows; 2. Calves; 3. Stable; 4. Straw barn; 5. Silo; 6. Foals; 7. Dairy; 8. Potato cellar; 9. Laundry; 10. Pigsty; 11. Piglets; 12. Farmhouse; 13. Old people; 14. Vegetable garden; 15. Hen house; 16. Workshop; 17. Garage; 18. Machine sheds; 19. Covered yard (redrawn from pencil originals in Häring Archive, Akademie der Künste, Berlin, photographed 1983).

most direct manner'.[34] He believed that from studying the details of the building's functional duty a shaping and hierarchy of elements could be deduced, accompanied by a logical and appropriate use of materials to generate the building's identity. Working from the inside out, and seeking form rather than imposing it, brought about a new kind of architecture. In 1925, with modernism as we know it yet to come, it was radical, contrasting both with style-driven ornament and the formalism of Beaux Arts planning. Aged forty-three, Häring was starting on the most fruitful eight years of his career, but it came to an end with Hitler, for between 1933 and 1945 he built only three private houses. Between 1935 and 1943 he took over the leadership of a private and liberal art school in Berlin, but it was bombed in 1943 so he returned to his native town of Biberach in the south, and deprived of useful work, diverted his creative energies into personal projects for a new architecture for realization after the war. Although his architectural essays or experiments were in a sense fantasies, they were projections of ways of life, organizationally conceived, technically informed, and expressed largely in terms of precisely drawn and dimensioned plan and section. Sitting in his attic flat, Häring could gain comfort from this imaginary world, planning dwellings for himself and others, eager to take on any proposition and exploring it in drawings. Among projects of 1943 are three farms, one drawn up in great detail that seems something of a re-run of Garkau (Figure 11.12). Whether this was an ideal project of his own or a general proposal for family friends, as his assistant Margot Aschenbrenner suggested, is unclear, but after three weeks of intensive work the delicate pencil drawings seem to have been put away untitled, leaving no record of an intended site or client.[35] The seriousness of the proposition is evident from the high level of detail, and the plans and sections show again concern with the storage and processing of crops, along with a will to engage changing agricultural processes with new machinery, but the sense of imagined habitation also remains strong, with telling details in the furnishing and textures. The crucial thing is that a rich architecture can once again be generated from the ordinary processes of life on a farm.

An apparently flat site and precise north–south orientation suggest a generic or ideal design rather than one for a specific place, but this is not surprising given Häring's regular practice of designing dwellings with an orientation but no site, not because he was uninterested in place – far from it – but because it was an unlocated project. It is surely telling in this case both that the entry drive is due south and that Häring chose to place his north point ceremoniously at the very centre of the farmyard (the *Hof*), declaring its hierarchical importance as an outdoor room and marking the crossing of the main axes. That running south–north is the main drive, which leads under the covered area for unloading. The cross-axis is the pedestrian entry to the building, celebrated in a symmetrical façade and two strategically placed trees. It leads into a kind of cross-passage running through and out the other side, both to divide and to connect: dwelling to south, animal husbandry to north. The north–south orientation sets the dwelling to face east and west, so bedrooms gain east light, while the kitchen faces west, controlling the approach. All beds are north-headed, a practice adopted by Häring from about 1936 onwards, and justified not only in terms of possible health benefits but also by accordance with the midday axis (*Mittagslinie*) and thus with the cosmos.[36] To the south the dwelling could open onto a large covered terrace. All this was in keeping with Häring's claim that:

A natural order will assert itself, with the tendency for each part to find its appropriate relation with the sun, so that the house opens towards the south and swings around from east to west, while it turns its back to the north. It behaves like a plant presenting its organs to the sun.[37]

There are separate living and dining areas, and an outside table for summer use. The end bedroom to the south has a small living room attached and was designated for 'old people', reflecting family inheritance as with the vernacular examples. The house interior seems generous and adequately laden with incident, but externally it is flat-roofed with repetitive windows, even if stone walls enliven the approach side. Margins are defined by the landscape treatment: to right and west of the drive a flower bed for display, by the east wall marked plots as vegetable gardens. That the house was left so plain suggests Häring sought to quieten it precisely to play up the farming end as more dramatic, displaying dairy production hierarchically as the central and primary task. Formally and spatially the cowhouse is the most dynamic element, and though Häring relied wholly on plans and sections, producing as far as we know neither a model nor a three-dimensional projection, there was a marginal sketch projection exploring the effect of the key semicircular element and its folded roof.

A small herd of twelve milking cows was envisaged with no bull. Keeping to the principles of Garkau, Häring placed them in a semicircle around their food, with clear routes in and out. Once again he set the hayloft above the cowhouse, with a central trapdoor dropping fodder onto the feeding floor below. Again the cowhouse ceiling sloped up to a ring of clerestory windows with separate vents, removing the rising breath of the cattle and giving maximum light for that given glass area. The conical floor of the hayloft above would guide the dry grass to the outlet like a funnel. Unlike at Garkau, where hand loading via side doors was needed, the hay was to be lifted by conveyor and dropped into the apex of the space, perfectly justifying the shape and height of the roof. The half-round container could be filled completely just by pitching the material onto the conveyor and letting it pile up, and it could be emptied by raising and lowering the hatch. The section (Figure 11.12b) shows the silo with the farmer feeding grass into a blower. Later he stands on the top of the silage and pitches it down a side shaft into a trolley operated by a woman: presumably his wife. The ghost of another kind of silo with an inverted pyramidal base is shown above the dairy. Both conveyor and blower were to be motor powered, either by electricity or by a small piston engine, but the carts drawn in the section are traditional wooden ones with wooden wheels, drawn by horses. A horse is shown in a stable at the north end with a pen for foals opposite. In the 1940s use of tractors was still limited.

By its hierarchy the plan states that the milking herd was the centre of the farm's production, including housing of calves in a subordinate bay to the north. The only other large animals included are pigs, in a series of five sties south of the cows, the larger central one presumably for the boar. Hens were placed on the west next to the entrance, their house helping to enclose the yard where they would wander and feed. The west edge of the complex was defined by semi-open sheds to house carts and machinery. Häring drew a number of sections that concentrate on the processes of bringing in foodstuffs, storing them, and distributing them to animals, all of which results in a long band of storage elements with an axial passage immediately behind them, linking domestic kitchen, laundry, potato cellar, dairy, and the various silos. From the suggestion in the silo section, this was the realm of the farmer's wife, moving to and fro tending animals and completing domestic tasks while her husband worked the fields. She fetches milk and potatoes to the domestic kitchen, then takes waste food back to the pigs before checking the laundry: all is laid out on a single axis. The south end terminates in the communal dining room and food on the table, the north end with the foddering of horses and calves. This gender division is not unlike that of the traditional farms examined earlier, and suggests Häring was merely following current practice.

Like the Lower Saxon Hall House, this already historic project belongs to a vanished age, albeit a more recent one, representing a way of life that has continued to change. But interest lies less in the possibility of reapplying any of the specifics than in considering the general approach: the idea that architecture can be derived from daily processes and rituals. Häring's functionalism certainly engaged directly with physical processes like the gravity filling and emptying of storage containers or the provision of light and ventilation, but it went further to generate territories with implicit relationships, embodying hierarchies and polarities similar to those that had evolved in vernacular tradition. Notable in the late farm design is the deployment of three main axes: the entrance, cross-passage, and food corridor, each with a functional rather than purely formal identity, and a strong sense of centre is given to the cowhouse, dramatized by its complex section. Without this dominating element the whole composition would fall apart, so the choice to make it focal is vital, even if other versions might take another emphasis. Häring developed his own terminology for this way of working, calling the more directly physical aspects *Organwerk* and the more abstract territorial ones *Gestaltwerk*:

> The exterior is no longer determined in advance, but arises in the same way as in all organic development [*Organwerk*]. The exterior does of course set limits on this organic development, but does not dictate its form … A natural order will assert itself, with the tendency for each part to find its appropriate relation, yet we have scarcely begun to take the next step, the development of *Gestaltwerk*. *Gestaltwerk* has a leading character. The spaces understand their serving role. They receive their form [*Gestalt*] from the inhabitants and their dwelling habits, they belong to life and take part in it. They become being-like [*wesenhaft*], no longer following the abstract structure of another world of forms.[38]

The building forms, by becoming 'what they want to be', escape the geometric straitjackets of structural grids or academic formal planning in the manner of J. N. L. Durand.[39] Häring believed that sufficient inspiration could be found in each task to provoke a specific architecture into existence, and he considered the farm a serious vehicle. We might recognize at this point that, just as it is possible to read a way of life from drawings of an existing architecture, so it is equally possible through drawings to project a new life within an imagined architecture. Thus Häring did this as prophet and spokesman for an organic modernist approach that enjoyed a greater flowering in the work of Hans Scharoun, as we shall see in the penultimate chapter.

Following the Second World War, farming across Europe underwent irreversible change, losing the charm of its vernacular identity along with the repression of its rituals, the mechanization of its methods, and the depletion of its communities. There is now neither shared work to celebrate nor anyone to celebrate it with. All too often, farm builders are compelled by economic pressures towards the most repetitive building systems, 'functional' in the most banal sense, and seldom given serious architectural consideration. In most parts of Europe, experience of the kind of world we have been looking at is limited to the open-air museum, where it is reassembled in an artificial way, tinged with romantic nostalgia.[40] Outside such cultural reservations, crops increasingly follow the economy of large-scale monoculture, erasing most traces of the cornucopia that went before, and of the variations in food that followed the seasons. Farmers today are often underpaid, under-respected, even suicidal. Combine harvesters remove the wheat effortlessly in hours. Field barns fall into ruin as crops are carted away in lorries, and instead of making hayricks, huge machines bundle the hay into black plastic rolls which lie haphazardly at corners of fields. In dairy farming, forced economies of scale are leading to entirely indoor farms with herds of 1,000, their food brought to them mechanically instead of the grassy field, and milk taken automatically three times a day. But this is highly controversial and protested against on grounds of animal welfare, and some small-scale producers are reinterpreting traditional methods in favour of raw milk as a niche product.[41] In general, though, only in market gardens, smallholdings and allotments does the tending of the land by hand produce the kind of identification I have been discussing.

Notes

1 Visser 1986, pp. 29–30.

2 Evans 1969 p. 64, with illustration. He spent years interviewing country people in East Anglia and recorded the results in several books: in chronological order: *Ask the Fellows Who Cut the Hay*, 1956; *The Farm and the Village*, 1969; *The Days That We Have Seen*, 1975; *Horse Power and Magic*, 1979; and *The Crooked Scythe*, 1993: all were published by Faber and Faber. Extensive material on 'Spirits of the Corn' was collected by James Fraser in *The Golden Bough*: see volumes 7 and 8 of the 1912 edition or more particularly pp. 526–37 of the 1963 abridged edition.

3 Cavalli-Sforza 2001, pp. 109–13.

4 Francis Pryor, writing recently of British archaeology, speculates about the uses of hazel both for coppicing as building material and for eating, for charred nuts have been found at ancient pre-agricultural sites, hazel trees would have been easy to propagate. See Pryor 2014, pp. 49–54.

5 Evans 1993, pp. 59, 61, emphasis in original.

6 Schinz 1996, pp. 70–1.

7 Lethaby 1923.

8 Ibid., p. 96.

9 Evans 1969, pp. 82–6.

10 Kaiser and Ottenjann 1985, pp. 144–5.

11 Evans 1969, p. 79.

12 It accompanied the art and architecture movement known as National Romanticism, see Lane 2000. I explained in my monograph on Gunnar Asplund (Blundell Jones 2006) how this affected that architect's later work.

13 Eitzen 2006.

14 Ibid., pp. 315–20.

15 Ibid., p. 316.

16 Kaiser and Ottenjann 1985, pp. 110–11.

17 Ibid., pp. 128–9.

18 Ibid., pp. 15–16.

19 Noted in relation to medieval halls like Penshurst, which had a louvre in the roof to exhaust

smoke. The ruins of Padley Hall, Derbyshire, c. 1350 still show the circular hearth stone despite the remains of decorated masonry which show that cash was not short.

20 Eitzen 2006, p. 316.

21 Ibid., pp. 316–17.

22 Examples are cited in Eitzen 2006, p. 313.

23 Eitzen 2006, p. 413

24 Typified for me by Pugin's drawing in *True Principles* which juxtaposes parody versions of Swiss Cottage, Brighton Pavilion, and Decimus Burton's classical palace-like housing side by side; Pugin 1853, opposite p. 47, fig. 1.

25 *The Architectural Review* July 1957, whole special issue entitled *The Functional Tradition*.

26 See Blundell Jones 2002, the chapter on the Bauhaus pp. 61–72.

27 See Blundell Jones 2002. Ludwig Mies van der Rohe, the high priest of flexibility, sought to avoid functional specificity. In an oral interview an ex-student reports asking him about the place of function, to which Mies scornfully replied: 'Function? That's sweeping dirt', Buch/Dressel interview.

28 Blundell Jones 1999, pp. 99–102.

29 *gut garkau das viehhaus* in Die Form, Berlin, 1925, the building and this text are discussed in English in Blundell Jones 1999, pp. 56–67.

30 *gut garkau das viehhaus* in Die Form, Berlin, 1925.

31 Häring claimed that the starting point had been the idea that cows gather in a circle around their food, but a circle would have been too large so it became an oval, but then thirdly the bull had to have a place. The clinching idea for the pear shape is therefore the relationship of cows to bull. I have analysed all this at greater length elsewhere, so I need only reiterate Häring's ideal of a self-generating architecture: see Blundell Jones 1999, pp. 56–67.

32 *gut garkau das viehhaus* in *Die Form*, Berlin, 1925.

33 Joedicke was presumably the instigator of its publication in *The Architectural Review* of 1960 probably edited by Peter Reyner Banham, who mentioned it favourably in his *Theory and Design in the First Machine Age* also published that year (Banham 1960).

34 *gut garkau das viehhaus* in *Die Form*, Berlin, 1925.

35 He had been running the art school Kunst und Werk in Berlin until it was bombed, then retreated to his home town of Biberach in Swabia and occupied himself with writing and producing endless drawings for houses and flats until the early 1950s. He hoped to execute some of them, but his only realized buildings of the period were the Schmitz houses of 1950. See Blundell Jones 1999, pp. 172–6. I reject Matthias Schirren's suggestion that this farm was a 'colonialist' scheme for new farms in territories taken over by the Third Reich (Schirren 2001, pp. 242–3), for which he presents no adequate evidence. The project is ideal rather than minimal, and the flat roofs would surely have been unacceptable to Nazi authorities. Margot Aschenbrenner, Häring's secretary who was with him during the period, suggested the family connection. Häring would have made inked top copies of the drawings and added titles had they been submitted, but no such versions have been found. There are also incomplete sets of drawings for two other farm projects made at the time, but frustratingly the plan of the most promising one is missing.

36 Evident from looking at the preserved projects in the Häring Archive, Akademie der Künste, Berlin, nearly all of which have north-headed beds from this time onwards. A short piece of text by Häring from 1954 cited in the compilation by Heinrich Lauterbach in *Bauwelt* no. 27, special issue on Häring, 4 July 1960, p. 780, includes the following: '... this north–south placing also concurs with the midday line of cosmic occurrence – by which day and night are divided into the two motions that dominate our whole life, which are decisive to give a settlement its cosmic backbone' (my translation). I would add that for an architect determined to find a basis for choice

of form it added a helpful design discipline. The anthropological record suggests that traditional dwellings in many or even most parts of the world were orientated for one reason or another.

37 Extract from 'Arbeit am Grundriss' 1952, first published in *Baukunst und Werkform* vol. 5, 1952; reprinted in Joedicke and Lauterbach 1965, p. 77, my translation.

38 Ibid.

39 I am thinking particularly of the gridded plan types depicted in his *Précis des Leçons* of 1802–5 which are purely formal and entirely empty, the prescription for an autistic architecture to come, see Durand 1802–5.

40 The first, and still very much the international model, is Skansen in Stockholm, set up by Artur Hazelius in 1891 as part of the tendency known as National Romanticism.

41 See Jon Henley, *The Guardian*, 2 October 2014. Available online: www.theguardian.com/uk-news/2014/…/-sp-battle-soul-british-milk.

CHAPTER 12
THE MODERNIST HOSPITAL

Figure 12.1. Wycombe General Hospital 1959–65, designed by Powell and Moya, view on approach by car (author's photograph 2012).

Figure 12.2. Zonnestraal Sanatorium, Utrecht, 1926 by Duiker and Bijvoet (author's photograph 1975).

Figure 12.3. Paimio Sanatorium 1928–31 by Alvar Aalto (photograph by Richard Weston).

The Hospital is a great white concrete structure with regular square windows and a flat roof. It was built not long ago and pictures of it appeared in the architectural reviews. There are a number of wings or transepts which jut out in different directions from the main block and cunningly divert the eye from the monotony of line. In the wells or gullies created by these transepts they have planted gardens, with grassy lawns and small trees which will one day be large trees, the preservation of which will be a matter endlessly debated by hospital committees torn between the therapeutic benefits of the charms of nature and the need to let a little more light into the wards on the lower floors.[1]

This is how Iris Murdoch presents the London hospital that appears almost as a character about three-quarters of the way through her first novel *Under the Net*, published in 1954. It has already loomed large from the window of the flat across the way, marking times of day by the way it reflects the sun, immovable in its blank purity:

towards evening the glare was withdrawn and a softer light glowed as if from within the concrete, showing up little irregularities in the stone … Nothing grew on the wall of the Hospital. Sometimes I tried to imagine that there was vegetation growing on a ledge … But in reality there was nothing there, and even in imagination the wall would resist me and remain smooth and white.[2]

Of all the institutions housed in the pure and abstract architecture of the Modern Movement, the hospital is perhaps the one that suits it best, and to which it gives an enduring image. The two early modernist hospitals that set the tone and appear most frequently in architectural history books are both tuberculosis sanatoria: Jan Duiker's Zonnestraal of 1926 and Alvar Aalto's Paimio of 1928 (Figures 12.2 and 12.3). In their white starkness they combine an image of hygienic purity with one of structural rationality, while also stressing the benefits of sunlight and air through a general openness, enormous windows, and bed-sized external terraces. Both were built in rural settings to assure clean air, and orientated to make best use of the sunlight that provided a valuable weapon against that dangerous disease before the age of antibiotics, for the tubercule bacillus is killed by ultraviolet light. The new architecture looked pure and clean both from the outside and within, lacking ledges and mouldings where dirt might gather, showing impermeable and apparently germ-free surfaces, and revelling in transparency. This ideal of cleanliness and purity was by the late 1920s well established. For three-quarters of a century there had been acute concern about hospital cross-infection, notably in the campaigns of Florence Nightingale following the scandal of Scutari in the Crimean War where the mortality rate of patients rose to over 40 per cent.[3] At first the processes of cross-infection were not understood, for only in 1866 was the water-borne character of cholera established, and not until the 1870s did Louis Pasteur start to identify bacilli,[4] but it was clear that something went through the air, and that dirty smelly conditions might be to blame, for unpleasant odours are directly perceptible, unlike germs. For Florence Nightingale even the exhaled breath of a healthy person was tainted, so that of the sick must be 'always highly morbid and dangerous'.[5] Everything therefore had to be clean and well-ventilated, and dirty corners or closets were insanitary as well as providing 'hiding or skulking places for patients or servants disposed to do wrong': note the moral and controlling tone.[6] Late-nineteenth-century hospitals therefore became dominated by 'miasma' theories and ventilation issues, built on spreading pavilion plans to isolate separate wards which were made long and thin to allow cross-ventilation. The Royal Herbert Hospital in Woolwich built between 1850 and 1864 was typical, with long, narrow, Nightingale wards strung out to either side of a long corridor divided by south-facing gardens for plenty of air (Figures 12.4 and 12.5). The mansion-like front block facing the street contained the administration, the short central block on axis behind it the dayroom and library, the main social rooms. Operating theatre and amphitheatre terminated the corridor's far right-hand end and a series of small isolation wards the left, while the last ward block on the front left was designated as the prison ward. A pair of covered ways, cloister-like, linked the administration with the ward block, the short wings in the corners being the pharmacy and the baths. This layout was axial and hierarchical, in keeping with earlier examples in this book, with an obvious articulation of content, but it was the perceived need for fresh air that spread it across the site. Some designs of that period even incorporated elaborate ventilation systems with basement intakes and roof exhaust stacks to ensure good airflow, and this became a dominant element in their architectural rhetoric.[7] By the mid-twentieth century, however, the nature of infectious diseases was better understood, and numerous drugs had been developed to combat them, but ventilation remained a critical requirement for hospitals, even if now mechanically driven and less evident. The sense of purity, of maintaining cleanliness and orderliness against the ever-present danger of disease, also prevailed. The hospital remained a highly ordered place, full of strict routines and social hierarchies, ruled by science and with little room for superstition. There could be no dirt, no 'matter out of place' to accept one of Mary Douglas's definitions.[8] It was all very 'high grid', to append another which she probably never intended in a directly architectural sense, but which brings to mind an image of small square bathroom tiles.[9]

The Hospital (always capitalized) of Iris Murdoch's novel is first introduced in the form of a monumental exterior, but it later becomes a somewhat oppressive interior when the hero takes a job there as an orderly. Its oppressiveness is not so much a matter of the architecture as of the social regime, run by a ward matron who was 'so august a person, so elderly and austere and with such a high notion of her own dignity, that the possibility of certain frictions was removed simply by the social distance which lay between us'.[10] In her charge are three ward sisters, whose lives are made a misery 'on the one hand by the Matron, who treated them with unremitting despotism, and on the other by the nurses who repaid them with continual veiled mockery for the pains which the Sisters, in order to recoup their own dignity, felt bound to inflict upon those beneath them'.[11] The novel's hero is tied to this little world, oblivious of the 'stratosphere' of the hospital hierarchy beyond, though witnessing doctors passing through to carry out their 'priest-like tasks', during which the doors of the rooms are always 'religiously' closed. His menial jobs include cleaning floors and washing up dishes, and sometimes he is even given the privilege of heating milk for the patients' drinks, but he is not allowed to serve it, or indeed to speak to them. He once enters into a conversation with a patient only to be ticked off immediately by Sister.

Suddenly one day a close friend from earlier in the story, with whom he had lost contact, is admitted with a minor head injury and taken to a single room. The hero feels an urgent need to speak to him, but is frustrated by their differently defined roles: 'It was an odd trick of fate that although we had been brought together it was under circumstances which made communication virtually impossible. We were placed here in the one relationship that totally debarred any exchange.'[12] Desperate to make contact, he decides to return at night, leaving a

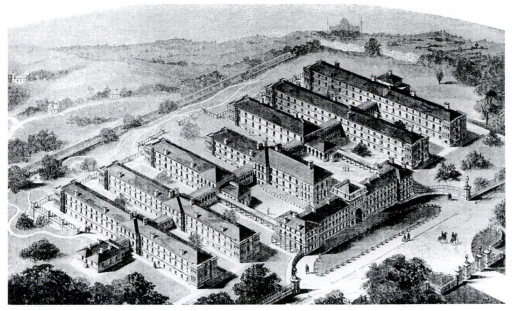

Figure 12.4 Royal Herbert Hospital in Woolwich 1859–64, the quintessential Florence Nightingale hospital, bird's-eye view (from *The Builder* 14 April 1864).

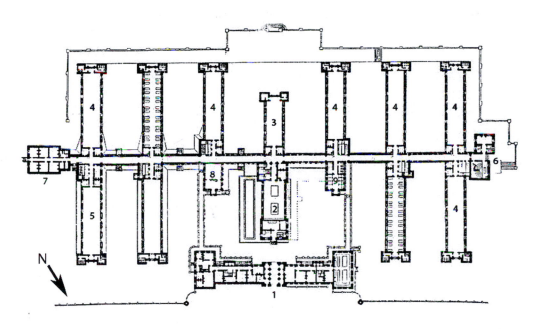

Figure 12.5. Royal Herbert Hospital, plan. Key: 1. Administration block; 2. Library; 3. Dayroom; 4. Ward block; 5. Prison ward; 6. Operating theatre and amphitheatre; 7. Isolation wards; 8. Pharmacy; 9. Baths (from *The Builder* 1864 relabelled).

ground floor window unlatched to effect an entrance. He makes his way to his friend's room undetected and they engage in a precarious conversation. The pair decide to make a break for it, but as they are sneaking out of the building they are spotted by the night porter and have to run for it, the hero in consequence losing his job. The reader accepts the hero's decision to break the rules rather than reappearing in the Hospital legitimately in the role of visitor and suffering the embarrassment of seeing this transition of his identity registered. The choice of the Hospital for this part of Murdoch's narrative contrasts with the other places chosen for the book, stressing the social control almost to the point of making it a prison. While this may be exaggerated, it certainly accords with others' experiences of the period, and reminds one of Erving Goffman's designation 'total institution'.[13] It is also completely and interestingly at variance with the view of a hospital presented in what will be the key source for the rest of this chapter: *Hospital Description: Wycombe General Hospital Phase One* by John Gainsborough, a booklet published by the King's Fund in 1968.[14]

Wycombe General 1966

The hospital in question was a new regional one at High Wycombe in Buckinghamshire designed by Powell and Moya, a nationally leading firm of architects who specialized in hospitals and whose partners later received the accolade of the RIBA Gold Medal. They designed it in the late 1950s, completing the phase of buildings described in 1966. It was chosen as the flagship project for a new kind of 'Hospital Description' which was intended to become a series, providing an accurate record of the hospital building process to help further hospital boards and their architects. It provides us with a very good set of drawings and other illustrations of a mid-1960s hospital, and includes much useful bureaucratic and technical information, but it is equally revealing by what it omits. Strangely missing from the 130-page document are any real sense of place, of the patient's experience, or any hint of the kind of social interactions so vividly portrayed in Murdoch's novel. Even more surprising, in view of the aim of the series, is the lack of any kind of general architectural critique or even justification of the main design decisions, despite the fact that the author was an architect and an expert on the subject who had recently co-written with his doctor brother a whole book: *Principles of Hospital Design*.[15] Did he feel in some way constrained by the high reputation of the architects? If so, he could at least have asked them for their version of the story and included it as such, but they have no presence. The report is couched in the language of scientific objectivity with much use of the passive 'it was decided that ...' and much parading of facts, and it contains far more about engineering and costing than about design, often concentrating on technical detail at the expense of the whole. Avoided are not only what would then have been deemed 'aesthetic' issues: missing is the whole rationale behind value judgements about what was put where and why. Why, for instance, put all the wards in a tower, and why put Gynaecology on the first floor along with the Psychiatric Ward? Such gaps in the narrative might be ignored as a shortcoming of this document were they not typical of the mindset among hospital makers of the period.

The main requirements of the brief were determined during the course of discussions and outline planning following the appointment of the architects, discussions in which

Figure 12.6. Wycombe General as presented in *The Hospital Description*: corner shot on approach (photograph by Bill Toomey, Powell and Moya Archive/John Haworth).

Figure 12.7. Wycombe General, architects' model showing main block with rooftop chapel, main block, operating suite and services beneath car park (photograph by Alfred Cracknell, Powell and Moya Archive/John Haworth).

Figure 12.8. Nurses' station in the ward block (photograph by Alfred Cracknell, Powell and Moya Archive/John Haworth).

Figure 12.9. Daylit pathology laboratory (photograph by Alfred Cracknell, Powell and Moya Archive/John Haworth).

the Ministry of Health, regional hospital board, hospital management committee, medical staff, officers and architects, were all closely involved. As was to be expected in a scheme of this complexity, the minutiae of the brief and operational policies only reached finality during the detailed planning period. Thus there was no formal briefing document available when the planning started. The briefing details which emerge from the recorded minutes are described below.[16]

This tells us nothing about which decisions were made, when and by whom, and how the various parties (which seem not to have included patients, the primary users) interacted. Yet it is Gainsborough's entire introduction to the section headed 'Design' before launching into a ten-page schedule of accommodation, listing room after room with basic quantities and their special technical requirements. Dermatology will serve as sample:

> The dermatological ward will need a treatment room with good ventilation. It should have a tiled floor with a gulley. There should be a couch provided in the centre of the room with fitting above for ultra-violet machine on pulleys. There should be a bathroom close to the treatment room. This ward will need a special examination room with a changing cubicle adjoining which will be used as a hot room having a temperature of approximately 100°F. Both the treatment room and the special examination room must be capable of being darkened. Minor operations will be undertaken in the special examination room.[17]

The accommodation list begins with the wards, continues with the operating theatre suite, goes on through pathology and pharmacy to the central sterile supply, then deals with the main entrance, service area, staff facilities and engineering services. This does not constitute any obvious hierarchy, except that it places the wards first as the substantial bulk of the accommodation, and the operating theatres second as the most highly serviced element. Otherwise it seems just a list, with the occasional hint about what needs to be adjacent to what, and then for purely technical and pragmatic reasons. Later there is a short description of the general composition, but its mere two paragraphs deal mainly with traffic zoning, economy of circulation, and the logistics of phased development. The sentence most revealing of the general strategy claims:

> The only repetitive units… are the wards and, because of the narrow site available, the architects adopted a compact block with a race-track plan for them. It has been possible to provide a majority of the beds on elevations other than the north and because of the open planning a high proportion of patients can enjoy sunshine. The outside form of the ward block was strongly influenced by the desire to combine the attractive characteristics of generous windows with privacy and protection from excessive sunlight… The aim has been to create buildings which not only satisfy functional requirements but which are also welcoming and have an atmosphere of a hotel rather than that of an institution.[18]

Apart from this brief concluding paragraph which risks open mention of an 'aesthetic' intention, there is little sense in the text of the building as a whole, or of how it came together.

What is more, two of the primary claims in it are demonstrably false: the aerial photo (Figure 12.10) reveals that there was plenty of site space available for a larger ward block, and wards look out evenly on all sides, regardless of orientation.[19] Subsequent parts of the text merely go into more detail about the structure, construction and technical operation, and are again presented as a list. It is almost as if Gainsborough believes that once you design the parts for their separate functions on a rational basis, the whole will take care of itself.[20] This was the way hospital building was heading at the time, with specialized design of each element through detailed technical research and development. First came definition in codes of practice, then 'solutions' were imposed as fixed tried and tested plan forms like the Nucleus Ward Template.[21] Gainsborough's text is also deficient in its treatment of place, showing more concern with description of the hospital's catchment area than with the actual site. Typically for the period, there had been an earlier intention to build on a greenfield site between Wycombe and Amersham which would have allowed quick emergency vehicle access and space for expansion, but the final site lay at the edge of the town, and is described by Gainsborough in a mere three paragraphs. These cover access roads, acreage available, and the problem of sloping ground. Missing is any sense of relation to the town: we are told only that it is a quarter of a mile from the centre and that 'a bus station occupies the north-east corner and there is a football ground to the west'.[22] Yet Gainsborough gives two whole pages to the engineers' report on ground conditions and boreholes. This was certainly a technical

Figure 12.10. Aerial photograph used to show the site, which gives no idea that High Wycombe town centre lies to the immediate right. In front of the new hospital is the local bus garage, behind it the earlier hospital building, beyond a playing field, above that nurses' accommodation by the same architects (Aerofilms, Powell and Moya Archive/John Haworth).

issue to be faced by future hospital planners, but as each site offered different conditions, it was hardly open to generic treatment. In contrast the question of urban integration enters the report not at all, though Powell and Moya were presumably interested, as they showed great sensitivity elsewhere.[23] Contextual issues were not on Gainsborough's horizon, nor did he show any interest in the existing hospital building to which the new one was being attached by umbilical link, a group of structures from the 1930s that appears in plans and photographs. Its character is ignored, and it appears in the text only to register the existence of the new access bridge. Any memories this older hospital might have borne seem to have been regarded as uninteresting and expendable. As well as being placeless, Gainsborough's *Description* is also timeless, setting out the prescription for a hospital in 1968 according to the latest knowledge and scientific techniques, in every sense 'current practice'. Concern for the future arises only in so far as expansion in future phases is considered, but this will be a consolidation of the current vision, not something recreated for a different era. As for the past, there is little sense in the *Description*, or even in Gainsborough's *Principles*, of the evolution of the hospital as a building type, and of the baggage that has come with it.[24] For example, the chapel on the roof at Wycombe gets barely a mention, and the uncomfortable way it doubles as a lecture hall for the medical centre passes unremarked, as does the presence of the Chaplain's office on the first floor next to the general office.[25] Until the nineteenth century a chapel was the hierarchical focus of nearly every hospital, just as the persisting designation 'Sister' speaks of nursing's origin in religious orders. The lurking presence of these religious elements is a reminder that questions of life and death have never gone away, for although by the mid-twentieth century more patients survived thanks to better treatment, increasing numbers of people were coming to die in hospitals under the benefit of palliative care.

Wycombe General from a reading of the drawings

By reading between the lines of Gainsborough's text and analysing the drawings, it is possible to assemble a fuller account of what the building was about. The first strategic decision seems to have been the placing of the wards in a six-storey tower rather than dispersing them about the site in separate pavilions like the hospitals of half a century earlier. This more compact arrangement allowed efficient servicing via a central core involving short distances, but made lifts compulsory and imposed the discipline of a regular structural grid (around 3.2 m) with consequent standardization of room widths between one and four bays (Figure 12.17). The vertical repetition forced a similarity between wards that provided a discipline for decision-making and economy in detailed design and production, but the four smaller wards had to be paired to fit in with the larger ones. Having decided on the tower, there arose the question of how to stack the wards. In a traditional building one mounts stairs to confront the *piano nobile* at first floor, and as upper floors are increasingly remote they become lower in status despite the principle of ranking by height. But lifts even out the effort of climbing. They even anaesthetize the sense of vertical progression, for one has to rely on the electric indicator to see which floor has been reached. Higher floors offer better views and more light, and they also head the accommodation list which maps one's way, and is read from the top down. The principle of ranking by height therefore reasserts itself, the rooms of highest prestige being at the top: in this case the general medical ward, general surgical ward, and orthopaedic ward,

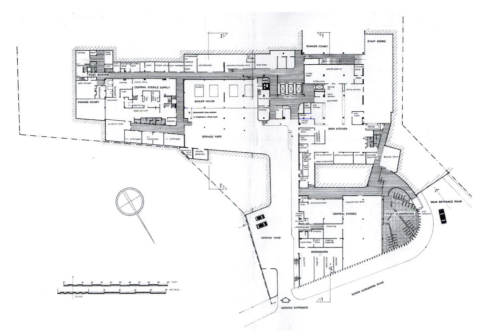

Figure 12.11. Wycombe General plan drawings as presented in *The Hospital Description*. Plan of the basement with services, deliveries, sterile store, kitchens, staff changing rooms, and staff canteen at bottom of stairs (Powell and Moya Archive/John Haworth).

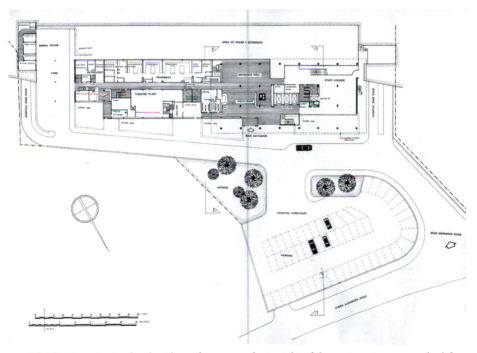

Figure 12.12. Plan at entry level with rooftop car park: to right of the main entrance are the lifts and the double-height staffroom with stairs down to the canteen, to left is the pharmacy with operating theatres over. The dotted line and column grid shows the outline of the ward block above (Powell and Moya Archive/John Haworth).

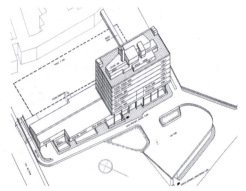

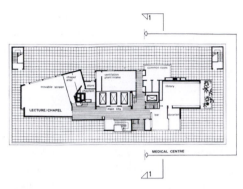

Figure 12.13. Axonometric projection showing the whole arrangement: ward block on columns, chapel and doctor's library on roof, operating wing to left, services under car park to right, and bridge connection behind (Powell and Moya Archive/John Haworth).

Figure 12.15. Plan of the rooftop floor with chapel doubling as lecture theatre and the doctors' library (Powell and Moya Archive/John Haworth).

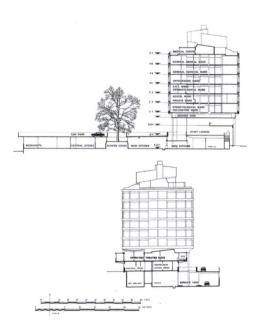

Figure 12.14. The top two floors of the ward block, General Surgical and General Medical (Powell and Moya Archive/John Haworth).

Figure 12.16. North-east to south-west section through basement and ward block (Powell and Moya Archive/John Haworth).

in that order. The two lower floors divide between lesser departments, the upper containing the hostel ward for convalescents and the private ward, which in an NHS hospital was obliged to be subordinate, if internally more luxurious.[26] The lowest floor contains Gynaecology and Psychiatry, the least important specialisms, the former reflecting the lower status of women in the 1960s, the latter the marginality of a discipline less firmly rooted in physical science. The ward designations evidently followed the established structure of hospital specialisms, a taxonomy no more questionable than the six departments of Chinese bureaucracy reported in Chapter 3.

The very idea of a ward starts with such large objects as beds and prompts standard planning in terms of bed units. The patient should enjoy light, view and air, while remaining close to the services and supervision on which she or he depends. The centre and periphery ward plan with its race-track corridor and pivotal nursing stations therefore had a distinct rationale, and the making of a discrete and repetitive freestanding block on a precisely double-square plan of 8 × 16 bays reflected the general rationalizing tendency of the Modern Movement and its myths about proportion. But Wycombe General is not just an autonomous ward block of pristine purity: it is a building in three parts with base, middle, and attic, and in the treatment of these parts the spirit of Le Corbusier is unmistakable. The recessed windows of the ward block, using the slab above as a sunshade, are a variant on Corbusian brise-soleil. The block stands on *pilotis*, allowing it to float above the basal parts of the building which are independently organized. Furthermore, the roof is surmounted by the sculptural masses of chapel, medical centre, library, and service stacks. Dedicated to discourse among the hospital élite – the doctors and surgeons – the medical centre makes a well-signalled head for the building. That the chapel is also there, sharing the tip of the hierarchy and approaching heaven, shows that ritual and symbolic significance is still attached, even if its sacred character is trumped by profane use as lecture theatre. All these rooftop elements emerge individualistically from the roof plane in a celebration of *plan libre* like the sculptural screens on Le Corbusier's Villa Savoye or the evocative rooftop world of the Marseilles Unité, examples with which the architects were doubtless familiar. Equally Corbusian is the deliberate variation of plan order between the three parts to obtain a decisive contrast between them.

The base of the building (Figure 12.11) is far more complex, and by its nature highly irregular in contrast with the pristine purity of the ward block. It has to absorb the irregularities of the ground and the need for several different kinds of approach and entrance for the various actors in the drama. Typical of the period, and more generally of the CIAM policy of zoning cities, is the assumption that everybody arrives by vehicle, resulting in differentiated traffic routes for users and deliveries on a one-way system. The vehicle flow pattern is actually the shaping motive of the lowest basement level, which is invisible as a building, being treated as a modified ground plane set behind a retaining wall, with a car park on the roof. Thus central stores, staff cloakrooms and kitchens are hidden out of sight as backstage elements that can best do their work undisturbed by the public gaze. For the architects this underworld permitted a convenient absorption of irregular and anomalous parts of the brief – those left over after pure finite entities like the ward block had been settled. Most deeply embedded in the ground at the extreme inner end, and therefore most secure, is the post-mortem room, which receives daylight only from its own sunken court. This secret and tomb-like position for the handling of the dead is the polar opposite in the spatial hierarchy of the chapel on the roof.

Arguably part of the base, with one end sliding beneath the ward block, is the two-storey linear wing housing the operating theatre suite and the pathology laboratory (Figure 12.19). Externally visible as a low extension to the ward block, it is distinguished in form by its roof lights and clerestories which bring daylight into its necessarily deep plan. With their undulating forms these might appear, at least from above, as junior cousins of the sculptural forms on the ward block roof, and for those in the know, they articulate externally the site of dramatic medical intervention. In plan the operating wing constitutes almost a separate building, linked to the rest only by an external gallery along the back. This is because its first-floor central axis linking the operating theatres is designated as a clean corridor, only accessible to staff divested of things polluted by the outside world and reclothed in the uniform of cleanliness. Nurses and surgeons have separate changing rooms, the surgeons granted additional cubicles in keeping with their higher status. Passage into the clean corridor is interrupted for each group by a bench at which boots must be changed, a firm reminder. They have separate rest rooms within the suite to avoid leaving the clean area, for this is a whole working world where they may remain all day or all night. Patients also need to cross the clean threshold, arriving on mobile beds at a transfer bay where they are moved onto a theatre trolley. Most hardly see the operating suite part, for sedated and bed-bound, they are wheeled across the corridor to the anaesthetic room to be deprived of all sensation, and they wake up in the recovery ward having recrossed the threshold in an unconscious state. On the far side of the operating theatres is a 'dirty corridor' for disposal of soiled material and used instruments between operations. There are separate clean and dirty service hoists to exchange materials with stores in the basement. All must be done in a careful and orderly fashion to avoid contamination. Ritual structures are rife.

To obtain two floor levels in the operating wing, the ward block had to be raised considerably on its *pilotis*, producing an open section two and a half storeys high around the main entrance, with further downward internal views in places to a third storey in the lower ground floor. This allowed the development of a double-height public entrance hall appropriate to such a large institution, spatially open, impressive, and welcoming. The visiting public gained a generous place of arrival where they could pause to take stock. On offer were enquiries, a tea-bar, and potential access to administrators around the first-floor gallery, all preparatory to taking the lifts up to the wards. The other part of the double-height volume to the right, at the north-west end, contained a generous split-level staff lounge with connecting staircase to the staff dining room below (Figure 12.20). This was architecturally one of the most impressive spaces, showing the importance of staff and their recreation. It also placed doctors and nurses at centre-stage in public view, perhaps as visual reinforcement of confidence in the system, reassuring visitors that their relatives were in good hands. If patients and visitors largely went in then up, doctors and nurses would experience the building laterally, moving between their recreational areas to the right and the hidden operating suite, pathology department, and pharmacy on the left. The experiences of building users also differed in time, doctors and nurses experiencing the hospital for years while taking its layouts and facilities for granted, the patient knowing it for perhaps a week without the freedom to wander, the visitor present for an hour, having to negotiate her or his way in and out. Playing their different roles, each group must have experienced a very different building, with varying proportions of frontstage and backstage, and competing advantages and disadvantages. This makes qualitative assessment all the more complicated.

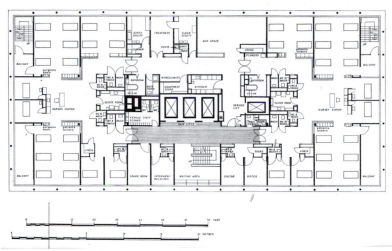

Figure 12.17 Detailed plan of a ward floor with central servicing and peripheral bedrooms, designed for efficient supervision by a nurse at each end. The blindness of the lift was compensated for by a good view across the stair and waiting area to the world outside (Powell and Moya Archive/John Haworth).

Figure 12.18. Operating theatre with north-north-east facing windows to the outside world and additional clerestory lighting. The architects placed these theatres in the top of the side wing in order to obtain the daylight and the orientation precludes sunlight (photograph by Alfred Cracknell, Powell and Moya Archive/John Haworth).

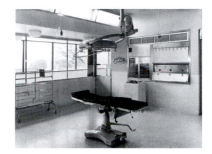

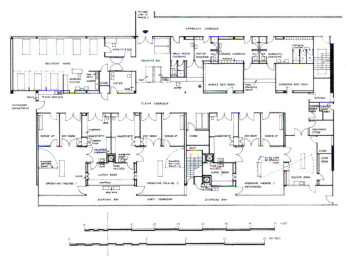

Figure 12.19. Detailed plan of the operating suite, showing the clean, dirty and approach corridors. The changing rooms for doctors and nurses are top right, with benches they have to swivel over while changing into surgical boots (Powell and Moya Archive/John Haworth).

Reflections on the modernist hospital

The majority of pages in Gainsborough's *Hospital Description* are given over to technical issues. To read them today is to be reminded of the unprecedented degree of servicing present in the modern hospital. Heating and ventilating gain a high priority, especially in operating theatres where positive pressure is required, but there are also many cold stores. Extensive hot and cold water supplies must be laid on everywhere, and piped surgical gases and suction to many parts. There have to be emergency generators, communications systems, hospital radio, even a pneumatic tube conveyor for documents. Quite unknown to the public is a basement area linked to the operating theatres by hoists where instruments are sterilized and fresh supplies gathered following the same ritualistic division of clean from dirty seen in the operating theatres. Everything must be done in strict sequence, and Gainsborough supplies a drawing showing the flow patterns (Figure 12.21). The enormous kitchen with its three preparation areas devoted to fish/meat, vegetables, and pastry (indicator of English eating habits in the 1960s) must deliver its 280 patient meals via a 'Ganymede' conveyor system. The specification goes on and on. It is easy to see why those two years of planning meetings so briefly passed over were necessary, yet the *Hospital Description* somehow loses the wood for the trees, and this is symptomatic of the way that hospital design in general became overwhelmed by technical issues and lost its sense of architecture. As skilled and sensitive architects, Powell and Moya produced a building that transcended the *Hospital Description*, but such architectural virtues as remained unidentified in that document were unlikely to be transmitted. The downplaying of the architects' role led to neglect of the need to coordinate the building as a whole, instead allowing the technical issues to play themselves out, in the process defining the territory in a way that gave them the stranglehold. This architectural development took place against an academic background that was science-based. The Oxford Conference on architectural education of 1958 determined that architecture should be set among the science departments of universities, demanding maths 'A' level of its entrants, and setting up number-crunching research programmes. These were famously promoted by Leslie Martin at Cambridge and Richard Llewelyn-Davies at the Bartlett in London, the latter being one of the leading figures in hospital research. It was part of an ideology that had become an orthodoxy in the Modern Movement, and that can be traced back to Hannes Meyer in 1928. In his famous manifesto *bauen* which marked the foundation of the Bauhaus's architecture department, Meyer declared that building was nothing more than function times economics, and that art and composition should have nothing to do with it.[27] He defined twelve functions to be considered in designing a dwelling and declared that there were only twelve. He demanded that the architect should draw up the 'function diagram, for the mother, the father, the child, the postman, the washerwoman, etc.'[28] continuing with a list of design parameters each to be defined and measured, with an implication that once all these issues had been quantified, the architectural 'solution' would automatically emerge.

Since the work of modernists like Pevsner's hero Walter Gropius was justified as 'scientific' and 'functional' in contrast with the superstition of the borrowed styles, a myth of scientific functionalism prevailed, with a concurrent compulsion to push architecture increasingly towards quantitative analysis. History was rejected as no longer relevant, and the will to personal expression was condemned as subjective in opposition to the presumed objectivity. It was a sin to be repressed, and Pevsner led the field in freely using the term 'Expressionism'

Figure 12.20. Staff lounge on the ground floor to right of the entrance. The double height was the result of raising the ward on *pilotis* and lent it a visible sense of generosity (photograph by Alfred Cracknell, Powell and Moya Archive/John Haworth).

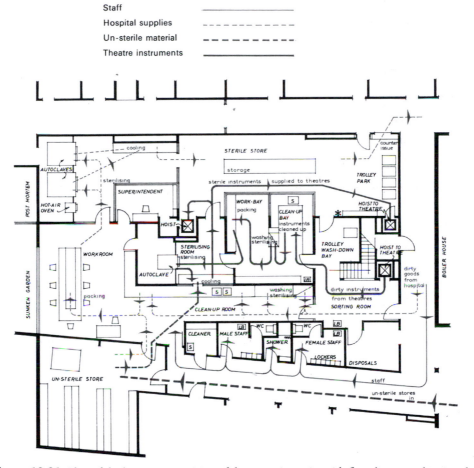

Figure 12.21. Plan of the basement servicing of the operating suite with flow diagrams showing the division of clean from dirty (Powell and Moya Archive/John Haworth).

as a dirty word to condemn work assumed to be 'wilful' or 'personal'.[29] Architecture was not only rational and scientific, but preferably pursued as teamwork, making it neutral or anonymous in expression. If dullness was not actually considered a virtue, certainly pursuit of interesting architectural form was considered suspect. Llewelyn Davies's partner John Weeks, in a supposedly scientific lecture about hospital design much geared to measurable effects and the virtues of centralized servicing, criticized Paul Nelson's oval operating theatres at St Lo as 'eccentric' and as a 'personal solution' without any specific argument. He then went on to praise an American ward plan as 'utterly direct, neither elegant nor inelegant', finding also that the exterior 'reflects the crispness and certainty of the interior organisation'. Reading between the lines, an aesthetic preference is revealed here, but it spells a rather puritanical renunciation. Weeks ended his lecture: 'A hospital is not the place for heroics. Everybody working there is doing a very important job of work and the architects's predilection for significant form may get in the way.'[30] The dominance of this kind of attitude by the mid-1960s led to a conspiracy of silence about the 'aesthetic' or 'expressive' aspects of architecture. A typical example recalled by both Richard MacCormac and John Sergeant was a student crit at the Llewelyn Davies dominated Bartlett involving the sociologist Jane Abercrombie. The student described his intention of providing a pool to reflect dancing sunbeams on the ceiling, whereupon Abercrombie demanded objective evidence that this experience would prove pleasurable. Since the student was unable to provide such evidence, his good intentions were set at nought. Even the act of marginalizing parts of architecture as 'aesthetic' or 'expressive' was part of this general ideological malaise, reflected in the art/science split famously identified by C. P. Snow.[31]

The problem with Hannes Meyer's method and its many progeny is that the required objectivity simply cannot be sustained. Some aspects of building performance are measurable and calculable, and it would be stupid not to measure them, yet even something as basic as structural strength routinely involves 'safety factors' that simply double the load, making a mockery of the precision of the calculations. Meyer's list of functions brings two serious difficulties: first that it cannot be reduced neatly to twelve but is endless, since more considerations impinging on a design can always be found. Second, it is implicitly hierarchical, accepting the first listed item as the most important. Yet more problematic is the comparison in value of unlike things, for the quantity of hot water obtainable from a tap can easily be calculated, but not the quality of the view from the window. In making a design, the architect may need to decide the priority of the two, which he or she can do intuitively on the basis of personal experience and empathy with the users, but turning it all into hard facts and calculation is difficult, not only because of the unmeasurables but also because of the relativities.

The conspiracy of silence of the period is evident in Gainsborough's *Description*, where the intention of making the building more like a hotel than an institution marks a rare 'subjective' moment at the end of the design text, rather than opening a fruitful discussion about what hospitals should be like and why. Giving priority to measurables inevitably meant that unmeasurables lost out. Consider, for example, the experience of the ward block in St Thomas's Hospital, London, of 1966, which still exists on the opposite bank of the Thames to the Palace of Westminster (Figures 12.22 and 12.23). It was an enlarged and further rationalized version of the hospital at Wycombe. The plan is much deeper, ten bays each side, allowing 112 beds per floor as opposed to Wycombe's forty, again sited all around the periphery with windows. The servicing is efficient, with a central core offering ten lifts and plenty of vertical ducts. But imagine arriving as a visitor in the central lobby, all artificially lit and ventilated with no views

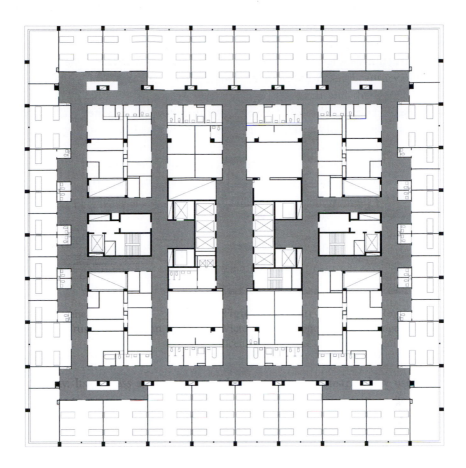

Figure 12.22. St Thomas's Hospital, Westminster, designed by Yorke Rosenberg and Mardall and completed in 1966, ward floor plan (redrawn by Diego Carrasco after a version in Thompson and Goldin 1975.

Figure 12.23. St Thomas's Hospital, Westminster, exterior (author's photograph 2012).

out. At Wycombe the lifts disgorged by a waiting area with windows to the outside world, an immediate point of reorientation, but visitors to St Thomas's must rely entirely on signs and numbers, because the labyrinth of parallel-sided corridors and right-angled corners gives no natural orientation. After a few turns it would appear confusingly endless. The plan of course makes logical sense to the god-like architect looking down on it, but for the person caught in its labyrinth there is no such reading. This is a clear instance of the kind of designed space criticized by Henri Lefebvre as a takeover of power from the ordinary person, a mapping of the world that speaks of power and control:

> It may be said of architectural discourse that it too often imitates or caricatures the discourse of power, and that it suffers from the delusion that 'objective' knowledge of 'reality' can be attained by means of graphic representations. This discourse no longer has any frame of reference or horizon ... Within the spatial practice of modern society, the architect ensconces himself in his own space. He has a representation of this space, one which is bound to graphic elements ... This conceived space is thought by those who make it to be true, despite the fact – or perhaps because of the fact – that it is geometrical: because it is a medium for objects, an object itself, and a locus of the objectification of plans.[32]

Consider also the plight of the poor doctors, nurses and the many medical students at St Thomas's – it is a teaching hospital – condemned eternally to meet and to work under artificial light in the rooms trapped between centre and periphery. Why should they complain when they get 300 lux on the work surface and ten air-changes an hour, the 1960s 'scientific' architect might ask. Yet most people would regard constant work under such conditions as deprivation, and psychological studies have shown that circadian rhythms are disrupted, while at the other end of the scale daylight and sunlight have a beneficial effect.[33] The variability of light and weather are reassuring, and from changes in the sky we also tell the time of day. In recent years the very pursuit of objective study in the psychological realm has begun to undermine the scientistic ideology of the 1960s and to prove the value of architectural qualities such as daylight, view, and easily navigable routes, matters that sensitive architects have always felt to be important. A milestone in such studies was work by Roger Ulrich about the view from a hospital bedroom. He studied a hospital with two identical rooms, one facing a garden view and the other a brick wall a short distance away. Both were in use by patients recovering from operations, with a quick enough turnover to allow a statistically significant number to be studied in a reasonable time. The result was that the patients in the room with the view went home on average a day earlier, which suddenly made the presence of the view economically significant.[34] Within the political and bureaucratic process that has evolved to determine the nature of hospitals, such hard evidence is probably needed to bring about changes of policy and design, but it confirms what we already knew intuitively. The work is valuable in reclaiming lost territory and rehumanizing some aspects of building, and it starts to contradict my earlier claim that views are not measurable, but note that it measures the quality of the view only in the crudest terms. It cannot put Hannes Meyer's programme of measuring everything back on the agenda. Measuring psychological aspects tends to be reductive and it is hindered in most situations by the sheer number of variables. In Ulrich's case the hospital proved a somewhat ideal subject because such a highly ritualized and controlled environment facilitates the kind of test where a single variable can be persuaded to stand out.

The fate of Wycombe General

Like many hospitals of the 1960s today, Wycombe has sprawled in an untidy way, and is surrounded by a sea of car parking. The original plans assumed vehicle access and no easily discernible pedestrian approach is evident, even though the hospital was placed close to the town centre. It was divided from it by the ring road and its principal roundabout, so vehicles gained complete priority over pedestrians. The original plans show a car park with a mere fifty-seven places, but this has expanded into every available space. The hospital was extended twice: once to the rear and more recently to the side, with buildings as large if not as high, though the original entrance is still the main one. Powell and Moya's building is looking tatty and poorly maintained on the outside (Figure 12.1), and doubtless it is thought by many to be an 'eyesore'. The roof now bristles with mobile telephone aerials, windows have been changed, and services added and re-routed in a piecemeal and pragmatic way. Although it operates internally much as intended, the wards still being wards and the theatre wing still the site of operations, there have been changes. The rooftop accommodation has become a charity-funded cancer centre, which allows patients peace and places them closer to heaven, while the chapel has been recreated at ground floor level near the entrance, its presence declared with an added stained glass window. Less sympathetic changes to the public areas have destroyed the generosity of the original concept and disrupted its clarity. Some, like glazed fire screens between lifts and stairs, result from changing perception of fire risk, despite lack of actual fires. When legislation is tightened in the name of safety there is substantial actual cost as well as a depletion in quality of life, but it becomes unquestionable once defined in terms of responsibility and insurance. Other changes are due to the takeover of spaces regarded as empty for short-term functionally pressing needs. The architects left a glazed 'waiting' space by the main stair on every floor, for example, so that you could see out across the city to get your bearings when leaving the lift, but these views are now blocked with closed rooms and there is no relief from the artificially lit corridor (Figure 12.24). On the ground floor a new wind lobby has been added that is out

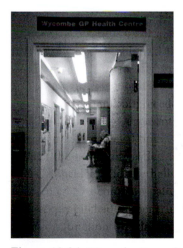

Figure 12.24. Wycombe General in 2012: viewless and artificially lit corridor now used as a waiting room (author's photograph).

Figure 12.25. Wycombe General in 2012: invasion of the formerly generous open-plan foyer by private food and drink outlets (author's photograph).

of sympathy with the original detailing, and the once generous foyer has been invaded by poorly planned encroachments (Figure 12.25). The largest is a franchise café, privatizing the former territory of the welfare state with its aggressive sales pitch: it is so normal today that we scarcely notice, as with the corner full of vending machines. Worst for the building is the complete loss of the double-height staff lounge, most impressive of the original rooms, and the concurrent isolation of the once grand staircase descending to the staff dining room. The basement cafeteria remains, but shoddily furnished and devoid of daylight. As attitudes to the welfare state have changed, it is hardly surprising that the original idealistic provision was compromised, but as so often, the pragmatic and short-term actions of building managers, irrespective of the original architects' intentions, has depleted quality to the point where people must wonder what the initial fuss was about. Memories are short and people soon adjust to a new arrangement, forgetting what they have lost. It is not that they failed to appreciate it, for users have little say in alterations and do not anticipate the effect. Transformed over fifty years from an exemplary model to an outdated and unloved hulk, Wycombe General now stands at a crossroads. Will it be demolished? It could probably be restored and recovered, but that would require sensitive negotiation between retaining the original architecture on the basis of a conservation proposal and meeting constantly updated medical and technical requirements. The human requirements may not have changed so very much.

Notes

1   Iris Murdoch *Under the Net*, Penguin edition 1960, p. 202.

2   Ibid., p. 197.

3   Thompson and Goldin 1975, p. 155.

4   For dates of these discoveries see Thompson and Goldin 1975, p. 189.

5   Thompson and Goldin 1975, p. 159.

6   Ibid.

7   Notably the Military hospital at Montpellier, 1884, p. 168, and the Johns Hopkins Hospital, Baltimore, USA, 1885, pp. 175 and 188.

8   Douglas 1966 *passim*.

9   Douglas 1982 pp. 1-8.

10   Murdoch 1960, p. 204.

11   Ibid., p. 205.

12   Ibid., p. 211.

13   Goffman 1968, pp. 13–22.

14   Gainsborough 1968.

15   Gainsborough and Gainsborough 1964.

16   Gainsborough 1968, p. 23.

17   Ibid., p. 25.

18   Gainsborough at his most human, 1968, p. 42.

19   The plans show rooms facing more or less equally in all directions, with one of the long sides facing disadvantageously north-east. Without a north point one would surely never guess the orientation.

20 Gainsborough was criticized precisely for this by Isadore Rosenfield, author of an American book on hospital design of 1969. Even so, from today's perspective their approaches seem similar: see Rosenfield 1969, p. 33.

21 A revealing glimpse of this development is given in a report of an RIBA discussion led by Richard Llewelyn Davies and John Weeks on hospital design in October 1958: see Richard Llewelyn Davies and John Weeks, 'Progress in planning hospitals', *Journal of the Royal Institute of British Architects* vol. LXVI, January 1959, pp. 79–92.

22 Gainsborough 1968, p. 19 and pp. 70–1.

23 Powell and Moya designed the wonderfully site-sensitive Cripps building at St John's College in Cambridge during the same period.

24 This is present but dealt with cursorily in Rosenfield's book, with a rather patronizing and dismissive attitude towards the pre-modern: but to be fair there was a lack of good general sources, for not until 1975 did Thompson and Goldin's authoritative history of the building type appear.

25 Gainsborough 1968, p. 29, one short paragraph on the whole top floor: 'The lecture theatre and the chapel should form a combined unit with the sanctuary area of the chapel so planned that it can be isolated from the lecture theatre when required.'

26 Interestingly private patients are given a flower shelf, in recognition of the flower ritual in hospital visiting, but places for flowers are not mentioned in relation to the general wards.

27 Hannes Meyer, *bauen*, published in translation in Conrads 1970, pp. 117–20.

28 Ibid.

29 For example, Pevsner in his Postscript to *Pioneers of Modern Design* condemned a wide range of 'expressionist' tendencies as 'attempts to satisfy the craving of architects for individual expression, the craving of the public for the surprising and fantastic, and for an escape out of reality into a fairy world', Pevsner 1960, p. 217.

30 Llewelyn Davies, and Weeks, 'Progress in planning hospitals'.

31 Snow 1964.

32 Lefebvre 1991, p. 361, emphasis in original.

33 K. M. Beauchemin, and P. Hays, 'Sunny hospital rooms expedite recovery from severe and refractory depressions'. *Journal of Affective Disorders* 40 (1996): 49–51.

34 R. S. Ulrich, 'View through a window may influence recovery from surgery'. *Science* 224 (1984): 420–1.

CHAPTER 13
THE OPERA AND THE CONCERT HALL

Figure 13.1. Paris Opéra by Charles Garnier 1875, the main staircase as presented by the architect in his celebratory portfolio of drawings (courtesy of Architectural Association Library, photograph Sue Barr).

Figure 13.2 Paris Opéra, main façade taking a prominent place in Haussmann's renewal of the city (author's photograph 2012).

Figure 13.3. Philharmonie Berlin, main entrance in 1973 before the addition of the Chamber Hall (Getty/Paul Banks).

This double case study looks at two relatively modern buildings in major cities dedicated to music and musical theatre. It concentrates mainly on how they serve the public ritual of an evening's entertainment, but also shows how they represent different stages in the development of the institution. Charles Garnier's Opéra in Paris (Figures 13.1 and 13.2) completed at the end of 1874 was the opera house that set a world standard and celebrated Georges-Eugène Haussmann's modernization of the city by terminating a nexus of Boulevards, while Hans Scharoun's Philharmonie in Berlin (Figure 13.3), completed in 1963, marked the recovery of West Germany and the return to a democratic ideal after the defeat of the Third Reich. In style and building technology the two buildings are worlds apart, for while the former marks the peak of Beaux Arts classicism, the latter is the key work of German organic modernism. Since the first serves the opera and the second orchestral concerts, they belong to different if closely related musical traditions, yet neither could have come about without a major city to provide a steady audience of wealthy patrons, let alone the economic support required for the large company of musicians, singers, administrators, stage-hands and others to put on nightly performances. In fact both were fuelled not just by local but by national funds: the Opéra commissioned by Napoleon III at the end of the Second Empire, the Philharmonie part of the special allowance permitted to West Berlin as a showcase within the East. Both architects were explicitly exercised by the social rituals of arrival, progression through the foyers, and meeting, about which Garnier provides an extraordinary level of detail in his book *Le Théâtre*. Both catered for people in their finery going to be seen as well as to see, but while Garnier accepted the bourgeois class hierarchy and need to pay homage to the Head of State, Scharoun pursued an egalitarian ideal. The two buildings in their respective cities housed prestigious performances, representing seemingly permanent and unchanging institutions, yet neither could have existed much earlier in history, and the century's gap between them reveals enormous changes not only in technical means, but in types of performance, attitudes towards representation, and social mores.

The Opéra and the concert hall exist to serve what is known as classical music, for many the most refined, most highly valued kind of music, which takes place in a specialized building as part of a ritual of entertainment regulated by an expensive ticket. In the designation 'classical' there is a curious but telling disparity between music and architecture. Classical architecture, if invented largely in and since the Renaissance, finds its primary examples in classical antiquity: but classical music, in the absence of antique examples, seems to centre on the works of Beethoven and Mozart around the year 1800, a mere couple of centuries ago.[1] Shared in both arts through the use of the word 'classic' is the notion of a fixed canon, of examples that, as Charles Reilly put it, have 'stood the test of time',[2] but perhaps the imagined stopping of the clock is a comforting delusion as well as representing the solidification of academic institutions. Within the development of human culture classical music is a relative newcomer, and was perhaps unprecedented in releasing music from its social context of feasts, marriages, funerals, worship, marching to war and finally even theatre.[3] Although it has brought great advances in composing extended works, scoring, playing, developing instruments, orchestration, personal expression by the composer, the symbolic representation of ideas, and so on, classical music fundamentally changed music's relationship with society, and despite the reification that makes musical works seem independent of time, its evolution has never ceased. Our two buildings represent different stages in the development of the musical arts, and as the concert hall is essentially the child of the opera house, it makes sense to deal with them in turn.[4]

Classical music and the birth of opera

Ludwig van Beethoven (1710–1827), cited above as the pinnacle of the classic, arrived just in time to take advantage of the new concert possibilities that had developed – instruments, orchestra, and score – but Johann Sebastian Bach (b. 1685) only one generation earlier and also certainly counted as 'classic', is less heard in the concert hall because the bulk of his output was for the Church. Works such as his 'well-tempered clavier' are a reminder too that the basic conventions of the Western musical scale were still being established. The origins of opera were earlier still. Its historians agree that the first operatic work was Claudio Monteverdi's *Orfeo* of 1607, though it drew on pre-existing Florentine musical theatre.[5] Born a century before Bach, Monteverdi also began his musical life in the Church before moving on to employment at the Court in Mantua: *Orfeo* was first presented for Duke Gonzaga as part of a wedding feast. Monteverdi, singer and viol player, was born in Cremona, the world centre of violin making: the first violin was made there by Amati only a dozen years earlier. Monteverdi was also a contemporary of Shakespeare, and Venice in 1600 was about the same size as London, the two port cities each having populations of around 150,000–200,000. The growth of such cities was needed to support specialized players and to provide an audience to fund productions, and in this respect the career of Monteverdi is pivotal, for the first public opera house in Venice was founded in 1637, less than ten years before his death, and his other surviving operas, *L'incoronazione di Poppea* and *Il ritorno d'Ulysse in patria*, were given there. It was left to his pupil Francesco Cavalli to exploit the new conditions and to develop the form, making a secular living by writing a couple of new operas a year.[6] The works became longer, the forces larger, the sets increasingly elaborate, and singers started to be celebrated as stars. By the end of the century there were ten opera houses in Venice, which had become the opera capital of the world. Works by Cavalli were performed also in Naples and Rome, and the composer was eventually lured to Paris to provide entertainment for Louis XIV, who granted the first patent for an opera house in 1669, which was to be 'like those in Italy'.

Royal money was needed, and the king had the power to grant a monopoly, so the institution which was at first the Académie d'Opéra, shortly afterwards renamed the Académie Royale de Musique, has existed ever since as the principal venue for opera and ballet in Paris, enduring through the Revolution, repossessed by Napoleon as the Académie Impériale de Musique in 1802, and redubbed royal after the restoration of 1814. From the start Louis XIV had intended to combine an academy with a public theatre, and its first home was a converted tennis court seating 1,200 people with added stage machinery – presumably one of very few interiors of adequate size. Its second home was purpose built, but occupied the site of another tennis court, and then it moved into a wing of the Royal Palace. Following the Revolution, the royal connection had hastily to be dropped, and the opera moved into the Théatre des Arts where it remained until 1820. The scandalous assassination of the Duc de Berry on the opera steps prompted a hasty move to the Salle Le Peletier, which was initially intended as temporary and accommodated an audience of 1900.[7] Napoleon III embarked on its replacement in 1858 as part of his modernization of Paris, resulting in the Palais Garnier, which was almost ready when the Salle Le Peletier succumbed to fire in 1873 – a frequent hazard for theatres at the time. Garnier's building was thus the final and appropriately grand home for what was intended as a leading representation of shared culture and national dignity, even if its fulfilment was delayed, and its impact dented, by the Franco-Prussian War and end of the Second Empire.

The story of the works played in these buildings and the advances in the art of opera between Monteverdi and the late-nineteenth century is too large a story to engage here: suffice it to say that as performances became increasingly sophisticated and spectacular, sets more elaborate, librettists and composers more inventive and daring, international competition more pressing, Paris took a leading role, particularly with the invention of 'Grand Opera' between the 1820s and the 1870s. Although the names of its leading librettist, Scribe, and its leading composer, Meyerbeer, are relatively unfamiliar today, the form had an international influence, paving the way for the great works of Verdi and Wagner. Stanley Sadie's *History of Opera* comments:

> The grand opera libretto as developed by Scribe was of large proportions, in four or five acts, usually with a historical or quasi-historical background, chosen to provide a succession of colourful scenes and the maximum scope for spectacle. It unfolded a drama of passionate human relationships impinged upon, most often with fatal results, by inexorable forces, usually involving the conflict of two peoples, religions or classes and having some relevance to contemporary conditions.[8]

Although Grand Opera reached its focus in the Opéra, there were numerous other forms of theatre and musical theatre taking place in the first half of the nineteenth century, and Gerhard identifies twenty-eight theatres that operated in central Paris in 1834,[9] catering for a huge audience which varied in its social composition, tickets for the Opéra (at the Salle Le Peletier) being the most expensive. Ten years after its inauguration in 1821 a refurbishment was made that reveals the changing hierarchy of places in the auditorium, for private boxes became less dominant, and stall places reserved for men were the most expensive seats in the house. Some boxes were removed and subdivided, and a form of more open box later readopted by Garnier, the *baignoire*, was invented. This was, according to Gerhard, an expression of 'the compromise between the concept of an auditorium as a place where the spectators could withhold themselves from the stares of other people and the one with which we are more familiar today, where members want, if anything, to be seen'.[10] He also comments on the increasing politeness of the audience, and their restraint from singing along with the performers or applauding indiscreetly.

Garnier and his book *Le Théâtre*

This hasty pre-history sets the scene for Garnier's appearance in the 1860s as the creator of the ideal venue for the Opéra, with a larger budget than ever before, the Emperor's blessing, the most prestigious possible site,[11] and the social rituals of opera-going both highly developed and well-understood. The Opéra was Garnier's masterpiece, won in a competition, occupying him for fifteen years,[12] and employing a design staff drawn from among the most talented alumni of the Beaux Arts school.[13] It has been considered one of the most distinguished examples to arise out of that institution,[14] but its presence in this book is due also to the text Garnier wrote about it, which explains his intentions in extraordinary detail. He visited two hundred theatres across Europe, and discusses many of their specific advantages and disadvantages in a text that repeatedly claims to be rational: a problem is posited, a range of

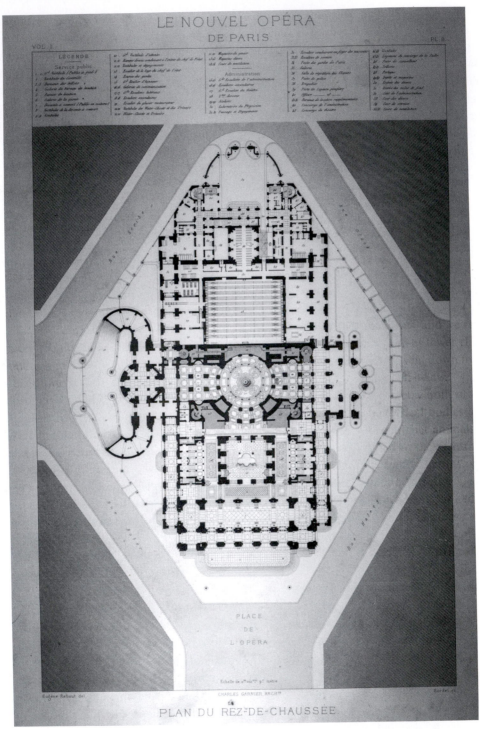

Figure 13.4. Paris Opéra, plan at ground floor level: pedestrians enter by the steps at the front, persons in carriages via the covered porch on the right, leading through to the circular hall and up steps to the main stair well. The ramped carriage entrance to the left is for the Head of State, with private foyers and stair above (courtesy of Architectural Association Library, photograph Sue Barr).

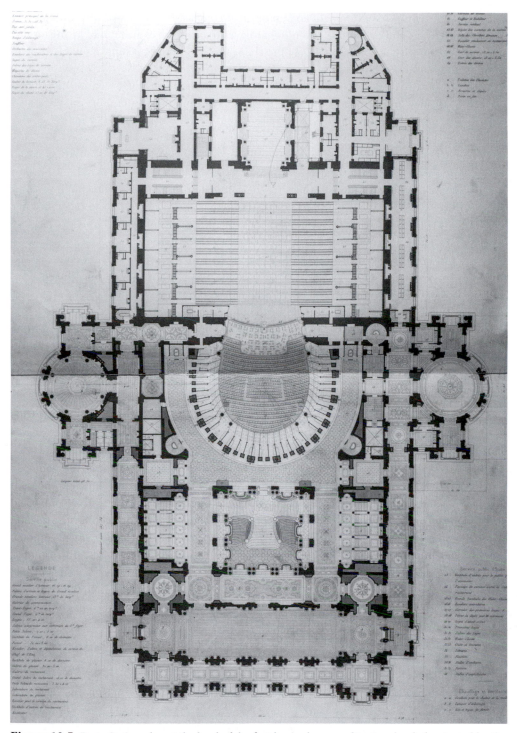

Figure 13.5. Paris Opéra, plan at the level of the first boxes, lower auditorium level, dominated by the central grand stair and the batteries of side stairs leading on to upper levels of boxes. The main foyer and its balcony looking back over the Place de l'Opéra are at the bottom (courtesy of Architectural Association Library, photograph Sue Barr).

solutions and examples is examined, and an optimal conclusion is reached. It is striking that the stylistic details and decorative scheme that have so exercised conventional art historians were hardly discussed, but rather relegated to the realms of art and personal choice.[15] Instead Garnier dedicates his 470 pages to essential matters of principle, technical issues, and the experience of the spectator. It is the latter that effectively structures the book, for nearly half of it charts progress from entry off the street to taking one's place in the auditorium, presented sequentially. Only thereafter does Garnier discuss auditorium and stage, and mainly under technical headings such as lighting, acoustics, heating and ventilating. He goes on to discuss curtain, stage, boxes, and administration, ending with long appendices of briefing information and statistics of other theatres. Despite such detail, he has little to say about how an opera is staged dramatically, perhaps because the conventions were well understood, perhaps because this was the province of other 'artists', but details such as how best to hang scenery, how to provide traps in the stage floor, and how to light the action by gas and electricity, are discussed. Reading between the lines, it is clear that a proscenium and illusionistic sets were assumed, and at one point the cloister from *Robert le Diable*, Meyerbeer's most famous opera, is cited as an especially effective piece of perspective.[16] When it came to stage machinery, Garnier was evidently obliged to choose among expertly developed systems,[17] but even with the auditorium he largely repeated the general layout and even details from the Salle Peletier. Garnier's main innovations lay rather in the front of house: in the entries, foyers and staircases, and in his great empathy for the audience's experience (Figures 13.1, 13.6 and 13.7). He frequently remarks how in earlier theatres such areas were cramped and mean, that one must have adequate space to develop them.[18] The book starts with a general claim on the universality of theatre:

> Put two or three persons together and theatre immediately results, at least in principle. Two of them interact, while the third who looks on and listens is the spectator; he who speaks is the poet, the place is the scene. This rudiment of drama contains the whole primitive idea of theatre … All that happens in the world is no more than theatre and representation: palace, tribune, church, meetings, discussions, all who speak and act, all is theatre at least in a general sense … To see and be seen, hear and be heard, is the fatal circle of humanity.[19]

By the end of the first chapter he is noting the effect of the building on the production, and justifying, in a way that fits perfectly the purposes of my book as well as his, how it works on people at an almost subconscious level:

> Architecture affects the emotions developed in drama, and scenic productions can be reinforced by the places in which they are held. When a hall is beautiful and of noble aspect, as for example with the new Opéra, the entering spectators suffer a kind of moral impression that they can hardly avoid. Contained and surrounded by this sort of elegant atmosphere, their thoughts, their character, even their speech and deportment are influenced. They sense instinctively that a certain dignity is required, and that loose behaviour would be unseemly. This feeling of reserve, this elevation of the spirit which arises spontaneously on entering the room, prepares one for the reception of great works. The influence of the setting dominates, and anything done carelessly brings the

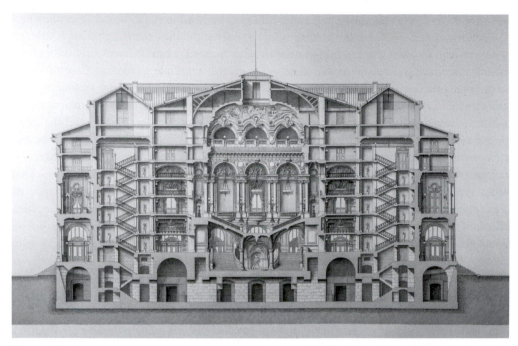

Figure 13.6. Paris Opéra, cross-section through the stairwell looking towards the front and foyers (courtesy of Architectural Association Library, photograph Sue Barr).

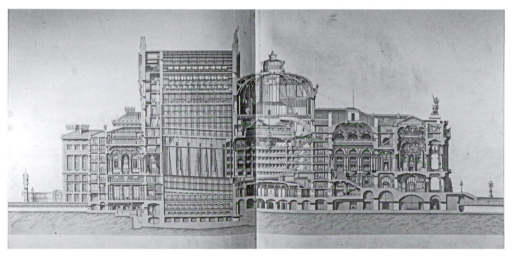

Figure 13.7. Long section with entrance and foyers right, auditorium central and stage with fly-tower left (courtesy of Architectural Association Library, photograph Sue Barr).

risk of finding oneself unwelcome. We can never disinterest ourselves completely from our surroundings, for the pleasures and pains we feel are excited or reduced by the character of the place, even if they are not perverse or troubling. One would find it as hard to sing a de profundis properly in a brilliant ballroom, as to dance with abandon in a funeral hall. There are places that predispose you powerfully towards joy or sadness, and no degree of rationality and philosophy can outweigh this influence.[20]

Moving on from his introduction, Garnier takes on the working of a theatre from the entry inwards, so the second chapter is entirely about covered porches, the third about vestibules. There is little discussion of the siting of the Opéra at this stage in the description,[21] for circulation, it seems, justifies the free-standing position, the island-like placing at the end of one of Haussmann's new axes being crucial to the development of entrances on all four sides to cater for different groups (Figure 13.4). The entrants were mainly audience members, for artists, musicians, administrators and other back-of-house persons entered behind the stage, and they were primarily divided between those arriving on foot and those by carriage, but differences were also noted in the habits of men and women, and there was need to accommodate servants of the wealthier patrons. The main front was given to pedestrians, who could straightforwardly follow the primary axial route up the steps from the square and through the long row of doors, while to avoid clashes Garnier restricted the carriage-borne to the sides. Those of highest status were subscribers with permanent boxes, whose private carriages would deposit them in a drive-through portal on the right-hand side of the building, set on the main cross-axis. Alighting there, they would follow a special spatial sequence centred on the large rotunda beneath the auditorium, the space that also served as waiting room on return while carriages were sought (Figure 13.4). In precisely the opposite position on the left side of the building lay the entrance for Napoleon III, instigator, paymaster and primary client. Garnier reserved an entire later chapter to the arrangements for him, including an almost excessive justification of why the Head of State's role needed to be celebrated.[22] Napoleon III needed not only a royal box but a royal entrance and a whole royal suite of rooms, being expected to arrive with his retinue in a line of no less than three carriages without getting caught up in the normal traffic.[23] So the entire left side of the Opéra was given over to a vast entry ramp sweeping up to his elevated entrance, with a special portal leading through to the Emperor's own grand stair and his imperial box near the stage. The symmetry of the building forced an equivalence between the simple arrival of the Emperor on the left and the protracted arrival of scores of lesser mortals coming by private coach on the right. The descriptions in Garnier's opening chapters show a commendable psychological insight as well as sensitivity to social conventions. The pedestrians must quickly get under the cover of a porch or gallery where, 'protected from the rain and wind, they can begin to take off their outdoor wear, find their tickets, then enter the theatre freed from these minor preoccupations'.[24] They move on through the doors to arrive in the grand vestibule, which is:

> the place of repose as one arrives at the theatre, it's the place to meet one's friends, the place where, secure at having arrived, one at least feels less rushed to find one's place, where one can wait a few moments or stroll about. But to facilitate this pause one must also be able to see the staircases and the control desks so that one's security is assured. One therefore knows where one is going to go, sees the route one should take, so one is less pressed, even invited.[25]

Next, the opera-goers move on through the ticket checks, set in desks to left and right so that they are obliged to look at their tickets and choose the direction indicated. After this they can move through to the staircases and on up to find their places. Meanwhile, as already described, those arriving in carriages on the right-hand side of the complex have a separate set of vestibules, and after this group have deposited their cloaks, greeted each other, and attended to

Figure 13.8 Paris Opéra, view of the main staircase (author's photograph 2012).

their toilette, they emerge on the lowest flights of the grand central stair to join the pedestrian group arriving from the front at the next level (Figure 13.9). Garnier devotes the whole of his fourth chapter to the stairs, half of which is devoted to analysing the many arrangements possible with their advantages and disadvantages, before he finally presents and justifies his own solution:

> The arrangement is simple: on the building's axis the arriving visitor encounters a great monumental flight of stairs. It rises to a landing in front of a first entrance, then the route divides, one flight rising to the right and the other to the left, both ending in galleries at the level of the first boxes … At the top of the first flight a central doorway leads to the baignoires and the stalls of the amphitheatre, and that accomplished, the lateral flights lead on up to the first boxes. Now as the two opposed flights and the landing between them only take about 20 metres, one arrives close to the median part of the corridors for the boxes. Before people reach the end of the two upper flights, the secondary stairs are visible directly opposite. Audience members stopping at the first boxes turn right or left … while those progressing to the second level of boxes continue straight on. There is again division of the crowd, generous facility of communication, and logical arrival at all seats. These conditions fulfilled, let us see if others are too, and if the communication of the boxes with the foyers is broad and easy. Since the width of the stair cage scarcely exceeds 20 metres, the galleries of the passage established to each side will align with the

Figure 13.9. Looking down on the main staircase, left side, where it comes up from the rotunda, showing the curved profile of the steps (Getty).

middle of the corridors of the hall, to give the greatest average proximity to the seats and proximity to the foyers, all with direct view of the route. There is no embarrassment, no detours to get from hall to foyers, so again the problem seems resolved.[26]

Reading through Garnier's comprehensive and well-argued text, with its constant concern for ease of movement, multiple routes, and avoidance of congestion and cross-flows, one at first almost misses the ambition of making the stair hall the central volume of the building with its major vertical void towering up to a skylight. With this design he opened up new social possibilities for people to parade and display themselves, and by the time the reader reaches the triumphant tailpiece to the chapter this has become the dominant theme. It was certainly recognized from the beginning by all commentators as the main glory of the building, making it, as Garnier says, 'a sumptuous and eventful place':

all persons circulating on every floor can if they wish find interest in the view of the grand stair and the incessant circulation of the crowd … On each floor the spectators leaning on the balconies decorate the walls and seemingly bring them to life, while others ascend or descend, adding further life. Finally with the addition of cloth and flowing draperies, with many-branched chandeliers, lustrous surfaces, marbles and flowers, colour throughout, one makes of the whole a brilliant and sumptuous composition reminiscent of canvases by Veronese. The light which sparkles, the resplendent costumes, the animated and smiling figures, the meetings and greetings: all give an atmosphere of feasting and pleasure, and without being conscious of the part played by the architecture in this magic effect, all enjoy themselves, in their happiness paying homage to this great art, so powerful in its manifestations, so elevated in its results.[27]

Despite such emphasis on togetherness, there is little doubt about the social hierarchy of the stair arrangements which followed the class structure of Parisian society, particularly the way the main flights provided a stage for the privileged, while the lesser orders looked on. It is also inescapable that the main stair served essentially the two favourite and most expensive levels of the baignoires and first boxes, the latter also setting the level of the extensive foyers as a clear *piano nobile* (Figure 13.7). This worked wonderfully for the overall hierarchy of the building and to create a general sense of location, but the auditorium provided seats at no less than five levels, so patrons in the upper three were obliged to use the batteries of secondary side stairs, which also efficiently absorbed much of the circulation load of departure following a performance. Garnier was sensitive about this hierarchy and a little too anxious to justify it:

whatever your feelings about the principles of equality, it must be admitted that in a theatre one can never make all seats equally good … The most rational method to split the crowd is to follow the seats, so the stairs divide into those serving ordinary seats and those serving luxurious ones. The route for each is defined, and confusion is avoided. I am well aware that some pedantic egalitarians will say this initial division disfavours part of the audience, and that the theatre should belong to all without distinction. I am not sure that any great harm is done to them, but if two or three thousand people are made to pass along the same route, that route will certainly be badly encumbered, and if everybody is treated the same, all are treated equally badly. I do not see therefore that it would achieve any increase in dignity. Since nobody is embarrassed to go to the stalls or to the third-level boxes, I see no reason why people should be embarrassed to take a route not shared with those going to the first level of boxes. When in the street I walk on the pavement, I do not feel insulted to leave the central carriageway to vehicles: it is a guarantee of security and makes circulation easier for everyone. Dignity is not involved.[28]

But of course at the Opéra dignity is involved, which becomes very clear later when Garnier comes to justify the special privileges given to the Head of State, deploying arguments similar to those of Thomas Carlyle in *Sartor Resartus*:

If social convention prevents a lawyer or a doctor donning the clothes of a labourer, it is also forbidden that a general should visit the tavern like a simple soldier, or that an archbishop remain in his seat to distribute holy water, so one recognizes that if those who represent the hierarchy of state, army or clergy have conventions to uphold, the one who represents all, officers or workers, should be subjected to many customs determined by practice, instinct or reason, which prevent him mixing with all. The principles of equality live in the exception, and this is the most legitimate and I would even say the most indispensable.[29]

Napoleon III never took up his box at the Opéra, being deposed, exiled and deceased long before it was opened, but the arrangements for the Emperor had been long agreed, and circumstances had only just changed when Garnier was writing.[30] He therefore argued that they should continue to apply to any Head of State, whose relative seclusion and complete protection from the crowd was essential. Napoleon III would have been on public view just three times on each visit, coming and going in his line of coaches for which the ramp was an appropriate platform of display, and appearing in the imperial box immediately to the left of the stage where he was revealed to the audience almost within the compass of the performance. This denied him the optimum viewpoint of the axis found in German ducal theatres, but it did make it unnecessary for the audience to turn and crane their necks to see him, and made him perhaps deliberately more a part of the show. Garnier's reluctance to admit to social hierarchy apart from the Head of State was strongly expressed in his ideas about the foyers for use in the interval, which he refused to subdivide between social ranks. Some of this was doubtless in the interests of architectural grandeur and wholeness, but there is also an overwhelming sense in his writing, committed to paper years before the building could be experienced, of the excitement to be had by the awareness of the whole crowd and its shared experience, not only as it gathered around the performance but also as people encountered each other during the intervals:

Some audience members relax without walking far, but stopping at points where they gain an advantageous view, and they take their distraction not from moving themselves but in watching the movement of others. But there are others who prefer, instead of just watching this general movement, to take part in it, to wander about seeking acquaintances whom they might have seen across the auditorium. Yet others look for more withdrawn places comfortably furnished where they can avoid the circulation of the crowd. There are others who quit these places or promenades in the foyers for a promenade or a place in the open air, and prefer the view of the outside world. Then there are also some who prefer to smoke, or to take refreshments standing before a long buffet or seated in a room ad hoc.[31]

He goes on to describe how all these activities can be pursued at will across the extensive foyers at first-box level, stretching around the main stairwell and across the front of the building, where members of the audience can also step outside and disport themselves on a gallery overlooking the square below with the long boulevard beyond, a position of advantage and privilege. But always the main staircase was intended to have a kind of gravitational pull:

> the grand staircase seems to have the position that allows an original and grandiose decoration, but also the different flights, variety of positions of people who circulate at different levels, the oppositions which arise between the horizontal or vertical parts with the oblique lines of the flights: all shows that this grand arrangement must offer a richness of view to attract those spectators who wish only to satisfy their eyes.[32]

Perhaps Garnier was right in his conviction that in the foyers the whole of society should be kept together rather than divided into different groups, so that in front of house as in auditorium the sense of a shared experience could continue, contributing to the communitas that potentially arises out of any theatrical event, when people are taken 'out of themselves' to share in an imagined other world.[33] Although the interval might offer a moment of relief to escape that imagined prospect, it gave the opportunity of an alternative one: partaking in the opera-going society, and that was best seen in its full scale and not subdivided. Certainly the Opéra worked well, gained international fame, and it became the model for opera houses around the world until the First World War, while the expanded front of house that Garnier had pioneered became widely adopted. In terms of stage and productions, the Opéra represented the state of the art for the 1860s, but it arose at a time when the leading creative impetus was already passing from Paris, Italy being in the ascendant with the rise of Giuseppe Verdi. Richard Wagner's first Bayreuth Festival, pushing the frontiers of the *Gesamtkunstwerk*, came only a year after the Opéra's opening. Social and technological conditions were on the move too, for the Paris of the Opéra was also that of railways, department stores, and electric lighting (by arc lamp), while the phonograph and cinema were almost waiting in the wings.[34]

The age of mechanical reproduction

By the time of our second main example, the Berlin Philharmonie of 1963, mechanical reproduction had radically changed the nature of performances and entertainments. Sound recording, which began with Edison's first voice recorder in 1877, became increasingly accurate and ubiquitous, with substantial sales of shellac discs by 1920. It allowed people to hear music when nobody was playing, so what had been evanescent was reified in a disc. It became possible to hear chosen performances repeatedly, to compare versions note for note, and the recording industry set new standards and expectations. The discophile could collect and possess endless works without witnessing a single live performance, and on disc the individual contributions of musicians could become blurred.[35] Music was more widely shared and readily available, but migration into the electronic world detached it from place and context. No longer compulsorily the primary experience, the live performance often became instead the confirmation of what was already known on disc. Popular music even originated within the disc culture, pushed into electronic form through amplification, then made visual through pop-videos on television and internet. So although the Glastonbury Festival undoubtedly remains effective for its sense of communitas, nobody arrives ignorant of the songs to be played. Nearly all are widely propagated in reproduced versions, and the audience even sing along.

What does all this do to the opera and the concert? Well, opera houses continue to exist and composers are still writing for them, but they serve a rather small and exclusive audience, still require substantial subventions, and the majority of works presented are 'classics', that is to say historic pieces, rather as in a museum, lacking immediacy and requiring an accompanying commentary.[36] More popular, relevant and experimental forms of musical theatre in the form of musicals coexist, but both are also served up in reproduced versions to be bought and owned. Mechanical reproduction has steadily grown, for already by the end of the 1920s cinema had overtaken in popularity live theatre, music hall and opera, and in the 1950s television began to overtake the cinema. For a few decades, with few channels and no way to store programmes, television events were still shared and held at specific times if in different places, but the home video-recorders of the 1980s made possible the personal ownership of cinematic material, which like sound records could be repeated and analysed, so losing any necessary connection with time and place. Today we face an endless cacophony of personal entertainment intertwined with a good deal of aggressive advertising, but the desire for a sense of occasion, of an experience physically shared – unlike reading a book, to remind readers that private consumption is not new – has provoked a rebirth of cinema, while opera and concerts also continue, perhaps as much for the communitas and social experience they bring as for the actual performance. In this respect the Berlin Philharmonie is not so different from the Paris Opéra.

Place, occasion and the Berlin Philharmonie

It was the Dutch architect Aldo van Eyck who around 1960 protested against Sigfried Giedion's 'space and time' by insisting that we should rather think in terms of 'place and occasion'.[37] Hans Scharoun was then at work on the construction of his masterpiece, the Berlin Philharmonic Orchestra's concert hall, fruit of an architectural competition in 1956, which is as dedicated to 'place and occasion' as the Opéra. Scharoun's organic architecture had been from the start concerned with specificity as opposed to the generality of the International Style, as he sought in each project to articulate whatever was special about the site and the programme, producing a highly irregular architecture that disdained the rational construction grid dominating orthodox modern architecture.[38] His work was often dismissed as 'personal' or 'expressionist', and it is true that he had been a significant member of Bruno Taut's *gläserne Kette* (Glass Chain) in the revolutionary period following the First World War, contributing some of the most famous watercolour images to that movement.[39] Certainly there was in the Philharmonie something of the *Volkshaus*, a kind of socialist cathedral represented in the

Figure 13.10. Public music in Budapest 1989, proof of Hans Scharoun's claim that the audience gather in a circle (author's photograph).

Figure 13.11. The Philharmonie during a concert seen from behind the orchestra. The audience, divided into 'vineyard terraces' surround the orchestra on all sides, replacing the opposition of producers and consumers with a single musical event (photograph Reinhard Friedrich, Scharoun Archive, Akademie der Künste, Berlin).

fantasies of 1918, but to dismiss the concert hall as merely a throwback to that period was to misunderstand Scharoun's whole subsequent development, and particularly his technique of working from the inside out, of thinking in terms of space, use and relationships, rather than the architectural object. Before the Philharmonie he had built neither theatre nor concert hall, but there had been a theatre project as early as 1920. He also produced over decades many fantasy drawings depicting both external forms and interiors with cascades of people on stairs, before he gained the chance to develop seriously worked-out designs in the period after the Second World War.[40] These began with competition projects in 1949 for an Opera House in Leipzig and the Liederhalle in Stuttgart, the latter winning first prize but remaining unbuilt. Then in 1952, with landscape architect Hermann Mattern, he won the competition project for the rebuilding of the theatre in Kassel. They spent more than a year developing it in detail before it was dropped under scandalous circumstances. This work prepared Scharoun and his office to undertake the competition for the National Theatre in Mannheim of 1953, his most radical theatre design, though the entry remained unplaced. Through these projects radically new approaches were developed to stage, foyer and site relationships, paving the way for the Philharmonie.[41]

From opera to concert

According to music historians Tim Carter and Erik Levi, substantial orchestras were first assembled for opera, and the 'conceding of aesthetic status and semiotic power to wordless music' began in the Baroque era, then orchestral music grew up with the new industrial society of the nineteenth century and its bourgeois audience. They note the inauguration of the London Philharmonic Society in 1813, the Paris Conservatoire of 1828 and the Vienna Philharmonic in 1842, but the last at first performed a mere two concerts per season.[42] The Berlin Philharmonic was founded in 1882 when fifty-four out of seventy musicians left a group called the Bilsesche Kapelle in protest against their tyrannical conductor. They became self-governed, voting in new members and also voting for their conductor, whose role nonetheless remained central. They first gained a high reputation under Hans von Bülow between 1887 and his death in 1894, and were then led by Arthur Nikisch until 1922, making their first recording in 1913 and establishing a vital relationship with the record company Deutsche Grammophon that has persisted to this day. The multiple discs of that occasion held Beethoven's Fifth Symphony and, mechanically recorded, were of poor quality, but Jon Tolanski claims to be able to discern 'pliant rhythmic flexibility and blending of inner parts'.[43] This suggests a distinct playing style, the crucial role of the conductor in moulding the 'instrument', and the growing importance held by recordings for the sake of identity, reputation and revenue. So it continued under Wilhelm Furtwängler in the 1920s, and radio broadcasts added a yet broader audience. Furtwängler maintained the high reputation and remained in charge throughout the Third Reich and beyond, despite his flight to Switzerland at the war's end and some awkward questions at Nuremberg. Then, following his death in 1954, Herbert von Karajan was voted in, the orchestra's most famous conductor of all, and doyen of the perfect recording. He was Hans Scharoun's principal client. The architectural competition of 1955 was destined to give the Berlin Philharmonic its first purpose-built home. From the beginning in 1882 its performances had been held in a converted ice rink on Bernburger strasse, and after the destruction

Figure 13.12. Main entrance to the Philharmonie, with welcoming canopy for arriving visitors and the hall rising behind (author's photograph 1993).

Figure 13.13 Model of the hall at competition stage, when it was destined for a more compact site and entered through the monumental building on the right (Scharoun Archive, Akademie der Künste, Berlin).

Figure 13.14. Model of hall in its new position at Tiergarten, initially a wasteland. Scharoun's intended square in front of the surviving church would have bound the composition together, but was never realized (Scharoun Archive, Akademie der Künste, Berlin).

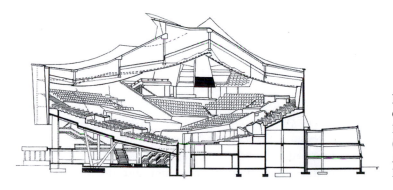

Figure 13.15. Cross-section of the Philharmonie as built (Scharoun Archive, Akademie der Künste, Berlin).

of that venue by bombing in 1944 the orchestra played temporarily in the opera house or the Titaniapalast, a former cinema. From 1949 on, funds were collected by a society of friends, and later in the midst of the German economic miracle the orchestra received unprecedented subsidy from the city,[44] but it was still a financial struggle to get the hall built at the end of the 1950s despite the fact that it was per seat the most economical of its time in Europe. The intended copper cladding had to be postponed.

Music in the centre

Right at the beginning of *Le Théâtre*, Garnier claims that the play naturally takes a circular form, for the crowd gather around the actor, people behind stretch up on their toes to see, then the actor steps onto a box to add some height.[45] Whether he had been reading Goethe's *Italian Journey* is not clear, but precisely the same idea is expressed there, and both were thinking of classical amphitheatres. Hans Scharoun had the same conviction when he commented:

> Is it just coincidence that whenever improvised music is heard people tend to gather around it in a circle? This wholly natural process, quite understandable from a psychological point of view, had to be carried over into a concert hall and that was the task we set ourselves, to take music as the spatial and optical centre … In the design of a concert hall there was no lack of examples to follow, but even the recent ones adopted the traditional division of space which was born of the theatre: the orchestra finds itself on a stage and the public sits in an auditorium. But the opera is visual, a show-piece (*Schau-spiel*), and needs the stage for all its technical apparatus, whereas the concert has no such requirement and the listener is instead a participant (*Zuschauer*). A room in which music is made and should be heard therefore demands quite a different concept.[46]

Deeply interested in the relation of audience to action in the design of his theatre projects, he had wished even there to break down the barrier between producers and consumers by eliminating the proscenium arch and extending the flexibility of staging. The Mannheim proposal went further, not only by offering an immensely wide stage but also by making the whole house asymmetrical: an intention he called 'aperspective theatre' in defiance of conventions held since the Renaissance (Figures 13.19 and 13.20).[47] Mannheim's former theatre had set the Duke's box on axis to enjoy the most privileged view, and also put the rest of the social hierarchy on display, but for the new theatre Scharoun sought an equality appropriate to restored democracy: each person was to have a different view but all of them should be equally good. The major innovation carried over to the Philharmonie was to divide the audience into separate terraces, which broke the great mass down into smaller groups, each sitting to face a slightly different direction. Giving each terrace a separate entrance and cloakroom arrangement not only solved the circulation problem but also gathered terrace members as a group. Because of the need to present theatrical performances visually, even the round amphitheatre at Epidaurus (Figure 2.26, p. 39) takes up scarcely more than half the circle, and although theatre in the round has in the past half century enjoyed some success through its sense of intimacy and immediacy, actors must deliver speeches with their backs to some of the audience. But orchestral music is arguably more omnidirectional, and though

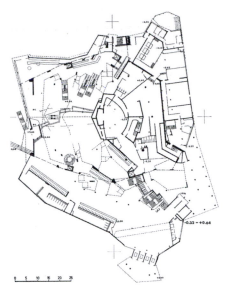

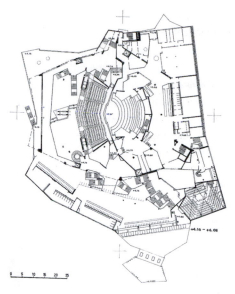

Figure 13.16. Plan of the Philharmonie at ground level, main entrance bottom: concert-goers either take the first bank of stairs and use cloakroom facilities on the first floor, or they cross the foyer to the stairs at the opposite end (Scharoun Archive, Akademie der Künste, Berlin).

Figure 13.17. Intermediate level with podium and lowest entries (Scharoun Archive, Akademie der Künste, Berlin).

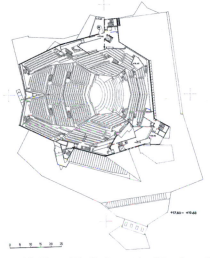

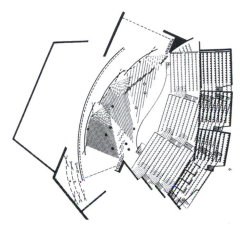

Figure 13.19. Plan of the auditorium of Scharoun's National Theatre project, Mannheim, 1953, in which the idea of the vineyard terraces originated (Scharoun Archive, Akademie der Künste, Berlin).

Figure 13.18. Full hall plan with all levels and upper staircases (Scharoun Archive, Akademie der Künste, Berlin).

Figure 13.20. Model of the auditorium of Scharoun's National Theatre project (photograph by Peter Lathey, University of Sheffield).

the best seats might be in front, it is better to sit behind and close than a long way off with the added advantage of facing the conductor. By surrounding the orchestra with the audience a more compact arrangement can be made, and by spreading them vertically in a bowl-shaped section everyone can gain a good line of sight and hearing (Figure 13.15). The glaring problem was one of acoustics, more essential to a concert hall than practically any other building, and greatly at risk with an untried arrangement. With the Opéra, Garnier claimed to have undertaken two years of study without being able to establish reliable principles, and the bewildering diversity of opinion justified the relative conservatism of his auditorium.[48] Scharoun, ever ready to experiment but aware of the importance of this issue, sought out Lothar Cremer, an acoustician of great intuitive as well as technical ability.[49] Cremer was initially doubtful of the centralizing concept, for some instruments are very directional, and singers even more so, but he made a pact with Scharoun that he would go along with it provided that he was given his way on the crucial acoustic issues.[50] In the general shaping of the hall it was important to prevent standing waves developing between parallel surfaces, and the ceiling was made convex rather than concave, with the potential focus between the curves broken by hanging reflectors, but the great acoustic success of the hall, it has been found since, depended on the early reflections from the fronts of the seating terraces. The surfaces were angled on Cremer's advice, but belonged to the 'vineyard terrace' arrangement first intended for entirely social reasons and carried over from the Mannheim project.[51]

Although the Mannheim auditorium design had been totally asymmetrical, Scharoun chose with the Philharmonie to respect the formal layout of the orchestra and its focus on the conductor, for whatever theories might now question the necessity of that role or the dominance in Berlin of that hitherto male figure, it had been essential to the orchestra's history and modus operandi: with von Karajan more so than ever.[52] So despite the idea of it being in-the-round, Scharoun adopted a strongly axial layout, and the crossing main axes in the plans remain the organizational reference point, even if the hall's axis does not dictate the rest of the surrounding building. He also accepted that the best seats are in front and that there should be more of them there than elsewhere, but by dividing them and swinging them to different angles he avoided direct confrontation with the orchestra, also preparing the way for the greater angle shifts that occur in the corner and side terraces, and so initiating the whole sense of rotation. The hall could therefore be called in the round with a frontal bias, while the terrace fronts remain straight to avoid acoustic foci. The several terraces are entered separately at different levels, which reduces circulation space within the hall and permits a rapid exit at the end of a concert, but more of that later in discussing the foyer.

Opinion seems divided on whether the Philharmonie is acoustically better than the much praised Vienna Musikverein, a direct contemporary of the Opéra built in 1870 to designs by Theophil Hansen, but the atmosphere of the two halls is utterly different (Figure 13.21). The Musikverein follows the shoebox principle, partly owing to the limited structural possibilities of the nineteenth century, but mainly to follow the classical precedent of the basilica. The flat layout of the main hall's seating directly confronts the orchestra on the stage in a classic division of producers and consumers, and the audience have neither as good a view of the action as in the Philharmonie, nor as good a view of each other. Because of its better sight-lines and careful handling of the sound-reflecting surfaces, the Philharmonie (Figure 13.22) offers greater consistency of seat quality, but also the possibility of many different experiences from different directions and distances.[53] But it is above all the sense of togetherness that

Figure 13.21. Vienna Musikverien, the classic 'shoebox' concert hall (photograph by Michael Barron).

Figure 13.22. Interior of the Philharmonie (author's photograph 1973).

Figure 13.23. Philharmonie foyer seen from the far end: the stairs and landings encourage exploration (author's photograph 1973).

distinguishes the Philharmonie, of being part of a great community of listeners, which is felt not only during the music but particularly during the applause as one looks across the sea of faces and registers agreement. This sharing of experience is perhaps all the more needed to enhance the excitement of live performance in the age of mechanical reproduction, for the aural quality can be almost as good at home with a hifi system or through headphones. The visual qualities of the hall are also vital to its atmosphere, particularly the spatial complexity and lack of perspective which make it difficult to judge the scale and position of events. One feels that one never quite grasps the room, and the music seems to fill it, almost as if it is a musical instrument in itself. The space both confirms the efficacy of the aperspective effect and adds to the music's ethereal quality. Its magic is widely appreciated, and half a century after its opening the Philharmonie had become the primary new model for the concert hall, its angled seating terraces adopted worldwide.

That the Opéra was axial and frontal, set up on an orthogonal system and made symmetrical in its massing at least from the front, followed the classical tradition as developed through the Beaux Arts. Even when faced with irregular sites, eighteenth- and nineteenth-century French architecture sought to suppress the anomalies, reimposing as much forced regularity as possible. As his early works show, Scharoun was from his education familiar with Beaux Arts techniques, but before the end of the 1920s he was reacting against such formal discipline, and he became the leading modernist master to break with the orthogonal, notoriously using whatever plan angles the site might suggest. This allowed him great freedom of invention, but also meant that the geometry of his buildings could be given over much more to 'fluidity' (das Flüchtige), that they could follow lines of movement and social processes rather than being constrained by Beaux Arts formal grids or Gropius's constructional rationality. So when he came to design foyers they were allowed to unfold along a route, taking in and celebrating the changing needs of the audience and guiding them to their places (Figures 13.23 and 13.24 and plans in Figures 13.16–13.18). This concern for user experience was essentially the same as Garnier's, and followed a similar progression of arrival, getting a ticket, depositing a coat, finding refreshment, and meeting friends in the interval. It was already a major consideration in designing the Kassel Theatre project of 1952 in which a special pedestrian bridge led through from the town centre, about which Scharoun remarked:

> The guiding of spectators over the footbridge or from the dropping off-point in the street below it, then on through foyer and cloakrooms into the auditorium, is not just functional, but serves their experience [Erleben]. All circulation and social rooms are optically connected to each other, while each retains its own identity. The rooms for movement unfold in the core-defining representative spatial progression, which includes foyer, refreshment room and smoking room. The refreshment room faces the front garden, the smoking room the valley, also open to the wider landscape. The enclosed court serves as yet another element to free-up and enrich the spatial sequence. The social task of the building is expressed additionally in the use of the theatre as Festival Site for the city. Therefore the provision of daylight is included, with help of a skylight, and in front is an ambulatory, along which a promenade can be made in favourable seasons with a view across the valley.[54]

In discussions of the Philharmonie it is often forgotten that the competition version of 1956 was designed for a different site (Figure 13.13). A surviving neoclassical building with columned portico was to be used as entrance, and the hall was to occupy the irregular space behind.[55] Always keenly concerned to integrate any building into its site, Scharoun accepted these conditions, which also fitted happily with the will to asymmetry he had exhibited since the late 1920s. It would have worked as an urban proposition, strengthening the new centre of West Berlin at Zoo Station and Kurfürstendamm, but on reconsideration it seemed better to place the hall where it would be closer to the city centre when Berlin was reunited, and so developed the idea of the Kulturforum at the corner of Tiergarten close to the edge of

Figure 13.24a, b, c, d, e. Philharmonie foyer at various levels (author's photographs 1973).

the western zone and the site of the Berlin Wall of 1961.[56] The hall was planned, as already explained, from the centre outwards, so the foyers in the competition design needed to link the main entrance given by the neoclassical portico to the many soundproof doors connected to the various levels of seating terraces, taking in ticket offices, cloakroom counters, lavatories and spaces for meeting and waiting in between. As proposed for the Kassel project, this was done in a fluid manner, using staircases as directional devices to guide the crowd and linking them with necessary landings. To deal with the crowd of two thousand and to capitalize on the basic symmetry of the hall, a double stair system was devised, with main foyers offering coat counters at both ground and first-floor level, but upper landings were made only as wide as needed, decreasing with reduced traffic, and all levels were left open to make it as transparent as possible. Owing to the shape of the first intended site, the centre of the hall was displaced to one side and the foyer began with stairs angled off to the left, necessarily developed in an asymmetrical manner. This asymmetry was carried over to the new site despite a fresh freedom to deploy the building in any direction, and the essential compactness of the whole was also retained, as was the asymmetry of the foyer layout with its double staircase system, half the crowd taking a stair near the entrance to ascend to cloakroom counters on the first floor, the other half proceeding across the ground floor to staircases on the other side, depositing their coats on the way (Figures 13.16, 13.23 and 13.24e). The upper levels consist of stairs and landings still visually open to the space below, so audience members see each other moving about, just as Garnier had intended with his stair at the Opéra, but they occupy a larger, more complex space freed from load-bearing solids and with a complex ever-changing envelope. The result is a space of unprecedented complexity which Frei Otto called 'the room of a thousand angles', but which is nonetheless navigable because of the logical sequence of stairs, each leading to the next. The larger scale statement of the hall's axis was made evident by the shape of its underbelly, its great V-shaped structural supports, and the symmetrically set coloured glass of the rear wall. It seems generally agreed that the complex fragmentation of the foyer space is a perfect foil to the unity of the hall, and in a concert interval people can be seen moving about, chatting, and leaning over the balustrade to view those below. The space positively encourages exploration, and the visual openness between levels makes it easier to discover friends.

The Philharmonie is most frequently criticized for a lack of urban integration, which was certainly not intended. The site was a complete wasteland first cleared for Speer's projected axis and by wartime destruction, then blighted by proximity to the Berlin Wall of 1961–89. Although Scharoun produced a general plan for the Kulturforum with a new square centred on the one surviving building, St Matthew's Church, it never happened (Figure 13.14). As with the Opéra, transport arrangements tended to make the hall into an island, especially the large car parks which took up much of the site. The addition of the musical instruments museum and Chamber Hall, posthumous works approved by Scharoun but carried out by Edgar Wisniewski, have added a local interior landscape, and Scharoun was also able to build the State Library opposite, but the motorway it was intended to set its back against was never completed, and instead the multi-lane Potsdamerstrasse runs in front. In the era of post-modernism the entire Kulturforum was dismissed as anti-urban, and following German reunification the Potsdamerplatz was rebuilt at too large a scale. To get any real idea of the potential effect of Scharoun's concept of city-landscape (*Stadtlandschaft*) you have to go to Wolfsburg to see how his theatre, completed in 1973, makes a new edge for the city, although everything is still too widely spread out thanks to the impact of the car. That theatre also has an extraordinarily successful foyer developed as a single linear sequence, though the stage is conventional to accommodate travelling productions.

Conclusion

The Opéra is effectively now a museum, visited daily by tourists and only used for a quarter of Paris's productions, since the Opéra Bastille with its larger seating capacity took over in 1990.[57] Garnier's building is now used for the period pieces for which it was built and offers the most appropriate staging, operas composed in the late-nineteenth century and earlier.[58] The Philharmonie is much younger and still allows for innovation, its orchestra still buoyed up by recording contracts, tours, and generous support from the Berlin Senate. Despite pressure from the audience to serve up classics, it has always striven to perform contemporary material, including unusual instrument combinations and electronic works.[59] The high reputation of Herbert von Karajan has been extended under Claudio Abbado and Sir Simon Rattle, making the institution more international and assuring that boundaries are still being pushed. Scharoun's building has suffered some minor damage and reconstruction owing to a damaged ceiling and later a fire, but it was repaired and is still going strong half a century later, widely respected both by musicians and by the general public. In the book *My Century*, a collection of fables social, political, and technological with which he mapped out German history year by year, Günter Grass gave it the honour of representing 1963. The tale is told by a music student unexpectedly recruited into acoustic tests by the architect and acoustic engineer, and how she returns repeatedly to experience 'how much music and architecture complement one another'.[60] Architects' attacks on Scharoun for being 'irrational' and for not attending to the imperatives of building construction have not altogether evaporated, but the use of free angles and intersecting spaces over the subsequent half century has become commonplace and is far less difficult technically, so it is much repeated, even if nobody has done it with greater panache or more sense of occasion. In the design of concert halls particularly, Scharoun's example has gradually become the primary new model developed in the twentieth century, imitated worldwide, and not least at Frank Gehry's Disney Hall. We began this chapter with Garnier's remark that when three people get together there is theatre. Theatre has always been a sharing of interactive experience, and despite the intervention of loudspeaker and video screen, there is still a special shared atmosphere when people get together around a theatrical event, perhaps in long-distant memory of those occasions when an entirely oral and performative culture was being passed on. I leave the final word to theatre director Peter Brook, who in talking about theatre in the 1980s said little about the building, but much about togetherness:

> I think that the moment the separation between any of the elements ceases, the moment there's no longer actor, author, subject, spectator; the moment all those fuse together into a new unity, and that unity has a taste that is different from a taste one can get from anywhere else in everyday life – then the theatre exists. At the beginning of a performance you have a number of people – 50, 500, 2000 people – all of whom are self-contained fragments with no natural flow going between them. In other words each one of us is like a car rushing along a highway, and even when one comes into a traffic jam one is completely cut off from the flow of life: one is in one's own little box, and that is in

a very crude way the way we live most of the time. One comes into a special surrounding which is an amphitheatre – an amphitheatre has only one virtue, it brings people together – and one sees that the more different the people together in the end, the better the result. And then, through a number of steps, through the fact that perhaps the theme, perhaps the rhythm, perhaps the work of the actor, the presence of the actor, all these together attract a common interest that becomes dynamic because the common interest turns into a common process and something begins to unroll and flow shared by everyone, and then you have, if you're lucky, like water coming to the boil, a change of state.[61]

Notes

1   In *The Cambridge Companion to the Orchestra*, Tim Carter and Erik Levi cite Beethoven and Mozart as 'emblematic of loftier musical principles' and a 'canon of great works' making up a 'museum repertory' beginning in the 1840s: see Lawson 2003, p. 12.

2   Charles Reilly was the Head of the Liverpool School of Architecture, the first in the UK to gain RIBA recognition in 1895, and was part of the institute's committee on architectural education in 1910.

3   To recapitulate cases already encountered, the Dong in China enact their courting rituals in song, a Dogon funeral with haunting horns was filmed by the BBC, Gould wrote of the deeply affecting power of an Aboriginal bull-roarer, and Stephen Hugh-Jones described how the ritual music of the Tukanoans was regarded as the voices of ancestors, their instruments exclusively for the purpose.

4   See Lawson 2003, pp. 2–3.

5   See Lindenberger 1998, pp. 13–19.

6   Sadie 1989, pp. 21–4.

7   Gerhard 1998, pp. 25–33.

8   Winton Dean, Dennis Libby and Ronald Crichton in Chapter XV of Sadie 1989, p. 204.

9   Gerhard 1998, p. 24.

10 Ibid., p. 25.

11 It lies at the intersection of several of Haussmann's Boulevards, with its front on an axis leading down to the Louvre. The diamond-shaped site was a key node in the new street pattern, requiring much demolition and rebuilding.

12 Initially Charles Rohault de Fleury had been commissioned by Louis-Napoleon, but he was displaced in 1860 in favour of the Empress's favourite Eugène Emmanuel Viollet-le-duc, who argued for a two-stage competition. This was duly held in 1860–1, and although Garnier only gained fifth place in the first round, he won unanimously in the second. The foundation stone was laid in 1862, though the building was not completed until 1875.

13 Grand Prix laureates Guadet, Noguet, Pascal, Bénard, Scellier de Gisors and Nénot all worked in Garnier's office on the Opéra, see Drexler 1977, p. 254.

14 It is the focus and culmination of David Van Zanten's long chapter 'Architectural Composition at the Ecole Des Beaux-Arts from Charles Percier to Charles Garnier' in Drexler 1977, pp. 111–324.

15 Much more about the decoration is discussed in his second book, *Le Nouvel Opéra de Paris* of 1878, written after the building was completed and employing a different chapter structure. I have chosen to draw from *Le Théâtre*, written during the construction, because it is more revealing of his design intentions.

16 Garnier 1871, p. 253.

17 Ibid., pp. 263–75.

18 Ibid., p. 10; pp. 39–41; pp. 57–8.

19 Ibid., pp. 1–2: my translation, as with all subsequent excerpts.

20 Ibid., pp. 16–17.

21 Garnier reserves the whole contextual aspect to a chapter near the end: there he acknowledges the importance of surrounding buildings, their consistency and scale. Perhaps with congested pre-Haussmann Paris in mind, he even goes out of his way in this late chapter to praise the picturesque integration of earlier monuments engulfed in the townscape, and regrets the way they had recently been laid bare, but in returning to discussion of the Opéra, he stresses the priority of circulation.

22 Garnier 1871, pp. 131–44.

23 Ibid., pp. 137–44.

24 Ibid., p. 43.

25 Ibid., p. 44.

26 Ibid., pp. 76–7.

27 Ibid., pp. 85–6.

28 Ibid., pp. 59–61, radically shortened.

29 Ibid., p. 132.

30 Ibid., footnote on p. 136.

31 Ibid., pp. 99–100.

32 Ibid., p. 100.

33 The term 'communitas' was coined by Victor Turner to describe the sense of togetherness that takes place in a theatre, a religious service or a pilgrimage and is central to his theory about the temporal unfolding of social events: for the use of the word and accompanying theory see *The Ritual Process: Structure and Anti-structure* (Turner 1969).

34 Edison's first voice recorder was made in 1877, only a couple of years after the Opéra, although it took twenty years to become commercially available, and yet another twenty to appear in popular form with shellac discs. Cinema appeared somewhat later, almost at the turn of the century, but it developed much more rapidly to become an international big business by 1910.

35 Even with a string quartet it is difficult to distinguish the first violin part from the second, and the recording allows only a poor impression of the concentrated coordination of the musicians, which in a live performance is exciting to watch. With large orchestral works the innocent listener has no easy way even to know which instrument is being played.

36 In period opera the plot and circumstances are so outdated as to require special explanation rather than being related to current experience. More generally the kind of criticisms made by Peter Brook in his description of 'The Deadly Theatre' in *The Empty Space* (Brook 1968) apply.

37 Aldo van Eyck, 'The Medicine of Reciprocity', *Forum*, nos 6–7 (1960–1), also *Architects' Year Book* 1962, pp. 173–8. He was criticizing Sigfried Giedion's famous book *Space, Time and Architecture*, one of the foundational texts of the Modern Movement.

38 For the development of Scharoun's career see Blundell Jones 1995.

39 See Pehnt, *Expressionist Architecture* (Pehnt 1973) for general coverage, Wendschuh 1993 for the watercolours.

40 See Wendschuh 1993.

41 More detail on all this can be found in Blundell Jones 1995, pp. 152–95.

42 Lawson 2003, pp. 5–12.

43 Ibid., p. 138.

44 'During von Karajan's tenure the Berlin Philharmonic's financial status and commercial prestige reached levels unprecedented in orchestral history … its subsidy from city of Berlin was far higher than any other municipality or state … an outstanding example of arts support' (Lawson 2003, p. 132).

45 Garnier 1871, pp. 5–6.

46 Hans Scharoun, 'Musik in Mittelpunkt', 19/7/1957 reprinted in *Pfankuch* 1974, p. 279, my slightly rearranged translation.

47 A whole chapter is devoted to the Mannheim Theatre Project in Blundell Jones 2002, pp. 189–202.

48 Garnier 1871, pp. 212–14.

49 Cremer evidently thought about acoustics constantly as an art, and not just positively as in concert halls but also negatively as in libraries. My memories of walking around with him at the opening of the Berlin Staatsbibliothek in 1979 include his concerns about 'sanitary noises' leaking from the lavatories, about photocopiers being placed not to disturb people, and that the string quartet engaged for the occasion had unfortunately been placed under an absorbent ceiling. Almost needless to say, in a giant library left open from the front door through to the reading room, and in which many small conversations inevitably take place, a quiet atmosphere prevails.

50 In a personal interview at Miesbach in the early 1980s Cremer told me that Scharoun had been the most flexibly minded architect he had ever worked with, always able somehow to accommodate a new demand without ruining his own conception.

51 For an acoustician's description see Barron 1993, pp. 95–100. Scharoun coined this landscape analogy in his own statements, but in my view this is a post-hoc description and not to be read as an inspiration, for the genesis of the idea is visible in the earlier projects.

52 I have several times heard it claimed that Herbert von Karajan favoured Scharoun's conception in the architectural competition because he was flattered by the tiny figure of himself at the focus of the model, but have no firm source for this. The later history suggests that von Karajan overreached himself, for despite having gained a lifetime post from the Senate he fell into disputes with the orchestra over recording contracts and he resigned in 1989.

53 This is explained in detail in relation to the specific seating banks by Edgar Wisniewski in his essay 'Raum, Musik, Mensch' included in the second *Philharmonischer Almanach*, Berliner Philharmonisches Orchester, Berlin 1983, pp. 30–2.

54 Extract from a text by Hans Scharoun in *Pfankuch* 1974, pp. 205–12, first published in *Bauwelt* 1952, vol. 44, pp.173ff, my translation.

55 The site was off Bundesallee and Schaperstrasse, entered through the Joachimsthalsen Gymnasium: it is now occupied by the Haus der Berliner Festspiele.

56 See Edgar Wisniewski, 'Philharmonie Berlin', 1964, reprinted in *Pfankuch* 1974, pp. 282–95.

57 Mitterand judged the Opéra's scope to be insufficient in 1982, and therefore organized a competition won by Carlos Ott for Opéra Bastille, which was built in 1984–9, the two houses becoming Opéra de Paris in 1990.

58 The 2014/15 season offers four productions at the Palais Garnier: Mozart, Humperdinck, Massenet, and Gluck, as opposed to twelve at Opéra Bastille.

59 Between 1955 and 1981 62 per cent of composers performed were contemporary and 48 per cent of performed works were by composers who had been alive in 1955 or still were: see Peter Girth, 'Die zeitgenösische Musik und das Berliner Philharmonische Orchester' in *Philharmonischer Almanack*, Berlin 1983, p. 87.

60 Grass 1999, pp. 162–4.

61 Peter Brook speaking on camera as part of Ronald Harwood's BBC television series *All the World's a Stage*, broadcast in 1984: transcribed by the author.

CHAPTER 14
THE FUN PALACE PROJECT, CENTRE POMPIDOU, AND PARADOXICAL IDEAS OF FREEDOM

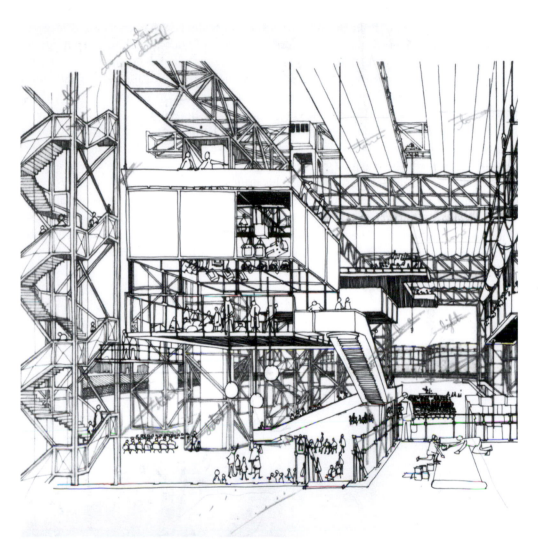

Figure 14.1 Cedric Price, Fun Palace: detail of interior perspective c. 1960–4. This drawing shows infrastructure, installations, and people. Pink and green coloured pencil on reprographic copy on paper 26.4 × 40.4 cm (DR1995:0188:525: 003:001, Cedric Price Fonds, Collection Centre Canadien d'Architecture/Canadian Centre for Architecture, Montréal).

If the Paris Opéra of the previous chapter represents an extreme version of a ritualized architecture, specialized for a particular kind of event and representing a stratified and hierarchical society, each level contained in its boxes and moving in its respective foyers, and if Hans Scharoun's Philharmonie offered a twentieth-century version socially more egalitarian but equally specific, Cedric Price and Joan Littlewood's Fun Palace project of 1964 was in contrast almost an anti-architecture, devised from the start to encourage people to generate their own social events with as little pre-framing as possible (Figures 14.1 and 14.2). It paralleled the theatrical experiments of Peter Brook, cited at the end of the last chapter, whose contemporaneous book *The Empty Space* of 1968 expresses in its very title the wish to clear things out and start again. Although the Fun Palace remained unbuilt, it represents that era and two of its creative spirits particularly well, and presents a curious paradox, for the romantic ideal pursued was freedom and cooperation, yet in practice the supporting hardware turned out overbearing, for the ideas behind the Fun Palace were put to the test in one of the most famous buildings of the century, Centre Pompidou in Paris by Renzo Piano and Richard Rogers. It monumentalized the idea in a way Price would never have endorsed, while the intended open-endedness has hardly been exploited. That the Fun Palace remained on paper at least allowed Price's vision to remain untarnished and left his principles intact.

The Fun Palace was a serious project developed over several years in some technical detail, but how exactly it would have worked remains open to speculation, particularly as it varied in its developing versions. The best known drawing (Figure 14.2) shows a great rectangular volume about ten storeys high flanked by pairs of diagonally braced service towers, further

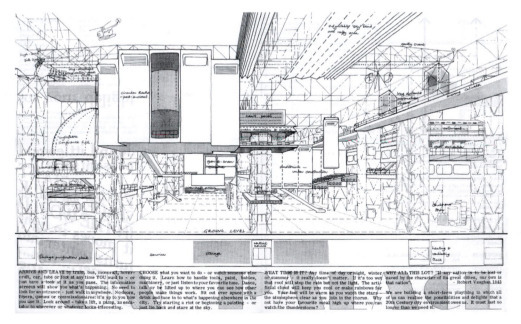

Figure 14.2 Cedric Price and Joan Littlewood, Fun Palace: promotional brochure 1964. This was the drawing published with text in the end plates of Joan Littlewood's autobiography. Black and red ink on reprographic copy on wove paper 36.2 × 59.8 cm (DR1995: 0188:525:001:023, Cedric Price Fonds, Collection Centre Canadien d'Architecture/Canadian Centre for Architecture, Montréal).

serviced by a travelling crane across the top which could move large elements of accommodation about. The space in the middle is occupied by suspended capsules and platforms of varying shapes and sizes with stairs and escalators running between them, and only parts of the volume are roofed, the rest being left open to the elements. In Price's perspective a hemispherical conference hall lies to the left, an auditorium is under construction in the middle, a restaurant and open exhibition area lie to the right, with a 'children's town' beneath. There is also a circular theatre (labelled 'part-enclosed') hanging in the foreground. Connecting these elements are escalators, landings, even moving catwalks, and people are milling about doing different things. Climb to the top and there is a 'long distance observation deck'. It makes an orderly perspective because the structure and supporting towers are arranged on a grid, but the entertainment units are disposed in an excitingly asymmetrical way and at varied heights. The interacting levels would have seemed more exciting in 1964, before the advent of the complex foyers, shopping malls and atria that have since become commonplace. Also shown in the drawing are suspended building components moving towards their points of installation, for a continuous state of construction and reconstruction was envisaged, adding to the general sense of excitement and without today's safety worries. The drawing's original accompanying text stresses the variety of experiences on offer, inviting joyful participation:

ARRIVE AND LEAVE by train, bus, monorail, hovercraft, car, tube, or foot at any time YOU want to – or just have a look at it as you pass. The information screens will show you what's happening. No need to look for an entrance – just walk in anywhere. No doors, foyers, queues or commissionaires: it's up to you how you use it. Look around – take a lift, a ramp, an escalator to wherever or whatever looks interesting.

CHOOSE what you want to do – or watch someone else doing it. Learn how to handle tools, paint, babies, machinery, or just listen to your favourite tune. Dance, talk or be lifted up to where you can see how other people make things work. Sit out over space with a drink and tune into what's happening elsewhere in the city. Try starting a riot or beginning a painting – or just lie back and stare at the sky.

WHAT TIME IS IT? Any time of day or night, winter or summer – it really doesn't matter. If it's too wet that roof will stop the rain but not the light. The artificial cloud will keep you cool or make rainbows for you. Your feet will be warm as you watch the stars – the atmosphere clear as you join in the chorus. Why not have your favourite meal high up where you can watch the thunderstorm?

WHY ALL THIS LOT? 'If any nation is to be lost or saved by the character of its great cities, our own is that nation.' Robert Vaughan 1843.
    We are building a short-term plaything in which all of us can realise the possibilities and delights that a 20th century city environment owes us. It must last no longer than we need it.[1]

More detail on what was intended appears in articles by both authors published in the *New Scientist* of May 1964. Joan Littlewood called it a 'university of the streets' with knowledge 'piped through jukeboxes'. There was to be a 'science playground', an agora for philosophers, and an 'acting area to afford the therapy of theatre for everyone ... but the essence of the place will be informality – anything goes... the whole plan is open ... so the greatest pleasure of traditional parks is preserved'. She also wrote enthusiastically about large screens showing by CCTV 'whatever is going on in or out of London ... it will be possible to see coalminers, woodsmen and dockers actually at work ... the comings and goings outside a local authority rest-centre ... the casualty ward of a hospital or a West End club', so that 'the curiosity that many people feel about their neighbours' lives can be satisfied instructively'. All this was to be 'without editing or art', so with hindsight the Fun Palace was about to embrace the coming media age, if also anticipating with naïve innocence the current surveillance and reality TV.[2] Price's text is rather more sober, promising 'self-participatory education and entertainment' and declaring that 'the activities designed for the site should be experimental, the place itself expendable and changeable. The organization of space and the object occupying it should, on the one hand, challenge the participants' mental and physical dexterity and, on the other, allow for a flow of space and time, in which passive and active pleasure is provoked'. He goes on to claim that there will be 'multi-directional movement and random pedestrian grouping, yet capable of programming'. As there are no doorways, one can 'choose one's own route and degree of involvement with the activities'.[3]

Joan Littlewood

Although Price briefly mentions rallies, concerts, conferences, theatre and screenings as events to be accommodated as a matter of course, Littlewood says surprisingly little about theatre, even suggesting that people will be 'drawn in' to spontaneously occurring events. 'In what has been called the acting area... there will be no rigid division between performers and audience – a generalisation of the technique used in Theatre Workshop for many years.'[4] As part of her life story concurrent with the beginnings of the Fun Palace, she describes an invited visit to Malmö University billed as a lecture, but which she had turned into an interactive session, inviting the students to fetch musical instruments and exchange possessions, and after a while leaving them to get on with it by themselves.[5] This shows the degree of destruc-turing she was prepared to promote. Price's drawing, though, is relatively more conservative, prioritizing a circular theatre as well as two other auditoria. Even so, the whole presentation stresses freedom of choice as if there were to be no performance times or ticket barriers. The emphasis on being able to do whatever you will has in the half century since the Fun Palace was proposed gained a surprisingly consumerist ring, yet this was long before museums gave precedence to their shops and cafés, or indeed started to be driven by visitor numbers.[6] It was intended as a generous socialist world, egalitarian and levelled, openly shared and with no hint of privilege. For both authors there was much 'tradition' from which to escape: Price didn't think much of 'The Theatre', and for theatre director Littlewood, already in her late forties, the traditional theatre building with its sharp proscenium dividing producers from consumers had long been a constraint, along with the polite bourgeois habits and assumptions that had developed around it. As a young woman she had visited Garnier's Opéra (see previous chapter), and been suitably impressed by the staircases, 'such curves, such splendour', but she later remembered finding the performance artificial and stilted:

It was not my impression that the French company could sing, and what else is there to do in opera? Such a damn silly story could hardly be acted, except as a comedy. But if anyone on that stage had ever given the job a thought, they showed no sign of it. They just stood around looking useless, waiting for the cue to open their mouths and let out those frightful sounds.[7]

For decades Littlewood had been working in temporary conditions across the country, leading politically radical groups such as Theatre of Action and Theatre Workshop, always on a shoestring and often down to their last penny,[8] and although they had finally in the 1950s found a more permanent home in the old Theatre Royal, Stratford East, successful productions there were transferred to the West End where they wilted under the dead hand of respectability, so the ideal venue had remained elusive. She sought an activist, cooperative, and political kind of theatre, and she had long been interested in its power as an educational tool. She wanted to engage the audience as directly as possible, if necessary on the street, and she had adopted new staging techniques following continental figures such as Brecht, Meyerhold and Laban. She encouraged improvisation and invention from her actors, but she was also a brilliant editor of texts, identifying new plays including Brendan Behan's *The Quare Fellow* and Shelagh Delaney's *A Taste of Honey* which she developed in collaboration with their authors.[9] Her most remembered production was *Oh What a Lovely War*, because it changed the way the so-called Great War was seen in the general culture. Originated at around the same time as the Fun Palace project, it was constructed around faithful but ironic use of sentimental songs from the First World War, one of which provided the title. As Nadine Holdsworth has commented:

> The most striking aspect … was the sheer audacity, confidence and variety of her theatrical vision. In this one production, she successfully combined all the theatrical elements she had previously experimented with … The traditions of popular entertainment – the seaside pierrot show, music hall, comic turns – sat alongside huge projected slides of recruiting posters and photographic evidence of trench life, whilst a ticker-tape newspanel flashed official death tolls, and statistics of battles fought, won and lost. These living newspaper techniques functioned in dynamic interplay with multi-faceted live action: a Master of Ceremonies' jocular interjections and actors performing satirical sketches, vaudevillian acts and realistic scenes of trench life… The overall result was a show that succeeded in being at once 'epic and intimate, elegantly stylized and grimly realistic; comic and tragi-comic, didactic and entertaining, educational and pleasurable, uproarious and deeply moving.[10]

Cedric Price

The first meeting between Joan Littlewood and Cedric Price was contrived by a mutual friend, journalist and Labour MP Tom Driberg, at a party in 1962. There the idea of the Fun Palace emerged, and she later recalled telling Price of:

> my idea of space where everybody might learn and play; where there could be every kind of entertainment, classical and ad lib, arty and scientific; where you could dabble

in paint or clay; attend scientific lectures and demonstrations; argue; show off; or watch the world go by.[11]

This varied and ambitious programme appealed to the young architect, twenty years her junior, and as it came from someone already so well known in the theatrical world, it suggested every hope of realization, though they had to finance its development themselves. Like Littlewood, Price was outspoken, energetic, something of a maverick, and a committed left-winger, even though his roots were middle class. Born in 1934 into an architect's family in Stoke-on-Trent, he had studied architecture first at Cambridge and then at the Architectural Association (AA), finishing in 1958. He reached maturity at a time of great social change in technology and society following the Second World War: a levelling of class and privilege, a willingness to work together for a better society and the welfare state, and a sense of urgent modernization. The growing prosperity brought pop music and the invention of youth culture, along with unprecedented changes in technology and communication. If Cambridge provided an elite arena of debate where Price could hone his intellectual and rhetorical skills, it also showed him the post-war British establishment in all its stratification and hierarchy, prompting a sense of rebellion that grew at the AA. He regarded the Cambridge teaching as old-fashioned, but even at the AA his projects were controversial, and he reported that Peter Smithson, leading progressive of the previous generation, walked out of his final review swearing in disgust.[12] This confrontation reflected perhaps an implicit threat to the creation of buildings as beautiful objects, still the goal of Le Corbusier-lover Smithson despite his well-rehearsed connections with pop-art and popular culture. Smithson claimed Price 'couldn't design', and Price was also criticized for having no taste. But in his personal dress, always the black and white shirt with detachable collar,[13] he was fastidious, in his presentations carefully edited, his rhetoric larded with a ready wit.[14] The confrontation at the AA was rather due to Price sensing and objecting to the aesthetic predisposition of Smithson and others. He wanted to be more open-minded about what kind of building came about – if indeed there were to be any building at all. For Price went beyond architecture, becoming an identifier of problems and a seeker of solutions, his aesthetic bent leaning towards the conceptual elegance of ideas rather than any resulting object. Perhaps no building was needed at all: the client should buy an old warehouse, or divorce his wife, or move to another city; that there could be some alternative strategy without constructing anything was the enduring legacy of Price's teaching at the AA.[15]

Anti-establishment

Price could perhaps be counted among those whom Christopher Booker designated as Neophiliacs[16] – in love with the new, and therefore at the same time iconoclastic – and he had close personal connections with personalities involved in the satire boom of the early 1960s. His long-term partner was Eleanor Bron, the actress whose reputation was made by the television show *That Was the Week That Was* of 1962–3,[17] and he frequented the ironically named Establishment Club,[18] started by comedian Peter Cook, whose career had begun with *Beyond the Fringe*, the runaway success of 1960.[19] It lampooned the War, the Church, Prime Minister Macmillan, and much more besides. Cook was also one of the founders of *Private Eye*, the satirical fortnightly started in 1961 that poked fun at politicians and published fearlessly about corruption and scandals. There had been humorous attacks on the establishment long before 1960, and there had also been a steady erosion of the old social hierarchies: for example the last year of the presentation of upper-class debutantes in 1957,[20] but only in the early 1960s did rebellion against the establishment become a popular wave, and with hindsight the Fun Palace marks its crest. Price's immersion in this social revolution as a fully paid up member of the Labour Party explains why, even though he recognized its power to shape society through social rituals, he saw permanent architecture as a constraint and a straitjacket.

Price's embrace of change also made him a pioneer in the matter of time: how long should a building last, he asked, for it becomes a burden after it has outlived its usefulness. As a champion of flexibility, he remained consistently outspoken, for example taking a perverse pride in the fact that the gutters of his computer centre in Southall were starting to fall off when it was eleven years old, for he had agreed with the clients a life of only ten years.[21] Ten years was also the intended lifetime of the Fun Palace, which seems rather short considering the estimated £5 million cost of the intended hardware. Price also constantly argued that architects must design for ease of demolition, and joined the society of demolition contractors. He took a consistent and extreme stand against conservation and historic listing,[22] and when some of his fans later argued for the retention of his Inter-action Centre, he refused his support, claiming it had served its purpose.[23] He is said to have dismissed Harvey Court, the new, and for its time progressive, Cambridge College by Leslie Martin, Colin St John Wilson and Patrick Hodgkinson designed in 1960, as 'the middle ages with 13 amp power points'.[24] It was monastic in concept and inward-looking despite the open site, but the permanence and old-fashioned wet-trades made it the butt of Price's criticism, for it was carefully constructed of brickwork and intended to last indefinitely.[25] Later, when working on his Potteries Thinkbelt Project, a university on rails, Price questioned the very existence of such halls of residence, criticizing them as 'monumental structures devoted to eating and sleeping'.[26] For him it was not merely a glorification of the unnecessary, for he saw only too keenly how institutions and their rituals could condition young minds in a set direction:

> Education is today little more than a method of distorting the individual's (mind and behaviour) to enable him to benefit from existing social and economic patternings. Such an activity, benevolently controlled and directed by an elite can… do little more than improve on the range and network of structures it already has under its control.[27]

The 'White Heat of Technology'[28]

The atom bomb, the space race, television, Technicolor, fast cars and ever proliferating gadgets made the late 1950s a time of evident change, and Price shared with the Archigram group and the historian Peter Reyner Banham a fascination with the liberation promised by new technologies. It had been a general mantra of the Modern Movement that factory production was coming, and that Henry Ford's economies would soon be applied to the construction industry. There were obvious economic advantages to making buildings in series as variations on a theme, lightweight and quickly assembled, for bricks and mortar construction was slow, depended on a dwindling supply of craftsmen, and was often curtailed by the weather. So former weapons factories were turned over to building components, moving the process indoors and speeding up assembly times. Prefabrication meant repetition and standard-ization, leading to the adoption of a regular grid as the means of coordination, which became a dominating discipline. Designing a system required concentration on standard joints between elements, and standard ways of handling corners. A key example was the Hertfordshire schools programme of the late 1940s and 1950s, which led on to further programmes across the country such as CLASP, all based on repetitive lightweight component systems.[29] These ideas fitted the revolutionary attitude of a younger generation of architects returning from the war who had absorbed Pevsner's enthusiasm for Walter Gropius, his grid-based rationality, and his belief in anonymous teamwork. Price was also particularly influenced by Buckminster Fuller in the United States and his ways of rethinking houses, cars, and ways of life using lightweight technology. Price even collaborated with Fuller on a project for a small domed theatre in Bath that would let people in and out by rising off the ground,[30] but the geodesic dome was too self-determined a form for Price, even if making it movable did fit in with his idea of variability.

Allied with prefabrication was the growth of services, documented in Giedion's book *Mechanisation Takes Command* and then in Banham's cri de coeur *The Architecture of the Well-tempered Environment*.[31] Until the late-nineteenth century there had been no wires and few pipes, and daylight provided most of the necessary illumination, so the only services to make themselves visible in buildings were the chimney stacks. All this changed quickly with lifts, electric lighting and air-conditioning, and deep plans became possible with the help of fluorescent tubes and electric fans, radically changing the massing of buildings. Although services had played little visible part in the works of the original modernist masters, Louis Kahn in the United States took servicing as primary theme in his Richards Laboratories of 1957–60, which was composed of alternating towers of served and serving spaces. He went on with buildings like the Kimbell Museum of 1958 to ally the servicing rationale with the primary structure, giving the pipes and wires logical and systematic locations within the geometric scheme, and even confining staircases to 'servant' bays.[32] Much of the point, even so, was to have noble unblemished 'served' rooms, and to provide a monumental structure to which the service elements could be subordinated, tidying them up as it were. Kahn was often criticized for this monumental tendency, but it now seems the strength of his work. In contrast, Price's great innovation with the Fun Palace was to get rid of these permanent rooms altogether, letting the servicing become the entirety of the building, so that the addition and subtraction of services became the essence of its variable life. He also negated the traditional assumption about primacy of shelter, setting everything in the open and adding roofs only where necessary. He intended to avoid thresholds by providing closure with invisible air curtains.

Development of the project

Price developed his ideas with leading engineer Frank Newby, and since complete variability with large elements was the goal, travelling cranes running on linear tracks became the main discipline, the spans being made as large as possible. This glorified a physical version of the Cartesian grid as the primary structure, both physically and intellectually. The developed version had fourteen 60-foot (18.3-metre) bays, each defined by four lattice columns flanking

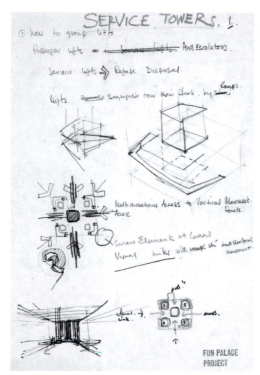

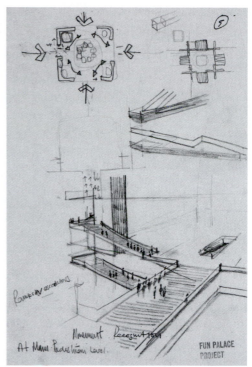

Figure 14.3 Cedric Price, Fun Palace: sketches for service towers c. 1963. The towers are shown as nodes in a universal grid that can extend equally on either axis. Graphite, red and purple pencil, blue and black ink on paper 38 × 25.3 cm (DR1995:0188:010, Cedric Price Fonds, Collection Centre Canadien d'Architecture/Canadian Centre for Architecture, Montréal).

Figure 14.4 Cedric Price, Fun Palace: sketches for vertical circulation or service towers c. 1963. This drawing shows service structures in plan, but also walkways and ramps in between. Graphite, red and purple pencil, blue and black ink on paper, 38.2 × 25.3 cm (DR1995:0188:013, Cedric Price Fonds, Collection Centre Canadien d'Architecture/Canadian Centre for Architecture, Montréal).

two larger spans of 120 feet (36.6 metres) within which main elements such as auditoria could be suspended (Figure 14.6). Not only did the moving and removing of such large and heavy elements produce many problems to be solved, but also the provision of access and the application of fire-proofing. The supporting towers had to be designed to lend structural support in a variety of ways, with pipes and wires in the corners, and lifts or staircases within allowing possible connections in any direction (Figures 14.3 and 14.4). The whole way of thinking about the hardware was dominated by a systematic rhythm and systematic connections that could be made and remade. As Littlewood wanted to get away from West End theatre and all its associations, an East End site was sought, and both she and Price agreed that the Fun Palace should be set by the river. The first site considered was on the Isle of Dogs, taking over some derelict dockland. It seemed ideal, and Littlewood managed to gain local support, but grey bureaucracies prevailed. After that fell through, locations in Battersea and the Lea Valley were found (Figure 14.5), researched, and argued over, but despite serious and intensive lobbying from influential friends, planning permissions officially applied for, constant work to make the project more feasible and appeals to influential politicians, it all fell through, even

Figure 14.5 Cedric Price, Fun Palace: perspective for the Lea River site 1961–5. Photomechanical print of a photomontage on Masonite board 63.3 × 121.5 cm (DR1995:0188:522, Cedric Price Fonds, Collection Centre Canadien d'Architecture/Canadian Centre for Architecture, Montréal).

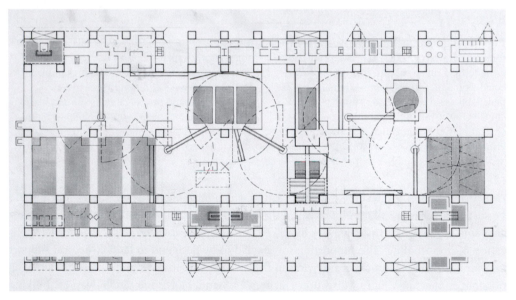

Figure 14.6 Cedric Price, Fun Palace: typical plan 1963. This plan drawing shows the service towers, two main spans, and some secondary elements, including diagonal escalators. Ink, screentone appliqué and graphite on translucent paper, 39.4 × 69.4 cm (DR1995:0188:235, Cedric Price Fonds, Collection Centre Canadien d'Architecture/Canadian Centre for Architecture, Montréal).

sub-projects for pilot versions.[33] Such a large and controversial project requiring public funds proved vulnerable to every kind of political chicanery and bureaucratic delay, but there also seems to have been a failure of credibility owing to the sheer open-endedness of its identity as a place. In August 1964, Reyner Banham wrote:

> [The] Fun Palace [does not offer] any kind of monument ... It really is a kit of parts, and for months now Cedric Price, the architect involved, has been driving architectural journalists mad by steadfastly refusing to release any picture of what the Fun Palace will actually look like. He may well not know, but that doesn't matter because it is not the point. Seven nights of the week it will probably look like nothing on earth from the outside: the kit of service towers, lifting gantries and building components exists solely to produce the kind of interior environments that are necessary and fitting to what is going on.[34]

Price and Littlewood's idea was that the users themselves should decide on which facilities were needed and when, and how they should be deployed. Obviously single individuals could not in a moment of whimsy move large auditoria about with travelling cranes, nor assemble halls with movable floors, walls and ceilings. Such things would require procedural planning, and Price sought to devise predictable systems that could be followed, enacted by the guardians, but without their assuming responsibility for every decision and reassuming the paternalistic model. With the help of cybernetics expert Gordon Pask, Price devised a programme based on mass user decisions determined by a punch-card system. It would calculate the preferences of the majority, changing the accommodation from day to day. The building would 'learn' what it wanted to be.[35] It would change its nature like a chameleon, even though it would have to start with a prescribed programme, with the danger that control could be manipulated by the technicians in charge. Price was ahead of the game in perceiving

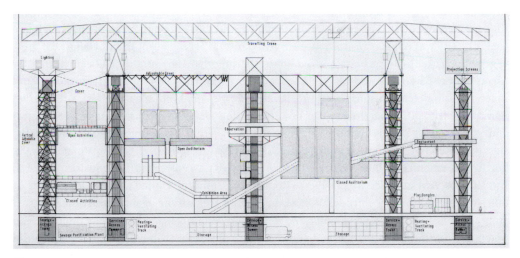

Figure 14.7 Cedric Price, Fun Palace: typical short section 21 April 1964. The section is dominated by the travelling crane; there was to be no general roof. This drawing is at a larger scale than the plan and runs vertically through it, identifiable by the five ranks of towers. Ink, screentone appliqué and graphite on translucent paper, 38.1 × 75.1 cm (DR1995:0188:197, Cedric Price Fonds, Collection Centre Canadien d'Architecture/Canadian Centre for Architecture, Montréal).

programming as a crucial discipline and in understanding the importance of algorithms when computer-usage was yet in its infancy, the PC still twenty years away. He also prefigured the operations of today's facilities managers, for whom the time schedule is as important as the space. The kind of popular choice he envisaged is also with us today in the running of the mass media. For example, to assess the reach of advertising, the relative popularity of commercial television programmes began long ago to be sampled, but this has now become the basis on which all public schedules are designed and programmes commissioned. Today's interactive technology allows viewers to choose material and to vote in contests, even if these are narrow choices. So-called 'reality TV' sustains the viewers' dreams about stepping through the screen, while the 'celebrities' made and perpetuated by television have become leading figures and role models in society. So in the virtual worlds of television and the web, where instant change is no problem and indeed is always expected, many aspects of the Fun Palace have come about without bodily participation. In the physical world, though, the dream of a great variable hardware was stillborn and remains largely restricted to container ports and building sites.

Centre Pompidou

The link between the Fun Palace and Centre Pompidou is not direct, though Pompidou's architects, Richard Rogers and Renzo Piano, freely admit to having been influenced by Price's ideas. Both are now world figures, but in 1971 they were just young architects scratching a living with small projects, struggling to keep small offices in London and Genoa going. When the competition for an Arts Centre at Plateau Beaubourg in Paris was announced they were even reluctant to enter, considering the odds too great. The essential catalyst was engineer Ted Happold, then working for Ove Arup and Partners, the world famous engineers responsible for building the Sydney Opera House. Happold saw the opportunity, persuaded the architects to join in, and paid the fee for the conditions personally. He thought they could at least make the top thirty out of a likely entry of more than 500, and thus obtain the recompense of a token fee.[36] The site was a then run-down area of east-central Paris adjacent to Les Halles, the great vegetable market that was being moved out to the suburbs. The ground had been cleared for use as a lorry park but could be reclaimed, allowing reconstitution of the city fabric without much need to defer to historic monuments. It was a personal initiative by President Georges Pompidou, who possessed the singular power to bestow an arts centre as a state-funded project and as a markedly populist gesture, avoiding the bureaucratic brake of local politics. From the start it was intended to include both an improved Museum of Modern Art and a major library, but it also embraced other institutions such as a design centre and the Musical Research Institute IRCAM intended to lure Pierre Boulez back from the United States. Although flexibility was not a primary consideration of the brief, it was on the agenda, and wholehearted embrace of it by Piano, Rogers, Arups and their team certainly helped avoid the difficulty and potential confusion of articulating a complex and constantly changing programme. Instead the architects absorbed everything within one large and generic whole, and the strong, simple idea stood out among the 681 competition entries, so that they won almost unanimously (Figure 14.8).[37] The moment for the idea had come, the technical utopianism of the image having been around for a decade not only with Price but in the publications of Archigram and others,[38] and the idea of a big media wall had already been much discussed but was yet unbuilt:

indeed projected film had been a tool of the Russian Constructivists. Without the backing of Arups the technical plausibility of the project would almost certainly have been in question, but the young architects who turned up in jeans to see the President seem to have represented for him the new youth culture, and a notional reconciliation with the events of 1968.[39]

Both Piano and Rogers had been interested in prefabrication and component systems: a world of grids and joints and shiny factory-made elements. This enthusiasm was shared by Happold and Peter Rice, the other main Arup engineer involved, though they took it to a larger scale, interested in the world competition in engineering large span structures like the tent roofs by Günter Behnisch and Frei Otto for the contemporary Munich Olympics. What one might call the techno-fetishism of the Centre Pompidou was therefore present from the start, in contrast with the more purely conceptual and aesthetically reticent stance of Cedric Price. But there were certainly also echoes of the spirit behind the Fun Palace, even if the social and political engagement of the architects was looser than that of Price and Littlewood. This is from a report by Rogers:

> The image of culture is static and elitist; our problem is to make it live to both entertain and inform ... We must all participate, not as separate watertight departments either more or less elegantly organised, but as a total centre, a new experiment ... Our building and what is around is a tool, not a rigid tailor-made architectural monument. It is fluid, flexible, easy to change, full of technical resources ... It is our belief that the people of today and tomorrow, the curators, the specialists, the amateurs, must have the possibility of designing their own changing needs into the building, as far as possible freed from the limitation of the architectural form.[40]

Perhaps the most important decision made by Piano and Rogers was to leave the west half of the former city block vacant as a public square (apart from the parking underneath), something attempted by hardly any other competitor. Not only did this produce the arena for public interaction that has since been lauded as an example for reawakening life in cities: it also gave their box-like building a clear front to contrast with its sides and back (Figure 14.10). Although, as with the Fun Palace, there were to be at first no doors, it allowed a degree of celebratory approach, and set some distance from which to read the intended media wall. In the official drawings originally published as part of the *Architectural Review*'s 21-page coverage of Centre Pompidou in 1977 – about as much page space as is ever given to any building – there are no plans of the five upper floors, only a single generic one without partitions (Figure 14.11).[41] The reader therefore cannot tell what is library and what art gallery or design centre, how they are disposed and how partitioned, or imagine progress around the building. Thus what we might for the purposes of this book call the ritual information is entirely missing, but this seems to have concerned neither the editors nor the architects, content to present the generic empty container. The essence of the design was that Piano and Rogers decided on five essentially identical upper floors each 7 metres high, and sought to achieve maximum flexibility with clear spans across the building's full 45 metre width (somewhat more than the Fun Palace's intended 36.6 metres). This was achieved with gigantic trusses, which deposited the structural loads on single external columns to each side (Figure 14.14). In the other direction the great box was divided into thirteen bays each of 12.8 metres, seemingly without concern for the number, or whether it was odd or even, since the middle went uncelebrated.[42] Initially

Figure 14.8 Piano and Rogers' bird's-eye view of Centre Pompidou with the activity square in front, as submitted for the competition (courtesy of Richard Rogers).

Figure 14.9 Elevation to the square, showing the structural cage and some applied elements, including variable signs and escalators, similar in conception to the Fun Palace (courtesy of Richard Rogers).

the whole was to be sheathed in glass, set in the same plane as the structure, but fire problems and detailing issues forced a separation of layers, and Arups invented a system of ingenious structural cantilever brackets called gerberettes which allowed the development of an open external aisle on each side and permitted the main trusses to be hung on pin-joints.[43] Within the front aisle facing the square the whole apparatus of circulation was applied, with escalators in transparent tubes climbing the façade. On the back, in contrast, was the whole servicing system in great pipes and ducts celebrated in bright colours.[44] The entire building and its large basement was air-conditioned by this machinery, so Banham's 'well-tempered environment' was a fundamental assumption. Rogers has always argued that the positioning of such service elements on the outside makes them easier to replace, and that this can therefore be done without disturbing the interior, but it also means that the ductwork has to be fully weather-proofed and designed for show rather than thrown together in the usual expedient fashion. Although he has continued with this policy in many later projects, it has not become standard practice.

Nathan Silver, in his monograph on Centre Pompidou, gives a sympathetic but sometimes harrowing account of the construction process with its uncertain budget, changes of programme, tight deadlines, and bewildering array of bureaucracies to contend with.[45] This taxed the young architects and their engineers to the limit. A particular French problem was getting around the system of the Bureau d'Etudes Techniques, specialist offices whose role was to deal with detail and control construction, removing such duties from the architect. In a building as innovative and dependent for its identity on detail, submitting to this would have been disastrous, but the necessary presence of Arups mitigated it, though they struggled over fees, and Happold, who had started the whole thing, eventually gave up and went home. There were problems of pricing the steel, tendered initially at 60 per cent over, but finally negotiated with Krupp.[46] There was a need to find specialized firms of service engineers to make the pipework both weatherproof and displayable, and difficult fireproofing issues which even threatened at one stage to change steel to concrete. There was the potential problem of the basement rising like a boat on the water table and the possible need to flood it which violated insurance provision. The most threatening blow of all was the death of the patron, Georges Pompidou, and his replacement by Giscard d'Estaing who wanted to cancel the project, then relented with the demand that it be reduced by a floor and that the exposed services be covered.[47] The removal of the top floor was resisted on grounds of engineering integrity, and the overcladding of the services was declared possible at extra expense. In the end it did not happen, so the building came to fruition in all its expressed mechanized glory, but the initial intention of having moveable floors had proved impossible, even the planned mezzanines between main levels were cancelled, and the intended open and doorless ground floor was closed off for security, with people queuing up to buy tickets at one main entrance. And finally there was little in the way of a media wall, because of not only expense but also issues of content and control.

When first opened the building was a sensation, but it was also controversial, soon dubbed the Pompidolium because it looked like an oil refinery. Visitors flocked to it not only for the exhibitions, but especially to ride the escalator to the top and look out over Paris (Figures 14.16 and 14.17). Since it stood just above the historic height limit of 31 metres which had long ago been dictated by the capabilities of fire-fighting equipment,[48] it gained the privilege both of seeing across the rooftops and of being visible from a distance, the twin advantages

Figure 14.10 Centre Pompidou as realized, seen from the well-animated square in front (author's photograph c. 1983).

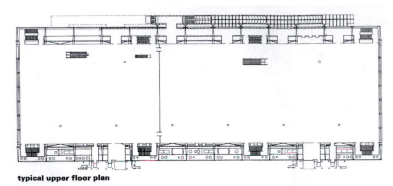

typical upper floor plan

Figure 14.11 'Typical Upper Floor Plan' with central open span and servicing in the side bays (*The Architectural Review* 1977).

Figure 14.12 The Musée d'Art Moderne in its initial form (author's photograph c. 1983).

Figure 14.13 The entrance hall in its initial form (author's photograph c. 1983).

enjoyed in a more extreme way by the Eiffel Tower.[49] The concentration of visitors brought life to the square below, which was soon full of acrobats, fire-eaters, ice-cream sellers and flâneurs, becoming a magnet to public life for the whole surrounding area. It created a vivid reminder of the street as public space, just at the time when architects' interest in 'the city' was being rekindled, with much discussion on the virtues of Nolli's Rome plan which had included public interiors.[50] The urban street had always been the place of public exchange, with markets, displays, entertainments, demonstrations, and every kind of public interaction. It was traditionally flexible, allowing one thing to happen one day and another the next, but modern life had reduced most city streets to domination by traffic and moved activities indoors, often simultaneously privatizing them.[51] The creation of an open reservoir of public space outside Pompidou remains the most effective legacy from Piano and Rogers's project, and the closest thing to fulfilling Joan Littlewood's ideas, even though the Fun Palace had no square, since freedom of use was meant to make it politically all 'street'.

The Musée d'Art Moderne and library moved in to the new Pompidou and were well patronized, but the museum required queues, tickets and security staff like any other, and the prestigious modern art collection seemed rather provisionally housed (Figure 14.12). Set on free-standing screens in the great open floors without much sense of route or progression, it was dwarfed by the huge trusses looming above, and lit almost entirely by artificial light. Neither the public nor the curators were much convinced by this Spartan arrangement, and within a decade the Italian designer Gae Aulenti, later author of Paris's Quai d'Orsay Museum, was brought in to effect a makeover, in other words to create the interior felt to be lacking within Piano and Rogers' shell.[52] As she belonged to the image-driven world of fashion and interior design, her work was at odds with Piano and Rogers' mechanistic integrity and Arups' structural rigour. Later, just before the millennium, another much larger makeover of the museum was undertaken, closing it for two years, including the addition of new circulation routes in the centre of the building that fundamentally violated the initial concept (Figure 14.18).[53] Some would argue that these changes proved the innate flexibility of the building, but they traduced the expected pattern of variations and possibilities. More importantly perhaps, the interchangeability of the component system – that dream of easy reconfiguration that lay at the centre of Price's thinking – was not fulfilled either. Furthermore, the building has spawned no progeny but remains a one-off monument, for neither did it become the model for arts centres elsewhere, nor did it turn out to be the demonstration of an economical component system that was repeated.

These unfulfilled promises beg the question of whether the entire architectural philosophy was worth it, for there were undoubtedly alternatives to the abdication from questions of context and content that Piano, Rogers and Arups considered so necessary a sacrifice in pursuing the project. For example, two art museums completed just as Pompidou was first conceived provided conditions much more conducive to the display of the kind of modernist paintings possessed by the Musée d'Art Moderne: The Nordjyllands Kunstmuseum at Aalborg in Denmark by Alvar Aalto (1958–72), and the Kimbell Museum at Fort Worth in the United States by Louis Kahn (1966–72) (Figures 14.19 and 14.20).[54] Late works by two modernist masters, both buildings reflected the optimism of a period in which there had been a harmonious relationship between abstract painting, sculpture, and architecture, when the art gallery had become a cultural building with almost sacred connotations. Both offered sequences of white rooms with variable partitions, but their dominant concern was daylight,

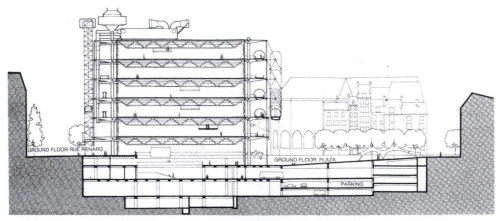

Figure 14.14 Centre Pompidou, cross-section, showing the long central span and side bands of servicing, but also the scale in relation to adjacent buildings (*The Architectural Review* 1977).

Figure 14.15 The entrance hall (author's photograph 2012).

Figure 14.16 The escalator, now mainly used for the view of Paris (author's photograph 2012).

Figure 14.17 Sculpture court and rooftop view (author's photograph 2012).

Figure 14.18 Refurbished gallery (author's photograph 2012).

long considered the optimum illumination for paintings, and exemplified by a venerable tradition of northlight windows for artists' studios. The problems of colour rendering with artificial light are still unsolved,[55] though conservators prefer it now because the level can be precisely controlled, and exhibitions are now almost universally plunged into gloom under the assumption that all art objects are highly vulnerable to light.[56] But the great virtue of both Aalto and Kahn's buildings is not just the inspiring quality of the light – that unfortunately hardly comes across in photographs – but that some relation to the outside world and the changing sky is perceptible, that the building exists as a kind of variable filter. Analysing the way sun angles changed through the seasons, Aalto devised elaborate sections employing deep curved reflectors to bounce light from clerestory roof lights onto the display walls. Kahn, building for a lower latitude and needing greater light attenuation, devised a system of concrete vaults to allow double reflection. Both buildings are admired as much for the atmosphere they produce as for the way they present the art, and each is orientated and well related to context. Concern for sequence of display and light has given each a purposeful character that differentiates it from other building types, and from the universal kind of 'well-tempered environment' cut off from the rest of the world. This is not to claim that the architects of Centre Pompidou should have concentrated on daylight or imitated Aalto and Kahn, just to point out how the pursuit of specificity allows engagement with the expectations of users and the rituals of use, in contrast with universal buildings that in claiming to be the Jack of all trades too often turn out to be the master of none.

'It is internationally accepted that the use of a large open space can offer 10% to 25% more usable space than a more articulated, broken-up space',[57] claimed Rogers, for large spans had become the holy grail of many architects following the universalist statements of Ludwig Mies van der Rohe and his famous collage of a 'concert hall' superimposing a few planar walls against the photographed interior of an aircraft factory. Factories and hangars certainly need big spans to accommodate the aircraft wingspan, but nothing in Centre Pompidou forced a 45-metre span. A single line of columns down the middle could have halved it, and the columns could easily have been absorbed within library and museum. At half the length, the trusses would have been smaller, cheaper, easier to bring from Germany by train and truck, and easier to crane into place. But this would have changed both the scale of the building and the purity of

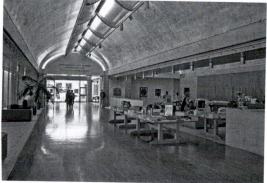

Figure 14.19 Interior of Nordjyllands Kunstmuseum at Aalborg in Denmark by Alvar Aalto, 1958–72 (author's photograph 2006).

Figure 14.20 Gallery interior at the Kimbell Museum, Forth Worth, 1966–72, by Louis Kahn (author's photograph 1989).

the concept, precluding many of the technical headstands for which Centre Pompidou is justly famous. For it is precisely the large span, rhetorical structural details, and expressed services that made the building the flagship of high-tech architecture, even if the original aim had been closer to the flexible, responsive, generous, social institution dreamed of by Littlewood and Price. Instead it has become a formal cultural monument in a continuing French tradition. Having decided not to monumentalize the complex and changeable programme, the architects monumentalized the technology instead, and it became a brand image which serves well in the age of the icon. Would the Fun Palace too have ended up as a monument? Certainly the technical apparatus would have been on the same scale and presumably as prominent, and it would also have been too costly for the mere ten-year lifetime predicted by Price: Piano's stated expectation with Pompidou was '300, 400, even 500 years'.[58]

Notes

1   Reproduced on endpapers of *Joan's Book*, by Joan Littlewood, London: Methuen, 1994.

2   Littlewood 1994, pp. 704–5.

3   Ibid., pp. 707–8.

4   Ibid., pp. 705–6.

5   Ibid., pp. 698–701.

6   It was in 1988 that an advertising campaign by Saatchi and Saatchi described the Victoria and Albert Museum controversially as 'an ace caff with quite a nice museum attached'.

7   Littlewood 1994, pp. 65–6.

8   Ibid., part 2, pp. 154–212.

9   A good general summary of her career can be found in Holdsworth 2006.

10   Holdsworth 2006, pp. 81–2.

11   Littlewood cited in Mathews 2007, p. 63.

12   Mathews p. 29.

13   Taken by Mathews as an emblem and used in a chapter title, see Mathews 2007, pp. 18ff.

14   'Style, through conscious action, exercises choice in the use of resources to translate the mundane into the generous ... Style is perceived in the sequence of time, whether evidenced, recorded, or experienced. Human involvement, together with movement in time, is therefore integral to true style. For example, style can be found in writing, cooking and dressing since the constituent parts, to be valid, must relate to an overall process requiring the passage of time ... A key field of style is that of manners. Whereas language can contain a message without style, the delivery of such a message with style requires a common code of manners to be shared by both the dispenser and the receiver', Cedric Price 1979, reprinted in Obrist 2003, number 50 of the chapter '73 snacks' (n.p.).

15   Personal experience: I was a student there from 1966 to 1972.

16   Booker 1992.

17   Produced by Ned Sherrin and David Frost (1939–2013). It was daringly loose in form and allowed the technology to show, in a way that doubtless appealed to Price.

18   Mathews 2007, p. 43.

19   The four principals were Peter Cook, Dudley Moore, Jonathan Miller and Alan Bennett, who all went on to enjoy enormous public careers and become household names: Cook and Moore

died early but the latter two have become current establishment figures and 'national treasures' lampooned in their turn.

20   See Fiona MacCarthy *The Last Curtsey*, 2006.

21   In an interview of 1978: I had been invited to write the entry on Price for the book *Contemporary Architects* (Emanuel 1988).

22   'It is socially, politically and economically more difficult to pull down a cathedral than a mountain', see Price, *The Case Against Conservation*, lecture extract cited in Obrist 2003, number 6 of the chapter '73 snacks', (n.p.).

23   Mathews 2007, p. 191.

24   A characteristic and fully credible quip that I was told decades ago, but I no longer remember by whom.

25   It still exists but has been subject to a restoration cum conversion: see Peter Blundell Jones, 'Court Circular: Levitt Bernstein updates a modern classic', *Architecture Today*, February 2012, pp. 40–9.

26   Mathews 2007, p. 200.

27   Price in *Architectural Design*, May 1968, p. 207, cited in Mathews 2007, pp. 198–9, his brackets.

28   Prime Minister Harold Wilson's phrase in October 1963 at the Labour Party Conference. The relationship between architecture and politics in that era is deftly described in Adam Sharr and Stephen Thornton's book *Demolishing Whitehall* (2013).

29   Saint 1987.

30   Mathews 2007, p. 26 and p. 40.

31   Giedion 1948 and Banham 1969.

32   See Blundell Jones 2002, pp. 229–40: the whole chapter is on the Kimbell Museum.

33   Mathews (2007) explains the history in detail in Chapters 2–6 of his book on Price. For Joan Littlewood's narrative see Littlewood 1994, pp. 701–19, 727–8, 731–3, 738–41 and 750–4.

34   Banham cited in Mathews 2007, p. 140.

35   Long before Brand's *How Buildings Learn*, 1994.

36   Silver 1994, pp. 13–17.

37   Ibid., pp. 38–47.

38   Reyner Banham put it into context in his celebratory article 'Enigma of the Rue Renard' in *The Architectural Review* May 1997, pp. 277–8.

39   Silver 1994, pp. 52–5.

40   Ibid., p. 102.

41   *The Architectural Review* Vol. CLXI, No. 963, May 1977, pp. 270–94.

42   Endless bays, extendable, is the character of a mechanical system, as opposed to the significant bay numbers of the Western Classical tradition and the Chinese tradition. More than seven bays is not perceptible without counting, and odd numbers are needed for a central entrance.

43   A precise and helpful summary of the technical solution is given by Arups and included in Silver 1994, pp. 132–7.

44   Steel requires painting, so colours had to be decided, and the main idea was to code them in relation to the functions of the services within, but there was much debate; see Silver 1994, pp. 150–4.

45   Silver 1994, Chapters 4 and 5.

46   Ibid., pp. 112–15.

47   Ibid., pp. 123–5.

48 A maximum height of 42 metres was allowed, calculated on the basis of fire access, Silver 1994, p. 100.

49 Eloquently explained in Roland Barthes's famous essay, in which he contrasts what one can see from the Eiffel Tower with where one can see it from: Barthes 1979.

50 Colin Rowe and Fred Koetter's book *Collage City* was published in 1978, just after Pompidou's completion.

51 Sennett 1992.

52 Gae Aulenti remake mid-1980s *Casabella* July/August, 1985.

53 See Mary Dejevsky, 'France confronts a blockage in the Pompidou pipe dream', *The Independent*, Friday 1 November 1996.

54 Blundell Jones 2002, pp. 229–40.

55 Jane Brox, *Brilliance: The Evolution of Artificial Light*, London: Souvenir Press, 2010, pp. 263–8.

56 An attitude now led by the insurance industry and their automatic imposition of stringent conditions and exaggeration of risk, 'to be on the safe side'.

57 Rogers in Silver 1994, p. 102.

58 Silver 1994, p. 180.

CHAPTER 15
CONCLUSION

Figure 15.1 Topping-out party at the half-built school hall, Evangelisches Gymnasium, Lippstadt, Germany, 2003 (courtesy of Peter Hübner).

Spatial and social patterns have appeared in this book repeatedly. They are particularly obvious on ceremonial occasions, but if you are looking for them they can be found ever present in the organization of institutions through room hierarchies, gender divisions, and personal roles. Persons take their allotted places, whether in a simple room like a yurt or a tipi, or at a large social occasion like the trial of Lord Lovat. The ordering may reflect gender, age, clan or rank: even wealth through the price of seats, as at the opera. It can operate at any scale from the humble family dining table to a national coronation. If in modern life we like to consider ourselves informal, a little reflection soon exposes this as merely a relative matter: we still know what it is to act or dress more formally, and social life is still full of manners. We do not see them much of the time, for as the saying goes, the fish is the last to know that he lives in water.[1] Their existence is much more easily shown in strange and unfamiliar examples from other times and other places. That is why the case studies in this book are drawn so broadly both from a wide geographical range and over a long timescale. A range of contrasting instances was needed to see how the relationship between people and the spaces they occupy might work. Detail was needed, to look at activities as well as buildings, to question order in time as well as in space, and to show how meanings become attached, detached, and reattached; how memories are preserved. Samples were chosen on the basis of spatial arrangements available on record, and sometimes an extensive anthropological context was needed to allow local ideas and *habitus* to be read. Descriptions therefore necessarily included not only spaces and practices but attitudes – prevailing beliefs behind the habits, particularly implicit ones. With such a wide compass it was often difficult to bring an increasingly rich investigation to a close. Readers will also have noticed that the choice of case studies cuts across customary categories of period such as traditional/modern/post-modern as well as the division between polite architecture and the vernacular. Sometimes it is advantageous to take a longer view and consider what has stayed the same rather than what is novel.

Although social relations can be construed in many different ways and according to a great diversity of possible rules, looking across the varied cases there appears to be an underlying substrate of common humanity which is both understandable and translatable, so that once you discern the rules you can imagine taking part. Even so, it is difficult to establish universals and even the attempt to do so can be damagingly reductive, with the danger that almost nothing is found at the bottom of the sieve. It hardly helps, for example, to note that important things happen at the ends of axes, that orientation tends to matter, that people acknowledge their worlds as having centres, or that they care about crossing thresholds: to be understood properly these issues have to be seen operating in specific cases. It is also easy to misunderstand and misplace 'others', and therefore wise to refrain from moralizing judgements based on too narrow and confident a position. Although one might wish to take an egalitarian stance, for example, hierarchies appear repeatedly and seem inevitable, not just politically, but as part of the operation of our attention and our selective perception, so we must live with them and try to use them wisely. It is evident that spatial order reflects social order and helps to recreate it, for buildings preserve memories of relationships through their very organization, thus defining roles and identities. With the political events described in the first part of the book, axial layouts appeared in every case, although the axes were differently exploited. The contrasting arrangements at Nuremberg and Westminster provoked a fresh respect for the balance between Queen and Speaker, but both are a reminder of the theatrical manner in which political power inevitably needs to show itself.[2] The proposed Chartist voting room introduced at the end of that chapter is the exception proving the rule, for not only does it place the ordinary citizen momentarily on axis at centre stage: it also makes this position temporary and open to each person in turn. We saw that processions give rise to spatial settings, transposing a dynamic order into a static one. Dances and games constitute mobile versions with their own spatial rules. They have an implicit geometry that is hard to record, but mostly does not need recording, being learned through practice and example.[3] The spatial arrangement for almost any social context – where you have to be, how you have to move, how to behave – is bodily engaged and learned from early childhood, then taken for granted as part of the general order of things. One does not need to think about how to pass through a door or how to hold a knife and fork, and if one did, life would be infinitely complicated. Nor does one think about the social structure of the house, the village, the town: it is simply there.

A sense of direction

Spatial orderings tend to be located, hierarchical, often dichotomous, and show a predisposition towards a combination of forward movement, symmetry and axiality, and/or centre versus periphery. There seems to be a universal differentiation between back and front, left and right, above and below, which can be identified as the three dimensions of space, but in a pre-Cartesian sense. Hunter-gatherer examples suggest they are pre-architectural and pre-civic, and imply a geometrical understanding that is pre-mathematical. This complies with Pierre Bourdieu's claim that the body is the first geometer, finding its way in the world in relation to movements forward and back, side to side, up and down.[4] These couples are also reflected in language as the basis of endless metaphors, so they lie also at the root of metaphorical or virtual space.[5] With our human existence there emerged a need to know where we are, how to get back home, at least how to rejoin the rest of the group, and also where to find food and water. So the body must engage also with world and cosmos to gain a sense of direction, and the movement of celestial phenomena provides both cardinal guidance and the measure of time. If then the body is the first geometer, its movements are compared with those in the sky as the second. Inside and out, equally essential, begins when we leave the womb, and is perceived in every kind of nesting series. As we move through the spatial order of our world, we must find our way, remembering landmarks, and we are able readily to reverse our route and find the way back. Hunter-gatherer examples suggest that the landscape was our original mnemonic and point of reference for sharing memories and perceptions, and our modern artificial landscapes of city architecture still bear at least some of this role. To explore and remember places is an ability commonly taken for granted, as one arrives at an unknown foreign city, walks around for hours, then finds one's way back to the hotel even without a map. This suggests that Stone Age way-finding skills and registry of place are still present, and that the role of experienced space in memory remains crucial. Further evidence is the preference of those undertaking feats of memory to use spatial models, placing items to be remembered in the rooms of an imaginary house. This indicates a persisting predisposition of brain capacity for this purpose. John O'Keefe's studies of the operation of neurons have revealed the existence of place cells and grid cells in the hippocampus of rodents, so there is also a physical basis for this memory process.[6]

The modern world

If this consciousness of place is so essential and still applies, the reader might ask, why does it need pointing out, and why does it seem neglected in so much building and architecture in the modern world? One obvious answer is that the way we officially understand and categorize space departs increasingly from an awareness of the body. In architecture and engineering technical geometry long ago created an abstract ordered world that could be recreated around us without reference to our sense of direction, our bodily geometry, or our sense of place, depending instead on abstract Cartesian coordinates. A recent extension is satellite navigation, which situates us in abstract space with more precision than ever, but leaves us in terms of bodily space completely lost. This is no mere choice of geometry in encountering the world, but a much more all-embracing and multifaceted issue. The relationship between people and buildings has changed, breaking local connections and small-scale traditions. This phenomenon can be taken under five headings: first the big issue of changing technology, second the social issue of clientship, procurement and bureaucracy, third the changing role of the architect and ideas about architecture, fourth the effects of growing communication and media, including the ways architectural ideas are transmitted and buildings presented, and fifth the pervading positivism that dictates a limited scientific version of reality and a narrow economic vision. These will be taken in turn.

Changing technology

At the beginning of the twentieth century it was above all technological development that provided the watershed and prevented buildings continuing as they were. Construction with steel and concrete allowed larger, taller structures and big spans, but also required larger building teams and more specialized equipment. Engineers were needed to calculate structures, architects to make drawings, construction managers to interpret them: it was no longer possible to proceed by oral communication and rule of thumb. The construction of eight or ten-storey buildings in places like Shanghai, for example, necessitated a wholesale adoption of Western methods, for traditional Chinese construction in wood was good only for two or three storeys.[7] Less immediately visible but finally greater in impact was technical equipment or 'services', which during the course of the twentieth century absorbed an ever increasing share of the building budget. To exceed four or five storeys lifts were needed, and once present they could proceed to a hundred. With the arrival of electricity the discipline of day lighting could be abandoned, totally internal rooms becoming acceptable. Central heating and air-conditioning replaced the focal role of the hearth with the so-called 'well-tempered environment', offering ideal standards of comfort, shirtsleeve temperature, and complete exclusion of the external world.[8] The distribution of services and factory production of components brought new modular planning disciplines to replace inherited patterns of use, and encouraged the development of flexible buildings undedicated to purpose. At the same time speed of construction became a priority, predisposing new buildings towards repetitive and standardized forms, and imposing the disciplines of the production line.

Clientship, procurement and bureaucracy

The anthropologist from Mars might point out that architectures always express the state of society and culture, so perhaps people get the architecture that they deserve. We can reply that we do not have to be so passive: that human decisions are made, and it is just as possible to produce poor and inappropriate buildings as good ones. Rich clients choose poor architects and despoil sites, competition juries are seduced by appearances and inappropriate designs; given the power and the money, it is even possible to build as wastefully and stupidly as Ceausescu with his emptily monumental palace for which a large part of old Bucharest was erased. Almost as oppressive is the housing for the masses put up by the Soviet regimes which defined the communist citizen by compressing people into racks of identical cells, but this was only a more extreme version of the workers' housing seen ever since the move into industrial cities, mean in character and cheaply contrived for 'average' persons. The problem is exacerbated with buildings developed speculatively, when profit wins over habitability and future occupants are unknown. The shoe-horning of activities forces people to adapt to the spaces given rather than welcoming their presence. In combination these factors have tended to produce neutral and abstract containers, unrelated to place and ritual. To make the new ways of deploying space safe and healthy, there also arose a plethora of rules and regulations, always well-meant but restrictive and expensive, imposing questionable standards, and sometimes dedicating disproportionate resources to minor risks. The degree to which our environment is dictated as opposed to merely modified by them has yet properly to be assessed and understood. The requirements of planning permission added an 'aesthetic' component that legislated on what buildings ought to look like. In theory this was democratic, but it compelled drawing in advance, necessitated judgement through often inadequate drawings, then building obediently with no deviation from what had been approved, in other words without improvisation. It also meant that appearance became geared to the tastes of planning committees rather than to the wishes of owners or their architects. The system has tended towards the uncontroversial, but we can hardly claim that the UK environment has become more beautiful since the Town and Country Planning Act of 1947, even if the preservation of some selected areas has been of great memorial value. Nowadays even a private citizen in possession of land and money cannot build as he or she wishes, because the building process necessitates an architect-like person to guide them through the maze of documentation. This reduces the chances for both social and self-expression, for learning by doing; it forbids improvisation and represses later ability to undertake maintenance.

The changing role of the architect

In the UK 'architect' was not a protected title until 1931, and the first university department to offer full-time approved courses was Liverpool in 1895, though the Académie d'Architecture in France went back a century earlier.[9] The origin of the role lies somewhere between master builder and gentleman amateur. Since it was at first driven largely by the needs of the wealthy for showy buildings, it gave rise to the idea that architects are responsible only for special buildings, and particularly for educated displays of style. Ordinary houses, farms, shops, mills – the majority of buildings in the landscape and townscape in fact – could be built by local builders with local materials. But during the twentieth century this changed, and the bureaucratic requirements described above now necessitate a whole team of people, with architect-like persons at the centre coordinating the design. The innocent builder has lost out, along with the cosy relationship to the prospective inhabitant or client, and though some of this interaction has passed to the architect, it is restricted to a few cases of largely domestic work. The architect now battles for supremacy against a legion of others each with their own interests and preferences, from planners and financiers to manufacturers of building systems.[10] To put it another way, the built environment is co-produced by a network of inter-acting social interests, and the architect, though wishing to be seen as leader and visionary, has often but a small part.

Since among the various specialists it is the architect whose education covers a general cultural responsibility and is informed by knowledge of history, it remains his or her duty to understand and give form to social processes. But that education has its limits. He or she is hampered first by always having to work on paper, comparing one putative proposal with another and undergoing years of education without necessarily engaging the physical world.[11] There are ways around this, such as engaging students in bricklaying or running live projects where they actually build something, but these are difficult to integrate with university procedures and generally end up marginal. Second, the burgeoning architect is encouraged by the prevalent culture towards self-expression on the model of heroes from Michelangelo to Le Corbusier or Zaha Hadid. This call for 'creativity' too often encourages him or her towards a kind of formalism, which can degenerate into mere pattern-making or play with shapes, pursued for purely 'aesthetic' effect. While passion, commitment and creativity are undoubtedly necessary to this education, aping the heroic role is not, and can lead to inappropriately selfish work. Third, the burgeoning architect is hampered by inadequate architectural history, which started a couple of centuries ago with excessive zeal for the Orders and the Grand Tour, then was downgraded by the modern movement in a bid to eliminate the useless 'styles' and to institute a supposedly scientific approach.[12] In the past fifty years, as the architect's role became more complex, an increasing range of sub-specialisms was added to courses and history was squeezed to the margin, as merely an ancillary subject rather than the primary source of understanding.[13]

Growing communication and media

In *Notre Dame de Paris* Victor Hugo declared 'Ceci tuera cela' meaning that once they possessed the Bible, people no longer needed to read biblical stories from sculptures on the front of cathedrals, and now few can.[14] Hugo's point was that the communicative potential of buildings had been replaced by written texts, which helps explain the decline in value of ornamentation, and in consequence of borrowed styles. Today most people are literate and used to reading written signs, guided everywhere from motorway and railway platform to the thousandth room in the hotel. Yet the signs' main use is on first visit, as thereafter we tend to revert to our memory of spatial progression. Differences between rooms or buildings, and the spatial sequences linking them, allow us to navigate through the city in a manner quite different from following signs, and signs are no substitute for substance. Decades ago when I discussed with James Gowan the issue of articulating the elements of a building in its external form, he remarked that if this were truly the intention, it would be simpler and clearer to write the rooms' names on the façade.[15] He was playing devil's advocate, but this idea neatly underlines the difference between reading a text message and reading a place with the eyes and the body, appreciating shapes and relationships, promised uses. Texts and buildings are not at all the same thing, despite a prolonged fashion for claiming buildings to *be* texts.[16] Architects are more dependent on print than perhaps they would care to admit, particularly on visual images.[17] This often leads them to neglect other senses like the aural and haptic, let alone the experience of a building in use.[18] If architecture is learned predominantly from texts and images, its identity is filtered through these media, and ever since the start of architectural education the majority of exemplary buildings discussed have passed unvisited. Long-standing textbooks like the definitive *Banister Fletcher* gathered a limited canon of examples presented through drawings and engravings, largely excised from context.[19] The limitations of printing technology meant they had to be redrawn in simplified form and in similar manner, whether or not they had originally been built from drawings. Photography, available from the mid-nineteenth century, was not trans-ferable effectively to the printed page until around 1920. The cubic buildings of the modernists then proved ideally suited to this new medium, and became known as 'the white architecture' despite the fact that many were coloured, simply because of photography in monochrome.[20] Published buildings remained predominantly in black and white until the 1980s, when cheap colour printing arrived and architects responded with a burst of colour. Until the end of the millennium, professional discourse took place largely through illustrated books and journals, most buildings still understood via drawings and photographs, and the actual visit could become a mere confirmation of what was already known from paper.[21] Since the mid-1990's television has changed public perception of architecture. There are popular programmes about people's struggles to build their own houses, sometimes with critic in tow, sometimes with the designer as solver of problems and purveyor of dreams. Other programmes, more consumerist in tone, document moves to the country following the London property boom. But as with drawings and photographs the bias of the medium applies. If possible the story is turned into a drama with difficulties exaggerated before being demonstrably resolved. Views of the buildings are limited to what camera and editor can convey, and the dominance of the presenter as king of taste for the celebrity age is taken for granted.

The computer has also imposed major changes. It has provided architects with new tricks, not least the ability to produce increasingly realistic images of unbuilt buildings by adding textures and reflections, images of light and shadow, sky, landscape, even people to a perspective projection. This has helped convince clients, but the publication of such images is disconcerting, for it begs two questions: 'is it actually built?', and 'why build it?', since the circle of dissemination has already been completed. The computer makes building production immensely quicker and more accurate, allowing sharing among specialists, instant editing, and direct transmission of data to cutting and shaping machines. It also allows a potential complexity of form impossible a few decades ago. But in the design studio it seems not yet to have replaced the drawing hand and three-dimensional spatial imagination, despite easing the production of perspectives and projections, even mobile fly-throughs. The trouble with these is that although a three-dimensional model is deployed in the machine, we see it only through the two-dimensional screen, limited in size and detail and rendered monocular. It evokes not so much the space we know with the body, as the familiar world of film and television in which one becomes passive spectator, and virtual space is constructed through montage.

The pervading positivism[22]

The changed technical aspects of our environment are everywhere evident, but behind them lies an ideological issue: the dominance of precise sciences and the attempt to make architecture fully scientific. The corollary of this is the dismissal of much carried-down knowledge and tradition, which the poet Stephen Spender already recognized in the heyday of modernism, 1951, with a certain irony:

> It was as though the nineteenth century had been a machine absorbing into itself at one end humanity dressed in fancy dress, unwashed, fierce and immoral, and emitting at the other modern men in their utilitarian clothes with their hygienic houses, their zeal for reform, their air of having triumphed by mechanical, economic and scientific means over the passionate, superstitious, cruel and poetic past.[23]

This opposition between science and 'superstition' remains, mostly without an awareness that the latter word arose in the Reformation, used by Protestants to dismiss the practices of Catholics, and that it often serves as the veiled insult of one ideology against another. Similarly, the word 'myth' is now used nearly always in a pejorative sense, to dismiss some idea or practice as necessarily untrue and therefore also useless, as if we possessed a secure basis of truth against which to measure it. Yet reality is not so finally definable, nor is a line so easily drawn between practical and 'religious' knowledge.[24] Just to take one example from this book, the stories of the dreamtime in Chapter 6 appear arrant nonsense against current conceptions of nature and history, but for the Australian Aboriginal People they constituted both a logical and a practical system, allowing life in a difficult environment and providing the vehicle for transmission of their culture.[25] 'Myth' was less a falsehood than a kernel of truth, and it does not allow the separation of parts deemed invalid by another knowledge system from parts deemed 'practical' without destroying the whole. Our age has become overconfident of the truth value of science, exacerbated by ahistorical teaching, which if noticing earlier versions at all, regards them not as alternatives but as beating a path to one's own door.[26] Allied with this is an implicit assumption that all things are measurable, resulting in an over-reliance on number and a concurrent over-reliance on economic factors.[27] This privileges a narrow range of supposed paths to truth, while other aspects of our accumulated culture are dismissed as invalid. Perhaps humanity has always tended to regard its knowledge as almost complete,[28] and perhaps people need to be wrong while believing they are right because they must make decisions on inadequate evidence,[29] but persistent claims from scientific as well as religious fundamentalists can provoke pause for thought. Immanuel Kant, the critic of pure reason, observed that we know the world only though the patterns and symbols we impose upon it, so it must always be subject to some kind of framing and classification. This should remind us that, in our reliance on a constructed model or conception of the world, we are not as far from the Aboriginal People as we thought.[30]

Seeing peoples trying to make sense of their worlds in diverse ways, anthropologists have long struggled with relativity. Evans-Pritchard, after living among the Azande, was prepared to remark that he found their order of things, including the complex social processes of witchcraft and the poison oracle, as good a way to conduct his life as any other.[31] Clifford Geertz, in the essay 'Anti-anti-relativism', retained unrepentantly the idea that there are many versions and endless translation between them.[32] Stanley Tambiah, in his long and cogently argued *Magic, Science, Religion and the Scope of Rationality*, pursued this issue through numerous examples, concluding in his chapter 'Multiple Orderings of Reality' with the identification of two complementary orientations to the world, which he sets in opposition as 'causality' and 'participation'. Causality is positivist science with its stance of detachment, its paradigm of evolution in space and time, its neutrality and fragmentation of phenomena. Participation is by contrast the religious view, with the observer involved with the world and immersed in it, using a language that expresses solidarity, unity and holism. It assumes continuity in place and time, and dependence on expressive action manifest through the telling of myths and the performance of rituals. In 'participation', phenomena are not fragmented but understood as wholes.[33] Tambiah regards the two attitudes as complementary, and crucially for our purposes, as equally valid. The anthropologist, of course, must be a participant, immersed in the situation, open to the contradictions between his or her world and the other's. The architect, to help in framing and giving shape to the lives of others, also needs to be so immersed. He or she cannot afford to ignore the calculations and benefits of the precise sciences, but must also attend to aspects less easily measurable though supported by shared experience and shared narrative.

Reconnection

Taken together these five issues have gradually expropriated us from decisions about our environment. Even in rural places local building traditions have collapsed, small builders are reduced to repairs and extensions, and indigenous materials have become uncompetitive or unavailable. Meanwhile volume house-builders with little local knowledge are constructing new estates for profit using international techniques to conjure up a sentimental and generalized vernacular image in line with fantasies presented on the media. Studies like the Dong village in Chapter 10 are needed just as a reminder of the degree to which a building culture *could* be integrated into society and reflect social values, with long-understood construction techniques carried out by local carpenters, clear and well-defined building types declarative of social structure, sensitivity to site and locality, and a building process integrated with the life of the community confirmed in rituals that give it definition and meaning at every stage. That old world is almost gone and we cannot return to it, but it provides lessons about scale, place and engagement. Perhaps the general evils of building too much, too fast, and at too unprecedented a scale are beyond mitigation, but small-scale examples could yet serve as oases of good practice as well as being kinder to the planet. The political and regulative aspects and the cost of bureaucratic processes might be given more critical scrutiny, and a limit could be set to the size of the rule book. But the best way to reduce the sense of expropriation and re-engage the public would be an increase in real user-participation. Experiments over the past forty years have shown repeatedly that when people become genuinely involved with decisions about their environment, they show interest, enthusiasm and continuing commitment which carries on into maintenance and repair.[34] I have written about this extensively elsewhere,[35] so here a tiny example must suffice: the school hall at Lippstadt in Germany, a project orchestrated by Peter Hübner, long a pioneer of participation, in 2002. The Evangelisches Gymnasium needed a hall for meetings and performances, but no state money

WILLKOMMEN IN UNSERER VISION

Figure 15.2 Participation in the construction of school hall, breaking the ground (courtesy of Peter Hübner).

WIR PACKEN AN
UND BAUEN UNSERE AULA SELBST
LASSEN SIE UNS NICHT IM REGEN STEHEN
Evangelisches Gymnasium · Lippstadt

Figure 15.4 Fundraising leaflet (courtesy of Peter Hübner).

Figure 15.3 School pupil building structural model (courtesy of Peter Hübner).

Figure 15.5 The model tested with the weight of two pupils (courtesy of Peter Hübner).

Figure 15.6 Participation in the construction of school hall, pupils celebrate completion of the structure (courtesy of Peter Hübner).

was forthcoming. The headmaster asked Hübner casually whether they might do something by themselves, and so started a series of meetings and brainstormings. These concerned not only what the building might be, but also how to raise funds and obtain materials. A campaign was started, a variety of donors were found, and a design was worked up by Hübner's office in close collaboration with the staff and pupils. It was constructed about 60 per cent by youth workers on a government work-creation scheme under a building master, but the other 40 per cent came from the school community and parents, often working at weekends. Hübner had a timber structure in mind, which could also become a visible demonstration of mutual support, and it was supported by twelve columns representing the apostles. His staff made a kit of parts for a scale model that was assembled in the school as a material demonstration and focus of will, but also as a celebration of the successful fundraising efforts (Figure 15.4). In the completed building, pupils' names were inscribed on the roof struts. The community's commitment was also expressed in a series of building rituals: not just a foundation laying and a topping-out, but two toppings-out (Figure 15.1). Concerts and social events occurred at each stage of its evolution: with structure but no roof deck, with roof but no walls, with the shell complete but no interior finishes. Although there was never much cash in hand, money kept coming in, and as completion approached sceptical sponsors joined in to share the success. The cost of half a million marks was only about 25 per cent of the average for the time, but more important was the project's social effect in uniting and empowering the community. Because of this valuable by-product, one can say with hindsight that it was better achieved this way than with full state funding. 'It's a big challenge for the architect to design the handover of the key' said Peter Hübner. For the final ritual marking the completion of the hall he obtained

Figure 15.7 The completed hall exterior (author's photograph 2004).

Figure 15.8 The completed hall interior (author's photograph 2004).

a long chain with on one end a large symbolic key, on the other the real key. Completing his speech, Hübner handed the ceremonial key to the Dean, remarking: 'This is the key of heaven'. As the Dean tore off the covering, the chain started to pull, drawing from the front rows a chain of children who represented every class in turn from the oldest to the youngest. Finally the smallest child handed over the real and earthly key. This moment underlined a communal enterprise in which everyone had played a part over nearly three years.

Notes

1   Said to be a Chinese proverb, used in recent history by Marshall McLuhan.

2   Clifford Geertz, in his book *Negara: The Theatre State in Nineteenth Century Bali*, makes the case that the theatrical display of politics is not so much the expression as the essential reality of it so that 'The king owned the country as he ruled it – mimetically: composing and constructing the very thing he imitated', Geertz 1980, p. 128.

3   There are graphic conventions for recording some kinds, used by choreographers to structure dance events, but they are not part of everyday discourse: see Tufte 1990, pp. 114–19.

4   Bourdieu 1977, pp. 114–24.

5   Lakoff and Johnson 1980.

6   He has recently won the Noble Prize for this, but the essential idea goes back to his book with Lynn Nadel of 1978 (O'Keefe and Nadel 1978).

7   Doctoral theses under my supervision at Sheffield, by Jayson Huang, Chomchon Fusinpaiboon, Bing Jiang, Derong Kong and Jianyu Cheng. Imperial China had no architects, only master carpenters, and buildings were predominantly single storey, alternating hall and courtyard.

8   Banham 1969.

9   On the general development of architectural education see Saint 2007, for detail on the Académie see Alex Griffin 'The Architectural Academy: Intellectual and social currents in academicism at the Académie Royale d'Architecture and Ecole des Beaux-Arts', PhD thesis University of Sheffield 2006.

10   They do not keep to a purely functional role but each, if good at the job, has also an aesthetic attitude, which we might call for example the aesthetic of good plumbing, or of neatly calculated quantities.

11   The French Beaux Arts system of examination in the nineteenth century showed this particularly. The students were given a simple brief and no site, and expected to design and draw in detail the whole building in just one sitting. The time limit, lack of access to references, and lack of site visit, assured that particular skills of memory and drawing were tested and displayed hermetically in the abstract. See Drexler 1977.

12   For a critique of this in relation to Harvard and Gropius see Herdeg 1983.

13   Architectural education before the Bauhaus assumed that the student should understand an inherited tradition, therefore the drawing of the orders and learning about history was paramount, even if the way it was done is now criticized. Technical and scientific disciplines are efficient because they concentrate on specific problems often with scant regard to history, ignoring the 'mistaken' paths of earlier researchers (see Kuhn 1962), but as I have tried to show repeatedly in this book, memory gives us our identity, both personally and as a society.

14   Hugo 1978.

15   Memory of a tutorial at the Architectural Association, London, c. 1971.

16   This claim is made, for example, by Suzanne Preston Blier in the preface to her otherwise

excellent book about the Batammaliba (Blier 1994). It accompanied a general and welcome rediscovery of the messaging power of buildings, but there are crucial differences in the ways buildings and texts work, as this book has attempted to show. My objections are threefold: first that buildings also function, second that text conventions are much more firmly established, third that giving priority to text might imply the priority of writing.

17 Evans 1997.

18 Pallasmaa 2005, Tanizaki 1977, Rasmussen 1959.

19 Banister Fletcher's *A History of Architecture on the Comparative Method*, was first published in 1896 and is still with us in a twentieth edition of 1996, the longest running and most widely used architectural history textbook. The two authors, father and son, were Banister Fletcher and Banister F. Fletcher, architects in the same practice, but the father was also the first Professor of Architecture at King's College London, where the son too became a lecturer. The latter, editing revised editions, became President of the RIBA and was also knighted. When I went to study at the Architectural Association in 1966 it was a compulsory purchase, regarded as definitive.

20 Colour transparencies existed in the form of autochromes, showable in a projector, but were not economically transferable to paper until much later.

21 See Peter Blundell Jones 'The Photo-dependent, the Photogenic and the Unphotographable: How our Understanding of the Modern Movement has been Conditioned by Photography' in Higgott and Wray, 2012, pp. 47–60.

22 Positivism was invented by Auguste Comte as a philosophical concept based on the new sciences, and in competition with religious knowledge: see Simpson 1969.

23 Spender 1951, p. 1.

24 Berger and Luckmann, *The Social Construction of Reality*, 1967.

25 As Enrico Guidoni put it: 'One of the reasons why a group is rooted in a specific area is because it *knows* how the territory was given its shape and form and because it descends from the one who made it', Guidoni 1975, p. 22, his emphasis.

26 T. S. Kuhn (1962) has already been mentioned, Gaston Bachelard (1963, 1987) comes to mind also as a historian of science trying to recover the value of the four elements. Koestler's book *The Sleepwalkers* (1959) about the history of cosmology is of interest because it shows successive attempts to frame the same material, revealing how the frame dominates.

27 In architectural theory traceable back to Hannes Meyer at the Bauhaus, 1928, see Conrads 1970, pp. 117–20; a later example is Friedman 1972. In the UK the Oxford Architectural Conference of 1958 marked a move by Leslie Martin, Richard Llewelyn-Davies and others to place architecture on a more scientific footing, see http://www.oxfordconference2008.co.uk/1958conference.htm, it is still going strong with the discipline of Space Syntax.

28 For example quotations from Planck, Hertz and others at http://amasci.com/weird/end.html.

29 Schulz 2010.

30 For a clearly expressed Neo-Kantian position see *Ways of Worldmaking*, Goodman 1978.

31 Evans-Pritchard 1937.

32 Geertz 1984.

33 Tambiah 1990, pp. 105–10.

34 See *Architecture and Participation*, Blundell Jones, Petrescu and Till, 2005.

35 'Student self-build in Stuttgart', *Architects Journal* 27 July 1983 pp. 32–50; 'Social process', *The Architectural Review* June 1985 pp, 76–81; *Architecture and Participation* (Blundell Jones et al. 2005); Hübner monograph (Blundell Jones 2007).

BIBLIOGRAPHY

Adams, Annmarie, *Architecture in the Family Way: Doctors, Houses, and Women, 1870–1900*. Kingston, Ontario: McGill-Queens University Press, 1996.

Alberti, Leone Batista, *The Ten Books of Architecture*. New York: Dover Books, 1986 (reprint of the Leoni edition of 1755).

Alford, B. W. E. and T. C. Barker, *A History of the Carpenters Company*. London: George Allen & Unwin Ltd, 1968.

Apter, Andrew, *Beyond Words: Discourse and Critical Agency in Africa*. Chicago and London: University of Chicago Press, 2007.

Bachelard, Gaston, *The Poetics of Space*. Boston, MA: Beacon Press, 1963.

Bachelard, Gaston, *The Psychoanalysis of Fire*. London: Quartet Books, 1987.

Banham, Peter Reyner, *Theory and Design in the First Machine Age*. London: Architectural Press, 1960.

Banham, Peter Reyner, *The Architecture of the Well-tempered Environment*. London: Architectural Press, 1969.

Banister Fletcher, Sir, *A History of Architecture on the Comparative Method*. 11th edn, London: Batsford, 1943.

Barron, Caroline M., *The Medieval Guildhall of London*. Corporation of London, 1974.

Barron, Michael, *Auditorium Acoustics and Architectural Design*. London: Spon Press, 1993.

Barry, Alfred, *The Life and Works of Charles Barry R.A., F.R.S., &c. &c.* London, 1857 (reprinted by Benjamin Blom, Inc., New York, 1972).

Barthes, Roland, *The Eiffel Tower and Other Mythologies*, translated by Richard Howard, New York: Hill and Wang, 1979.

Bartlett, F. C., *Remembering*. Cambridge: Cambridge University Press, 1932.

Bell, Catherine, *Ritual Theory, Ritual Practice*. Oxford and New York: Oxford University Press, 1992.

Bell, Diane, *Daughters of the Dreaming*. Sydney: McPhee Gribble/George Allen & Unwin, 1983.

Bennett, Eric, *The Worshipful Company of Wheelwrights of the City of London 1670–1970*, Newton Abbot: David & Charles, 1970.

Berger, Peter and Thomas Luckmann, *The Social Construction of Reality*. Harmondsworth: Penguin, 1967.

Bergson, Henri, *Time and Freewill*. London: George Allen & Unwin, 1910.

Biddle, Martin, Daphne Hudson and Caroline Heighway, *The Future of London's Past: A Survey of the Archaeological Implications of Planning and Development in the Nation's Capital*. Rescue Publications no. 4, 1973.

Blier, Suzanne Preston, *The Anatomy of Architecture: Ontology and Metaphor in Batammaliba Architectural Expression*. Chicago: University of Chicago Press, 1994.

Bloch, Maurice, *Ritual, History and Power*. London: Athlone Press, 1989.

Blundell Jones, Peter, *Hans Scharoun*. London: Phaidon, 1995.

Blundell Jones, Peter, *Hugo Häring*. Fellbach: Axel Menges, 1999.

Blundell Jones, Peter, *Modern Architecture Through Case Studies*: Oxford: Architectural Press, 2002.

Blundell Jones, Peter, *Gunnar Asplund*. London: Phaidon, 2006.

Blundell Jones, Peter, *Peter Hübner: Building as a Social Process*. Stuttgart: Axel Menges, July 2007.

Blundell Jones, Peter and Eamonn Canniffe, *Modern Architecture Through Case Studies 1945–1990*. Oxford: Architectural Press, 2007.

Blundell Jones, Peter and Mark Meagher, eds, *Architecture and Movement*. London: Routledge, 2015.

Blundell Jones, Peter, Doina Petrescu and Jeremy Till, eds, *Architecture and Participation*. London and New York: Spon Press, 2005.

Bibliography

Bond, Maurice and David Beamish, *The Gentleman Usher of the Black Rod*. London: Her Majesty's Stationary Office, 1976.

Booker, Christopher, *The Neophiliacs: The Revolution in English Life in the Fifties and Sixties*. London: Pimlico Books, 1992.

Bourdieu, Pierre, *Algeria 1960*. Cambridge: Cambridge University Press, 1963.

Bourdieu, Pierre, *Outline of a Theory of Practice*. Cambridge: Cambridge University Press, 1977.

Bourdieu, Pierre, *Distinction, A Social Critique of the Judgement of Taste*. London: Routledge and Kegan Paul, 1984.

Bourke, Joanna, ed., *Ritual: Thematic Studies in Architecture*. New Jersey: The Princeton Journal, Princeton Architectural Press, 1983.

Brand, Stewart, *How Buildings Learn, What Happens After They're Built*. London: Viking Press, 1994.

Brook, Peter, *The Empty Space*. New York: Simon & Schuster, 1968.

Brox, Jane, *Brilliance: The Evolution of Artificial Light*. London: Souvenir Press, 2010.

Carlyle, Thomas, *Sartor Resartus*. Oxford: Oxford University Press, 1987 (first published 1833–4).

Carsten, Janet and Stephen Hugh-Jones, *About the House: Levi-Strauss and Beyond*. Cambridge: Cambridge University Press, 1995.

Cassirer, Ernst, *Language and Myth*. New York: Dover Books, 1953.

Cavalli-Sforza, Luigi Luca, *Genes, People and Languages*. London: Penguin, 2001.

Chatwin, Bruce, *The Songlines*. London: Franklin Press, 1986.

Chi Yün, *Shadows in a Chinese Landscape*. New York: East Gate Books, 1999.

Colvin, H. M., J. Mordaunt Crook and H. M. Port, *The History of the King's Works*, Volume VI, 1782–1851. London: Her Majesty's Stationery Office, 1973.

Conrads, Ulrich, ed., *Programmes and Manifestoes on 20th Century Architecture*. London: Lund Humphries, 1970.

Crump, Thomas, *The Anthropology of Numbers*. Cambridge: Cambridge University Press, 1990.

Davies, Jon, *Death, Burial and Rebirth in the Religions of Antiquity*. London: Routledge 1999.

Dawson, Raymond, *The Chinese Experience*. London: Phoenix Press, 1978.

Day, Barry, *This Wooden 'O': Shakespeare's Globe Reborn*. London: Oberon Books, 1996.

DeMallie, Raymond. J., *The Sixth Grandfather: Black Elk's Teachings Given to John G. Neilhardt*. Lincoln, NB: University of Nebraska Press, 1984.

Denis, Marie Noele, and Marie Claude Groshens, *L'architecture rurale francaise: corpus des genres, des variantes. Alsace*. Paris: Berger-Levrault, 1978.

DeRoo, Rebecca J., *The Museum Establishment and Contemporary Art: The Politics of Artistic Display in France after 1968*. Cambridge: Cambridge University Press, 2006.

De Zurko, Edward Robert, *Origins of Functionalist Theory*. New York: Columbia University Press, 1957.

Donald, Merlin, *Origins of the Modern Mind: Three Stages in the Evolution of Culture and Cognition*. Cambridge, MA: Harvard University Press, 1991.

Douglas, Mary, *Purity and Danger*. London: Routledge and Kegan Paul, 1966.

Douglas, Mary, *Rules and Meanings*. Harmondsworth: Penguin, 1973 (republished by Routledge as part of Douglas's Collected Works vol. IV in 2003).

Douglas, Mary, *Implicit Meanings*. London: Routledge and Kegan Paul, 1975.

Douglas, Mary, *Essays in the Sociology of Perception*. London: Routledge and Kegan Paul, 1982.

Draaisma, Douwe, *Metaphors of Memory: A History of Ideas about the Mind*. Cambridge: Cambridge University Press, 2001.

Drexler, Arthur, *The Architecture of the Ecole Des Beaux Arts*: London: Secker and Warburg, 1977.

Dummelow, John, *The Wax Chandlers of London*. London and Chichester: Phillimore, 1973.

Durand, J. N. L., *Précis des leçons d'architecture données à l'Ecole royale polytechnique*. Paris, 1802–5 (modern reprints).

Durkheim, Emile and Marcel Mauss, *Primitive Classification*. London: Cohen & West, 1963 (translated by Rodney Needham; first French edition 1901–2).

Eichhorn, Ernst, Rudolf Käs, Bernd Ogan, Klaus-Jürgen Sembach, Wolfgang W. Weiss and Siegfried Zelnhefer, *Kulissen der Gewalt: Das Reichsparteitagsgelände in Nürnberg*. Munich: Hugendubel, 1992.

Eitzen, Gerhard, *Bauernhausforschung in Deutschland, gesammelte Aufsätze 1938 bis 1980*. Heidenau: PD-Verlag, 2006.

Eliade, Mircea, *Patterns in Comparative Religion*. London: Sheed and Ward, 1958.

Emanuel, Muriel, ed., *Contemporary Architects*. London: St Martin's Press, 1988.

Evans, George Ewart, *The Farm and the Village*. London: Faber and Faber, 1969.

Evans, George Ewart, *The Crooked Scythe*. London: Faber and Faber, 1993.

Evans, Robin, *The Fabrication of Virtue, English Prison Architecture from 1750 to 1840*. Cambridge: Cambridge University Press, 1982.

Evans, Robin, *Translation from Drawing to Building and Other Essays*. Cambridge, MA: MIT Press, 1997.

Evans-Pritchard, E. E., *Witchcraft, Oracles and Magic among the Azande*. Oxford: Oxford University Press, 1937.

Faegre, Torvald, *Tents: Architecture of the Nomads*. London: John Murray, 1979.

Feuchtwang, Stephan, *The Imperial Metaphor: Popular Religion in China*. London: Routledge, 1992.

Forde, Daryll, *African Worlds*. Oxford: International African Institute/Oxford University Press, 1954.

Foucault, Michel, *Discipline and Punish: The Birth of the Prison*. London: Penguin Books, 1979

Fraser, Douglas, *Village Planning in the Primitive World*. London: Studio Vista, 1968.

Fraser, James, *The Golden Bough, A Study in Magic and Religion*: London: Macmillan, 1912.

Friedman, Yona, *Toward a Scientific Architecture*. Cambridge, MA: MIT Press, 1972.

Fu, Anhui and Dazhong Yu, *Customs of Nine Stockaded Village*. Guiyang, Guizhou People's Press, 1997.

Gainsborough, John, *Hospital Description: Wycombe General Hospital Phase One*. London: King's Fund, 1968.

Gainsborough, John, and Hugh Gainsborough, *Principles of Hospital Design*. London: Architectural Press, 1964.

Garnier, Charles, *Le Théâtre*. Paris: Librarie Hachette et Cie, 1871.

Garnier, Charles, *Le Nouvel Opéra de Paris*. Paris: Portfolio of printed drawings, 1875.

Geary, Norman; Ruth B. Geary, Ou Chaoquan, Long Yaohong, Jiang Daren and Wang Jiying, *The Kam People of China: Turning Nineteen*. London: Routledge Curzon, 2003.

Geertz, Clifford, *Negara: The Theatre State in Nineteenth Century Bali*. Princeton, NJ: Princeton University Press, 1980.

Geertz, Clifford, *Local Knowledge: Further Essays in Interpretive Anthropology*. New York: Basic Books, 1983.

Geertz, Clifford, 'Anti-anti-relativism', *American Anthropologist* vol. 86, no. 2, June 1984.

Geertz, Clifford, *The Interpretation of Cultures*. London: Fontana Press, 1993 (1st edn New York 1973).

Gerhard, Anselm, *The Urbanisation of Opera: Music Theatre in Paris in the Nineteenth Century*. Chicago: University of Chicago Press, 1998.

Giedion, Sigfried, *Mechanisation Takes Command, A Contribution to Anonymous History*. Oxford: Oxford University Press, 1948.

Goffman, Erving, *The Presentation of the Self in Everyday Life*. Edinburgh University Social Science Centre, Edinburgh 1956 (later editions, Harmondsworth: Allen Lane, 1959; US edition New York: Doubleday, 1959).

Goffman, Erving, *Asylums: Essays on the Social Situation of Mental Patients and Other Inmates*. Harmondsworth: Penguin, 1968.

Gombrich, Ernst, *Meditations on a Hobby Horse*. London: Phaidon, 1963.

Goodman, Nelson, *Languages of Art*, Indianapolis: Hackett Publishing, 1976.

Goodman, Nelson, *Ways of Worldmaking*, Indianapolis: Hackett Publishing, 1978.

Goodman, Nelson and Catherine Elgin, *Reconceptions in Philosophy and Other Arts and Sciences*. London: Routledge, 1988.

Goody, Jack, *The East in the West*. Cambridge: Cambridge University Press, 1996.

Gould, Richard A., *Yiwara: Foragers of the Australian Desert*. London and Sydney: Collins, 1969.

Gould, Richard A., *Living Archaeology* Cambridge: Cambridge University Press, 1980.

Graham, Clare, *Ordering Law: The Architectural and Social History of the English Law Court to 1914*. Aldershot: Ashgate, 2003.

Bibliography

Grass, Günter, *My Century*. London: Faber and Faber, 1999.

Greenough, Horatio, *Form and Function: Remarks on Art*, edited by Harold A. Small. Berkeley: University of California Press, 1947.

Griaule, Marcel, *Dieu d'Eau, Entretiens avec Ogotemmêli*, 1948 (Paris: Librarie Arthème Fayard, 1975, web version by Pierre Palpant).

Griaule, Marcel, *Conversations with Ogotemmêli*. Oxford: Oxford University Press, 1965.

Griaule, Marcel, and Germaine Dieterlen, *The Pale Fox*, English edition translated by Stephen C. Infantino, Baltimore: Afrikan World Books, 1986.

Grinnell, George Bird, *The Cheyenne Indians: Their History and Lifeways*. Bloomington: World Wisdom, 2008 (modern abridged edition, original 1923).

Grout, Donald Jay, *A Short History of Opera*. New York: Columbia University Press, 1971.

Guidoni, Enrico, *Primitive Architecture*. Milan: Faber/Electa, 1975.

Harris, John Arthur, *Ceremonials of the Corporation of London, A Handbook prepared by authority of the Court of Lord Mayor and Aldermen for the guidance of the Lord Mayor etc…* Corporation of London, 1991.

Hastings, Maurice, *Parliament House: The Chambers of the House of Commons*. London: The Architectural Press, 1950.

Herdeg, Klaus, *The Decorated Diagram: Harvard Architecture and the Failure of the Bauhaus Legacy*. Cambridge, MA: MIT Press, 1983.

Herrmann, Wolfgang, ed., *In What Style Should We Build? The German Debate on Architectural Style*. Santa Monica, CA: Getty Centre, 1992.

Hevia, James L., *English Lessons: The Pedagogy of Imperialism in Ninetenth-century China*. Durham, NC: Duke University Press, 2003.

Hiatt, L. R., *Arguments About Aborigines*. Cambridge: Cambridge University Press, 1996.

Higgott, Andrew and Timothy Wray, eds, *Camera Constructs: Photography, Architecture and the Modern City*. Farnham: Ashgate, 2012.

Hill, Rosemary, *God's Architect: Pugin & the Building of Romantic Britain*. London and New Haven, CT: Yale University Press, 2007.

Hobsbawm, Eric and Terraece Ranger, *The Invention of Tradition*. Cambridge: Cambridge University Press, 2012.

Hoffecker, John F. *Landscape of the Mind: Human Evolution and the Archaeology of Thought*. New York: Columbia University Press, 2011.

Holdsworth, Nadine, *Joan Littlewood*. London: Routledge, 2006.

Hone, William, *Ancient Mysteries Described*. London: William Reeves, 1823.

Huang, Liuhung, *A Complete Book Concerning Happiness and Benevolence: A Manual for 17th Century Magistrates*, translated by Djang Chu. Tucson, AZ: University of Arizona Press, 1984.

Hugh-Jones, Christine, *From the Milk River: Spatial and Temporal Processes in Northwest Amazonia*. Cambridge: Cambridge University Press, 1979.

Hugh-Jones, Stephen, *The Palm and the Pleiades: Initiation and Cosmology in Northwest Amazonia*. Cambridge: Cambridge University Press, 1979.

Hugo, Victor, *Notre Dame of Paris*. Harmondsworth: Penguin Books, 1978.

James, E. O., *Seasonal Feasts and Festivals*. London: Thames and Hudson, 1961.

Jaskot, Paul B., *The Architecture of Oppression: The SS, Forced Labor and the Nazi Monumental Building Economy*. London: Routledge, 2000.

Jencks, Charles and George Baird, *Meaning in Architecture*. London: Barrie and Jenkins, 1970.

Joedicke, Jürgen and Heinrich Lauterbach, *Hugo Häring: Schriften, Entwürfe, Bauten*. Stuttgart: Karl Krämer Verlag, 1965.

Jones, Christopher, *The Great Palace: The Story of Parliament*: London: British Broadcasting Corporation, 1983.

Jones, Martin, *Feast: Why Humans Share Food*: Oxford: Oxford University Press, 2007.

Jordan, Thomas, *London's Glory or the Lord Mayor's Show etc*. London: John and Henry Playford, 1680.

Josephy, Alvin M. Jr., *500 Nations: An Illustrated History of North American Indians*. London: Hutchinson Pimlico, 1995.

Jupp, Edward, and William Pocock, *An Historical Account of the Worshipful Company of Carpenters*: London: Pickering and Chatto, 1887.

Kahneman, Daniel, *Thinking, Fast and Slow*: London: Allen Lane, 2011.

Kaiser, Hermann and Helmut Ottenjann, *Museumsfüher*. Museumsdorf Cloppenburg, Niedersächsisches Freilichtmuseum, 1985.

Kelley, Klara Bonsack and Harris Francis, *Navajo Sacred Places*. Bloomington and Indianapolis: Indiana University Press, 1994.

Kershaw, Ian, *Hitler: 1889–1936 Hubris*. Harmondsworth: Allen Lane, 1998.

Kertzer, David L., *Ritual, Politics & Power*. New Haven, CT: Yale University Press, 1988.

Koestler, Arthur, *The Sleepwalkers*. Harmondsworth: Penguin, 1959.

Kostof, Spiro, *The City Shaped: Urban Patterns and Meanings Through History*: London: Thames & Hudson, 1991.

Kostof, Spiro, *The City Assembled: The Elements of Urban Form Through History*. London: Thames & Hudson, 1999.

Kuhn, T. S., *The Structure of Scientific Revolutions*: Chicago: University of Chicago Press, 1962.

Kurz, Philip, ed., *Scharoun, Geschwister-Scholl-Schule: Die Geschichte einer Instandsetzung*. Stuttgart: Kraemerverlag (Baudenkmale der Moderne), 2014.

Lakoff, George and Mark Johnson, *Metaphors We Live By*. Chicago: University of Chicago Press, 1980.

Lakoff, George and Rafael E. Nunez, *Where Mathematics Comes From: How the Embodied Mind Brings Mathematics into Being*. New York: Basic Books, 2000.

Lane, Barbara Miller, *National Romanticism and Modern Architecture in Germany and the Scandinavian Countries*. Cambridge: Cambridge University Press, 2000.

Lao Tzu, *Tao Te Ching*, translated by D. C. Lau. Harmondsworth: Penguin, 1963.

Lauber, Wolfgang, ed., *Architektur der Dogon: Traditioneller Lehmbau und Kunst in Mali*. Munich: Prestel, 1998.

Laubin, Reginald and Gladys Laubin, *The Indian Tipi: Its History Construction and Use*. Norman: University of Oklahoma Press, 1957/1989.

Lawson, Bryan, *The Language of Space*. Oxford: Architectural Press, 2001.

Lawson, Colin, ed., *The Cambridge Companion to the Orchestra*. Cambridge: Cambridge University Press, 2003.

Lefebvre, Henri, *The Production of Space*. Oxford: Blackwell, 1991.

Lethaby, William Richard, *Form in Civilisation*. Oxford: Oxford University Press, 1922.

Lethaby, William Richard, 'Home and Country Arts', *Home and Country,* the N.F.W.I. magazine, London 1923.

Lethaby, William Richard, *Philip Webb and His Work*. Oxford: Oxford University Press, 1935.

Lethaby, William Richard, *Architecture, Nature and Magic*, London: Duckworth, 1956.

Levi-Strauss, Claude, *Structural Anthropology*, Harmondsworth: Penguin, 1968.

Levi-Strauss, Claude, *The Raw and the Cooked*. London: Jonathan Cape, 1970.

Levi-Strauss, Claude, *Tristes Tropiques*. London: Jonathan Cape, 1973.

Li, Xuemei, *The Life Bridge: An Anthropology of the Origins of the Dong 'Wind and Rain' Bridge in Southern China*, PhD thesis, University of Sheffield, 2008.

Lindenberger, Herbert, *Opera in History from Monteverdi to Cage*. Stanford: Stanford University Press, 1998.

Littlewood, Joan, *Joan's Book: Joan Littlewood's Peculiar History as She Tells It*. London: Methuen, 1994.

Longford, Lord, *A History of the House of Lords*. London: Collins, 1988.

Lowenthal, David, *The Past is a Foreign Country*. Cambridge: Cambridge University Press, 1985.

Lowie, Robert,*The Crow Indians*. Lincoln, NB and London: University of Nebraska Press, 1935/1983.

Luo, Tinghua and Shengxian Wang, *Dong History, Culture and Customs* (Chinese texts), edited by Tinghua Luo and Shengxian Wang. Guiyang: Guizhou Peoples' Press, 1989.

MacCarthy, Fiona, *The Last Curtsey*. London: Faber and Faber, 2006.

Mackay, David, *Trial of Simon, Lord Lovat of the '45*. Edinburgh and Glasgow: William Hodge, 1911.

Markus, Thomas A., *Buildings and Power*. London: Routledge, 1993.

Bibliography

Marti, Monserrat Palau, *Les Dogon*. Paris: Presses Universitaires de France, 1957.

Mathews, Stanley, *From Agit-Prop to Free Space: The Architecture of Cedric Price*. London: Black Dog, 2007.

McClintock, James, ed., *The Stonehenge Companion*. London: Think Publishing/English Heritage, 2006.

McNaughton, Patrick R., *The Mande Blacksmiths: Knowledge, Power and Art in West Africa*. Bloomington: Indiana University Press, 1988.

Meggitt, M. J., *Desert People: A Study of the Walbiri Aborigines of Central Australia*. Chicago and London: University of Chicago Press, 1962.

Mertes, Kate, *The English Noble Household 1250–1600: Good Governance and Politic Rule*. Oxford: Basil Blackwell, 1988.

Meyer, Leonard B., *Emotion and Meaning in Music*. Chicago: University of Chicago Press, 1956.

Miyazaki, Ichisada, *China's Examination Hell: The Civil Service Examinations in Imperial China*. New Haven, CT: Yale University Press, 1976.

Moore, Sally and Barbara Myerhoff, *Secular Ritual*. Amsterdam: Van Gorcum, 1977.

Murdoch, Iris, *The Bell*. Harmondsworth: Penguin, 1958.

Murdoch, Iris, *Under the Net*. Harmondsworth: Penguin, 1960.

Nabokov, Peter and Robert Easton, *Native American Architecture*. New York and Oxford: Oxford University Press, 1989.

Needham, Joseph, *Science and Civilisation in China, Volume 2*. Cambridge: Cambridge University Press, 1956.

Needham, Rodney, ed., *Right and Left: Essays on Dual Symbolic Classification*. Chicago: University of Chicago Press, 1973.

Neihardt, John G. *Black Elk Speaks, Being the Life Story of a Holy Man of the Oglala Sioux*. Lincoln, NB and London: University of Nebraska Press, 1932/1960/1979.

Obrist, Hans Ulrich, *Re: CP*. Basel, Boston and Berlin: Birkhäuser, 2003.

O'Keefe, John, and Lynn Nadel, *The Hippocampus as a Cognitive Map*. Oxford: Clarendon Press, 1978.

Pallasmaa, Juhani, *The Eyes of the Skin: Architecture and the Senses*. Chichester: Wiley, 2005.

Paxton, Robert O., *The Anatomy of Fascism*. Harmondsworth: Penguin Books, 2004.

Pearson, Michael Parker, and Colin Richards, *Architecture and Order: Approaches to Social Space*. London: Routledge, 1994.

Pedley, John, *Sanctuaries and the Sacred in the Ancient Greek World*. Cambridge: Cambridge University Press, 2005.

Pehnt, Wolfgang, *Expressionist Architecture*. London: Thames and Hudson, 1973.

Pevsner, Nikolaus, *Pioneers of Modern Design: From William Morris to Walter Gropius*. Harmondsworth: Pelican Books, 1960.

Pevsner, Nikolaus, *An Outline of European Architecture*. Harmondsworth: Penguin Books, 1963 (1st edn 1943).

Pevsner, Nikolaus, *The Buildings of England: London, Volume One*. Harmondsworth: Penguin Books, 1973.

Pevsner, Nikolaus, *Building Types*. Harmondsworth: Penguin Books, 1976.

Pfankuch, Peter, ed., *Hans Scharoun: Bauten, Entwürfe, Texte*. Berlin: Akademie der Künste, 1974, revised edition with updated worklist 1993.

Port, M. H., *The Houses of Parliament*. New Haven, CT, and London: Yale Studies in British Art, 1976.

Price, John Edward, *A Descriptive Account of the Guildhall of the City of London*. Corporation of the City of London, 1886.

Pryor, Francis, *Home: A Time Traveller's Tales from British Prehistory*. London: Allen Lane, 2014.

Pugin, Augustus Welby Northmore, *Contrasts, or a Parallel between the Noble Edifices of the Middle Ages and Corresponding Buildings of the Present Day*. London: Charles Dolman, 1841 (first edition 1836, facsimile reprint Leicester University Press, 1969).

Pugin, Augustus Welby Northmore, *The True Principles of Pointed or Christian Architecture*, London: Henry G. Bohn, 1853 (first edition 1841, facsimile reprint Blackwell 1969).

Rasmussen, Steen Eiler, *Experiencing Architecture*. London: Chapman and Hall, 1959.

Rees, J. Aubrey, *The Worshipful Company of Grocers: An Historical Retrospect 1345–1923*, London and Sydney: Chapman and Dodd, 1923.

Reichel, Peter, *Der schöne Schein des Dritten Reiches: Gewalt und Faszination des deutschen Faschismus.* Hamburg: Ellert & Richter, 2006.

Reichel-Dolmatoff, Gerardo, *Amazonian Cosmos: The Sexual and Religious Symbolism of the Tukano Indians.* Chicago: University of Chicago Press, 1971.

Reichel-Dolmatoff, Gerardo, *Rainforest Shamans: Essays on the Tukano Indians of the Northwest Amazon.* Totnes: Themis Books, 1997.

Riding, Chistine and Jacqueline Riding, eds, *The Houses of Parliament, History, Art Architecture.* London: Merrell Publishers, 2000.

Rosenfield, Isadore, *Hospital Architecture and Beyond.* New York: Van Nostrand Reinhold, 1969.

Rowe, Colin and Fred Koetter, *Collage City*, Cambridge, MA: MIT Press, 1978.

Ruan, Xing, *Allegorical Architecture: Living Myth and Architectonics in Southern China.* Honolulu: University of Hawaii Press, 2006.

Ruitenbeek, Klaas, *The Lu Ban Jing: A Fifteenth-century Chinese Carpenter's Manual,* Rijksuniversiteit te Leiden, 1989.

Rykwert, Joseph, *The Idea of a Town.* Cambridge, MA: MIT Press, 1976.

Sadie, Stanley, ed., *History of Opera.* London: Macmillan, 1989.

Sahlins, Marshall, *Stone-age Economics.* New Brunswick, NJ: Transaction Publishers, 1972.

Saint, Andrew, *Towards a Social Architecture.* New Haven, CT: Yale University Press, 1987.

Saint, Andrew, *Architect and Engineer: A Study in Sibling Rivalry.* New Haven, CT: Yale University Press, 2007.

Schinz, Alfred, *The Magic Square, Cities in Ancient China.* Stuttgart: Edition Axel Menges, 1996.

Schirren, Matthias, *Hugo Häring, Architekt des neuen Bauens.* Ostfildern-Ruit: Hatje Cantz, 2001.

Schultheis, Franz and Christine Frisinghelli, eds, *Pierre Bourdieu in Algerien: Zeugnisses der Enwurzelung,* Graz: Camera Austria, 2003.

Schulz, Kathryn, *Being Wrong: Adventures in the Margin of Error, the Meaning of Error in an Age of Certainty.* London: Portobello Books, 2010.

Sennett, Richard, *The Fall of Public Man.* New York: Norton, 1992.

Sharar, Meir and Robert P. Weller, *Unruly Gods: Divinity and Society in China.* Honolulu: University of Hawaii Press, 1996.

Sharr, Adam and Stephen Thornton, *Demolishing Whitehall: Leslie Martin, Harold Wilson and the Architecture of White Heat.* London: Ashgate, 2013.

Shirer, William L., *Berlin Diary: The Journal of a Foreign Correspondent 1934–41.* London: Hamish Hamilton, 1941.

Sicheng, Liang, *Chinese Architecture: A Pictorial History,* edited by Wilma Fairbank. Cambridge, MA: MIT Press, 1984.

Silver, Nathan, *The Making of Beuabourg: A Building Biography of the Centre Pompidou Paris.* Cambridge, MA, and London: MIT Press, 1994.

Simpson, George, *Comte, Sire of Sociology.* New York: Crowell, 1969.

Sinyavsky, Andrei, *Ivan the Fool: Russian Folk Belief.* Moscow: Glas Publishers, 2007 (original French edn, 1990).

Skinner, William G., *The City in Late Imperial China.* Stanford, CA: Stanford University Press, 1977.

Smelser, Neil and Paul Baltes, eds, *International Encyclopaedia of the Social and Behavioural Sciences.* Amsterdam: Elsevier, 2001.

Smith, Jonathan Z., *To Take Place: Toward Theory in Ritual.* Chicago and London: University of Chicago Press, 1987.

Snow, C. P., *The Two Cultures and a Second Look.* Cambridge: Cambridge University Press, 1964.

Sontag, Susan, *Under the Sign of Saturn.* New York: Farrar, Strauss and Giroux, 1980.

Speer, Albert, *Erinerrungen.* Berlin: Propyläen Verlag, 1969.

Speer, Albert, *Inside the Third Reich.* London: Sphere Books, 1971.

Speer, Albert, *Spandau: The Secret Diaries.* London: Collins, 1976.

Spencer, Baldwin and F. J. Gillen, *The Native Tribes of Central Australia.* London: Macmillan 1899.

Bibliography

Spender, Stephen, *World Within World*. London: Faber and Faber, 1951.

Stafford, Charles, *Separation and Reunion in Modern China*. Cambridge: Cambridge University Press, 2000.

Standing Bear, Luther, *My People the Sioux*. Lincoln, NB and London: University of Nebraska Press, 1975 (1st edn, 1928).

Standing Bear, Luther, *Land of the Spotted Eagle*. Lincoln, NB and London: University of Nebraska Press, 1978 (1st edn, 1933).

Steadman, Philip, *The Evolution of Designs: Biological Analogy in Architecture and the Applied Arts*. Cambridge: Cambridge University Press, 1979.

Summerson, John, *Heavenly Mansions and Other Essays on Architecture*. London: The Cresset Press, 1949.

Tambiah, Stanley, *Magic, Science, Religion and the Scope of Rationality*. Cambridge: Cambridge University Press, 1990.

Tanizaki, Junichiro, *In Praise of Shadows*. London: Vintage Books, 1977/2001.

Tanner, Adrian. *Bringing Home Animals: Religious Ideology and Mode of Production of the Mistassini Cree Hunters*. London: C. Hurst, 1979, republished in Canada by Memorial University of Newfoundland.

Täubrich, Hans-Christian, ed., *Fascination and Terror: Documentation Centre, Nazi Party Rally Grounds Nuremberg*. Nuremberg: Druckhaus Nürnberg, 2006.

The Microcosm of London, T. Rowlandson and A. C. Plugin, King Penguin reprint with text by John Summerson London 1943.

Thompson, John D. and Grace Goldin, *The Hospital: A Social and Architectural History*. New Haven, CT: Yale University Press, 1975.

Thompson, Michael, *The Medieval Hall, the Basis of Secular Domestic Life, 600–1600 AD*. Aldershot: Scolar Press, 1995.

Thornbury, Walter, *Old and New London*, Volume 1. London: Cassell, Petter and Galpin, 1871.

Thornton, Robert J., *Space Time and Culture among the Iraqw of Tanzania*. New York: Academic Press, 1980.

Till, Jeremy, *Architecture Depends*. Cambridge, MA: MIT Press, 2009.

Tufte, Edward R. *Envisioning Information*. Cheshire, CT: Graphics Press, 1990.

Turner, Victor, *The Ritual Process: Structure and Anti-structure*. Chicago: Aldine, 1969.

Unschuld, Paul W. *Huang di nei jing su wen: Nature, Knowledge, Imagery in an Ancient Chinese Medical Text*. Berkeley: University of California Press, 2003.

Unwin, George, *The Gilds and Companies of London*. London: Methuen, 1908.

Van Gennep, Arnold, *The Rites of Passage*. London: Routledge and Kegan Paul, 1960 (1st edn 1908).

Visser, Margaret, *Much Depends on Dinner*. Harmondsworth: Penguin, 1986.

Visser, Margaret, *The Rituals of Dinner*, Penguin, Harmondsworth, 1991.

Waley, Arthur, *The Analects of Confucius*. London: George Allen & Unwin, 1964.

Walker, James R. *Lakota Belief and Ritual*, edited by Raymond J. DeMallie and Elaine A. Jahner. Lincoln, NB and London: University of Nebraska Press, 1980.

Wang, Mingming, *Empire and Local Worlds: A Chinese Model of Long-Term Historical Anthropology*. Walnut Creek, CA: Left Coast Press, 2009.

Wedgwood, Alexandra, *Rebuilding the Houses of Parliament, Drawings from the Kennedy Albums and the Thomas Greene Papers*. House of Lords Record Office Memorandum No. 69, House of Lords Record Office, 1984.

Wendschuh, Achim, ed., *Hans Scharoun Zeichnungen, Aquarelle, Texte*. Berlin: Akademie der Künste, 1993.

Wheatley, Paul, *The Pivot of the Four Quarters: A Preliminary Enquiry into the Origins and Character of the Ancient Chinese City*. Edinburgh: Edinburgh University Press, 1971.

Wilson, Peter, ed., *The Greek Theatre and Festivals*. Oxford: Oxford University Press, 2007.

Wu, Dingguo (A), 'Liping Dong Funeral Customs' (Chinese texts), in *Dong History, Culture and Customs*, edited by Tinghua Luo and Shengxian Wang. Guiyang: Guizhou Peoples' Press, 1989.

Wu, Dingguo (B), 'Guizhou Liping "Tian Fu" Dong Birth Customs', in *Dong History, Culture and Customs*, edited by Tinghua Luo and Shengxian Wang. Guiyang: Guizhou Peoples' Press, 1989.

Xiao, Bin, 'Reciting Dong Funeral', (Chinese text) Dong Custom and Culture http://www.dongzu8.com/forum.php?mod=view thread&tid=46260 (accessed 30 September 2010).

Xu, X. G. *Drum Tower: The Cultural Field of Conclusion and Implementation of Dong Customary Law*, in Politics and Law of Analects 10/2009, pp. 51–4.

Yang, Zhuhui, *Record of Dong Customs* (Chinese text). Beijing: Central University of Nationalities Press, 1999.

Yu, Dazhong, *Dongzu Minju* (The Dwellings of the Dong). Guiyang: Huaxia Wenhua Yishu Press, 2001.

Zhang, Juwen, *A Translation of the Ancient Chinese Book of Burial by Guo Pu (276–324)*. Lampeter: Edwin Mellen Press, 2004.

INDEX

Index

Index

Index